Programming .NET 3.5

Other Microsoft .NET resources from O'Reilly

Related titles

.NET Windows Forms in a Nutshell

ADO.NET 3.5 Cookbook™

ADO.NET 3.5 in a Nutshell

Building a Web 2.0 Portal with ASP.NET 3.5

Learning ASP.NET 3.5

Programming ASP.NET AJAX

.NET Books Resource Center

dotnet.oreilly.com is a complete catalog of O'Reilly's books on .NET and related technologies, including sample chapters and code examples.

ONDotnet.com provides independent coverage of fundamental, interoperable, and emerging Microsoft .NET programming and web services technologies.

Conferences

O'Reilly brings diverse innovators together to nurture the ideas that spark revolutionary industries. We specialize in documenting the latest tools and systems, translating the innovator's knowledge into useful skills for those in the trenches. Visit *conferences.oreilly.com* for our upcoming events.

Safari Bookshelf (*safari.oreilly.com*) is the premier online reference library for programmers and IT professionals. Conduct searches across more than 1,000 books. Subscribers can zero in on answers to time-critical questions in a matter of seconds. Read the books on your Bookshelf from cover to cover or simply flip to the page you need. Try it today for free.

Programming .NET 3.5

Jesse Liberty and Alex Horovitz

O'REILLY®

Beijing · Cambridge · Farnham · Köln · Sebastopol · Taipei · Tokyo

Programming .NET 3.5
by Jesse Liberty and Alex Horovitz

Copyright © 2008 Jesse Liberty and Alex Horovitz. All rights reserved.
Printed in the United States of America.

Published by O'Reilly Media, Inc., 1005 Gravenstein Highway North, Sebastopol, CA 95472.

O'Reilly books may be purchased for educational, business, or sales promotional use. Online editions are also available for most titles (*safari.oreilly.com*). For more information, contact our corporate/institutional sales department: (800) 998-9938 or *corporate@oreilly.com*.

Editor: John Osborn
Production Editor: Rachel Monaghan
Copyeditor: Rachel Head
Proofreader: Rachel Monaghan

Indexer: Ellen Troutman Zaig
Cover Designer: Karen Montgomery
Interior Designer: David Futato
Illustrator: Jessamyn Read

Printing History:

July 2008:   First Edition.

 This book uses RepKover™, a durable and flexible lay-flat binding.

ISBN: 978-0-596-52756-3
[M]

This book is dedicated to the simple idea of human respect, which entails the incredibly difficult process of actually listening to one another with an open mind.

—Jesse Liberty

To my spouse, Torri, and my three boys, Daniel, Zachary, and Jason. Together our adventure continues. Each day brings new opportunities and the chance to build on the accomplishments of the day before. Never stop living to make today the best day of your life.

—Alex Horovitz

Table of Contents

Part II.   Interlude on Design Patterns

Part III.   The Business Layer

Preface

This book tells the story of .NET 3.5. We will not try to sell you on why .NET 3.5 is great, why it will make you more productive, why you should learn it, why your company should invest in incorporating this new technology, and so on. Microsoft has lots of folks selling .NET 3.5, and they are quite good at their jobs, so we'll leave that to them. Nor will we regurgitate the Microsoft documentation; you can get that for free on the Internet. Finally, while we hope you will return to this book often and keep it on your desk as a useful reference, our goal is *not* to provide a compendium, but simply to introduce you to .NET 3.5, speaking as one programmer to another.

In the early days of personal computing, the hard part was finding the information you needed, because so little was published. Today, the hard part is separating the nuggets of wheat from the mountains of chaff. There is a blizzard of information out there (books, articles, web sites, blogs, videos, podcasts, sky writing…), but the signal-to-noise ratio approaches zero (while the metaphors are beginning to pile up under your feet!). Our aim is to provide you with the key information you need, together with a context for that information: a scaffolding into which you can fit what you learn to make you more productive and to make your programs *better*.

It is our belief that .NET 3.5 in general, and Silverlight in particular, will change programming more significantly than anything that has come from Microsoft for at least a decade.

The advent of .NET 3.5 marks a turning point in how we approach programming—one we embrace with great enthusiasm. From one perspective, .NET 3.5 is nothing more than a collection of disparate technologies:

- Windows Presentation Foundation (WPF) for writing Windows applications
- Silverlight for delivering Rich Internet Applications (RIAs) via the Web, across browsers and platforms
- Windows Communication Foundation (WCF) for creating contract-based web services and implementing Service-Oriented Architectures (SOAs)
- Windows Workflow Foundation (WF) for defining the workflow in an application

- CardSpace for creating user-negotiated identities on the Web
- ASP.NET/AJAX for rich-client web applications

You can expect to see many books that treat each of these technologies individually, but in this book we have instead chosen to take an integrated approach. This book has two goals. The first, as we have intimated, is to tell the real story of .NET 3.5, rather than simply repeating what you can find in the documentation. We will provide the essential information that you need to make solid, practical, reliable use of all of the technologies we've just mentioned, while providing a clear picture of which problems each of the technologies solves, either alone or working with others.

The second goal is to show that, rather than truly being a collection of isolated technologies, the various parts of .NET 3.5 can be stitched together into a coherent whole with a pair of common themes:

- .NET 3.5 fosters the development of better-architected applications (leveraging MVC, n-tier, SOA, and other industry-tested patterns).
- .NET 3.5 augments object-oriented programming with a big dose of declarative programming.

Together, these changes—which lead to better-architected applications that leverage a rich declarative extensible markup language—combine to foster the creation of richer applications that break traditional platform boundaries and, perhaps more importantly, applications that are brought to market more quickly and are easier to scale, extend, modify, and maintain.

So, buckle your seat belts...this is going to be a blast!

Who This Book Is For

This book is intended for experienced .NET programmers who have written Windows applications and/or web applications for the Windows platform and who are at least comfortable with either the C# or the Visual Basic language.

In truth, highly motivated Java™ programmers should have little trouble either; experience with .NET will make life easier, but the motivated Java-experienced reader should find few areas of confusion.

How This Book Is Organized

This book will take a goal- and objective-oriented approach to the .NET 3.5 suite of framework and related technologies, and will focus implicitly on an MVC/n-tier and SOA approach to building applications. We will make best practices and pattern-based programming techniques explicit from the very beginning, without letting these architectural design patterns get in the way of straightforward explanations of the new classes and how to put them to work.

We will urge you, as developers, to stop thinking about "desktop versus web" applications and to think instead about the problem to be solved, the model or engine that represents the solution, and from there to proceed downward to persistence and upward to presentation.

A range of presentation choices is available, including Windows Forms, WPF, Silverlight, ASP.NET/AJAX, and ASP.NET. We will not demonstrate the use of Windows Forms or ASP.NET, as familiarity with these technologies is assumed; we will focus instead on WPF, AJAX, and Silverlight. This approach will enable you to extract maximum value from learning the new technologies without getting bogged down in the technologies of the past.

The book consists of 14 chapters organized into three parts.

Part I, Presentation Options

Chapter 1, *.NET 3.5: A Better Framework for Building MVC, N-Tier, and SOA Applications*
> This chapter provides a short observation on the real power of .NET 3.5.

Chapter 2, *Introducing XAML: A Declarative Way to Create Windows UIs*
> The single biggest change in the presentation layer that .NET 3.5 provides is the ability to create a desktop-based presentation using a declarative syntax. XAML—which originally stood for eXtensible Application Markup Language—is the declarative thread that runs through WPF, WF, and Silverlight. This chapter discusses the advantages of declaring objects in XAML, while exploring the XAML syntax and the tools you will use to create objects and move fluidly between XAML and managed code (C#).
>
> In addition, this chapter provides a solid introduction to elements; attributes; attached and binding properties; events and event handlers; layout positioning; stacks, grids, and other essential elements; switching between XAML, design, and code view; and debugging XAML.

Chapter 3, *Introducing Windows Presentation Foundation: A Richer Desktop UI Experience*
> Windows Presentation Foundation is the rich-user-interface technology that provides developers with triggers, 2-D and 3-D objects, rich text, animation, and much more—all built on top of XAML. In this chapter we'll look at the use of styles, triggers, resources, and storyboards in WPF, and at how XAML is put to work to build rich desktop applications.

Chapter 4, *Applying WPF: Building a Biz App*
> In this chapter we expand on the material in Chapter 3, building a rich desktop application using WPF.

Chapter 5, *Introducing AJAX: Moving Desktop UIs to the Web*

This chapter provides an introduction to the Microsoft AJAX library and includes a rant on our premise that using AJAX should be dead simple. We explore the script manager and the extended AJAX controls and discuss why we believe AJAX is a .NET 3.5 technology, even if no one else at Microsoft does (hint: it fosters the kinds of programming that .NET 3.5 is so good at, and it works and plays well with all of the rest of .NET 3.5).

Chapter 6, *Applying AJAX: ListMania*

In this chapter we build on the discussion in Chapter 5 by developing a real-world, web-based AJAX-enhanced application.

Chapter 7, *Introducing Silverlight: A Richer Web UI Platform*

This chapter introduces you to Silverlight. Leveraging many of the advantages of .NET 3.5, Silverlight delivers all the deployment and platform-agnostic benefits that come with a browser-deployed application—and it does so without giving up the rich interactivity of WPF.

Part II, Interlude on Design Patterns

Chapter 8, *Implementing Design Patterns with .NET 3.5*

This chapter discusses the ways in which .NET 3.5 promotes the implementation of architectural patterns in day-to-day programming. Our thesis is that while we have been paying lip service to Model-View-Controller and n-tier programming for the past decade, .NET 1.0 and 2.0 did not foster this approach, and many .NET programs were, inevitably and as a direct result of the framework itself, really two-tier at best.

Part III, The Business Layer

Chapter 9, *Understanding LINQ: Queries As First-Class Language Constructs*

This chapter shows you how to replace the cumbersome ADO.NET database classes with embedded SQL using .NET 3.5's built-in support for Language INtegrated Query (LINQ).

Chapter 10, *Introducing Windows Communication Foundation: Accessible Service-Oriented Architecture*

This chapter defines SOA and explains the problem it solves. It then shows how WCF can be used to implement SOA, exploring such key topics as the service model as a software resource, binding a service for accessing the resource, using the service, and hosting the service in IIS. The chapter also describes the ABCs (access, bindings, and contract) of creating a web service.

Chapter 11, *Applying WCF: YahooQuotes*

This chapter builds on the concepts explained in the previous chapter, presenting a complete example of a WCF application.

Chapter 12, *Introducing Windows Workflow Foundation*
> What is workflow, and how might you use it? How could it serve as a business layer in your application? This chapter explores the use of workflow in human interaction, business processes, software processes and development, and more. We discuss various types of workflow, with an emphasis on sequential processing.

Chapter 13, *Applying WF: Building a State Machine*
> In this chapter we build a complete workflow application, demonstrating all the concepts explained in the previous chapter.

Chapter 14, *Using and Applying CardSpace: A New Scheme for Establishing Identity*
> CardSpace is based on identity selectors that allow a user to present any of numerous identities to a web site, based on the level of trust required and the user's willingness to trade some level of privacy for some return of value.
>
> When a user logs into a CardSpace-aware web site, the CardSpace service is displayed, and the user picks an identity card to pass to the web site, much as you might choose between a general ID, a government-issue ID, or a credit card from your wallet, depending on with whom you are interacting.

What You Need to Use This Book

To work through the examples in this book you will need a computer running Windows Vista, Windows XP (SP2), or Windows Server 2003 SP1.

You'll also need to ensure that you've installed .NET Framework 3.5 and Visual Studio 2008, both of which are available from Microsoft.

Conventions Used in This Book

The following typographical conventions are used in this book:

Italic
> Indicates new terms, URLs, email addresses, filenames, file extensions, pathnames, directories, and Unix utilities.

`Constant width`
> Indicates commands, options, switches, variables, attributes, keys, functions, types, classes, namespaces, methods, modules, properties, parameters, values, objects, events, event handlers, XML tags, HTML tags, the contents of files, or the output from commands.

`Constant width bold`
> Shows commands or other text that should be typed literally by the user. Also used for emphasis in code samples.

`Constant width italic`
> Shows text that should be replaced with user-supplied values.

This icon signifies a tip, suggestion, or general note.

This icon indicates a warning or caution.

Using Code Examples

This book is here to help you get your job done. In general, you may use the code in this book in your programs and documentation. You do not need to contact us for permission unless you're reproducing a significant portion of the code. For example, writing a program that uses several chunks of code from this book does not require permission. Selling or distributing a CD-ROM of examples from O'Reilly books *does* require permission. Answering a question by citing this book and quoting example code does not require permission. Incorporating a significant amount of example code from this book into your product's documentation *does* require permission.

We appreciate, but do not require, attribution. An attribution usually includes the title, author, publisher, and ISBN. For example: "*Programming .NET 3.5* by Jesse Liberty and Alex Horovitz. Copyright 2008 Jesse Liberty and Alex Horovitz, 978-0-596-52756-3."

If you feel your use of code examples falls outside fair use or the permission given above, feel free to contact us at *permissions@oreilly.com*.

Comments and Questions

Please address comments and questions concerning this book to the publisher:

O'Reilly Media, Inc.
1005 Gravenstein Highway North
Sebastopol, CA 95472
800-998-9938 (in the United States or Canada)
707-829-0515 (international or local)
707-829-0104 (fax)

We have a web page for this book, where we list errata, examples, and any additional information. You can access this page at:

http://www.oreilly.com/catalog/9780596527563/

To comment or ask technical questions about this book, send email to:

bookquestions@oreilly.com

For more information about our books, conferences, Resource Centers, and the O'Reilly Network, see our web site at:

http://www.oreilly.com

Safari® Books Online

 When you see a Safari® Books Online icon on the cover of your favorite technology book, that means the book is available online through the O'Reilly Network Safari Bookshelf.

Safari offers a solution that's better than e-books. It's a virtual library that lets you easily search thousands of top tech books, cut and paste code samples, download chapters, and find quick answers when you need the most accurate, current information. Try it for free at *http://safari.oreilly.com*.

Acknowledgments

Many people helped us along with this book. Thanks to our family members and editors, who helped us bring this book to life; our friends, who gave technical input and practical advice; and our early Rough Cut readers, who gave great feedback and made this a better book.

Presentation Options

CHAPTER 1

.NET 3.5: A Better Framework for Building MVC, N-Tier, and SOA Applications

The release of .NET 3.5 represents one of the most significant advances for Windows and web development in the last decade (arguably since the release of .NET itself). Yet in many ways, it has been lost in the excitement and confusion over the release of constituent and related products. That is, many developers have focused on the trees (e.g., WPF or WCF) rather than on the forest of .NET 3.5.

Granted, it can all be a bit overwhelming. Within less than a year, .NET developers were faced with various previews, betas, and release versions of:

- The Vista operating system
- Windows Presentation Foundation (WPF)
- Windows Communication Foundation (WCF)
- Windows Workflow Foundation (WF)
- CardSpace
- C# 3.0
- VB 9
- Visual Studio 2008
- AJAX
- Silverlight
- ASP.NET/MVC
- XAML

Technically, the .NET 3.5 release is dominated by four new frameworks—WPF, WCF, WF, and CardSpace—which made their first appearances in .NET 3.0. But these libraries were released as part of a commitment to more expressive programming and a greater reliance on industry standards that is clearly expressed, for example, in the release of the AJAX libraries, Silverlight, and the MVC libraries.

It is a major premise of this book that there is one key and unique aspect of .NET 3.5 that sets it apart from previous versions: the level of maturity of its component frameworks and libraries, which is now sufficient to fully support—indeed, to foster—the industry-accepted design patterns we've all been struggling to implement for the past decade.

Specifically, we believe that while .NET programmers have, since version 1, been working to build .NET applications that are n-tier, scalable, and maintainable, the .NET frameworks have not been of sufficient help. Consequently, many .NET programs are two-tier applications that mix the code for data access and business logic with the code that handles the presentation of the user interface. .NET 3.5, however, offers programmers an extensive set of tools and libraries that not only foster n-tier and/or MVC programming, but provide much of the infrastructure and plumbing needed to make true separation of responsibility the natural outcome.

Integration Versus Silos

One perfectly valid approach to .NET 3.5 is to write about each of the .NET technologies individually. We call books that take this approach—including such worthwhile and in-depth titles as Chris Sells's and Ian Griffiths's *Programming WPF*, Juval Lowy's *Programming WCF Services* (both O'Reilly), and others—"silo books," because they isolate the technologies from one another, like separate types of grains in their individual silos. What these books lose in their integrated perspectives, they make up for in tremendous depth.

This book, however, takes a different approach. Our aim is to show you enough about each of these technologies to enable you to make practical use of them. Rather than considering them in isolation, we will endeavor to tie them together with the common thread of showing how they each contribute to building robust, scalable, maintainable, high-quality applications.

Big Ideas, Small Examples

The paradox in weaving together these ideas and teaching these disparate technologies is that exploring a single application in all its complexity actually gets in the way of understanding each of the building blocks. Thus, we will keep our examples simple and focused. We will, however, take every opportunity as we move from framework to framework to show how they work together, offering an integrated approach.

In Chapter 8 we provide an explicit review of some of the most common and well-established (some might say cherished) programming patterns and show how .NET 3.5 fosters their implementation.

It Ain't Just the Framework

Because this book is targeted at working .NET programmers, we've used the broadest definition of .NET 3.5—that is, we've attempted to include the full breadth of .NET technologies currently available.

It's a Moving Target

Microsoft's research and development budget is roughly equivalent to the GDP of a small European country, so the pace of innovation can be staggering. Over the past decade, "Windows" developers have been offered massive improvements ranging from the move from C++ and the MFC to C# and Windows Forms, to the maturation of C# and the introduction of WPF. On the web side, we've seen the introduction of ASP and then ASP.NET, the addition of AJAX, and now the introduction of Rich Internet Application (RIA) programming with Silverlight. Access to data and decoupling of business logic from underlying data structures have undergone similar transitions, with the progression from ADO to ADO.NET to LINQ. The list of improvements goes on and on, including better and more sophisticated mechanisms to manage metadata, reflection, threading, networking, web services, business objects, and more.

This book had to be *completely* revised even before it was released just to keep up with the changes in the technologies that occurred during the process of developing it. In a sense, you are actually already reading the second edition.

Fortunately, four forces are now working to make mastering these technologies more manageable:

- The greater coherence and maturation of the .NET technologies, which will naturally make new offerings easier to integrate into what you already know
- An increased commitment from Microsoft to providing information and support, as exemplified by sites such as Silverlight.net, ASP.net, and so forth
- Better-informed and higher-quality books throughout the technical publishing industry, such as those offered by O'Reilly, A-Press, Addison-Wesley, and others
- A far higher signal-to-noise ratio in the blogosphere

What? All That in One Book?

A perfectly reasonable question to ask before plunking down your money is, "If 600-page books have been written about *each* of these technologies, how can you hope to teach anything useful about *all* of them in a single volume (though it is obviously an incredibly well-written book, I must admit)?"

The answer is, fortunately for us both as authors and as developers, that these seemingly disparate frameworks have a great deal in common; our goal is to show you the 25% that you will use 85% of the time. We don't pretend that this is the only book you will ever need on all of these topics, though it may well be the only book you need to consult about those parts of .NET that are not central to your business.

But let us be clear: this is not an overview, nor do we intend it to be read by pointy-headed managers. This is a book *by* developers *for* developers that is meant to be a useful reference and to provide you with sufficient core capability in each area to enable you to write real-world commercial applications.

CHAPTER 2

Introducing XAML: A Declarative Way to Create Windows UIs

Before the appearance of .NET 3.0, web applications were written with "markup languages" such as HTML and Windows applications were not. We may have dragged controls onto forms, but the creation of the controls and their properties was managed by the development environment, or you instantiated them programmatically at runtime.

.NET 3.0 changed all that with the introduction of the eXtensible Application Markup Language, or XAML (pronounced "zamel," to rhyme with "camel"). There are two key things to know about XAML:

1. It is a markup language for creating Windows applications, just as HTML is a markup language for creating web applications.

2. Almost every XAML object has a corresponding Common Language Runtime (CLR) object; most of what you can create declaratively in XAML you can also create programmatically in C#, and vice versa.

The goal of this chapter is to provide an overview of XAML and how it is used in creating user experiences. By the end of this chapter you should have an appreciation of XAML as a declarative language, an understanding of the basic elements and attributes that you are likely to encounter when writing a .NET 3.5 application, and a fundamental appreciation for hand-crafting meaningful XAML applications. We will not cover every element in the XAML vocabulary, but we will cover the entire landscape of XAML, demonstrating all of its significant capabilities.

 For a detailed treatment of the XAML markup language, we highly recommend *XAML in a Nutshell*, by Lori A. MacVittie (O'Reilly).

XAML 101

Historically, developers have often had a difficult time translating user interface designers' ideas into an implementation that worked on a specific development platform. Designers, for their part, were often forced to compromise their designs to accommodate the limitations of software tools. In short, the worlds of design and development did not share a common border, and this created significant frustration. XAML, a new declarative programming language, was specifically designed to provide that common border.

Interface Versus Implementation

A *declarative* programming language is a high-level language that describes a problem rather than defining a solution. In other words, declarative programming languages deal with the "what" (i.e., the goals of your program), and *imperative* programming languages deal with the "how" (the details of achieving those goals). Declarative code is typically used to design the interface, while programming code (e.g., C#) is typically used to provide the implementation.

Purely declarative languages, in general, do not "compute" anything; rather, they specify relationships. For example, in a declarative language you might say "a text box with a one-pixel border will be drawn here," while in an imperative language you would specify the algorithm for drawing the text box.

HTML is declarative, because you use it to specify how a web page will look (but not how to implement that presentation). XAML is also a declarative language, but most of its elements correspond exactly to objects in an imperative language (e.g., C#). This makes it a tremendously powerful and flexible markup language, as you can declare in your markup how Windows pages will appear as well as behave.

Consider a wristwatch, as shown in Figure 2-1. The user or designer is most interested in the interface. (Is it easy to tell the time? Are the numbers clear? Can I distinguish the hour hand from the minute hand? Are the numbers in the conventional places? What font is used?)

Figure 2-1. Interface versus implementation

The developer, on the other hand, may be more interested in the implementation. (How do I create a mechanism that will ensure that the watch tells the correct time, all the time, while meeting all the design requirements for cost, size, reliability, and so on?)

XAML greatly improves collaboration between designers and developers because it is, as Microsoft describes it, "toolable" (that is, it can be manipulated by software tools). This helps foster the separation of the interface design from the implementation: it encourages companies to build some tools targeted at designers and other tools targeted at programmers, all of which can interact with the same underlying XAML.

For example, in some companies designers work with UI tools (such as Microsoft's Blend) to create the UI, and then generate XAML that developers can import into code-oriented tools such as Visual Studio.

 So, you might ask, why didn't Microsoft leverage an existing markup language such as HTML for creating the user interface? The short answer is that HTML simply wasn't rich enough to express everything that is required for a Windows application. HTML was intended from the outset to be a "cut-down" and simplified markup language. XAML, on the other hand, builds on the industry-standard XML and is inherently extensible.

With XAML, most interfaces have representations, and each interface property is represented by an XML element and/or attribute. All of the information about a XAML-based application window is contained in the XAML file itself, and a single XAML file can contain all that the parser needs to know to render the view.

Each view will contain XAML elements, nodes, and other components, organized hierarchically. A XAML-based view also describes an *object model*, which creates the window at runtime. Each of the elements and nodes described in the XAML document is instantiated and the object model is created in memory. This allows for programmatic manipulation of the object model: the programmer can add and remove elements and nodes, changing the page and re-rendering it as it changes.

Looking at XAML in terms of its relationship to CLR objects and types, WPF defines types to represent controls and other UI elements, and the XAML parser simply maps tags to types. For example, the following code for a <Button> tag sets a few properties of a Button control:

```
<Button Width="20" Height="10">OK Button</Button>
```

XAML element names are mostly one-to-one mappings of CLR type names. Similarly, the attributes of each element are mappings of the members exposed by the object referenced in the element name. The net effect is that there is a single unified API; XAML objects are CLR objects, and vice versa.

Getting Yourself Up and Running

To follow along with the examples in this chapter, you will need a machine running Vista. Please make sure you also have:

- .NET Framework 3.5
- Microsoft Windows Software Development Kit for Windows Vista and .NET Framework 3.0 Runtime Components (*http://tinyurl.com/y7hudw*)

 It is very important that your .NET Framework, SDK, and Visual Studio extensions all be from the same release. Please check the Microsoft documentation for more information to make sure you have the right versions properly loaded. Even though this is a book about .NET 3.5 (and you will need that SDK and Framework as well), we'll be using XAMLPad for the examples in this chapter, and at the time of this writing, XAMLPad is available only as part of the .NET 3.0 SDK.

Simple XAML Done Simply

Markup languages combine information about the UI elements (text, images, etc.) with attribute information (boldness, opacity, etc.). In HTML you might write the following:

```
<b><i>XAML is a markup language</i></b>
```

This would lead to a web browser displaying the text as follows:

XAML is a markup language

The text is augmented by markup that tells the browser to render it in bold italics.

The same combination of UI elements and markup applies to XAML, making it a very convenient way to approach the presentation layer of your Windows applications. Consider this simple XAML example:

```
<Page xmlns="http://schemas.microsoft.com/winfx/2006/xaml/presentation"
    xmlns:x="http://schemas.microsoft.com/winfx/2006/xaml" >
  <Grid>
     <Label
         Content="Hello World"
         FontFamily="Verdana"
         FontSize="32pt" />
  </Grid>
</Page>
```

This displays "Hello World" in 32-point Verdana, as shown in Figure 2-2.

Figure 2-2. Simple XAML example

The `<Label />` tag represents a standard `System.Windows.Controls` label. Therefore, you can expect that through the attributes of the tag, you will have access to all the members exposed by the `Label` type. You can set them declaratively (as shown here with the `Content`, `FontFamily`, and `FontSize` attributes), or you can manipulate them programmatically at runtime.

In general, you will find that XAML obeys completely the XML syntax rules.

 Naming each element that you create using the `ID` or `Name` attribute will allow you to refer to the element in code. We recommend using self-documenting naming conventions rather than cryptic names that require explanatory comments.

Because XAML effectively *is* XML, your documents must be "well formed." While the total set of rules can be complex,[*] the principal things to keep in mind are:

- Element and attribute names need to be cased correctly.
- Attribute values must be in quotes.
- Elements may not overlap (though they may be nested).

XAML elements fall into a limited number of categories: root elements, control elements, panel elements, shape and geometric elements, and document elements. Taken together, these five categories provide user interface designers with some spectacular opportunities to create rich user experiences.

 As we move further into this chapter, the examples will get much longer. Please take the time to download the *.xaml* files from *http://tinyurl.com/35yrm5*.

---

[*] See *http://www.w3.org/TR/REC-xml/* for more information.

Panel Elements

A *panel element* is a container, designed to support the layout and placement of elements on a page. Panels come in several different shapes and sizes. Depending on how you exercise them, they are useful for laying out different types of elements.

As an example, open up XAMLPad and type the following (broken) code into the code window (replacing whatever code was already there):

```
<Window
    xmlns="http://schemas.microsoft.com/winfx/2006/xaml/presentation"
    xmlns:x="http://schemas.microsoft.com/winfx/2006/xaml"
    Title="My Window" Height="300" Width="300"
    >
    <Grid Name="AGrid" Background="AntiqueWhite">

</Window>
```

As you can see in Figure 2-3, the Auto Parse mode allows you to see syntax errors immediately as you enter XAML.

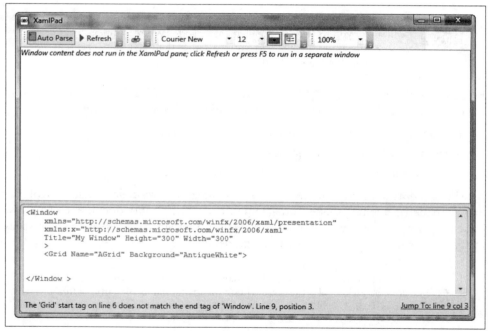

Figure 2-3. XAMLPad shows errors automagically

If an error is encountered, the entire XAML content is displayed in red, and the status information at the bottom of the XAMLPad window displays the specific syntax error. A hyperlink to the right of the displayed error allows you to jump to the area of XAML content that contains the error.

In our broken code example, the status information indicates that the `<Grid>` start tag on line 6 does not match the end tag of `</Window >`. This message is—as error messages often are—a little misleading; what it means is that there is no close tag for the Grid element. To fix this, you can add a close grid tag (`</Grid>`) after the opening `<Grid>` tag and before the close window tag (`</Window>`). Once you've corrected this error, your XAMLPad window should look like Figure 2-4.

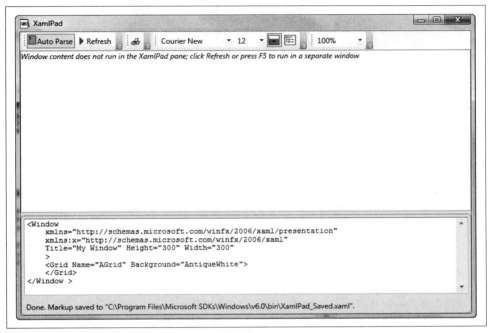

Figure 2-4. XAML with no errors displays without an error message

Now, if you click the Refresh button, XAMLPad will instantiate a window labeled "My Window" with an off-white background, as shown in Figure 2-5.

Root Elements

Root elements are special derivations of panel elements. They serve as the fundamental containers for pages. Every page requires exactly one root element. In the next chapter, when we build an application with Visual Studio, you will notice that the default root element is Grid. It is not uncommon for other panel elements (e.g., StackPanel, DockPanel, or Canvas, as well as Page and Window) to serve as root elements. The root element must contain a reference to the namespace needed by the other elements in the container.

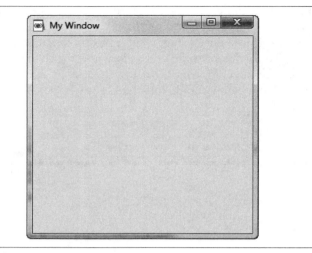

Figure 2-5. My Window

You should be able to type the following code into XAMLPad and get a result similar to the Hello World text we showed previously:

```
<Page
    xmlns="http://schemas.microsoft.com/winfx/2006/xaml/presentation"
    xmlns:x="http://schemas.microsoft.com/winfx/2006/xaml"
    Title="Hello" Height="300" Width="300"
    >
    <Grid Name="HelloWorldGrid">
        <Label
            Name="HelloWorldLabel"
            Content="Hello World"
            FontFamily="Verdana"
            FontSize="32pt"
        />
    </Grid>
</Page>
```

This time we did not use a Window container, but rather a Page container. Your XAMLPad display should automatically have rendered "Hello World" in 32-point Verdana, as shown in Figure 2-6.

All XAML documents expect that the elements contained inside the root element be appropriately referenced via namespace declarations. We do this here by declaring the namespace(s) for our controls as attributes of the Page:

```
xmlns="http://schemas.microsoft.com/winfx/2006/xaml/presentation"
```

If the provided elements are too rudimentary for you, you can create custom elements by deriving new classes from Page or Window and exposing them as XAML elements. Indeed, for very sophisticated user interactions where the standard features may not suffice, this is probably the desired course of action.

Figure 2-6. Hello World

Control Elements

Control elements are user-manipulated objects that help with data or user interactions. Controls can be differentiated into five types based on their support of the Content, Header, and Item attributes:

- Simple controls
- Content controls
- Item controls
- Headered item controls
- Headered content controls

Simple controls

A *simple control* does not have Content, Header, or Item attributes. Controls like images, frames, and scroll bars all fall into this category. The next snippet shows an example of an Image control in a window:

```
<Window
    xmlns="http://schemas.microsoft.com/winfx/2006/xaml/presentation"
    xmlns:x="http://schemas.microsoft.com/winfx/2006/xaml"
    Title="Image" Height="100" Width="200"
    >
    <Grid Name="StuffToBuy">

    <Image
        Source="http://www.oreilly.com/images/oreilly/add_to_cart.gif"
        Height="33"
        Width="142"
        />

    </Grid>
</Window>
```

If you run this in XAMLPad, you should get something like Figure 2-7.

Figure 2-7. An image embedded in a window

While this code just displays an image, it is easy to see how you could make this functional in your application by embedding the Image inside a Button control:

```
<Button Height="33" Width="142" Background="Transparent">
    <Image
        Source="http://www.oreilly.com/images/oreilly/add_to_cart.gif"/>
</Button>
```

Change your code in XAMLPad and hit Refresh. You should get a clickable button similar to Figure 2-8. Note that it registers the mouse click by changing the button's color.

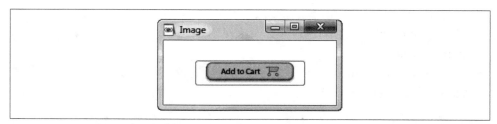

Figure 2-8. Image control embedded in a Button control

Content controls

Content controls display some sort of content. They fall into two categories: simple and complex. *Simple content controls* display single elements. They include TextBoxes, Buttons, and Labels. *Complex content controls* can display multiple elements. DockPanel and StackPanel are two of the most important complex content controls.

We'll begin with an example of a simple content control. There are two ways to set the content of a Button control. The first is to place it between the open and close element tags:

```
<Button Height="30" Width="100">
    Click on Me
</Button>
```

The second is to use the Content attribute:

```
<Button Height="30" Width="100" Content="Click on Me" />
```

Most content controls have a Content attribute; they may also have Header and/or Item attributes. You can also embed controls inside the open and close element tags:

```
<Button Height="30" Width="150" Background="Transparent">
    <TextBox>Click to type in here</TextBox>
</Button>
```

(Although I must confess I don't know why you would ever want a text box inside a button, from a design point of view.)

Now let's look at a complex content control. If we start with a DockPanel and add an image and our crazy Button with the TextBox, we'll wind up with code like this:

```
<Window
    xmlns="http://schemas.microsoft.com/winfx/2006/xaml/presentation"
    xmlns:x="http://schemas.microsoft.com/winfx/2006/xaml"
    Title="Dock Panel" Height="100" Width="400"
    >
<Grid Name="StuffToBuy">
<DockPanel>
    <Image
        Source="http://www.oreilly.com/images/oreilly/add_to_cart.gif"
        Height="33" Width="142" />
    <Button Height="30" Width="150" Background="Transparent">
        <TextBox>Click to type in here</TextBox>
    </Button>
</DockPanel>
</Grid>
</Window>
```

A job the DockPanel can do nicely is to render the elements in the order in which they are declared, from left to right. (You may use attributes of the DockPanel to alter the relative positions of the child elements.)

The result is shown in Figure 2-9.

Figure 2-9. Complex content control using a DockPanel

Now change the DockPanel to a StackPanel and change the height and width of the Window to 120 and 170, respectively. You will see a difference in how the user interface is rendered: while the DockPanel by default orients its child objects horizontally, the StackPanel by default orients its children vertically, as shown in Figure 2-10.

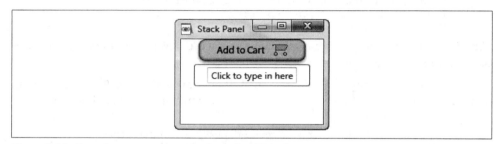

Figure 2-10. Complex content control using a StackPanel

Item controls

Item controls have children, including controls with collections. *Headered item controls* have no Content attributes, but they do have Header and (optionally) Item attributes. As an example, a Menu is an item control, and it contains a collection of MenuItem(s). MenuItem(s) are headered item controls, as shown in the following example:

```
<Window
    xmlns="http://schemas.microsoft.com/winfx/2006/xaml/presentation"
    Title="Hello and Goodbye" Height="300" Width="300"
    >
<StackPanel
    Name="HelloWorldGrid"
    Background="AntiqueWhite"
    >
```

```
<Menu
    Height="21" Margin="0,0,0,0">
    <MenuItem Header="Say Hello">
        <MenuItem Header="Hello Jesse" />
        <MenuItem Header="Hello Alex" />
    </MenuItem>
    <MenuItem Header="Say Goodbye">
        <MenuItem Header="Goodbye Jesse" />
        <MenuItem Header="Goodbye Alex" />
    </MenuItem>
</Menu>
<Label
    Content="Hello Goodbye"
    FontFamily="Verdana"
    FontSize="32"
/>
</StackPanel>
</Window>
```

When you launch this code from XAMLPad, you get a window that looks like
Figure 2-11. You can see how the Menu control exposes its list of MenuItem(s). We
have used the implicit Item declaration of MenuItem to expose the child menu items:

```
Pseudocode to follow:
MenuItem Header="Parent">
    <MenuItem Header="Child">
        <MenuItem Header="Grandchild">
            <MenuItem Header="Great Grandchild" />
        </MenuItem>
    </MenuItem>
</MenuItem>
```

Figure 2-11. Item controls and headered item controls in the form on a menu

To keep the example focused, the menus drop down but do not change the text in the main window.

Headered content controls

Headered content controls can have a `Header` attribute and a `Content` attribute but no `Item` attribute. Like a content control, a headered content control can have only one child in its `Content` attribute, and you can set the content implicitly or explicitly. For example, you could set the content of an `Expander` control like this:

```
<Expander Height="50"
    Name="MyExpander"
    VerticalAlignment="Bottom" >
        When you click on an expander it shows its content.
</Expander>
```

or like this:

```
<Expander Height="50"
    Name="MyExpander"
    VerticalAlignment="Bottom"
    Content="When you click on an expander it shows its content."
/>
```

Document Elements

Document elements are another interesting aspect of XAML. Most of us are familiar with the first case of the document element, the `FixedDocument`. This is the traditional *what you see is what you get* (WYSIWYG) view of a document that we all know and love. The example presented here uses a `FlowDocument`, which provides much greater flexibility in how the document is rendered and improves user experience.

Coupled with a rich set of controls, a flow document can make for a very pleasant reading experience. Things are going to get a bit recursive here, as we look at how the first part of this chapter might look as a flow document.

The complete code for XAMLPad follows (you can find it in the source you downloaded for this chapter). You may want to enter each paragraph in turn and then press F5 to watch the demonstration grow one step at a time. You don't have to type in all the text between the `<Paragraph>` and `</Paragraph>` tags to get the full effect of this example. Here's the code:

```
<Window
    xmlns="http://schemas.microsoft.com/winfx/2006/xaml/presentation"
    xmlns:x="http://schemas.microsoft.com/winfx/2006/xaml"
    Title="Programming .NET 3.5 | Chapter 3">
<FlowDocument>
```

```
<Paragraph FontSize="28" Foreground="Red">
    Introducing XAML: A Declarative Way to Create Windows UIs
</Paragraph>
<Paragraph>
    Before the appearance of .NET 3.0, web applications were written with "markup
    languages" such as HTML and Windows applications were not. We may have
    dragged controls onto forms, but the creation of the controls and their
    properties was managed by the development environment, or you instantiated
    them programmatically at runtime.
</Paragraph>
<Paragraph>
    .NET 3.0 changed all that with the introduction of the eXtensible Application
    Markup Language, or XAML (pronounced "zamel," to rhyme with "camel"). There
    are two key things to know about XAML:
</Paragraph>
<Paragraph>
    1. It is a markup language for creating Windows applications, just as HTML is
    a markup language for creating web applications.
</Paragraph>
<Paragraph>
    2. Almost every XAML object has a corresponding Common Language Runtime (CLR)
    object; most of what you can create declaratively in XAML you can also create
    programmatically in C#, and vice versa.
</Paragraph>
<Paragraph>
    The goal of this chapter is to provide an overview of XAML and how it is used
    in creating user experiences. By the end of this chapter you should have an
    appreciation of XAML as a declarative language, an understanding of the basic
    elements and attributes that you are likely to encounter when writing a .NET
    3.5 application, and a fundamental appreciation for hand-crafting meaningful
    XAML applications. We will not cover every element in the XAML vocabulary,
    but we will cover the entire landscape of XAML, demonstrating all of its
    significant capabilities.
</Paragraph>
<Paragraph>
    For a detailed treatment of the XAML markup language, we highly recommend XAML
    in a Nutshell, by Lori A. MacVittie (O'Reilly).
</Paragraph>
<Paragraph FontSize="24" Foreground="Red">
    XAML 101
</Paragraph>
<Paragraph>
    Historically, developers have often had a difficult time translating user
    interface designers' ideas into an implementation that worked on a specific
    development platform. Designers, for their part, were often forced to
    compromise their designs to accommodate the limitations of software tools. In
    short, the worlds of design and development did not share a common border,
    and this created significant frustration. XAML, a new declarative programming
    language, was specifically designed to provide that common border.
</Paragraph>
<Paragraph FontSize="18" Foreground="Red">
    Interface Versus Implementation
</Paragraph>
```

```
<Paragraph>
   A declarative programming language is a high-level language that describes a
   problem rather than defining a solution. In other words, declarative
   programming languages deal with the "what" (i.e., the goals of your program),
   and imperative programming languages deal with the "how" (the details of
   achieving those goals). Declarative code is typically used to design the
   interface, while programming code (e.g., C#) is typically used to provide the
   implementation.
</Paragraph>
<Paragraph>
   Purely declarative languages, in general, do not "compute" anything; rather,
   they specify relationships. For example, in a declarative language you might
   say "a text box with a one-pixel border will be drawn here," while in an
   imperative language you would specify the algorithm for drawing the text box.
</Paragraph>
<Paragraph>
   HTML is declarative, because you use it to specify how a web page will look
   (but not how to implement that presentation). XAML is also a declarative
   language, but most of its elements correspond exactly to objects in an
   imperative language (e.g., C#). This makes it a tremendously powerful and
   flexible markup language, as you can declare in your markup how Windows pages
   will appear as well as behave.
</Paragraph>
<Paragraph>
   Consider a wristwatch, as shown in Figure 2-1. The user or designer is most
   interested in the interface. (Is it easy to tell the time? Are the numbers
   clear? Can I distinguish the hour hand from the minute hand? Are the numbers
   in the conventional places? What font is used?)
</Paragraph>
<BlockUIContainer>
   <Image Height="184" Width="202"
      Source=" http://alexhorovitz.com/oop/ivi_watch.gif" />
</BlockUIContainer>
<Paragraph FontSize="15" Foreground="Blue">
   Figure 3-1. Interface vs. implementation
</Paragraph>
<Paragraph>
   The developer, on the other hand, may be more interested in the
   implementation. (How do I create a mechanism that will ensure that the watch
   tells the correct time, all the time, while meeting all the design
   requirements for cost, size, reliability, and so on?)
</Paragraph>

</FlowDocument>
</Window>
```

Enter this code in XAMLPad and click the Refresh button. XAMLPad will launch a window that can, through the use of the embedded flow document reader controls, be made to look like Figure 2-12.

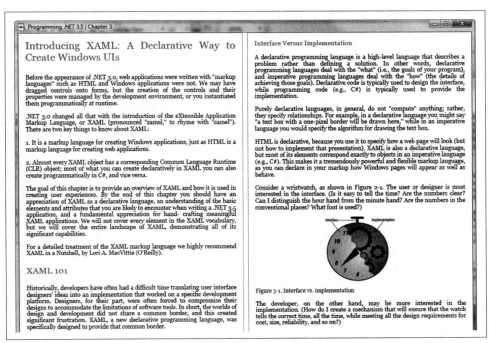

Figure 2-12. FlowDocument version of the opening pages of this chapter

Over Here...No, Wait, I Meant Over There!

One of the major tasks involved in software user experience design is determining what goes where, and why. Once you know what you want to show to a user and why you want to show it, you need a mechanism to address screen size and resolution. Fortunately, XAML (as part of WPF) addresses both these issues automagically.

XAML is rich with options for grouping page resources conveniently and ensuring that layout elements are positioned in a manner to enhance user experience. In addition, XAML elements by default dynamically size to fit their environment. As you can see, with XAML you can easily accommodate the most demanding UI designer's requirements.

When laying out a simple application's user interface, it's convenient to call on two subclasses of `Panel` to do your heavy lifting: `DockPanel` and `StackPanel`. For more complex applications, `Grid` is likely a smarter choice. As you might have guessed from their names, the primary function of these controls is the positioning of elements. They have the added feature of automatically placing elements in the order of their declaration in the XAML.

Review: In our examples, DockPanel is used to lay out elements left to right (although attributes can be used to dock the elements to any border—left, right, top or bottom), while StackPanel is used to stack elements one on top of the other.

We're going to use a fictional employee directory to explore how these controls interoperate with other elements and how they assist in the layout of the user experience.

StackPanel and DockPanel

The first step is to divide the window into three content areas using StackPanel and DockPanel.

Begin by creating a Window element in XAMLPad. Give it a title of "Employee Directory":

```
<Window
    xmlns="http://schemas.microsoft.com/winfx/2006/xaml/presentation"
    Title="Employee Directory" Height="480" Width="640"
    >
```

Then insert a Grid element along with the DockPanel that will contain the three content areas:

```
<Grid>
    <DockPanel LastChildFill="False">
```

Grid is a souped-up form of StackPanel that allows you to orient your layout both horizontally and vertically. Be careful not to confuse this with DataGrid, which, surprisingly, is not present in WPF (yet).

Next, add three Border elements. Border inherits from Decorator and is used to draw a border around an element. It can also be used to provide a background color for an element.

Border, like almost all elements in a DockPanel, has a DockPanel.Dock attribute that you can use to specify its position within the DockPanel. Set the three Border elements' DockPanel.Dock attributes to Top, Left, and Right, respectively, to indicate their desired docking locations. Then add a Label element inside each Border:

```
<Border
    DockPanel.Dock="Top"
    BorderBrush="Black"
    BorderThickness="1"
    Height="70">
    <Label
        FontFamily="Verdana"
        FontSize="32"
        HorizontalAlignment="Center"
    >Top</Label>
</Border>
```

```
<Border
    DockPanel.Dock="Left"
    BorderBrush="Black"
    BorderThickness="1"
    Width="400">
    <StackPanel>
    <Label
        FontFamily="Verdana"
        FontWeight="Bold" FontSize="18"
        HorizontalAlignment="Center"
    >Left</Label>
    </StackPanel>
</Border>
<Border
    DockPanel.Dock="Right"
    BorderBrush="Black"
    BorderThickness="1"
    Width="240">
    <StackPanel>
    <Label
        FontFamily="Verdana"
        FontWeight="Bold" FontSize="18"
        HorizontalAlignment="Center"
    >Right</Label>
    </StackPanel>
</Border>
```

Close the opened tags from the start and test the program:

```
</DockPanel>
```

```
</Grid>
</Window>
```

Assuming you've typed everything correctly, you should end up with a window that looks like the one in Figure 2-13.

As you can see, layout in XAML is not very different from layout in HTML. If you are going to code XAML without the aid of a layout tool, it's helpful to envision the layout in terms of columns and rows.

XAML also combines the x,y layout positioning you get with CSS, so you can be very precise in the placement of your elements.

Moving beyond columns and rows

The first enhancement we'll make to our Employee Directory is to add an image that we'll pull from a web site. In part, this is to demonstrate that .NET 3.5 applications can mix and match resources: you can reference images locally, but you can also reference remote images using a number of protocols. In this case, we're going to retrieve an image via an HTTP request.

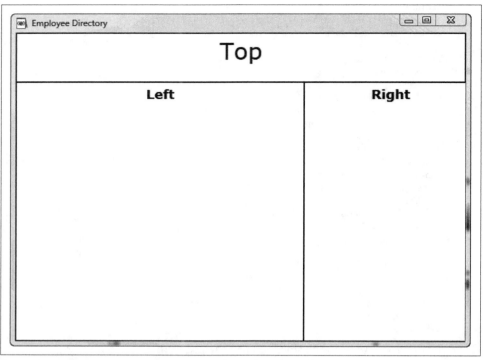

Figure 2-13. Three content sections using Border and DockPanel

In the "right" DockPanel, inside the Border, add a StackPanel and an Image (delete the Label that was there previously):

```
<Border
    DockPanel.Dock="Right"
    BorderBrush="Black"
    BorderThickness="1"
    Width="240">
  <!-- New Content -->
  <StackPanel>
    <Image Name="EmployeePicture"
        Margin="0,10,0,0"
        Height="200"
        HorizontalAlignment="Center"
        VerticalAlignment="Top"
        Width="200"
        Source="http://alexhorovitz.com/DotNet3/Alex_w200.jpg"/>
  </StackPanel>
  <!-- End New Content -->
</Border>
```

Note that we set the Margin attribute to ensure that the image appears at least 10 pixels from the top of the Border container. We also used the HorizontalAlignment and VerticalAlignment attributes to ensure the image is positioned correctly relative to the container. It is important to understand that all positioning happens relative to the parent container.

When you run this code, you will get a window that looks like Figure 2-14.

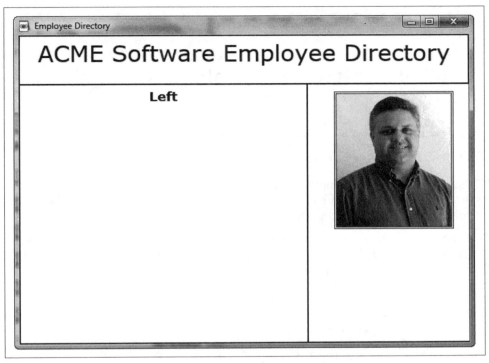

Figure 2-14. The Employee Directory with a picture from an HTTP request

Now we'll fill in the other `Border` containers, using a smattering of XAML elements and attribute formatting to create a nice user experience.

We'll start with the `Border` that has been attached to the "top" of our dock panel. Here, we're going to change the existing `Label` and set the font. This will give us the desired effect on the text of the label:

```
<Border
    DockPanel.Dock="Top"
    BorderBrush="Black"
    BorderThickness="1"
    Height="70">
    <Label
        FontFamily="Verdana"
        FontSize="32pt"
        HorizontalAlignment="Center"
    >
    ACME Software Employee Directory
    </Label>
</Border>
```

When you run this again in XAMLPad, you will see a nice banner across the top dock panel that says in a 32-point Verdana font "ACME Software Employee Directory," as shown in Figure 2-15.

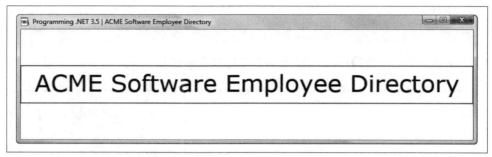

Figure 2-15. ACME Software Employee Directory banner in 32-point Verdana

Things are a little more complicated in the "left" Border, as this will display rows and columns of information. We'll use a series of StackPanel, DockPanel, and Separator elements to get the desired look and feel.

We want the elements in this Border to flow vertically as opposed to horizontally, so we'll use a StackPanel at the top. We'll also introduce some Separator elements to further visually divide this column:

```
<StackPanel>
  <Label
      FontFamily="Verdana"
      FontWeight="Bold" FontSize="18"
      HorizontalAlignment="Left"
  >Name: Alex Horovitz</Label>
  <Separator
      Height="5"
      Margin="2,0,40,0"
      Name="s1"
      VerticalAlignment="Bottom"
  />
  <Label
      FontFamily="Verdana"
      FontSize="14"
      HorizontalAlignment="Left"
  >Department: Software Engineering</Label>
  <Label
      FontFamily="Verdana"
      FontSize="14"
      HorizontalAlignment="Left"
  >Location: Acton, MA</Label>
  <Label
      FontFamily="Verdana"
      FontSize="14"
      HorizontalAlignment="Left"
  >Email: alex@alexhorovitz.com</Label>
```

```
<Separator
    Height="5"
    Margin="2,0,40,0"
    Name="s2"
    VerticalAlignment="Bottom"
/>
```

This section is pretty straightforward.

We want to place icons near some of the contents of this section, so we're going to want to control the layout at a finer granularity here. In this case, we'll introduce a series of DockPanel elements inside the current StackPanel (immediately following the last Separator). These will contain Border elements, creating a hierarchy that provides us with very fine-grained control over the layout:

```
<DockPanel>
    <Border DockPanel.Dock="Left" BorderThickness="0">
        <Image Width="80"
            Source="http://alexhorovitz.com/DotNet3/Nortel_Phone.gif"/>
    </Border>
    <Border DockPanel.Dock="Right" BorderThickness="0">
        <Label FontFamily="Verdana" FontSize="14"
            HorizontalAlignment="Left"
            VerticalAlignment="Center"
            >978 555 1111</Label>
    </Border>
</DockPanel>
<DockPanel>
    <Border DockPanel.Dock="Left" BorderThickness="0">
        <Image Width="80"
            Source="http://alexhorovitz.com/DotNet3/X-Phone_r2_c3.gif"/>
    </Border>
    <Border DockPanel.Dock="Right" BorderThickness="0">
        <Label FontFamily="Verdana" FontSize="14"
            HorizontalAlignment="Left"
            VerticalAlignment="Center"
            >978 555 1212</Label>
    </Border>
</DockPanel>
<DockPanel>
    <Border DockPanel.Dock="Left" BorderThickness="0">
        <Image Width="80"
            Source="http://alexhorovitz.com/DotNet3/fax.gif"/>
    </Border>
    <Border DockPanel.Dock="Right" BorderThickness="0">
        <Label FontFamily="Verdana" FontSize="14"
            HorizontalAlignment="Left"
            VerticalAlignment="Center"
            >978 555 1313</Label>
    </Border>
</DockPanel>
</StackPanel>
```

This code renders in XAMLPad as shown in Figure 2-16.

Figure 2-16. Full-blown Employee Directory in XAML

Here is the complete code for this example:

```xml
<Window
    xmlns="http://schemas.microsoft.com/winfx/2006/xaml/presentation"
    Title="Employee Directory" Height="480" Width="640"
    >
<Grid>
    <DockPanel>
      <Border
          DockPanel.Dock="Top"
          BorderBrush="Black"
          BorderThickness="1"
          Height="70">
          <Label
              FontFamily="Verdana"
              FontSize="32"
              HorizontalAlignment="Center"
          >ACME Software Employee Directory</Label>
      </Border>
      <Border
          DockPanel.Dock="Left"
          BorderBrush="Black"
          BorderThickness="1"
          Width="400">
          <StackPanel>
```

```
        <Label
            FontFamily="Verdana"
            FontWeight="Bold" FontSize="18"
            HorizontalAlignment="Left"
        >Name: Alex Horovitz</Label>
        <Separator
            Height="5"
            Margin="2,0,40,0"
            Name="s1"
            VerticalAlignment="Bottom"
        />
        <Label
            FontFamily="Verdana"
            FontSize="14"
            HorizontalAlignment="Left"
        >Department: Software Engineering</Label>
        <Label
            FontFamily="Verdana"
            FontSize="14"
            HorizontalAlignment="Left"
        >Location: Acton, MA</Label>
        <Label
            FontFamily="Verdana"
            FontSize="14"
            HorizontalAlignment="Left"
        >Email: alex@alexhorovitz.com</Label>
        <Separator
            Height="5"
            Margin="2,0,40,0"
            Name="s2"
            VerticalAlignment="Bottom"
        />
<DockPanel>
    <Border DockPanel.Dock="Left" BorderThickness="0">
        <Image Width="80"
            Source="http://alexhorovitz.com/DotNet3/Nortel_Phone.gif"/>
    </Border>
    <Border DockPanel.Dock="Right" BorderThickness="0">
        <Label FontFamily="Verdana" FontSize="14"
            HorizontalAlignment="Left"
            VerticalAlignment="Center"
        >978 555 1111</Label>
    </Border>
</DockPanel>
<DockPanel>
    <Border DockPanel.Dock="Left" BorderThickness="0">
        <Image Width="80"
            Source="http://alexhorovitz.com/DotNet3/X-Phone_r2_c3.gif"/>
    </Border>
    <Border DockPanel.Dock="Right" BorderThickness="0">
        <Label FontFamily="Verdana" FontSize="14"
            HorizontalAlignment="Left"
            VerticalAlignment="Center"
        >978 555 1212</Label>
    </Border>
```

```
          </DockPanel>
          <DockPanel>
             <Border DockPanel.Dock="Left" BorderThickness="0">
                <Image Width="80"
                      Source="http://alexhorovitz.com/DotNet3/fax.gif"/>
             </Border>
             <Border DockPanel.Dock="Right" BorderThickness="0">
                <Label FontFamily="Verdana" FontSize="14"
                      HorizontalAlignment="Left"
                      VerticalAlignment="Center"
                   >978 555 1313</Label>
             </Border>
          </DockPanel>
          </StackPanel>
      </Border>
      <Border
          DockPanel.Dock="Right"
          BorderBrush="Black"
          BorderThickness="1"
          Width="240">
          <StackPanel>
             <Image Name="EmployeePicture"
                   Margin="0,10,0,0"
                   Height="200"
                   HorizontalAlignment="Center"
                   VerticalAlignment="Top"
                   Width="200"
                   Source=" http://alexhorovitz.com/DotNet3/Alex_w200.jpg"/>
          </StackPanel>
      </Border>
    </DockPanel>

  </Grid>
  </Window>
```

It's Alive! (Or, How I Learned to Stop Worrying and Love Animation)

XAML is a very powerful declarative language. As we have seen, it allows you to create complex layouts and absorb resources both locally and remotely. But one of the truly amazing things about XAML is that it enables you to animate your user experience.

Our next example will demonstrate how to animate a fairly simple window, with a focus on the nuts and bolts of animation. The XAML code might seem a little daunting at first, but hang in there; you'll come to see that most of it has to do with positioning and the timing of effects.

When you run this example, you should notice that the user interface elements fade in rather than appearing abruptly, and that the artwork in the product name banner is gently animated.

The human eye can process visual information at an astonishing rate, but there are limits. Traditionally, most applications present all UI elements simultaneously. The overloaded eye doesn't know where to look first, and the user is temporarily overwhelmed. By making the UI elements appear in a logical sequence, you can help the user see the story of your presentation.

Animation Overview

We'll go into animation in more detail in the next chapter, but we want to give you a taste now of how much you can do with XAML. Some of the concepts illustrated here aren't discussed fully until the next chapter. Bear with us; they'll be made clear soon.

Two techniques are used for animation. In the first, known as *From/To/By animation*, you transition from a starting to an ending value (these are called the "target values"). You can specify either an endpoint (from here to there) or a By property (from here, offset by this much).

The second technique, called *keyframe animation*, lets you specify more than two values (i.e., more than just a start and stop position). It also lets you specify the interpolation method:

Linear interpolation
    Animation at a constant rate

Discrete interpolation
    Animation jumping from one value to the next without interpolation

Splined interpolation
    The most realistic animation, in which there are both acceleration and deceleration effects

The example we'll show here is a keyframe animation using splined interpolation.

The Animation Storyboard

The first part of creating an animated user experience is deciding what will be animated, how it will be animated, and in what order the animation will occur. The more common name for this collection of information is a *storyboard*.

Just for fun, in this example you're going to mock up a splash page for an O'Reilly book. You'll have some text, and some branding in the form of a red gradient opaque banner. And what example would be complete without a hexatarsier (Figure 2-17)?

Figure 2-17. The world-renowned hexatarsier

In your storyboard, you're first going to add the bit of XAML that will help you rotate our friend the hexatarsier. You'll need a `DoubleAnimationUsingKeyFrames` object, comprised of two `SplineDoubleKeyFrame` objects:

```
<DoubleAnimationUsingKeyFrames Storyboard.TargetName="Gear1"
    Storyboard.TargetProperty="(UIElement.RenderTransform).
        (TransformGroup.Children)[3].(RotateTransform.Angle)"
    BeginTime="00:00:00"
    RepeatBehavior="Forever">
    <SplineDoubleKeyFrame KeySpline="0.5,0.5,0.5,0.5" Value="0"
        KeyTime="00:00:00"/>
    <SplineDoubleKeyFrame KeySpline="0.5,0.5,0.5,0.5" Value="360"
        KeyTime="00:01:18"/>
</DoubleAnimationUsingKeyFrames>
```

Note that the `Storyboard.TargetName` value of the `DoubleAnimationUsingKeyFrames` object ("Gear1") refers to the target of the behavior, the image of the hexatarsier:

```
<Image IsEnabled="True" HorizontalAlignment="Left" VerticalAlignment="Top"
    RenderTransformOrigin="0.5,0.5" x:Name="Gear1" Margin="0,-100,0,0"
    Width="192" Height="187" Opacity="1">
    <Image.Source>
        <BitmapImage
            UriSource="http://alexhorovitz.com/DotNet3/rotate_tarsier.png"/>
    </Image.Source>
```

```
<Image.RenderTransform>
  <TransformGroup>
    <TranslateTransform X="0" Y="0"/>
    <ScaleTransform ScaleX="1" ScaleY="1"/>
    <SkewTransform AngleX="0" AngleY="0"/>
    <RotateTransform Angle="0"/>
    <TranslateTransform X="0" Y="0"/>
    <TranslateTransform X="0" Y="0"/>
  </TransformGroup>
</Image.RenderTransform>
</Image>
```

The `KeySpline` values of the `SplineDoubleKeyFrame` objects define cubic Bézier curves. The resulting curves specify how an animation is interpolated during a time segment; that is, the curve represents the rate of change in the animation's target attribute over the time segment. In this case, you are simply rotating the image 360 degrees over the course of one minute and 18 seconds.

You're going to make five animated gears in your storyboard and label them *Gear1* through *Gear4*.

You're also going to animate the other aspects of the UI. The text logo and the content grid will fade in using opacity:

```
<DoubleAnimationUsingKeyFrames Storyboard.TargetName="TextLogo_png1"
    Storyboard.TargetProperty="(UIElement.Opacity)" BeginTime="00:00:00">
  <SplineDoubleKeyFrame KeySpline="0.5,0.5,0.5,0.5" Value="0"
    KeyTime="00:00:00"/>
  <SplineDoubleKeyFrame KeySpline="0.5,0.5,0.5,0.5" Value="0"
    KeyTime="00:00:01.5"/>
  <SplineDoubleKeyFrame KeySpline="0.5,0.5,0.5,0.5" Value="1"
    KeyTime="00:00:02.5"/>
</DoubleAnimationUsingKeyFrames>
<DoubleAnimationUsingKeyFrames Storyboard.TargetName="ContentGrid"
    Storyboard.TargetProperty="(UIElement.Opacity)" BeginTime="00:00:00">
  <SplineDoubleKeyFrame KeySpline="0.5,0.5,0.5,0.5" Value="0"
    KeyTime="00:00:00"/>
  <SplineDoubleKeyFrame KeySpline="0.5,0.5,0.5,0.5" Value="0"
    KeyTime="00:00:01"/>
  <SplineDoubleKeyFrame KeySpline="0.5,0.5,0.5,0.5" Value="1"
    KeyTime="00:00:02"/>
</DoubleAnimationUsingKeyFrames>
```

You'll do the same thing for the red gradient box using `RedGradient` and `WhiteKnockOut`:

```
<DoubleAnimationUsingKeyFrames Storyboard.TargetName="RedGradient"
    Storyboard.TargetProperty="(UIElement.Opacity)" BeginTime="00:00:00">
  <SplineDoubleKeyFrame KeySpline="0.5,0.5,0.5,0.5" Value="0"
    KeyTime="00:00:00"/>
  <SplineDoubleKeyFrame KeySpline="0.5,0.5,0.5,0.5" Value="1"
    KeyTime="00:00:01"/>
</DoubleAnimationUsingKeyFrames>
```

```
<DoubleAnimationUsingKeyFrames Storyboard.TargetName="WhiteKnockout"
    Storyboard.TargetProperty="(UIElement.Opacity)" BeginTime="00:00:00">
    <SplineDoubleKeyFrame KeySpline="0.5,0.5,0.5,0.5" Value="0"
        KeyTime="00:00:00"/>
    <SplineDoubleKeyFrame KeySpline="0.5,0.5,0.5,0.5" Value="1"
        KeyTime="00:00:00.5830000"/>
</DoubleAnimationUsingKeyFrames>
<DoubleAnimationUsingKeyFrames Storyboard.TargetName="TextBlock2"
    Storyboard.TargetProperty="(UIElement.Opacity)" BeginTime="00:00:00">
    <SplineDoubleKeyFrame KeySpline="0.5,0.5,0.5,0.5" Value="0"
        KeyTime="00:00:00"/>
    <SplineDoubleKeyFrame KeySpline="0.5,0.5,0.5,0.5" Value="0"
        KeyTime="00:00:01.3330000"/>
    <SplineDoubleKeyFrame KeySpline="0.5,0.5,0.5,0.5" Value="1"
        KeyTime="00:00:02.3330000"/>
</DoubleAnimationUsingKeyFrames>
<DoubleAnimationUsingKeyFrames Storyboard.TargetName="TextBlock3"
    Storyboard.TargetProperty="(UIElement.Opacity)" BeginTime="00:00:00">
    <SplineDoubleKeyFrame KeySpline="0.5,0.5,0.5,0.5" Value="0"
        KeyTime="00:00:00"/>
    <SplineDoubleKeyFrame KeySpline="0.5,0.5,0.5,0.5" Value="0"
        KeyTime="00:00:01.9990000"/>
    <SplineDoubleKeyFrame KeySpline="0.5,0.5,0.5,0.5" Value="1"
        KeyTime="00:00:02.3330000"/>
</DoubleAnimationUsingKeyFrames>
<DoubleAnimationUsingKeyFrames Storyboard.TargetName="PDFImage"
    Storyboard.TargetProperty="(UIElement.Opacity)" BeginTime="00:00:00">
    <SplineDoubleKeyFrame KeySpline="0.5,0.5,0.5,0.5" Value="0"
        KeyTime="00:00:00"/>
    <SplineDoubleKeyFrame KeySpline="0.5,0.5,0.5,0.5" Value="0"
        KeyTime="00:00:01.6660000"/>
    <SplineDoubleKeyFrame KeySpline="0.5,0.5,0.5,0.5" Value="1"
        KeyTime="00:00:02.3330000"/>
</DoubleAnimationUsingKeyFrames>
```

You create the red gradient box using XAML and color offsets:

```
<Rectangle Stroke="{x:Null}" StrokeMiterLimit="2" x:Name="RedGradient"
    Margin="0,90,0,0" HorizontalAlignment="Stretch" VerticalAlignment="Top"
    Width="Auto" Height="90" Opacity="1">
<Rectangle.Fill>
    <LinearGradientBrush StartPoint="0,0.5" EndPoint="1,0.5">
        <LinearGradientBrush.GradientStops>
            <GradientStopCollection>
                <GradientStop Color="#FF0000" Offset="0"/>
                <GradientStop Color="sc#1, 1, 1, 0.768538356"
                    Offset="0.10256410256410256"/>
                <GradientStop Color="#FF0000" Offset="0.60897435897435892"/>
                <GradientStop Color="#FF0000" Offset="0.79487179487179482"/>
                <GradientStop Color="#FF0000" Offset="1"/>
                <GradientStop Color="#FF0000" Offset="0.25"/>
                <GradientStop Color="#FF0000" Offset="0.44230769230769229"/>
            </GradientStopCollection>
        </LinearGradientBrush.GradientStops>
    </LinearGradientBrush>
</Rectangle.Fill>
```

```
<Rectangle.OpacityMask>
    <LinearGradientBrush StartPoint="0,0.5" EndPoint="1,0.5">
        <LinearGradientBrush.GradientStops>
            <GradientStopCollection>
                <GradientStop Color="sc#1, 1, 0.987141, 0"
                    Offset="0.39743589743589741"/>
                <GradientStop Color="sc#0.7, 1, 0.658374846, 0" Offset="1"/>
            </GradientStopCollection>
        </LinearGradientBrush.GradientStops>
    </LinearGradientBrush>
</Rectangle.OpacityMask>
</Rectangle>
```

Because you tie these effects to the keyframes, they are produced in sequence. So, not only do the hexatarsiers rotate, but (equally impressive to the viewer, though more subtle), the entire presentation seems to fade in, with each segment appearing in turn as shown in Figure 2-18 (your book may not show color or the actual animation, depending on how much you paid for it).

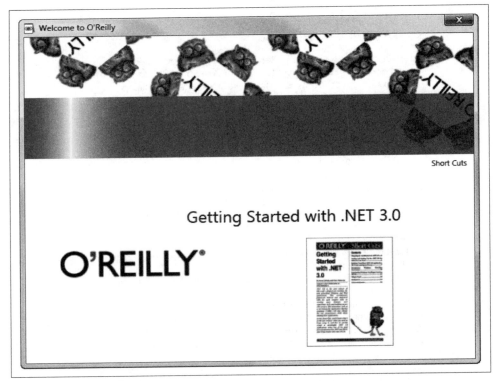

Figure 2-18. Animated images

Example 2-1 shows the complete code for this animation example. You don't need to type it all into XAMLPad (it's very long); if you've downloaded the source for this chapter, you can just open the file *AnimationExample.xaml*.

Example 2-1. Keyframe animation using splines

```xml
<Window
    xmlns="http://schemas.microsoft.com/winfx/2006/xaml/presentation"
    xmlns:x="http://schemas.microsoft.com/winfx/2006/xaml"
    xmlns:System="clr-namespace:System;assembly=mscorlib"
    x:Name="RootWindow"
    Title="Welcome to O'Reilly"
    SizeToContent="WidthAndHeight" ResizeMode="NoResize" >
  <Window.Resources >

    <System:Double x:Key="LargeText">14</System:Double>

    <Storyboard x:Key="OnLoaded">
      <DoubleAnimationUsingKeyFrames Storyboard.TargetName="Gear1"
          Storyboard.TargetProperty="(UIElement.RenderTransform).
            (TransformGroup.Children)[3].(RotateTransform.Angle)"
          BeginTime="00:00:00"
          RepeatBehavior="Forever">
        <SplineDoubleKeyFrame KeySpline="0.5,0.5,0.5,0.5" Value="0"
            KeyTime="00:00:00"/>
        <SplineDoubleKeyFrame KeySpline="0.5,0.5,0.5,0.5" Value="360"
            KeyTime="00:01:18"/>
      </DoubleAnimationUsingKeyFrames>
      <DoubleAnimationUsingKeyFrames Storyboard.TargetName="Gear2"
          Storyboard.TargetProperty="(UIElement.RenderTransform).
            (TransformGroup.Children)[3].(RotateTransform.Angle)"
          BeginTime="00:00:00"
          RepeatBehavior="Forever">
        <SplineDoubleKeyFrame KeySpline="0.5,0.5,0.5,0.5" Value="0"
            KeyTime="00:00:00"/>
        <SplineDoubleKeyFrame KeySpline="0.5,0.5,0.5,0.5" Value="-360"
            KeyTime="00:01:18"/>
      </DoubleAnimationUsingKeyFrames>
      <DoubleAnimationUsingKeyFrames Storyboard.TargetName="Gear3"
          Storyboard.TargetProperty="(UIElement.RenderTransform).
            (TransformGroup.Children)[3].(RotateTransform.Angle)"
          BeginTime="00:00:00"
          RepeatBehavior="Forever">
        <SplineDoubleKeyFrame KeySpline="0.5,0.5,0.5,0.5" Value="0"
            KeyTime="00:00:00"/>
        <SplineDoubleKeyFrame KeySpline="0.5,0.5,0.5,0.5" Value="360"
            KeyTime="00:01:18"/>
      </DoubleAnimationUsingKeyFrames>
      <DoubleAnimationUsingKeyFrames Storyboard.TargetName="Gear4"
          Storyboard.TargetProperty="(UIElement.RenderTransform).
            (TransformGroup.Children)[3].(RotateTransform.Angle)"
          BeginTime="00:00:00"
          RepeatBehavior="Forever">
        <SplineDoubleKeyFrame KeySpline="0.5,0.5,0.5,0.5" Value="0"
            KeyTime="00:00:00"/>
        <SplineDoubleKeyFrame KeySpline="0.5,0.5,0.5,0.5" Value="-360"
            KeyTime="00:01:18"/>
      </DoubleAnimationUsingKeyFrames>
```

Example 2-1. Keyframe animation using splines (continued)

```xml
<DoubleAnimationUsingKeyFrames Storyboard.TargetName="Gear1"
    Storyboard.TargetProperty="(UIElement.Opacity)" BeginTime="00:00:00">
  <SplineDoubleKeyFrame KeySpline="0.5,0.5,0.5,0.5" Value="0"
      KeyTime="00:00:00"/>
  <SplineDoubleKeyFrame KeySpline="0.5,0.5,0.5,0.5" Value="1"
      KeyTime="00:00:01"/>
  <SplineDoubleKeyFrame KeySpline="0.5,0.5,0.5,0.5" Value="1"
      KeyTime="00:01:18"/>
</DoubleAnimationUsingKeyFrames>
<DoubleAnimationUsingKeyFrames Storyboard.TargetName="Gear2"
    Storyboard.TargetProperty="(UIElement.Opacity)" BeginTime="00:00:00">
  <SplineDoubleKeyFrame KeySpline="0.5,0.5,0.5,0.5" Value="0"
      KeyTime="00:00:00"/>
  <SplineDoubleKeyFrame KeySpline="0.5,0.5,0.5,0.5" Value="0"
      KeyTime="00:00:00.5000000"/>
  <SplineDoubleKeyFrame KeySpline="0.5,0.5,0.5,0.5" Value="1"
      KeyTime="00:00:01.5420000"/>
  <SplineDoubleKeyFrame KeySpline="0.5,0.5,0.5,0.5" Value="1"
      KeyTime="00:01:18"/>
</DoubleAnimationUsingKeyFrames>
<DoubleAnimationUsingKeyFrames Storyboard.TargetName="Gear3"
    Storyboard.TargetProperty="(UIElement.Opacity)" BeginTime="00:00:00">
  <SplineDoubleKeyFrame KeySpline="0.5,0.5,0.5,0.5" Value="0"
      KeyTime="00:00:00"/>
  <SplineDoubleKeyFrame KeySpline="0.5,0.5,0.5,0.5" Value="0"
      KeyTime="00:00:01.4580000"/>
  <SplineDoubleKeyFrame KeySpline="0.5,0.5,0.5,0.5" Value="1"
      KeyTime="00:00:02.5000000"/>
  <SplineDoubleKeyFrame KeySpline="0.5,0.5,0.5,0.5" Value="1"
      KeyTime="00:01:18"/>
</DoubleAnimationUsingKeyFrames>
<DoubleAnimationUsingKeyFrames Storyboard.TargetName="Gear4"
    Storyboard.TargetProperty="(UIElement.Opacity)" BeginTime="00:00:00">
  <SplineDoubleKeyFrame KeySpline="0.5,0.5,0.5,0.5" Value="0"
      KeyTime="00:00:00"/>
  <SplineDoubleKeyFrame KeySpline="0.5,0.5,0.5,0.5" Value="0"
      KeyTime="00:00:02"/>
  <SplineDoubleKeyFrame KeySpline="0.5,0.5,0.5,0.5" Value="1"
      KeyTime="00:00:03"/>
  <SplineDoubleKeyFrame KeySpline="0.5,0.5,0.5,0.5" Value="1"
      KeyTime="00:01:18"/>
</DoubleAnimationUsingKeyFrames>
<!--Text logo fade in-->
<DoubleAnimationUsingKeyFrames Storyboard.TargetName="TextLogo_png1"
    Storyboard.TargetProperty="(UIElement.Opacity)" BeginTime="00:00:00">
  <SplineDoubleKeyFrame KeySpline="0.5,0.5,0.5,0.5" Value="0"
      KeyTime="00:00:00"/>
  <SplineDoubleKeyFrame KeySpline="0.5,0.5,0.5,0.5" Value="0"
      KeyTime="00:00:01.5"/>
  <SplineDoubleKeyFrame KeySpline="0.5,0.5,0.5,0.5" Value="1"
      KeyTime="00:00:02.5"/>
</DoubleAnimationUsingKeyFrames>
```

Example 2-1. Keyframe animation using splines (continued)

```
<!--Content area (UI) fade in-->
<DoubleAnimationUsingKeyFrames Storyboard.TargetName="ContentGrid"
    Storyboard.TargetProperty="(UIElement.Opacity)" BeginTime="00:00:00">
    <SplineDoubleKeyFrame KeySpline="0.5,0.5,0.5,0.5" Value="0"
        KeyTime="00:00:00"/>
    <SplineDoubleKeyFrame KeySpline="0.5,0.5,0.5,0.5" Value="0"
        KeyTime="00:00:01"/>
    <SplineDoubleKeyFrame KeySpline="0.5,0.5,0.5,0.5" Value="1"
        KeyTime="00:00:02"/>
</DoubleAnimationUsingKeyFrames>
<DoubleAnimationUsingKeyFrames Storyboard.TargetName="RedGradient"
    Storyboard.TargetProperty="(UIElement.Opacity)" BeginTime="00:00:00">
    <SplineDoubleKeyFrame KeySpline="0.5,0.5,0.5,0.5" Value="0"
        KeyTime="00:00:00"/>
    <SplineDoubleKeyFrame KeySpline="0.5,0.5,0.5,0.5" Value="1"
        KeyTime="00:00:01"/>
</DoubleAnimationUsingKeyFrames>
<DoubleAnimationUsingKeyFrames Storyboard.TargetName="WhiteKnockout"
    Storyboard.TargetProperty="(UIElement.Opacity)" BeginTime="00:00:00">
    <SplineDoubleKeyFrame KeySpline="0.5,0.5,0.5,0.5" Value="0"
        KeyTime="00:00:00"/>
    <SplineDoubleKeyFrame KeySpline="0.5,0.5,0.5,0.5" Value="1"
        KeyTime="00:00:00.5830000"/>
</DoubleAnimationUsingKeyFrames>
<DoubleAnimationUsingKeyFrames Storyboard.TargetName="TextBlock2"
    Storyboard.TargetProperty="(UIElement.Opacity)" BeginTime="00:00:00">
    <SplineDoubleKeyFrame KeySpline="0.5,0.5,0.5,0.5" Value="0"
        KeyTime="00:00:00"/>
    <SplineDoubleKeyFrame KeySpline="0.5,0.5,0.5,0.5" Value="0"
        KeyTime="00:00:01.3330000"/>
    <SplineDoubleKeyFrame KeySpline="0.5,0.5,0.5,0.5" Value="1"
        KeyTime="00:00:02.3330000"/>
</DoubleAnimationUsingKeyFrames>
<DoubleAnimationUsingKeyFrames Storyboard.TargetName="TextBlock3"
    Storyboard.TargetProperty="(UIElement.Opacity)" BeginTime="00:00:00">
    <SplineDoubleKeyFrame KeySpline="0.5,0.5,0.5,0.5" Value="0"
        KeyTime="00:00:00"/>
    <SplineDoubleKeyFrame KeySpline="0.5,0.5,0.5,0.5" Value="0"
        KeyTime="00:00:01.9990000"/>
    <SplineDoubleKeyFrame KeySpline="0.5,0.5,0.5,0.5" Value="1"
        KeyTime="00:00:02.3330000"/>
</DoubleAnimationUsingKeyFrames>
<DoubleAnimationUsingKeyFrames Storyboard.TargetName="PDFImage"
    Storyboard.TargetProperty="(UIElement.Opacity)" BeginTime="00:00:00">
    <SplineDoubleKeyFrame KeySpline="0.5,0.5,0.5,0.5" Value="0"
        KeyTime="00:00:00"/>
    <SplineDoubleKeyFrame KeySpline="0.5,0.5,0.5,0.5" Value="0"
        KeyTime="00:00:01.6660000"/>
    <SplineDoubleKeyFrame KeySpline="0.5,0.5,0.5,0.5" Value="1"
        KeyTime="00:00:02.3330000"/>
</DoubleAnimationUsingKeyFrames>

</Storyboard>
```

Example 2-1. Keyframe animation using splines (continued)

```xml
    <Style x:Key="HeaderedContentControlStyle1"
        TargetType="{x:Type HeaderedContentControl}">
        <Setter Property="Template"
            Value="{DynamicResource HeaderedContentControlControlTemplate1}"/>
    </Style>
    <ControlTemplate x:Key="HeaderedContentControlControlTemplate1"
        TargetType="{x:Type HeaderedContentControl}">
        <BulletDecorator x:Name="BulletDecorator1"
            RenderTransformOrigin="0.5,0.5">
            <BulletDecorator.Bullet>
                <ContentControl Content="{TemplateBinding Header}" Width="Auto"
                    Height="Auto" VerticalAlignment="Center" Margin="0,0,0,0"/>
            </BulletDecorator.Bullet>
                <ContentControl Content="{TemplateBinding Content}"
                    VerticalAlignment="Stretch" Margin="4,4,4,4"
                    HorizontalAlignment="Left"/>
        </BulletDecorator>
    </ControlTemplate>

</Window.Resources>
<Window.Triggers >
    <EventTrigger RoutedEvent="FrameworkElement.Loaded">
        <EventTrigger.Actions>
            <BeginStoryboard x:Name="_OnLoaded"
                Storyboard="{DynamicResource OnLoaded}"/>
        </EventTrigger.Actions>
    </EventTrigger>
</Window.Triggers>
<Grid x:Name="DocumentRoot" Width="640" Height="480">
    <Grid.ColumnDefinitions>
        <ColumnDefinition/>
    </Grid.ColumnDefinitions>
    <Grid.RowDefinitions>
        <RowDefinition Height="*"/>
    </Grid.RowDefinitions>

    <Rectangle Fill="#FFFFFFFF" StrokeMiterLimit="2"
        x:Name="GearBackgroundRectangle" RenderTransformOrigin="0.5,0.5"
        HorizontalAlignment="Stretch" VerticalAlignment="Top" Width="Auto"
        Height="175" Margin="0,0,0,0" Opacity="1"/>
    <Image IsEnabled="True" HorizontalAlignment="Left" VerticalAlignment="Top"
        RenderTransformOrigin="0.5,0.5" x:Name="Gear1" Margin="0,-100,0,0"
        Width="192" Height="187" Opacity="1">
        <Image.Source>
            <BitmapImage
                UriSource="http://alexhorovitz.com/DotNet3/rotate_tarsier.png"/>
        </Image.Source>
        <Image.RenderTransform>
            <TransformGroup>
                <TranslateTransform X="0" Y="0"/>
                <ScaleTransform ScaleX="1" ScaleY="1"/>
                <SkewTransform AngleX="0" AngleY="0"/>
```

Example 2-1. Keyframe animation using splines (continued)

```xaml
                    <RotateTransform Angle="0"/>
                    <TranslateTransform X="0" Y="0"/>
                    <TranslateTransform X="0" Y="0"/>
                </TransformGroup>
            </Image.RenderTransform>
        </Image>
        <Image IsEnabled="True" HorizontalAlignment="Left" VerticalAlignment="Top"
            RenderTransformOrigin="0.5,0.5" x:Name="Gear2" Margin="169,-4,0,0"
            Width="192" Height="187" Opacity="1">
            <Image.Source>
                <BitmapImage
                    UriSource="http://alexhorovitz.com/DotNet3/rotate_tarsier.png"/>
            </Image.Source>
            <Image.RenderTransform>
                <TransformGroup>
                    <TranslateTransform X="0" Y="0"/>
                    <ScaleTransform ScaleX="1" ScaleY="1"/>
                    <SkewTransform AngleX="0" AngleY="0"/>
                    <RotateTransform Angle="0"/>
                    <TranslateTransform X="0" Y="0"/>
                    <TranslateTransform X="0" Y="0"/>
                </TransformGroup>
            </Image.RenderTransform>
        </Image>
        <Image IsEnabled="True" HorizontalAlignment="Left" VerticalAlignment="Top"
            RenderTransformOrigin="0.5,0.5" x:Name="Gear3" Margin="339,-101,0,0"
            Width="192" Height="187"  Opacity="1">
            <Image.Source>
                <BitmapImage
                    UriSource="http://alexhorovitz.com/DotNet3/rotate_tarsier.png"/>
            </Image.Source>
            <Image.RenderTransform>
                <TransformGroup>
                    <TranslateTransform X="0" Y="0"/>
                    <ScaleTransform ScaleX="1" ScaleY="1"/>
                    <SkewTransform AngleX="0" AngleY="0"/>
                    <RotateTransform Angle="0"/>
                    <TranslateTransform X="0" Y="0"/>
                    <TranslateTransform X="0" Y="0"/>
                </TransformGroup>
            </Image.RenderTransform>
        </Image>
        <Image IsEnabled="True" HorizontalAlignment="Right" VerticalAlignment="Top"
            RenderTransformOrigin="0.5,0.5" x:Name="Gear4" Margin="0,-4,-60,0"
            Width="192" Height="187" Opacity="1">
            <Image.Source>
                <BitmapImage
                    UriSource="http://alexhorovitz.com/DotNet3/rotate_tarsier.png"/>
            </Image.Source>
```

Example 2-1. Keyframe animation using splines (continued)

```
    <Image.RenderTransform>
      <TransformGroup>
        <TranslateTransform X="0" Y="0"/>
        <ScaleTransform ScaleX="1" ScaleY="1"/>
        <SkewTransform AngleX="0" AngleY="0"/>
        <RotateTransform Angle="0"/>
        <TranslateTransform X="0" Y="0"/>
        <TranslateTransform X="0" Y="0"/>
      </TransformGroup>
    </Image.RenderTransform>
  </Image>

  <Rectangle StrokeMiterLimit="2" x:Name="WhiteKnockout"
    RenderTransformOrigin="0.5,0.5" Margin="0,176,0,0"
    HorizontalAlignment="Stretch" VerticalAlignment="Stretch" Width="Auto"
    Height="Auto" Opacity="1" Fill="#FFFFFFFF"/>
  <Rectangle Stroke="{x:Null}" StrokeMiterLimit="2" x:Name="RedGradient"
      Margin="0,90,0,0" HorizontalAlignment="Stretch" VerticalAlignment="Top"
      Width="Auto" Height="90" Opacity="1">
    <Rectangle.Fill>
      <LinearGradientBrush StartPoint="0,0.5" EndPoint="1,0.5">
        <LinearGradientBrush.GradientStops>
          <GradientStopCollection>
            <GradientStop Color="#FF0000" Offset="0"/>
            <GradientStop Color="sc#1, 1, 1, 0.768538356"
                Offset="0.10256410256410256"/>
            <GradientStop Color="#FF0000" Offset="0.60897435897435892"/>
            <GradientStop Color="#FF0000" Offset="0.79487179487179482"/>
            <GradientStop Color="#FF0000" Offset="1"/>
            <GradientStop Color="#FF0000" Offset="0.25"/>
            <GradientStop Color="#FF0000" Offset="0.44230769230769229"/>
          </GradientStopCollection>
        </LinearGradientBrush.GradientStops>
      </LinearGradientBrush>
    </Rectangle.Fill>
    <Rectangle.OpacityMask>
      <LinearGradientBrush StartPoint="0,0.5" EndPoint="1,0.5">
        <LinearGradientBrush.GradientStops>
          <GradientStopCollection>
            <GradientStop Color="sc#1, 1, 0.987141, 0"
                Offset="0.39743589743589741"/>
            <GradientStop Color="sc#0.7, 1, 0.658374846, 0" Offset="1"/>
          </GradientStopCollection>
        </LinearGradientBrush.GradientStops>
      </LinearGradientBrush>
    </Rectangle.OpacityMask>
  </Rectangle>
```

Example 2-1. Keyframe animation using splines (continued)

```xml
<Grid x:Name="ContentGrid" Width="640" Height="480"
    RenderTransformOrigin="0.5,0.5" Opacity="1">
    <Grid.RenderTransform>
        <TransformGroup>
            <TranslateTransform X="0" Y="0"/>
            <ScaleTransform ScaleX="1" ScaleY="1"/>
            <SkewTransform AngleX="0" AngleY="0"/>
            <RotateTransform Angle="0"/>
            <TranslateTransform X="0" Y="0"/>
            <TranslateTransform X="0" Y="0"/>
        </TransformGroup>
    </Grid.RenderTransform>
</Grid>

<Image IsEnabled="True" HorizontalAlignment="Left" VerticalAlignment="Top"
    RenderTransformOrigin="0.5,0.5" x:Name="TextLogo_png1"  Width="369"
    Height="69" Margin="50,300,0,0" Opacity="1">
    <Image.Source>
        <BitmapImage
        UriSource="http://www.oreilly.com/images/oreilly/oreilly_large.gif"/>
    </Image.Source>
</Image>

<TextBlock x:Name="TextBlock2" Margin="0,185,10,0"
    HorizontalAlignment="Right" VerticalAlignment="Top" Width="290"
    Height="21" Text="Short Cuts" TextAlignment="Right" FontSize="11"
    Opacity="1"/>
<TextBlock x:Name="TextBlock3" Margin="0,250,10,0"
    HorizontalAlignment="Right" VerticalAlignment="Top" Width="400"
    Height="40" Text="Getting Started with .NET 3.0" TextAlignment="Left"
    FontSize="24" Opacity="1"/>
<Image x:Name="PDFImage" IsEnabled="True" HorizontalAlignment="Left"
    VerticalAlignment="Top" RenderTransformOrigin="0.5,0.5"
    Source="http://www.oreilly.com/catalog/covers/059652921X_cat.gif"
    Margin="400,300,10,20" Opacity="1"/>
    </Grid>
</Window >
```

Hooked Yet?

This chapter has provided only a taste of what can be done with XAML. In the next chapter we'll explore the library Microsoft built to help you utilize XAML to construct your presentation layer: the Windows Presentation Foundation, which is provided as part of .NET 3.5.

Be prepared—all your existing Windows applications are about to look *very* old. Don't you hate it when that happens?

CHAPTER 3

Introducing Windows Presentation Foundation: A Richer Desktop UI Experience

Unlike Windows Forms applications, but much like ASP.NET applications, Windows Presentation Foundation (WPF) applications contain both "markup" (XAML) and the "code-behind" that together correspond to the .NET class libraries. As demonstrated in the previous chapter, you can use XAML to create very powerful layouts and displays. However, WPF goes beyond that, using XAML and code-behind to create complete applications that provide enhanced text, 2-D and 3-D graphics, and much more.

The best way to think about WPF is as a framework of classes that Microsoft provides for you. You implement these classes either programmatically, by instantiating them in code, or declaratively, by using XAML.

In Chapter 4 you'll build a significant business application that uses many features of WPF. To prepare you for that, this chapter will build on the previous chapter and introduce more of the features of WPF that you are likely to use in creating your applications.

Note About the Examples

More experienced readers will note that the examples in this chapter utilize some XAML elements in a less than highly optimized manner. This is intentional, to allow you to better visualize how things fit together. Often, we choose to use elements that best show off the intermediate states of the examples and, ultimately, create better results from a visual perspective.

Starting Simple: Panels

One challenge with every markup language is achieving precise layout of the elements for display. The approach taken with XAML is to use panel elements, as touched on in the previous chapter.

Perhaps the most flexible panel is the Grid, which gives you control of both columns and rows (not unlike a table in HTML). Enter the code shown in Example 3-1 into XAMLPad and run it.

Example 3-1. Grid example

```
<Window
    xmlns="http://schemas.microsoft.com/winfx/2006/xaml/presentation"
    xmlns:x="http://schemas.microsoft.com/winfx/2006/xaml"
    Title="Programming .NET 3.5 | Understanding Grids">
  <Grid>
    <Grid.RowDefinitions>
      <RowDefinition/>
      <RowDefinition/>
      <RowDefinition/>
    </Grid.RowDefinitions>
    <Grid.ColumnDefinitions>
      <ColumnDefinition/>
      <ColumnDefinition/>
      <ColumnDefinition/>
    </Grid.ColumnDefinitions>

    <TextBlock TextBlock.FontSize="36"
        TextBlock.Foreground="White"
        Background="Blue"
        Grid.Column="0"
        Grid.Row="0"
        Grid.RowSpan="2">1</TextBlock>

    <TextBlock TextBlock.FontSize="36"
        Background="Gold"
        Grid.Column="1"
        Grid.Row="0" >2</TextBlock>

    <TextBlock TextBlock.FontSize="36"
        TextBlock.Foreground="White"
        Background="Crimson"
        Grid.Column="2"
        Grid.Row="0" >3</TextBlock>

    <TextBlock TextBlock.FontSize="36"
        Background="White"
        Grid.Column="1"
        Grid.Row="1"
        Grid.ColumnSpan="2">4</TextBlock>
```

Example 3-1. Grid example (continued)

```
<TextBlock TextBlock.FontSize="36"
    TextBlock.Foreground="White"
    Background="Purple"
    Grid.Column="0"
    Grid.Row="2" >5</TextBlock>

<TextBlock TextBlock.FontSize="36"
    TextBlock.Foreground="White"
    Background="Green"
    Grid.Column="1"
    Grid.Row="2" >6</TextBlock>

<TextBlock TextBlock.FontSize="36"
    TextBlock.Foreground="White"
    Background="Black"
    Grid.Column="2"
    Grid.Row="2" >7</TextBlock>

    </Grid>
</Window>
```

What you get should look like Figure 3-1 (only colorful).

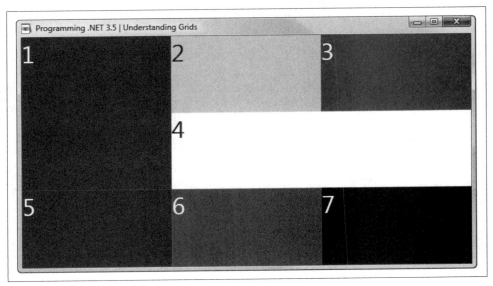

Figure 3-1. A colorful grid

This example starts by declaring a Grid element, then declares a set of three RowDefinitions (each with no properties) and three ColumnDefinitions (also with no properties).

Below these row and column definitions, you declare TextBlocks. Let's examine the first TextBlock. Its FontSize is specified as 36 (this is used for the numeral), and its Background is set to Blue (which is much more effective when you can see the colors!). Its row/column position in the grid is also stated, and it includes a RowSpan attribute whose value is set to 2 (the fourth TextBlock demonstrates the corresponding ColumnSpan attribute). Finally, you set its text. For those of you who come from the world of HTML markup, all of this should seem quite familiar.

In summary, the code indicates that the first TextBlock will display the numeral "1" with a font size of 36 on a blue background. The block will be placed in column 0, row 0 of the grid and will span two rows. All of this is consistent with what you saw in Figure 3-1.

Interestingly, the grid itself has no colors. The TextBlocks placed inside the grid provide the color; the grid just supplies the structure.

DockPanel

A key property of the DockPanel element is that you can "dock" its contents to specific edges of the panel, as illustrated in Example 3-2. Take special note of the DockPanel declaration (in bold) and its attribute LastChildFill="True"—this ensures that the last child of the panel will fill whatever space is left.

Example 3-2. A DockPanel

```
<Window
    xmlns="http://schemas.microsoft.com/winfx/2006/xaml/presentation"
    xmlns:x="http://schemas.microsoft.com/winfx/2006/xaml"
    Title="Programming .NET 3.5 | Layout: DockPanel">

    <DockPanel LastChildFill="True">
      <TextBlock DockPanel.Dock="Top" Background="LightCoral">
        I am the top...</TextBlock>
      <TextBlock DockPanel.Dock="Bottom" Background="LightCoral">
        I am the bottom...</TextBlock>
      <TextBlock DockPanel.Dock="Left" VerticalAlignment="Center">
        I am the left...</TextBlock>
      <TextBlock DockPanel.Dock="Right" VerticalAlignment="Center">
        I am the Right...</TextBlock>
      <Button Height="40" Width="200">
        I am the Fill (or the center)</Button>
    </DockPanel>

</Window>
```

As promised, the Button placed as the final element in the DockPanel appears in the center, as shown in Figure 3-2.

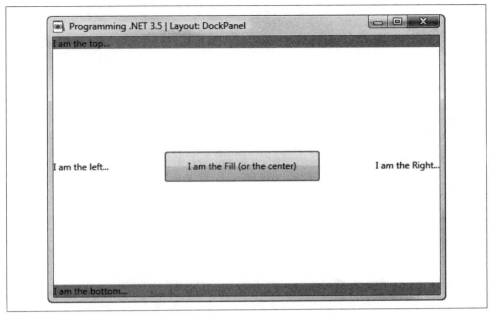

Figure 3-2. A simple DockPanel with the top and bottom specified first

Order of declaration is important

If you change the DockPanel slightly and declare the left and right TextBlocks before the top and bottom TextBlocks, you change the area devoted to each. Effectively, the DockPanel devotes a full column each to the left and right TextBlocks and then allocates the top and bottom blocks from the remaining space, as shown in Figure 3-3.

 To create this effect, modify the code in Example 3-2 so that the first two text blocks swap places with the third and fourth (that is, right and left are declared before top and bottom).

If you modify the declarations of the right and left TextBlocks to set the background color:

```
Background="lightblue"
```

it is easy to see that the area of the right and left columns is exactly the area taken away from the top and bottom blocks. As illustrated in Figure 3-4, there are full columns on the left and right extending up to the top and down to the bottom.

As you can see, the DockPanel can be instrumental in many applications; for example, with the left (or right) column reserved for a menu or site map, the top reserved for a header or tabs, the bottom reserved for a status bar, and the center used to present the application's contents.

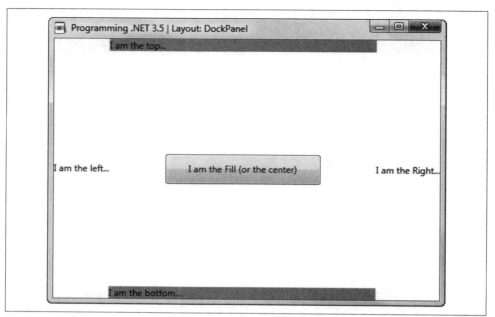

Figure 3-3. The same DockPanel with the left and right specified first

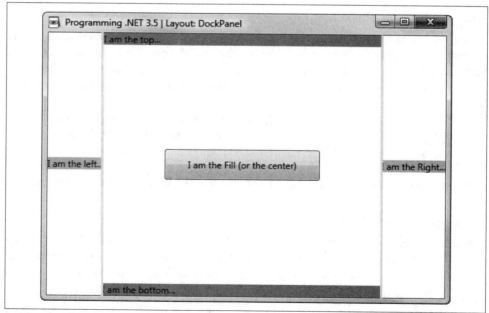

Figure 3-4. Visualizing the columns in a DockPanel

StackPanel

A StackPanel (like all panels) can be used on its own or inside other containers. Later you'll use a StackPanel inside a Button, but for now, we'll show one inside a DockPanel.

In this example, we'll create an advertising page for an O'Reilly book. First create the DockPanel, then add two TextBlocks. Dock one to the top of the DockPanel; you'll use it to display the O'Reilly logo. Dock the other one to the bottom; it will show the copyright and trademark notifications. Here's the code:

```
<Window
    xmlns="http://schemas.microsoft.com/winfx/2006/xaml/presentation"
    xmlns:x="http://schemas.microsoft.com/winfx/2006/xaml"
    Title="Programming .NET 3.5 | Layout: StackPanel and the FlowDocumentReader">

    <DockPanel LastChildFill="True">
        <TextBlock
            DockPanel.Dock="Top"
            Background="White"
            TextBlock.FontFamily="Verdana"
            TextBlock.FontSize="48"
            VerticalAlignment="Center">
            <Image
                Source="http://www.oreilly.com/images/oreilly/oreilly.gif"
                Width="287"
                Height="67"/>
        </TextBlock>
        <TextBlock DockPanel.Dock="Bottom"
            Background="DarkRed"
            Foreground="White" >
        &#169; 2008 O'Reilly Media, Inc.
        All trademarks and registered trademarks appearing on
        oreilly.com are the property of their respective owners.
        </TextBlock>
    </DockPanel>

</Window>
```

Now add a StackPanel immediately following the last TextBlock, and dock it to the left of the DockPanel. Within that StackPanel, place an Image to hold the book cover image:

```
<StackPanel
    DockPanel.Dock="Left"
    VerticalAlignment="Center"
    Margin="5">
    <Image
        Source="http://www.oreilly.com/catalog/covers/059652921X_cat.gif"
        Height="223"
        Width="180" />
</StackPanel>
```

At this point, you should have a screen that looks something like Figure 3-5.

Figure 3-5. A DockPanel with an embedded StackPanel

Now add a `FlowDocumentReader` as the final element in the `DockPanel` (right after the `StackPanel`). Because you specified `LastChildFill="True"` as an attribute of the `DockPanel`, the `FlowDocumentReader` will, as the last child, fill all the space that hasn't been occupied by the other children. (This is actually the default value, but we wanted to call it to your attention.)

`FlowDocumentReader` is a powerful document-presentation tool. Here, it contains a single `FlowDocument`, which in turn holds a handful of `Paragraph` elements (you don't have to type in all the paragraphs, or all the text within them, to see the effect of this example):

```
<FlowDocumentReader>
  <FlowDocument>
    <Paragraph>
      <Bold></Bold>
    </Paragraph>
    <Paragraph>
      <Paragraph.FontFamily>Verdana</Paragraph.FontFamily>
      <Paragraph.FontSize>36</Paragraph.FontSize>
      <Bold>Getting Started with .NET 3.0</Bold>
    </Paragraph>
    <Paragraph>
      <Paragraph.FontFamily>Verdana</Paragraph.FontFamily>
      <Paragraph.FontSize>18</Paragraph.FontSize>
      <Bold>Writing Your First .NET 3.0 Application</Bold>
    </Paragraph>
    <Paragraph>
      <Paragraph.FontFamily>Verdana</Paragraph.FontFamily>
      <Paragraph.FontSize>18</Paragraph.FontSize>
      By Jesse Liberty and Alex Horovitz<LineBreak />
      September 2006<LineBreak />
      Pages: 56 <LineBreak />
    </Paragraph>
    <Paragraph>
```

```
            Learn how to create more dynamic user experiences
            and build secure web services using Windows Communication
            Foundation (WCF) and Windows Presentation Foundation (WPF),
            two of the foundational pillars of .NET 3.0,
            with this succinct and well-written PDF document.
        </Paragraph>
        <Paragraph>
            Co-authored by best-selling author Jesse Liberty,
            this document gets right to the point helping you build a
            meaningful Windows application. It walks you through the
            terminology, concepts, and software you need to get started
            and then jumps to creating Me!Trade, a portfolio management
            tool.
        </Paragraph>
        <Paragraph>
            As a bonus, this Short Cut also introduces two additional
            pillars of .NET 3.0: Windows Workflow Foundation and
            Windows Card Services.
        </Paragraph>
        <Paragraph>
            Take the mystery out of .NET 3.0 and get started today.
        </Paragraph>
    </FlowDocument>
</FlowDocumentReader>
```

Now your output should look like Figure 3-6.

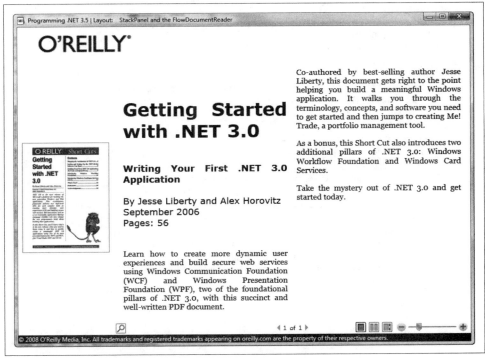

Figure 3-6. Incorporating a FlowDocumentReader into the simple app

Example 3-3 shows the complete XAML code listing.

Example 3-3. A StackPanel inside a DockPanel

```xml
<Window
    xmlns="http://schemas.microsoft.com/winfx/2006/xaml/presentation"
    xmlns:x="http://schemas.microsoft.com/winfx/2006/xaml"
    Title="Programming .NET 3.5 | Layout: StackPanel and the FlowDocumentReader">

    <DockPanel LastChildFill="True">
        <TextBlock
            DockPanel.Dock="Top"
            Background="White"
            TextBlock.FontFamily="Verdana"
            TextBlock.FontSize="48"
            VerticalAlignment="Center">
            <Image
                Source="http://www.oreilly.com/images/oreilly/oreilly.gif"
                Width="287"
                Height="67"/>
        </TextBlock>
        <TextBlock DockPanel.Dock="Bottom"
            Background="DarkRed"
            Foreground="White" >
        &#169; 2008 O'Reilly Media, Inc.
        All trademarks and registered trademarks appearing on
        oreilly.com are the property of their respective owners.
        </TextBlock>
        <StackPanel
            DockPanel.Dock="Left"
            VerticalAlignment="Center"
            Margin="5">
            <Image
              Source="http://www.oreilly.com/catalog/covers/059652921X_cat.gif"
              Height="223"
              Width="180" />
        </StackPanel>
        <FlowDocumentReader>
            <FlowDocument>
                <Paragraph>
                    <Paragraph.FontFamily>Verdana</Paragraph.FontFamily>
                    <Paragraph.FontSize>36</Paragraph.FontSize>
                    <Bold>Getting Started with .NET 3.0</Bold>
                </Paragraph>
                <Paragraph>
                    <Paragraph.FontFamily>Verdana</Paragraph.FontFamily>
                    <Paragraph.FontSize>18</Paragraph.FontSize>
                    <Bold>Writing Your First .NET 3.0 Application</Bold>
                </Paragraph>
                <Paragraph>
                    <Paragraph.FontFamily>Verdana</Paragraph.FontFamily>
```

Example 3-3. A StackPanel inside a DockPanel (continued)

```
                <Paragraph.FontSize>18</Paragraph.FontSize>
                By Jesse Liberty and Alex Horovitz<LineBreak />
                September 2006<LineBreak />
                Pages: 56 <LineBreak />
            </Paragraph>
            <Paragraph>
                Learn how to create more dynamic user experiences
                and build secure web services using Windows Communication
                Foundation (WCF) and Windows Presentation Foundation (WPF),
                two of the foundational pillars of .NET 3.0,
                with this succinct and well-written PDF document.
            </Paragraph>
            <Paragraph>
                Co-authored by best-selling author Jesse Liberty,
                this document gets right to the point helping you build a
                meaningful Windows application. It walks you through the
                terminology, concepts, and software you need to get started
                and then jumps to creating Me!Trade, a portfolio management
                tool.
            </Paragraph>
            <Paragraph>
                As a bonus, this Short Cut also introduces two additional
                pillars of .NET 3.0: Windows Workflow Foundation and
                Windows Card Services.
            </Paragraph>
            <Paragraph>
                Take the mystery out of .NET 3.0 and get started today.
            </Paragraph>
        </FlowDocument>
    </FlowDocumentReader>
  </DockPanel>

</Window>
```

Canvas and ViewBox

When discussing simple 2-D graphics, we are particularly fond of using little green men. To get started, you'll use the Canvas layout control, which allows for absolute positioning of child elements. You can greatly enhance this control by placing it inside a Viewbox, which, when used in conjunction with an interactive control such as a Window (as shown in Example 3-4), gives you great control over stretching and scaling of the child elements.

Example 3-4. Canvas and ViewBox: Little green men

```
<Window
    xmlns="http://schemas.microsoft.com/winfx/2006/xaml/presentation"
    xmlns:x="http://schemas.microsoft.com/winfx/2006/xaml"
    Title="Programming .NET 3.5 | Layout: I'm So Happy! ">
    <Viewbox>
```

Example 3-4. Canvas and ViewBox: Little green men (continued)

```
        <Canvas Width="180" Height="180" VerticalAlignment="Center">
            <Ellipse Canvas.Left="10"
                Canvas.Top="10"
                Width="160"
                Height="160"
                Fill="LimeGreen"
                Stroke="Black" />
            <Ellipse Canvas.Left="45"
                Canvas.Top="50"
                Width="25"
                Height="25"
                Fill="Black"
                Stroke="Black" />
            <Ellipse Canvas.Left="77.5"
                Canvas.Top="50"
                Width="25"
                Height="25"
                Fill="Black"
                Stroke="Black" />
            <Ellipse Canvas.Left="110"
                Canvas.Top="50"
                Width="25"
                Height="25"
                Fill="Black"
                Stroke="Black" />
            <Path Data="M 50,100 A 30,30 900 0 0 130,100"
                Stroke="Black"/>
        </Canvas>
    </Viewbox>
</Window>
```

An `Ellipse` object draws an ellipse (surprise!). You place it on the canvas using its position relative to the upper-left corner of the canvas.

 All shape objects (Ellipse, Line, Path, Polygon, Polyline, and Rectangle) share common properties. Three of the most frequently used are:

- `Stroke`, which dictates how the shape's outline will be drawn
- `StrokeThickness`, which determines the thickness of the shape's outline
- `Fill`, which indicates how the shape's interior will be painted

All of the properties for coordinates and vertices are measured in device-independent pixels.

The `Viewbox` implements the facilities that enable users to stretch and resize its contents. In this case, the contents are the canvas on which the little green man is drawn.

(I grew up being called "four-eyes"; think of this as my revenge!) Because you've placed your canvas in a Viewbox, resizing is automagic. Figure 3-7 shows the initial view; stretching the Viewbox results in the display shown in Figure 3-8.

Figure 3-7. Small LGM

Figure 3-8. Large LGM

Control Presentation

WPF and XAML give you tremendous and precise control (pardon the expression)[*] over the appearance of controls. To demonstrate, we'll start with a simple button, as shown in Example 3-5.

---

[*] Despite the incredible breadth of the English language, even resorting to the astonishingly useful Visual-Thesaurus (*http://www.VisualThesaurus.com*) didn't yield a better word than "control" to use in this sentence!

Example 3-5. A simple button

```
<Window
    xmlns="http://schemas.microsoft.com/winfx/2006/xaml/presentation"
    xmlns:x="http://schemas.microsoft.com/winfx/2006/xaml"
    Title="Programming .NET 3.5 | Adding flavor to controls">
    <StackPanel Height="200">
        <Button Width="200" VerticalAlignment="Center">Press Me!</Button>
    </StackPanel>
</Window>
```

When you run this code in XAMLPad a button is rendered, as shown in Figure 3-9. No surprises here!

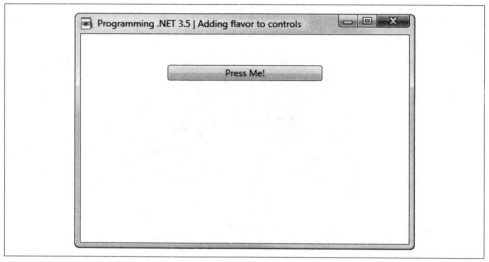

Figure 3-9. A standard button

You can now style this button using gradients, to improve (and professionalize) its look. Example 3-6 shows how to do this. An in-depth discussion follows the code.

Example 3-6. Adding gradients to the Button class

```
<Window
    xmlns="http://schemas.microsoft.com/winfx/2006/xaml/presentation"
    xmlns:x="http://schemas.microsoft.com/winfx/2006/xaml"
    Title="Programming .NET 3.5 | Adding flavor to controls">

    <Window.Resources>

        <LinearGradientBrush
            x:Key="ButtonGradient"
            StartPoint="0,0"
            EndPoint="0,1">
```

Example 3-6. Adding gradients to the Button class (continued)

```xml
    <GradientStop
        Color="#FDB6CADF"
        Offset="0" />
    <GradientStop
        Color="#FCC3C5FF"
        Offset="0.1" />
    <GradientStop
        Color="#FCC4D0EF"
        Offset="0.3" />
    <GradientStop
        Color="#FDB7C2DF"
        Offset="0.6" />
    <GradientStop
        Color="#FE95B3CF"
        Offset="0.8" />
    <GradientStop
        Color="#FE96AACF"
        Offset="1" />
</LinearGradientBrush>

<LinearGradientBrush
    x:Key="ButtonUpGradient"
    StartPoint="0,0"
    EndPoint="0,1">
    <GradientStop
        Color="Transparent"
        Offset="0" />
    <GradientStop
        Color="#33000000"
        Offset="1" />
</LinearGradientBrush>

<LinearGradientBrush
    x:Key="ButtonDownGradient"
    StartPoint="0,0"
    EndPoint="0,1">
    <GradientStop
        Color="#10000000"
        Offset="0" />
    <GradientStop
        Color="#20000000"
        Offset="1" />
</LinearGradientBrush>

<LinearGradientBrush
    x:Key="ButtonDisabledGradient"
    StartPoint="0,0"
    EndPoint="0,1">
    <GradientStop
        Color="#10302A90"
        Offset="0" />
```

Example 3-6. Adding gradients to the Button class (continued)

```
        <GradientStop
            Color="#10201040"
            Offset="1" />
    </LinearGradientBrush>

    <!-- BUTTON TEMPLATE -->
    <Style TargetType="{x:Type Button}">
        <Setter Property="Template">
            <Setter.Value>
                <ControlTemplate TargetType="{x:Type Button}">
                    <Border
                        x:Name="OuterBorder"
                        CornerRadius="3"
                        Background="{DynamicResource ButtonGradient}">
                        <Border
                            x:Name="InnerBorder"
                            CornerRadius="3"
                            Background="{DynamicResource ButtonUpGradient}"
                            Padding="{TemplateBinding Padding}">
                            <ContentPresenter
                                x:Name="ContentSite"
                                HorizontalAlignment="Center"
                                VerticalAlignment="Center" />
                        </Border>
                    </Border>
                    <ControlTemplate.Triggers>
                        <Trigger Property="IsPressed" Value="true">
                            <Setter
                                TargetName="InnerBorder"
                                Property="Background"
                                Value="{DynamicResource ButtonDownGradient}"/>
                        </Trigger>
                        <Trigger Property="IsEnabled" Value="false">
                            <Setter
                                TargetName="InnerBorder"
                                Property="Background"
                                Value="{DynamicResource ButtonDisabledGradient}"/>
                            <Setter Property="BorderBrush" Value="Silver"/>
                            <Setter Property="Foreground" Value="SlateGray"/>
                        </Trigger>
                    </ControlTemplate.Triggers>
                </ControlTemplate>
            </Setter.Value>
        </Setter>
        <Setter Property="Height" Value="18" />
        <Setter Property="Foreground" Value="MidnightBlue" />
    </Style>

</Window.Resources>
<StackPanel Height="200">
```

Example 3-6. Adding gradients to the Button class (continued)

```
    <Button Width="200" Height="40"
        VerticalAlignment="Center">Press Me!
    </Button>
    </StackPanel>
</Window>
```

This code will be a lot more familiar to those readers who are comfortable with Cascading Style Sheets (CSS) than to those who come to WPF from Windows Forms.

 We strongly recommend reading Eric Meyer's *CSS: The Definitive Guide* (O'Reilly) for a solid introduction to CSS, and Dave Shea and Molly Holzschlag's *The Zen of CSS Design: Visual Enlightenment for the Web* (Peachpit Press) for insight into how CSS can help you create magnificent web sites.

Let's walk through this XAML section by section to see what it does.

Resources

The first set of steps is to declare the Window, put in the customary namespaces, and then declare a Resources section. Resources provide the ability to share styles or elements throughout the UI. In this case, you are declaring resources for the Window:

```
<Window
    xmlns="http://schemas.microsoft.com/winfx/2006/xaml/presentation"
    xmlns:x="http://schemas.microsoft.com/winfx/2006/xaml"
    Title="Programming .NET 3.5 | Adding flavor to controls">

    <Window.Resources>
```

The first resource you declare is a LinearGradientBrush, which, as you've probably guessed, is a specialized brush for creating LinearGradients—that is, gradients that fall off at a steady rate.

Linear Gradients

A linear gradient paints a color along a line, with that color changing gradually from one value to another as it moves along the line. (The gradual change can be interrupted by abrupt changes to a new color using GradientStop objects.)

A linear gradient is typically applied along a diagonal, though this is not required. The line is determined by a start point and an endpoint, gradually indicated by a pair of x,y coordinates designating the upper-left and lower-right corners of the area being filled, as illustrated in Figure 3-10.

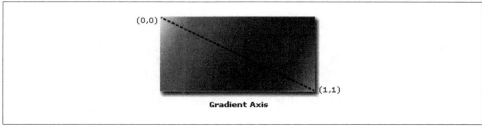

Figure 3-10. Linear gradient illustration from Microsoft

When creating a LinearGradient, you declare the start and endpoints (as described in the previous sidebar "Linear Gradients"); then, within the definition of the LinearGradientBrush, you declare one or more GradientStop elements. These correspond to the collection of GradientStop objects associated with a LinearGradientBrush object. Each GradientStop specifies both a color and an offset along the gradient axis:

```
<LinearGradientBrush x:Key="ButtonGradient"
    StartPoint="0,0"
    EndPoint="0,1">

    <GradientStop Color="#FDB6CADF"
        Offset="0" />
```

In short, the LinearGradientBrush determines the rate of change of the gradient, and the GradientStops determine the color transitions and where along the gradient the colors change. In this example, you declare LinearGradientBrush objects for each state of the button: the button in its initial (unclicked) state, and then the button when pressed (ButtonDownGradient), when released (ButtonUpGradient), and, for completeness, when disabled (ButtonDisabledGradient).

Styles

The first line in the next section indicates that you are defining a global *style* and that the target of the style is a Button. The target is set by the property TargetType and identified by the Type attribute within the namespace *http://schemas.microsoft.com/winfx/2006/xaml* (for which we created the alias "x" at the top of the file):

```
<Style TargetType="{x:Type Button}">
```

Below this line you add a Setter element. In general, a Setter sets a property; in this case the Setter is used to specify the target of the style, identifying the specific instance whose property is being set. Table 3-1 explains how the Setter is used in this example, line by line.

Table 3-1. Setter element explanation, line by line

<Setter Property="Template">	The keyword Property is required and names the property being set. In this case, you are indicating that Style is being used as a template.
<Setter.Value>	The Template value is being set as an explicit property with an opening tag and a closing tag and any number of properties and elements within them.

Table 3-1. Setter element explanation, line by line (continued)

`<ControlTemplate` `TargetType="{x:Type Button}">`	A `ControlTemplate` is used to simplify the creation of the `ButtonTemplate`. The `ControlTemplate` has a property, `TargetType`, that requires that you specify the type for which this `ControlTemplate` will be used (`Button`).

`<Border x:Name="OuterBorder"`
    `CornerRadius="3"`
    `Background="{DynamicResource`
        `ButtonGradient}">`
	In this `Template` the button will have a border that we've (arbitrarily) named `OuterBorder` and that we've defined as having a corner radius of 3 (that is, it will be a rounded rectangle). We've defined the background inline, so it will be utilized as a `DynamicResource`.
	
	Note to reader: to see the effect of the rounding, try changing the `CornerRadius` value to 10, making the button look more like a bullet.

`<Border x:Name="InnerBorder"`
    `CornerRadius="3"`
    `Background="{DynamicResource`
        `ButtonUpGradient}"`
    `Padding="{TemplateBinding`
        `Padding}">`
 	
    `<ContentPresenter`
        `x:Name="ContentSite"`
        `HorizontalAlignment=`
          `"Center"`
        `VerticalAlignment="Center"`
    `/>`
`</Border>`
	Next, you define a second `Border` object to sit atop the first. This sets the background, this time using `ButtonUpGradient`.
	
	`Padding` is used to put padding around the content, and `ContentPresenter` is used to display the text of the button.

`<ControlTemplate.Triggers>`	`Triggers` are the mechanism by which properties change and animations are started in response to events or changes in other properties. We've included `Triggers` even though we don't call them in this example, because you will be using them in future examples to create interaction effects.

`<Trigger Property="IsPressed"`
    `Value="true">`
    `<Setter`
        `TargetName="InnerBorder"`
        `Property="Background"`
        `Value="{DynamicResource`
          `ButtonDownGradient}"`
    `/>`
`</Trigger>`
	When the button is pressed, this `Trigger` causes the `ButtonDownGradient` to be drawn in the `InnerBorder`.

`<Trigger Property="IsEnabled"`
    `Value="false">`
    `<Setter`
        `TargetName="InnerBorder"`
        `Property="Background"`
        `Value="{DynamicResource`
          `ButtonDisabledGradient}"`
    `/>`
    `<Setter Property="BorderBrush"`
        `Value="Silver"/>`
    `<Setter Property="Foreground"`
        `Value="SlateGray"/>`
`</Trigger>`
	This `Trigger` sets the `Background` property of the `Border` control named `InnerBorder` to change in response to the `IsEnabled` property becoming `False`. The actual change is that the `InnerBorder`'s `Background` property is set to the `DynamicResource` value `ButtonDisabledGradient`, the `BorderBrush` is set to `Silver`, and the `Foreground` color is set to `SlateGray`.

Table 3-1. Setter element explanation, line by line (continued)

| ```
</ControlTemplate.Triggers>
</ControlTemplate>
</Setter.Value>
</Setter>
``` | We've finished specifying the Setter; it's now time to close all the open tags. |
|---|---|
| ```
<Setter Property="Height"
    Value="18"/>
<Setter Property="Foreground"
    Value="MidnightBlue"/>
``` | Two more Setters are used to set general style properties of the button. |
| ```
</Style>
</Window.Resources>
<StackPanel Height="200">
    <Button Width="200"
        VerticalAlignment=
            "Center">
      Press Me!
    </Button>
</StackPanel>
</Window>
``` | The Style element is closed off, the Resources element is closed off, and a StackPanel in which a button is nested is created. That finishes off the Window. |

All of this may look a bit daunting at first, but notice that at no time did you have to go into a drawing program and create an image button; you *described* an image button in XAML and it was drawn for you based on that description. That's pretty neat. The result is shown in Figure 3-11.

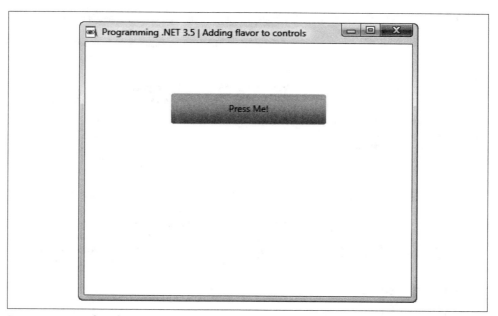

Figure 3-11. Gradient button
```

Making effects more pronounced

We strongly encourage you to play with these examples to make the effects more pronounced and see what happens. For example, to make the gradient effect much more obvious I modified the colors, substituting primary rainbow colors:

```
<LinearGradientBrush x:Key="ButtonGradient"
    StartPoint="0,0"
    EndPoint="0,1">

    <GradientStop Color="Red"
        Offset="0" />
    <GradientStop Color="Orange"
        Offset="0.1" />
    <GradientStop Color="Yellow"
        Offset="0.3" />
    <GradientStop Color="Green"
        Offset="0.6" />
    <GradientStop Color="Blue"
        Offset="0.8" />
    <GradientStop Color="Violet"
        Offset="1" />
</LinearGradientBrush>
```

and greatly increased the size of the button:

```
    <Setter Property="Height" Value="40" />
    <Setter Property="Foreground" Value="BLUE" />
</Style>
</Window.Resources>
<StackPanel Height="400">
```

The result is shown in Figure 3-12.

Figure 3-12. Rainbow button

Nesting

Switching gears for a moment, it is possible and legal to nest one control (or graphic element) within another. This allows you to place, for example, a StackPanel inside a Button, and then place other controls or graphics within that StackPanel.

Either on its own or used in conjunction with templates and styles, this is a very powerful technique for making combined, nearly custom controls on the fly. In the next example, we'll put a horizontally oriented StackPanel inside a button.

We'll then place a Canvas within that StackPanel, and in the Canvas we'll put a set of converging Ellipses to create a bull's eye. Using the StackPanel, we'll put a TextBlock next to the Canvas to print a message. This produces an interesting effect with minimal effort, as shown in Figure 3-13.

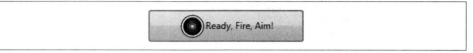

Figure 3-13. Ready, Fire, Aim!

The complete code is shown in Example 3-7.

Example 3-7. Graphics within controls

```
<Window
    xmlns="http://schemas.microsoft.com/winfx/2006/xaml/presentation"
    xmlns:x="http://schemas.microsoft.com/winfx/2006/xaml"
    Title="Programming .NET 3.5 | Programming Methodology Graphic">

  <StackPanel Height="200">
    <Button Width="200" VerticalAlignment="Center">
      <StackPanel Orientation="Horizontal">
        <Canvas Width="30"
            Height="30"
            VerticalAlignment="Center"
            Margin="3">
          <Ellipse Canvas.Left="1"
              Canvas.Top="1"
              Width="30"
              Height="30"
              Fill="White"
              Stroke="Black" />
          <Ellipse Canvas.Left="4"
              Canvas.Top="4"
              Width="24"
              Height="24"
              Fill="Black"
              Stroke="Black" />
          <Ellipse Canvas.Left="8"
              Canvas.Top="8"
              Width="16"
              Height="16"
              Fill="Blue"
              Stroke="Blue" />
          <Ellipse Canvas.Left="11"
              Canvas.Top="11"
              Width="10"
              Height="10"
              Fill="Red"
              Stroke="Red" />
```

Example 3-7. Graphics within controls (continued)

```
                <Ellipse Canvas.Left="14"
                    Canvas.Top="14"
                    Width="4"
                    Height="4"
                    Fill="Yellow"
                    Stroke="Yellow" />
            </Canvas>
            <TextBlock VerticalAlignment="Center"> Ready, Fire, Aim!</TextBlock>
        </StackPanel>
    </Button>
  </StackPanel>
</Window>
```

Resources

Resources provide your XAML with a way to define and share objects. You can share resources at the page (window) level, or throughout an entire application (or even across an entire system!).

The Resources section of your XAML is sometimes referred to as the "resource dictionary." To create a resource that is scoped to a single window, you use this element:

```
<Window.Resources>
```

as shown in Example 3-8.

Example 3-8. A static resource scoped to a single window

```
<Window
    xmlns="http://schemas.microsoft.com/winfx/2006/xaml/presentation"
    xmlns:x="http://schemas.microsoft.com/winfx/2006/xaml"
    Title="Programming .NET 3.5 | Resources">
  <Window.Resources>
     <SolidColorBrush x:Key="GreenBrush" Color="Green" />
  </Window.Resources>
  <Viewbox>
     <TextBlock Foreground="{StaticResource GreenBrush}">
         Little Green Men
     </TextBlock>
  </Viewbox>
</Window>
```

The resource is applied to a TextBlock by setting the foreground value to the resource itself. The keyword StaticResource indicates that the resource will be set at compile time and cannot be updated by associating a different resource with the resource key at runtime. In contrast, dynamic resources can usually be defined at runtime. If you make all your skinnable properties DynamicResource references, you will be able to change the skin just by dropping in a different resource dictionary. WPF will automatically update all the properties when you do this.

The result of applying the GreenBrush resource to the TextBlock is shown in Figure 3-14.

Figure 3-14. A StaticResource used to color the text

Transformations

While there is much that can be written about 2-D graphics, one of the more interesting (and at times confusing) aspects of taking control of graphics is transformations. Here, we'll look at an example of the art of transforming the up/down orientation of the page.

WPF makes simple transformations very simple, as shown in Example 3-9.

Example 3-9. A simple transformation

```
<Window
    xmlns="http://schemas.microsoft.com/winfx/2006/xaml/presentation"
    xmlns:x="http://schemas.microsoft.com/winfx/2006/xaml"
    Title="Programming .NET 3.5 | Transformations: Rotate">
  <Border Margin="30"
      HorizontalAlignment="Left" VerticalAlignment="Top"
      BorderBrush="Black" BorderThickness="1" >
    <StackPanel Orientation="Vertical">
      <Button Content="Top Button" Opacity="1" />
      <Button Content="Middle Button" Opacity="1" />
      <Button Content="Rotated Button">
        <Button.RenderTransform>
          <RotateTransform Angle="45" />
        </Button.RenderTransform>
      </Button>

    </StackPanel>
  </Border>
</Window>
```

This example creates three buttons. The third button has a RenderTransform applied to it, and the RenderTransform has a child element, RotateTransform, whose attribute is an angle (in this case, 45 degrees). The button is rendered with a 45-degree clockwise rotation, as shown in Figure 3-15.

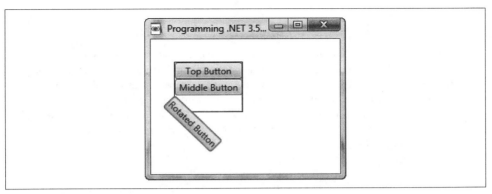

Figure 3-15. A 45-degree rotation

Animation

The power of transformations is greatly enhanced when they are combined with animation. Rotate an object? Interesting. Rotate an object in front of my eyes? Much more interesting.

To be animated in WPF, an object must meet just three requirements:

- It must have a dependency property (see the upcoming sidebar "Dependency and Attached Properties").
- It must belong to a class that inherits from DependencyObject and implements IAnimatable (controls such as Button, Panel, and Shape all inherit from DependencyObject and implement IAnimatable, so this is almost never a problem).
- There must be a compatible animation type available (or you can create your own).

The typical first step for animation is to pick a property to animate. In the next example, you'll animate a Button's rotation by changing its angle. The Angle value is of type Double, so you'll use a DoubleAnimation to create a transition between the starting and ending values (referred to as the From and To properties). You must also specify a Duration—that is, the time it takes to go from the starting value to the destination value. The longer the Duration is, the slower the animation is.

The second step is to create a Storyboard, inside which you will place the DoubleAnimation. The DoubleAnimation designates where to apply the animation (the Storyboard.TargetName)—in other words, it specifies the object to animate (in this case, the button).

The final step is to associate the Storyboard with a Trigger (i.e., the event that will kick off the animation). This is all illustrated in Example 3-10.

Dependency and Attached Properties

Dependency properties provide support for value expressions, property invalidation, and dependent-value coercion, as well as for default values, inheritance, data binding, animation, property change notification, and styling. Dependency properties allow for the creation of "attached properties"—that is, they indicate the ability of one class to "attach" properties to another. This is what allows a Canvas, for example, to "attach" properties to a control such as an Ellipse, so that you can write code like this:

```
<Canvas Width="180" Height="180"
    VerticalAlignment="Center">
  <Ellipse Canvas.Left="10" Canvas.Top="10" Width="160"
      Height="160" Fill="LimeGreen" Stroke="Black" />
```

Ellipse does not have a Left or Top property, but as this snippet shows, the Canvas can attach its Left and Top properties to the Ellipse.

Example 3-10. Rotating a button on click

```
<Page
    xmlns="http://schemas.microsoft.com/winfx/2006/xaml/presentation"
    xmlns:x="http://schemas.microsoft.com/winfx/2006/xaml"
    Title=" Programming .NET 3.5 | Graphics: Animated Rotation"
    Background="White" Margin="50">
  <StackPanel>

      <Button Content="Slow Spinning Button" Width="200"
          RenderTransformOrigin="0.5,0.5">
        <Button.RenderTransform>
          <RotateTransform x:Name="AnimatedRotateTransform" Angle="0" />
        </Button.RenderTransform>
        <Button.Triggers>
          <EventTrigger RoutedEvent="Button.Click">
            <BeginStoryboard>
              <Storyboard>
                <DoubleAnimation
                    Storyboard.TargetName="AnimatedRotateTransform"
                    Storyboard.TargetProperty="Angle"
                    To="360" Duration="0:0:5" FillBehavior="Stop" />
              </Storyboard>
            </BeginStoryboard>
          </EventTrigger>
        </Button.Triggers>
      </Button>

  </StackPanel>
</Page>
```

If you run this code in XAMLPad and then click the button, it will rotate 360 degrees in five seconds.

Simultaneous Animations

Your Storyboard need not be restricted to running a single DoubleAnimation, nor need it stop after a single well-defined activity (e.g., one complete rotation). You can combine movement vertically with movement horizontally to create diagonal movement, for example, and you can repeat that movement indefinitely, as shown in Example 3-11.

Example 3-11. Diagonal movement through paired DoubleAnimations

```xml
<Window
    xmlns="http://schemas.microsoft.com/winfx/2006/xaml/presentation"
    xmlns:x="http://schemas.microsoft.com/winfx/2006/xaml"
    Title="Programming .NET 3.5 | Simple LGM Animation"
    Background="White" Margin="50">

    <Window.Triggers>
        <EventTrigger RoutedEvent="Window.Loaded">
            <BeginStoryboard Name="LGMMoverStoryboard" >
                <Storyboard>
                    <DoubleAnimation
                        Storyboard.TargetName="LGMCanvas"
                        Storyboard.TargetProperty="Height"
                        From="10" To="600"
                        Duration="0:0:5"
                        RepeatBehavior="Forever" />

                    <DoubleAnimation
                        Storyboard.TargetName="LGMCanvas"
                        Storyboard.TargetProperty="Width"
                        From="10" To="600"
                        Duration="0:0:5"
                        RepeatBehavior="Forever" />
                </Storyboard>
            </BeginStoryboard>
        </EventTrigger>
    </Window.Triggers>

    <Canvas
        Width="180"
        Height="180"
        VerticalAlignment="Center"
        x:Name="LGMCanvas">
        <Ellipse
            Canvas.Left="10"
            Canvas.Top="10"
            Width="160"
            Height="160"
            Fill="LimeGreen"
            Stroke="Black" />
        <Ellipse
            Canvas.Left="45"
            Canvas.Top="50"
```

Example 3-11. Diagonal movement through paired DoubleAnimations (continued)

```
            Width="25"
            Height="25"
            Fill="Black"
            Stroke="Black" />
        <Ellipse
            Canvas.Left="77.5"
            Canvas.Top="50"
            Width="25"
            Height="25"
            Fill="Black"
            Stroke="Black" />
        <Ellipse
            Canvas.Left="110"
            Canvas.Top="50"
            Width="25"
            Height="25"
            Fill="Black"
            Stroke="Black" />
        <Path
            Data="M 50,100 A 30,30 900 0 0 130,100"
            Stroke="Black"/>
    </Canvas>

</Window>
```

Notice that the trigger for this event is loading the Window itself:

```
    <EventTrigger RoutedEvent="Window.Loaded">
```

This animation begins as soon as the Window loads and continues until the Window is closed. You will need to run the example to see what it does—a screenshot won't show the animation.

A Composite Control

Once you're familiar with WPF controls, drawing capabilities, and resources, you can mix, match, and combine them, adding subtle animations to create composite user interfaces. These will provide you with very powerful presentation mechanisms that you can reuse in many different formats. To illustrate this idea, let's create a slider-like interface that displays images of the presidents of the United States retrieved from the White House web site; we'll reuse this code in the example in the next chapter.

Figure 3-16 shows what the finished product will look like.

The complete code is shown in Example 3-12.

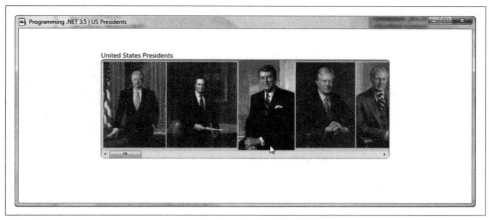

Figure 3-16. U.S. Presidents—a preview

Example 3-12. Composite control: image slider

```
<Window
    xmlns="http://schemas.microsoft.com/winfx/2006/xaml/presentation"
    xmlns:x="http://schemas.microsoft.com/winfx/2006/xaml"
    Title="Programming .NET 3.5 | US Presidents"
    Background="White"
    Margin="50">
  <Window.Resources>

    <LinearGradientBrush x:Key="ListBoxGradient"
        StartPoint="0,0"
        EndPoint="0,1">

      <GradientStop Color="#90000000"
          Offset="0" />
      <GradientStop Color="#40000000"
          Offset="0.005" />
      <GradientStop Color="#10000000"
          Offset="0.04" />
      <GradientStop Color="#20000000"
          Offset="0.945" />
      <GradientStop Color="#60FFFFFF"
          Offset="1" />

    </LinearGradientBrush>

    <Style
        x:Key="SpecialListStyle"
        TargetType="{x:Type ListBox}">
      <Setter Property="Template">
        <Setter.Value>
          <ControlTemplate TargetType="{x:Type ListBox}" >
```

Example 3-12. Composite control: image slider (continued)

```
            <Border
                BorderBrush="Gray"
                BorderThickness="1"
                CornerRadius="6"
                Background="{DynamicResource ListBoxGradient}" >
                <ScrollViewer VerticalScrollBarVisibility="Disabled"
                    HorizontalScrollBarVisibility="Auto">
                    <StackPanel
                        IsItemsHost="True"
                        Orientation="Horizontal"
                        HorizontalAlignment="Left" />
                </ScrollViewer>
            </Border>
        </ControlTemplate>
    </Setter.Value>
    </Setter>
</Style>

<Style x:Key="SpecialListItem"
    TargetType="{x:Type ListBoxItem}">
    <Setter Property="MaxHeight"
        Value="75" />
    <Setter Property="MinHeight"
        Value="75" />
    <Setter Property="Opacity"
        Value=".75" />
    <Style.Triggers>
        <EventTrigger RoutedEvent="Mouse.MouseEnter">
            <EventTrigger.Actions>
                <BeginStoryboard>
                    <Storyboard>
                        <DoubleAnimation Duration="0:0:0.2"
                            Storyboard.TargetProperty="MaxHeight"
                            To="85" />
                        <DoubleAnimation Duration="0:0:0.2"
                            Storyboard.TargetProperty="Opacity"
                            To="1.0" />
                    </Storyboard>
                </BeginStoryboard>
            </EventTrigger.Actions>
        </EventTrigger>
        <EventTrigger RoutedEvent="Mouse.MouseLeave">
            <EventTrigger.Actions>
                <BeginStoryboard>
                    <Storyboard>
                        <DoubleAnimation Duration="0:0:1"
                            Storyboard.TargetProperty="MaxHeight" />
                        <DoubleAnimation Duration="0:0:0.2"
                            Storyboard.TargetProperty="Opacity" />
                    </Storyboard>
                </BeginStoryboard>
```

Example 3-12. Composite control: image slider (continued)

```
            </EventTrigger.Actions>
        </EventTrigger>
    </Style.Triggers>
</Style>

</Window.Resources>

<Grid Width="300"
    Height="150">
    <StackPanel>
        <TextBlock FontSize="14">United States Presidents</TextBlock>
        <ListBox
            Style="{StaticResource SpecialListStyle}"
            Grid.Row="1"
            Grid.ColumnSpan="3"
            Name ="PhotoListBox"
            Margin="0,0,0,20"
            ItemsSource="{Binding }"
            ItemContainerStyle="{StaticResource SpecialListItem}"
            SelectedIndex="0">

            <Image Source=
                "https://www.naymz.com/media/images/306/portrait-portrait.jpg"/>
            <Image Source=
                "http://www.whitehouse.gov/history/presidents/images/bc42.gif"/>
            <Image Source=
                "http://www.whitehouse.gov/history/presidents/images/gb41.gif"/>
            <Image Source=
                "http://www.whitehouse.gov/history/presidents/images/rr40.gif"/>
            <Image Source=
                "http://www.whitehouse.gov/history/presidents/images/jc39.gif"/>
            <Image Source=
                "http://www.whitehouse.gov/history/presidents/images/gf38.gif"/>
            <Image Source=
                "http://www.whitehouse.gov/history/presidents/images/rn37.gif"/>
            <Image Source=
                "http://www.whitehouse.gov/history/presidents/images/lj36.gif"/>
            <Image Source=
                "http://www.whitehouse.gov/history/presidents/images/jk35_1.gif"/>
            <Image Source=
                "http://www.whitehouse.gov/history/presidents/images/gw1.gif"/>
        </ListBox>
    </StackPanel>
</Grid>

</Window>
```

Nothing in this code is new; the components have just been put together in new ways. You start with the resource dictionary, in which you declare a LinearGradientBrush with GradientStops for the colors you want along the gradient.

You then create a Style for the list of presidents and target it at the ListBox, setting the border color to Gray and the border thickness to 1 and rounding the corners. You also turn off the vertical scroll bar and set the horizontal scroll bar to automatic (so that if the width of the control is insufficient to show all the images, the user can scroll through them).

Next, you create a second Style for the items in the ListBox, setting their minimum and maximum heights as well as their opacity and setting a trigger for when the mouse passes over the items. When this event fires (i.e., when the user hovers the mouse pointer over an image), an animation begins that inflates the image to its maximum height and increases its opacity to 100%.

You also set a second trigger that fires when the user moves the mouse pointer away from the image, causing the image to deflate to the minimum size and the opacity to be reduced to 75% (making the image somewhat less vivid). You can see the effect quite clearly when you refresh the window in XAMLPad.

Data Binding

Sooner or later (sooner, if you are writing typical commercial applications), you'll need to associate your presentation widgets with persistent data. That data may come from the Internet, or it may come from XML files, email, your operating system, or a database. OK, let's be blunt: most often it will come from a relational database, and if you're programming in the Microsoft world, we'll go so far as to say that it will most often come from SQL Server (though both authors have written commercial applications that used gigabytes of data from databases that were not written in Redmond!).

The ability to *bind* a control to a data source (of whatever type) is critical in creating efficient professional programs, and WPF would be nothing more than a very impressive toy if it did not support the sophisticated data binding capabilities to which ASP.NET and Windows Forms programmers have grown accustomed.

Data binding in WPF allows you to decouple your user interface from the underlying data (whether it is from SQL Server, an XML file, or some other data source); it thus scales better, performs better, and is more maintainable than more tightly coupled approaches.

Creating a CheckOut Application in Visual Studio

For the next example, you're going to combine XAML and a business class to display a simple shopping cart, as shown in Figure 3-17. You will populate the listbox by binding to a data source you'll declare in the XAML.

Fire up Visual Studio and create a new WPF application named *CheckOut*. Begin by creating a new class, *ShoppingCartItem.cs*, as shown in Example 3-13.

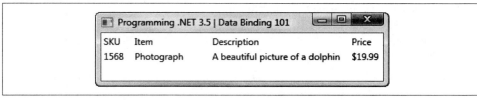

Figure 3-17. A simple shopping cart

Example 3-13. ShoppingCartItem.cs

```csharp
using System;
using System.Collections.Generic;
using System.Linq;
using System.Text;

namespace CheckOut
{

    public class ShoppingCartItem
    {

        public ShoppingCartItem( )
        {
            this.Item = string.Empty;
            this.Value = string.Empty;
            this.ShortDescription = string.Empty;
            this.SKU = -1;
            this.LongDescription = string.Empty;
        }

        public string Item
        {
            get;
            set;
        }
        public string Value
        {
            get;
            set;
        }
        public string ShortDescription
        {
            get;
            set;
        }
        public int SKU
        {
            get;
            set;
        }
        public string LongDescription
```

Example 3-13. ShoppingCartItem.cs (continued)

Example 3-13. ShoppingCartItem.cs (continued)

```
    {
        get;
        set;
    }
}

}
```

This class has nothing but four properties: three strings and an integer.

In the *Window1.xaml* file, add the XAML code to define the presentation layer. This code is shown in Example 3-14.

Example 3-14. XAML for the shopping cart

```
<Window x:Class="CheckOut.Window1"
    xmlns="http://schemas.microsoft.com/winfx/2006/xaml/presentation"
    xmlns:x="http://schemas.microsoft.com/winfx/2006/xaml"
    xmlns:local="clr-namespace:CheckOut"
    Title="Programming .NET 3.5 | Data Binding 101" Height="100" Width="380" >
    <Window.Resources>
        <local:ShoppingCartItem x:Key="Cart"
            SKU="1568"
            Item="Photograph"
            Value="$19.99"
            ShortDescription="A beautiful picture of a dolphin"/>
    </Window.Resources>

    <Grid DataContext="{StaticResource Cart}"
        Margin="3"
        Width="360"
        HorizontalAlignment="Left">
        <Grid.RowDefinitions>
            <RowDefinition Height="20"/>
            <RowDefinition Height="20"/>
            <RowDefinition/>
        </Grid.RowDefinitions>
        <Grid.ColumnDefinitions>
            <ColumnDefinition Width="40"/>
            <ColumnDefinition Width="100"/>
            <ColumnDefinition />
            <ColumnDefinition Width="40"/>
        </Grid.ColumnDefinitions>

        <TextBlock Grid.Column="0"
            Grid.Row="0">SKU</TextBlock>
        <TextBlock Grid.Column="1"
            Grid.Row="0">Item</TextBlock>
        <TextBlock Grid.Column="2"
            Grid.Row="0">Description</TextBlock>
        <TextBlock Grid.Column="3"
            Grid.Row="0">Price</TextBlock>
```

Example 3-14. XAML for the shopping cart (continued)

```
    <TextBlock Grid.Column="0"
        Grid.Row="1"
        Text="{Binding Path=SKU}" />
    <TextBlock Grid.Column="1"
        Grid.Row="1"
        Text="{Binding Path=Item}" />
    <TextBlock Grid.Column="2"
        Grid.Row="1"
        Text="{Binding Path=ShortDescription}" />
    <TextBlock Grid.Column="3"
        Grid.Row="1"
        Text="{Binding Path=Value}" />

</Grid>

</Window>
```

In the Resources section you declare an instance of a shopping cart, setting the various properties declaratively. You then create a Grid, setting its DataContext to the Cart you declared in the Resources section (and thus binding the data from the Resources section to the presentation you are now declaring).

Next, you define a pair of rows and four columns. That done, you define your first four TextBlocks and assign them to the four columns, all within the first row; these serve as headers.

In the second set of TextBlocks, you set the Text using the binding syntax:

```
    <TextBlock Grid.Column="0"
        Grid.Row="1"
        Text="{Binding Path=SKU}" />
```

This places the TextBlock in column 0 of row 1 and states that the Text will come from binding to a data source whose path is set in the resource named earlier as "SKU." We saw that definition of SKU in the Resources section:

```
    <Window.Resources>
        <local:ShoppingCartItem x:Key="Cart"
            SKU="1568"
            Item="Photograph"
            Value="$19.99"
            ShortDescription="A beautiful picture of a dolphin"/>
```

In this case the value for SKU is defined in place, but it could also be dynamically retrieved from a database or web service.

When you run this code, a window is opened and the Grid is filled with both the header row and the second row bound to the ShoppingCartItem, as shown in Figure 3-18.

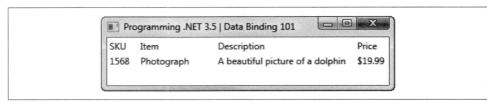

Figure 3-18. The results of our simple data binding

Binding to a List

A much more powerful (and real-world) capability is to bind the listbox to a dynamic collection. In this example, you'll modify the listbox so it can include multiple items from a collection without knowing the size of the collection in advance. Figure 3-19 shows what the listbox will look like.

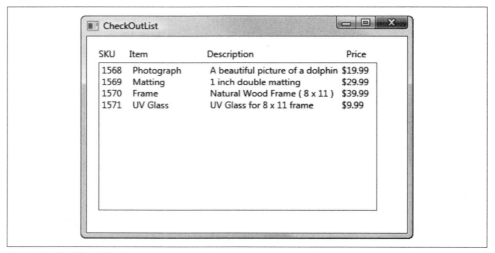

Figure 3-19. CheckOutList—a preview

To create a list of items in the shopping cart, you need to make only one change to the C# code: add a class called ShoppingCart and derive it from List<ShoppingCartItem>. Here's the code:

```
namespace CheckOut
{
    public class ShoppingCart : List<ShoppingCartItem>
    {
    }

    public class ShoppingCartItem
    {
// ...
```

The next step is to modify the resources in your XAML file to create a collection of ShoppingCartItems (we're recommending this only to get a working example up and running, not because it is a good idea to hardcode your lists in your presentation layer!):

```
<Window.Resources>
    <local:ShoppingCart x:Key="Cart">
        <local:ShoppingCartItem SKU="1568"
            Item="Photograph"
            Value="$19.99"
            ShortDescription="A beautiful picture of a dolphin"/>
        <local:ShoppingCartItem SKU="1569"
            Item="Matting"
            Value="$29.99"
            ShortDescription="1 inch double matting"/>
        <local:ShoppingCartItem SKU="1570"
            Item="Frame"
            Value="$39.99"
            ShortDescription="Natural Wood Frame ( 8 x 11 ) "/>
        <local:ShoppingCartItem SKU="1571"
            Item="UV Glass"
            Value="$9.99"
            ShortDescription="UV Glass for 8 x 11 frame"/>
    </local:ShoppingCart>
</Window.Resources>
```

You are now ready to display these items. You can't just use TextBlocks in a grid, though, since in theory (eventually) you won't know how many items you're going to display.

What you want to do is is use an ItemsControl. In this case you are going to create a ListBox and display the items in it. That doesn't mean you have to give up control of the display layout, however. While a DataTemplate in a ListBox can only have one control within it (in our case, a StackPanel whose orientation will be Horizontal to hold one "row"), *that* control can itself have many child controls.

Give the StackPanel four child StackPanels, each set to a Vertical orientation and each with a width equal to that of the header column so that the values line up nicely, as shown in Example 3-15.

Example 3-15. XAML for displaying a list of items

```
<Window x:Class="CheckOutList.Window1"
    xmlns="http://schemas.microsoft.com/winfx/2006/xaml/presentation"
    xmlns:x="http://schemas.microsoft.com/winfx/2006/xaml"
    xmlns:local="clr-namespace:CheckOut"
    Title="CheckOutList" Height="300" Width="430"
    >
    <Window.Resources>
        <local:ShoppingCart x:Key="Cart">
            <local:ShoppingCartItem SKU="1568"
                Item="Photograph"
                Value="$19.99"
                ShortDescription="A beautiful picture of a dolphin"/>
```

Example 3-15. XAML for displaying a list of items (continued)

```xaml
            <local:ShoppingCartItem SKU="1569"
                Item="Matting"
                Value="$29.99"
                ShortDescription="1 inch double matting"/>
            <local:ShoppingCartItem SKU="1570"
                Item="Frame"
                Value="$39.99"
                ShortDescription="Natural Wood Frame ( 8 x 11 ) "/>
            <local:ShoppingCartItem SKU="1571"
                Item="UV Glass"
                Value="$9.99"
                ShortDescription="UV Glass for 8 x 11 frame"/>
        </local:ShoppingCart>
</Window.Resources>

<!-- the heading -->
<Grid DataContext="{StaticResource Cart}"
    Margin="15"
    Width="430"
    HorizontalAlignment="Left">
    <Grid.RowDefinitions>
        <RowDefinition Height="20"/>
        <RowDefinition Height="200"/>
        <RowDefinition/>
    </Grid.RowDefinitions>
    <Grid.ColumnDefinitions>
        <ColumnDefinition Width="40"/>
        <ColumnDefinition Width="100"/>
        <ColumnDefinition Width="180" />
        <ColumnDefinition Width="40"/>
    </Grid.ColumnDefinitions>

    <TextBlock Grid.Column="0"
        Grid.Row="0">SKU</TextBlock>
    <TextBlock Grid.Column="1"
        Grid.Row="0">Item</TextBlock>
    <TextBlock Grid.Column="2"
        Grid.Row="0">Description</TextBlock>
    <TextBlock Grid.Column="3"
        Grid.Row="0">Price</TextBlock>

<!-- the listbox to display all the contents of the cart -->
    <ListBox Grid.Column="0"
        Grid.Row="1"
        Grid.ColumnSpan="4"
        ItemsSource="{Binding}"
        Width="360">
        <ListBox.ItemTemplate>
          <DataTemplate>

              <!-- the outer StackPanel (one per row) -->
              <StackPanel Orientation="Horizontal" Width="350">
```

Example 3-15. XAML for displaying a list of items (continued)

```xaml
                    <!-- the inner stack panels - one per column -->
                    <StackPanel Orientation="Vertical" Width="40">
                      <TextBlock Text="{Binding Path=SKU}" />
                    </StackPanel>
                    <StackPanel Orientation="Vertical" Width="100">
                      <TextBlock Text="{Binding Path=Item}" />
                    </StackPanel>
                    <StackPanel Orientation="Vertical" Width="170">
                      <TextBlock Text="{Binding Path=ShortDescription}" />
                    </StackPanel>
                    <StackPanel Orientation="Vertical" Width="40">
                      <TextBlock Text="{Binding Path=Value}" />
                    </StackPanel>

                </StackPanel>

            </DataTemplate>
        </ListBox.ItemTemplate>
    </ListBox>

  </Grid>
</Window>
```

The leap of imagination you must make is that you can bind to an unknown number of items. This listbox will simply add each item, one by one, with the outer StackPanel describing what each entry in the listbox looks like and the inner StackPanels describing what each "column" of information (the SKU, item, short description, and value) looks like and where they are placed. The result is shown in Figure 3-20.

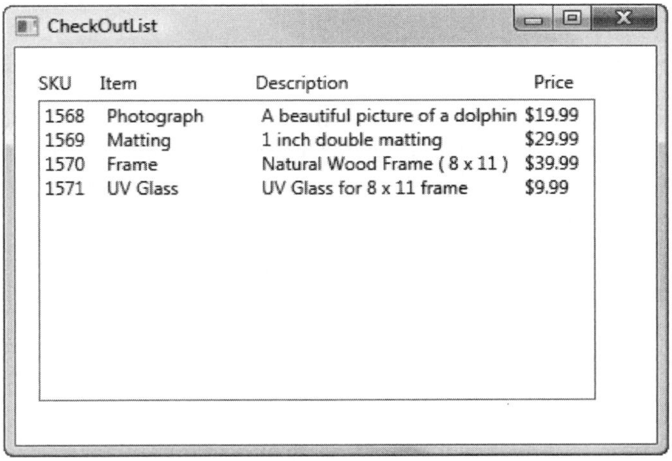

Figure 3-20. CheckOutList—final result

Master/Detail Records

One of the most common and powerful data representations is the master/detail or order/detail record. A classic example is looking at recent orders on Amazon.com—mine are shown in Figure 3-21.

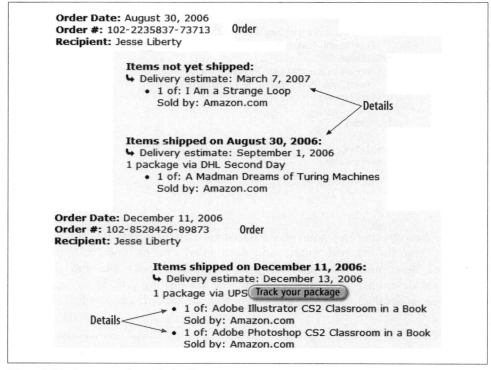

Figure 3-21. Amazon order with details

As you can see, each order can have more than one item within it. These items themselves have valuable information associated with them, including the shipping date (or estimated delivery date) and more. It is very common to have this kind of master/detail relationship throughout virtually any serious business database.

In the next example, we'll assume that some detail is too big to put into the listbox and must be reserved for when the user clicks on an item, thereby requesting more information. To handle this, you're going to add a long description for each item; it will display below the listbox, as you see in Figure 3-22.

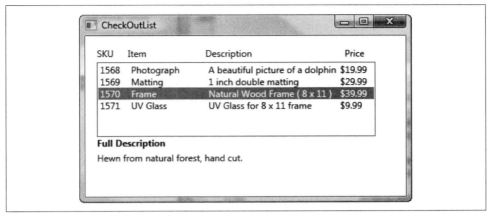

Figure 3-22. Master/detail list binding—a preview

The first step is to modify the previous example, adding a `LongDescription` property to the `ShoppingCartItem` class:

```
public string LongDescription
{
    get;
    set;
}
```

You will need to update both constructors to initialize this property correctly:

```
namespace CheckOut
{
    public class ShoppingCartItem
    {
        public ShoppingCartItem( )
        {
            this.Item = string.Empty;
            this.Value = string.Empty;
            this.ShortDescription = string.Empty;
            this.SKU = -1;
            this.LongDescription = string.Empty;
        }

        public ShoppingCartItem(
            string item,
            string value,
            string shortDescription,
            int sku,
            string longDescription)
```

```
    {
        this.Item = item;
        this.Value = value;
        this.ShortDescription = shortDescription;
        this.SKU = sku;
        this.LongDescription = longDescription;
    }
    // ...
    }
}
```

That done, you'll need to make more substantial changes to the *Window1.xaml* page. The first change is to add a LongDescription to each ShoppingCartItem in the Resources section. For example:

```
<local:ShoppingCartItem SKU="1570"
    Item="Frame"
    Value="$39.99"
    ShortDescription="Natural Wood Frame ( 8 x 11 )"
    LongDescription="Hewn from natural growth forest, hand cut. " />
```

You'll also need to modify the Grid's row definition to make room for the details below the listbox. Let's shorten the listbox row's height from 200 to 100 and add a row for the description:

```
<Grid.RowDefinitions>
    <RowDefinition Height="20"/>
    <RowDefinition Height="100"/>
    <RowDefinition Height="20"/>
    <RowDefinition/>
</Grid.RowDefinitions>
```

While you're at it, you can make the headers bold by adding the FontWeight style to each header's TextBlock:

```
<TextBlock Grid.Column="0" FontWeight ="Bold"
    Grid.Row="0">SKU</TextBlock>
```

Event handling

One way you can ensure that the FullDescription is displayed when the user clicks on an item in the listbox is to take these steps:

1. Add an event handler to *Window1.xaml.cs* (the code-behind for the window).

2. Add a delegate to the ListBox telling it which event handler to call when its selection changes.

3. Add a TextBlock in the form where you can place the long description when a choice is made in the listbox.

Actually, you'll need to add two TextBlocks. Below the ListBox, but before you close the Grid, add one TextBlock as a header for the long description, and one to hold the long description when the user clicks in the listbox:

```
<TextBlock Grid.Column="0" Grid.ColumnSpan="2" FontWeight="Bold"
    Grid.Row="2">Full Description</TextBlock>
<TextBlock Grid.Column="0"
    Grid.ColumnSpan="4"
    Grid.Row="3"
    Name="LongDescriptionLabel" />
```

Next, modify the ListBox declaration to call a method that you'll add to the code-behind file:

```
<ListBox Grid.Column="0"
    Grid.Row="1"
    Grid.ColumnSpan="4"
    ItemsSource="{Binding}"
    SelectionChanged="ShoppingCartSelection"
    Width="360">
```

You must now implement the ShoppingCartSelection( ) method as a member of the Window1 class in *Window1.xaml.cs*. It will examine the ListBox control, see what was selected, extract the LongDescription from that object (which will be of type ShoppingCartItem), and place that long description into the TextBlock you just added to the form. This method is shown in Example 3-16.

Example 3-16. ShoppingCartSelection in Window1.xaml.cs

```
private void ShoppingCartSelection(object sender, RoutedEventArgs e)
{
    ListBox lb = sender as ListBox;
    ShoppingCartItem scItem = lb.SelectedItem as ShoppingCartItem;
    LongDescriptionLabel.Text = scItem.LongDescription.ToString( );
}
```

The old C hacker in me is tempted to write the method as follows:

```
private void ShoppingCartSelection(
    object  sender, RoutedEventArgs e)
{
    LongDescriptionLabel.Text =
        ((sender as ListBox).SelectedItem as
        ShoppingCartItem).LongDescription.ToString( );
}
```

But that would be evil.

When the user clicks on an item in the listbox, the SelectionChanged event is fired, and ShoppingCartSelection( ) is called in *Window1.xaml.cs*. The listbox is retrieved, the selected ShoppingCartItem is identified, and its LongDescription is extracted. That string is then placed into the TextBlock and displayed, as shown in Figure 3-23 (which is the same as Figure 3-22, now that this example is complete).

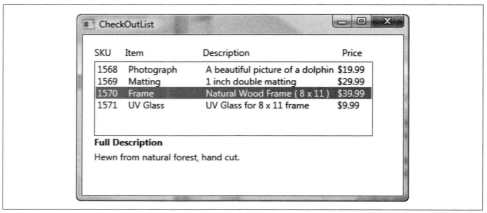

Figure 3-23. Master/detail list binding—final result

Applying WPF: Building a Biz App

The previous chapter introduced various aspects of working with WPF. In this chapter you're going to build a larger desktop application that has two significant "pages": on the first page (shown in Figure 4-1), users will be able to choose among photographs, crop them, and then add prints and related items to the shopping cart; on the second page (shown in Figure 4-2), users will pay for the items in their carts using a credit card.

Figure 4-1. Page 1

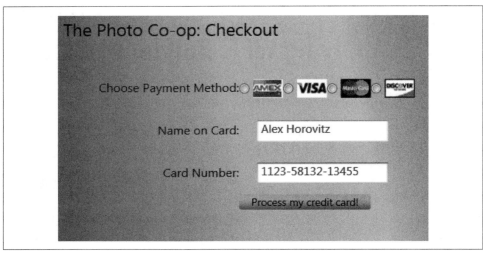

Figure 4-2. Page 2

Breaking the Application into Pieces

This application clearly lends itself to being developed in a number of pieces. The first division is between the first page, in which the user adds items to the shopping cart, and the second page, in which the user pays for those items.

Page 1, in turn, can easily be divided into its component parts: the photo slider you developed in the last chapter, the central photo display, the shopping cart area, and the surrounding areas.

To begin, create a new WPF Application called *PhotoCooperative*. You will use this project as a container for the code you create and evaluate along the way.

Adorners

The spec for this project states that the user can drag a cropping rectangle within any photograph and then click the Crop button to crop the photo, as shown in Figure 4-3.

To accomplish this, you'll need to be able to create and display a "rubberband" on mouse down and mouse drag, and leave it in place on mouse up (activating the Crop button)—and you'll need to be able to "crop" the photo to its new rectangle.

You'll implement the rubberband as an *adorner*. Adorners are, essentially, elements that are rendered "on top of" existing elements (or collections of elements). You can think of WPF as having what amounts to an acetate layer of adorners that can be laid on top of adorned elements, with the adorners positioned relative to the elements that are being adorned.

Figure 4-3. Cropping a photo

Adorners are often used to create element-manipulation handles (like rotation handles or resizers) or visual feedback indications. A rubberband for cropping is an excellent example. In fact, Microsoft offers sample code that you can "borrow" and adapt for the purposes of this application, as shown in Example 4-1.

Example 4-1. The rubberband adorner

```
using System;
using System.IO;
using System.Windows;
using System.Windows.Input;
using System.Windows.Media;
using System.Windows.Documents;

namespace PhotoCooperative
{
    public class RubberbandAdorner : Adorner
    {
        public Window1 Window { set; get; }
        private RectangleGeometry geometry;
        public System.Windows.Shapes.Path Rubberband { get; set; }
        private UIElement adornedElement;
        private Rect selectRect;
        public Rect SelectRect { get { return selectRect; } }
        protected override int VisualChildrenCount { get { return 1; } }
        private Point anchorPoint;

        public RubberbandAdorner(UIElement adornedElement) : base(adornedElement)
        {
            this.adornedElement = adornedElement;
            selectRect = new Rect();
            geometry = new RectangleGeometry();
```

Example 4-1. The rubberband adorner (continued)

```
      Rubberband = new System.Windows.Shapes.Path( );
      Rubberband.Data = geometry;
      Rubberband.StrokeThickness = 2;
      Rubberband.Stroke = Brushes.Yellow;
      Rubberband.Opacity = .6;
      Rubberband.Visibility = Visibility.Hidden;
      AddVisualChild(Rubberband);
      MouseMove += new MouseEventHandler(DrawSelection);
      MouseUp += new MouseButtonEventHandler(EndSelection);
   }

   protected override Size ArrangeOverride(Size size)
   {
      Size finalSize = base.ArrangeOverride(size);
      ((UIElement)GetVisualChild(0)).Arrange(new Rect(new Point( ), finalSize));
      return finalSize;
   }

   public void StartSelection(Point anchorPoint)
   {
      this.anchorPoint = anchorPoint;
      selectRect.Size = new Size(10, 10);
      selectRect.Location = anchorPoint;
      geometry.Rect = selectRect;
      if (Visibility.Visible != Rubberband.Visibility)
          Rubberband.Visibility = Visibility.Visible;
   }

   private void DrawSelection(object sender, MouseEventArgs e)
   {
      if (e.LeftButton == MouseButtonState.Pressed)
      {
         Point mousePosition = e.GetPosition(adornedElement);
         if (mousePosition.X < anchorPoint.X)
         {
            selectRect.X = mousePosition.X;
         }
         else
         {
            selectRect.X = anchorPoint.X;
         }
         if (mousePosition.Y < anchorPoint.Y)
         {
            selectRect.Y = mousePosition.Y;
         }
         else
         {
            selectRect.Y = anchorPoint.Y;
         }
         selectRect.Width = Math.Abs(mousePosition.X - anchorPoint.X);
         selectRect.Height = Math.Abs(mousePosition.Y - anchorPoint.Y);
         geometry.Rect = selectRect;
```

Example 4-1. The rubberband adorner (continued)

```
            AdornerLayer layer = AdornerLayer.GetAdornerLayer(adornedElement);
            layer.InvalidateArrange( );
        }
    }

    private void EndSelection(object sender, MouseButtonEventArgs e)
    {
        const int MinSize = 3;

        if (selectRect.Width <= MinSize || selectRect.Height <= MinSize)
        {
            Rubberband.Visibility = Visibility.Hidden;
        }
        else
        {
            Window.CropButton.IsEnabled = true;
        }
        ReleaseMouseCapture( );
    }

    protected override Visual GetVisualChild(int index)
    {
        return Rubberband;
    }
  }
}
```

Let's unpack a bit of this code. You begin by creating a few private member variables:

```
        private RectangleGeometry geometry;
        private UIElement adornedElement;
        private Point anchorPoint;
```

The Geometry class is used to describe a 2-D shape. In this case, you'll use the RectangleGeometry class to constrain the rubberband to draw a rectangle as the user drags the mouse across the photograph (as you saw in Figure 4-3).

The private member variable adornedElement is the element that will be adorned (i.e., the element on which the Rubberband will act). This value is passed into the constructor, which sends it along to the abstract base class (Adorner):

```
        public RubberbandAdorner( UIElement adornedElement ) : base( adornedElement )
```

anchorPoint is the starting point for the rectangle, established by an initial mouse-down event similar to this:

```
        private void OnMouseDown( object sender, MouseButtonEventArgs e )
        {
            Point anchor = e.GetPosition( CurrentPhoto );

        }
```

The constructor attaches the RubberbandAdorner to the adornedElement (in this case, the current photo) and creates a new rectangle:

```
this.adornedElement = adornedElement;
selectRect = new Rect( );
```

It then sets the Rubberband property to a new Path object (a Path is used to describe a complex geometric figure; the segments within a path are combined to create a single shape):

```
Rubberband = new System.Windows.Shapes.Path( );
```

In this case, you set the Data for the Path to geometry, which you'll remember is just a RectangleGeometry (that is, the data to create a rectangle shape). The Path also takes a StrokeThickness (the width of the rectangle's border), a Stroke (the color), an Opacity (the level of transparency), and a Visibility (it starts out hidden):

```
geometry = new RectangleGeometry( );

Rubberband.Data = geometry;
Rubberband.StrokeThickness = 2;
Rubberband.Stroke = Brushes.Yellow;
Rubberband.Opacity = .6;
Rubberband.Visibility = Visibility.Hidden;
```

Next, you add the rubberband member variable to the adorner by calling its AddVisualChild( ) method:

```
AddVisualChild( Rubberband );
```

This adds the Path to the adorner's collection of visual elements.

Finally, you add two event handlers, MouseMove (which calls DrawSelection( )) and MouseUp (which calls EndSelection( )):

```
MouseMove += new MouseEventHandler( DrawSelection );
MouseUp += new MouseButtonEventHandler( EndSelection );
```

StartSelection( ) is called by the OnMouseDown handler in Window1, as you'll see later in this chapter.

Here is the complete listing of the constructor:

```
public RubberbandAdorner(UIElement adornedElement) : base(adornedElement)
{
    this.adornedElement = adornedElement;
    selectRect = new Rect( );

    Rubberband = new System.Windows.Shapes.Path( );

    geometry = new RectangleGeometry( );

    Rubberband.Data = geometry;
    Rubberband.StrokeThickness = 2;
    Rubberband.Stroke = Brushes.Yellow;
    Rubberband.Opacity = .6;
    Rubberband.Visibility = Visibility.Hidden;
```

```
AddVisualChild(Rubberband);
MouseMove += new MouseEventHandler(DrawSelection);
MouseUp += new MouseButtonEventHandler(EndSelection);
    }
```

To place each visual child element, you call the base class's `ArrangeOverride( )` method and pass in the `Size` object you are given, getting back a `Size` object representing the area you have to work with. You then obtain each visual child in turn and call `Arrange( )` on them, passing in a `Rectangle`. Finally, you return the `Size` object obtained from the base class:

```
protected override Size ArrangeOverride(Size size)
{
    Size finalSize = base.ArrangeOverride(size);
    ((UIElement)GetVisualChild(0)).Arrange(new Rect(new Point( ), finalSize));
    return finalSize;
}
```

Business Classes

To support the user interface, you need a set of simple business classes representing the photographs and the items the user can purchase based on each photo. These are collected in the *StoreItems.cs* file, shown in Example 4-2.

Example 4-2. StoreItems.cs

```
using System;
using System.Collections.Generic;
using System.Text;
using System.IO;
using System.Collections.ObjectModel;
using System.ComponentModel;
using System.Windows.Media.Imaging;
using System.Collections.Specialized;
using System.Windows.Controls;

namespace PhotoCooperative
{
    public class ImageFile
    {
        public String Path { get; set; }
        public Uri TheUri { get; set; }
        public BitmapFrame Image { get; set; }

        public ImageFile(string path)
        {
            Path = path;
            TheUri = new Uri(Path);
            Image = BitmapFrame.Create(TheUri);
        }

        public override string ToString( )
```

Example 4-2. StoreItems.cs (continued)

```
        {
            return Path;
        }
    }

    public class PhotoList : ObservableCollection<ImageFile>
    {
        DirectoryInfo theDirectoryInfo;

        public PhotoList() { }

        public PhotoList(string path) : this(new DirectoryInfo(path)) { }

        public PhotoList(DirectoryInfo directory)
        {
            theDirectoryInfo = directory;
            Update();
        }

        public string Path
        {
            set
            {
                theDirectoryInfo = new DirectoryInfo(value);
                Update();
            }
            get { return theDirectoryInfo.FullName; }
        }

        public DirectoryInfo Directory
        {
            set
            {
                theDirectoryInfo = value;
                Update();
            }
            get { return theDirectoryInfo; }
        }

        private void Update()
        {
            foreach (FileInfo f in theDirectoryInfo.GetFiles("*.gif"))
            {
                Add(new ImageFile(f.FullName));
            }
        }
    }
```

Example 4-2. StoreItems.cs (continued)

```csharp
public class PrintType
{
    public String Description { get; set; }
    public double Price { get; set; }

    public PrintType(string description, double price)
    {
        Description = description;
        Price = price;
    }

    public override string ToString()
    {
        return Description;
    }

}

public class PrintTypeList : ObservableCollection<PrintType>
{
    public PrintTypeList()
    {
        Add(new PrintType("5x7 Print", 0.49));
        Add(new PrintType("Holiday Card", 1.99));
        Add(new PrintType("Sweatshirt", 19.99));
    }
}

public class PrintBase : INotifyPropertyChanged
{
    private BitmapSource aPhoto;
    private PrintType aPrintType;
    private int aQuantity;

    public PrintBase(BitmapSource photo, PrintType printtype, int quantity)
    {
        Photo = photo;
        PrintType = printtype;
        Quantity = quantity;
    }

    public PrintBase(BitmapSource photo, string description, double cost)
    {
        Photo = photo;
        PrintType = new PrintType(description, cost);
        Quantity = 0;
    }

    public BitmapSource Photo
```

Example 4-2. StoreItems.cs (continued)

```
        {
            set { aPhoto = value; OnPropertyChanged("Photo"); }
            get { return aPhoto; }
        }

        public PrintType PrintType
        {
            set { aPrintType = value; OnPropertyChanged("PrintType"); }
            get { return aPrintType; }
        }

        public int Quantity
        {
            set { aQuantity = value; OnPropertyChanged("Quantity"); }
            get { return aQuantity; }
        }

        public event PropertyChangedEventHandler PropertyChanged;

        private void OnPropertyChanged(String info)
        {
            if (PropertyChanged != null)
                PropertyChanged(this, new PropertyChangedEventArgs(info));
        }

        public override string ToString()
        {
            return PrintType.ToString();
        }
    }

    public class Print : PrintBase
    {
        public Print(BitmapSource photo) : base(photo, "5x7 Print", 0.49) { }
    }

    public class GreetingCard : PrintBase
    {
        public GreetingCard(BitmapSource photo) : base(photo, "Greeting Card", 1.99)
        { }
    }

    public class SShirt : PrintBase
    {
        public SShirt(BitmapSource photo) : base(photo, "Sweatshirt", 19.99) { }
    }

    public class PrintList : ObservableCollection<PrintBase> { }
}
```

There's nothing terribly surprising in this code. In the `ImageFile` constructor, you first define the `ImageFile` object (the picture) based on its disk location. You create a URI from the path to the file on disk, and you create a `BitmapFrame` from that URI:

```
public ImageFile(string path)
{
    Path = path;
    TheUri = new Uri(Path);
    Image = BitmapFrame.Create(TheUri);
}
```

The `PhotoList` class represents an `ObservableCollection` of `ImageFiles`:

```
public class PhotoList : ObservableCollection<ImageFile>
```

`ObservableCollection` is a generic collection that implements the Observer pattern (discussed in Chapter 8); that is, it notifies interested (registered) objects when items are added or removed, or when the list is refreshed. This will come in handy later, when you create the scrolling listbox of photos from which the user can choose. Because the list is observable, when an item is selected an event will be raised. You can set an event handler accordingly:

```
<ListBox Style="{DynamicResource PhotoListStyle}"
    Grid.Row="1"
    Grid.ColumnSpan="3"
    Name ="PhotoListBox"
    Margin="0,0,0,20"
    DataContext="{Binding Source={StaticResource Photos}}"
    SelectionChanged ="PhotoListSelection"
    ItemsSource="{Binding }"
    ItemContainerStyle="{DynamicResource PhotoListItem}"
    SelectedIndex="0" />
```

You'll need one more business class, to validate credit cards, but we'll delay discussion of that until you're ready to build the second page.

Page 1—Adding Items to the Shopping Cart

With the business classes in place in *StoreItems.cs*, you're ready to build the first page. Open up *Window1.xaml*, as shown in Figure 4-4.

Now, edit this file to create a slider for the photographs. You'll do this by adapting the image list created in the previous chapter to display the U.S. presidents.

In that example you had a `Grid` with a `StackPanel`, and inside that was a `ListBox` with `ListBox` items. In this case, rather than explicitly naming the items in the listbox, you're going to bind the `ListBox` to a data source (a static resource called `Photos`). You'll put the `ListBox` inside a `Grid`, and you'll put that inside a `ViewBox` so the user can resize the entire thing. This will be done in two steps, with the first one allowing you to visualize the `Grid`.

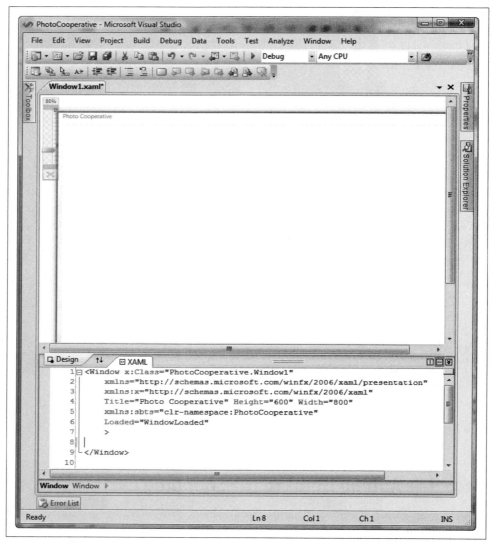

Figure 4-4. The Photo Cooperative

```xml
<Viewbox VerticalAlignment="Top" Stretch="Uniform">

<Grid Margin="20" Width="620" ShowGridLines="True" >
  <Grid.RowDefinitions>
    <RowDefinition Height="Auto" />
    <RowDefinition Height="120" />
    <RowDefinition Height="Auto" />
    <RowDefinition Height="250" />
```

```
        <RowDefinition Height="15" />
        <RowDefinition Height="Auto" />
        <RowDefinition Height="*" />
    </Grid.RowDefinitions>
    <Grid.ColumnDefinitions>
        <ColumnDefinition/>
        <ColumnDefinition Width="400" />
        <ColumnDefinition Width="160" />
    </Grid.ColumnDefinitions>
    <TextBlock Grid.Row="0" Grid.ColumnSpan="3"
        Style="{DynamicResource TitleText}">
        <Span>The Photo Co-op: </Span>
        <Span FontStyle="Italic"> your pictures your way</Span>
    </TextBlock>
</Grid>

</Viewbox>
```

If you run the application now, you should see something like Figure 4-5. You won't want the gridlines to be visible, though—to turn them off, set the ShowGridLines property of the Grid to False.

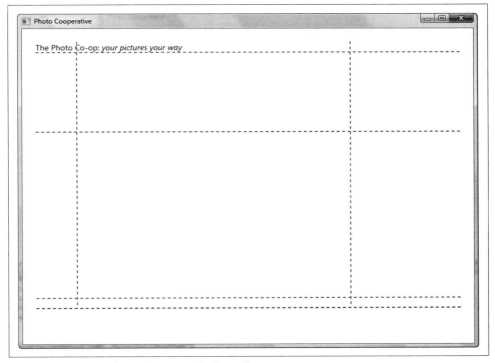

Figure 4-5. Running the application with the gridlines on

Next, you need to deal with some of the resources that the Window will use (specifically, DynamicResource and PhotoListStyle). It is helpful to understand that you simply need to add these resources to a Window.Resources section. You'll put this section just below your Window class declaration:

```
<Window x:Class="PhotoCooperative.Window1"
    xmlns="http://schemas.microsoft.com/winfx/2006/xaml/presentation"
    xmlns:x="http://schemas.microsoft.com/winfx/2006/xaml"
    Title="Photo Cooperative" Height="600" Width="800"
    xmlns:sbts="clr-namespace:PhotoCooperative"
>
    <Window.Resources>

        <!-- PHOTOLIST TEMPLATE -->

        <Style x:Key="PhotoListStyle" TargetType="{x:Type ListBox}">
            <Setter Property="Template">
                <Setter.Value>
                    <ControlTemplate TargetType="{x:Type ListBox}" >
                        <Border
                            BorderBrush="Gray"
                            BorderThickness="1"
                            CornerRadius="6"
                            Background="{DynamicResource ListBoxGradient}" >
                            <ScrollViewer
                                VerticalScrollBarVisibility="Disabled"
                                HorizontalScrollBarVisibility="Auto">
                                <StackPanel
                                    IsItemsHost="True"
                                    Orientation="Horizontal"
                                    HorizontalAlignment="Left" />
                            </ScrollViewer>
                        </Border>
                    </ControlTemplate>
                </Setter.Value>
            </Setter>
        </Style>

        <!-- PHOTOLIST STORYBOARDS -->

        <Style x:Key="PhotoListItem" TargetType="{x:Type ListBoxItem}">
            <Setter Property="MaxHeight" Value="75" />
            <Setter Property="MinHeight" Value="75" />
            <Setter Property="Opacity" Value=".75" />
            <Style.Triggers>
                <EventTrigger RoutedEvent="Mouse.MouseEnter">
                    <EventTrigger.Actions>
                        <BeginStoryboard>
                            <Storyboard>
                                <DoubleAnimation
                                    Duration="0:0:0.2"
                                    Storyboard.TargetProperty="MaxHeight"
                                    To="85" />
```

```
                    <DoubleAnimation
                        Duration="0:0:0.2"
                        Storyboard.TargetProperty="Opacity"
                        To="1.0" />
                </Storyboard>
            </BeginStoryboard>
        </EventTrigger.Actions>
    </EventTrigger>

    <EventTrigger RoutedEvent="Mouse.MouseLeave">
        <EventTrigger.Actions>
            <BeginStoryboard>
                <Storyboard>
                    <DoubleAnimation
                        Duration="0:0:1"
                        Storyboard.TargetProperty="MaxHeight" />
                    <DoubleAnimation
                        Duration="0:0:0.2"
                        Storyboard.TargetProperty="Opacity" />
                </Storyboard>
            </BeginStoryboard>
        </EventTrigger.Actions>
    </EventTrigger>
  </Style.Triggers>
 </Style>
</Window.Resources>
```

At this point you will need to add the ListBox code mentioned earlier to your *Window1.xaml* file, right below the TextBlock inside the Grid:

```
<ListBox Style="{DynamicResource PhotoListStyle}"
    Grid.Row="1"
    Grid.ColumnSpan="3"
    Name ="PhotoListBox"
    Margin="0,0,0,20"
    DataContext="{Binding Source={StaticResource Photos}}"
    SelectionChanged ="PhotoListSelection"
    ItemsSource="{Binding }"
    ItemContainerStyle="{DynamicResource PhotoListItem}"
    SelectedIndex="0" />
```

Note the SelectionChanged attribute. This indicates that you need an event handler for when the selection changes in the photo display. Put that in *Window1.xaml.cs*:

```
private void PhotoListSelection( object sender, RoutedEventArgs e )
{
    String path = ( ( sender as ListBox ).SelectedItem.ToString( ) );
    BitmapSource img = BitmapFrame.Create( new Uri( path ) );
}
```

Recall that in *StoreItems.cs* you declared a class of type PhotoList:

```
public class PhotoList : ObservableCollection<ImageFile>
```

In *Window1.xaml.cs*, create a member variable that is an instance of this class:

```
public partial class Window1 : System.Windows.Window
{
    public PhotoList Photos;
```

The business class also defines an ImageFile class (see the listing for *StoreItems.cs*), but your Resources section needs to define a DataTemplate for binding to an ImageFile:

```
<!-- DATA TEMPLATES -->

<DataTemplate DataType="{x:Type sbts:ImageFile}">
    <Border VerticalAlignment="Center"
        HorizontalAlignment="Center"
        Padding="4"
        Margin="2"
        Background="White">
        <Image Source="{Binding Image}" />
    </Border>
</DataTemplate>
```

The rest is just aesthetics. You'll want to define styles both for the Window itself and for the Title text:

```
<!-- STYLES -->

<Style TargetType="{x:Type sbts:Window1}">
    <Setter Property="Background"
        Value="{DynamicResource WindowGradient}" />
</Style>

<Style x:Key="TitleText"
    TargetType="{x:Type TextBlock}" >
    <Setter Property="FontFamily"
        Value="Segoe Black" />
    <Setter Property="FontSize"
        Value="20px" />
    <Setter Property="Foreground"
        Value="MidnightBlue" />
</Style>
```

Also, both the ListBox and the Window use gradients, so these must be defined as well. Add these brushes to the top of the Window.Resources section:

```
<!- LINEAR GRADIENT BRUSHES -->
<LinearGradientBrush x:Key="WindowGradient"
    StartPoint="0,0.3"
    EndPoint="1,0">
    <GradientStop Color="#B2B6CAFF"
        Offset="0" />
    <GradientStop Color="#BFC3D5FF"
        Offset="0.1" />
    <GradientStop Color="#E0E4F0FF"
        Offset="0.3" />
```

```
        <GradientStop Color="#E6EAF5FF"
            Offset="0.5" />
        <GradientStop Color="#CFD7E2FF"
            Offset="0.6" />
        <GradientStop Color="#BFC5D3FF"
            Offset="0.8" />
        <GradientStop Color="#C4CBD8FF"
            Offset="1" />
    </LinearGradientBrush>

    <LinearGradientBrush x:Key="ListBoxGradient"
        StartPoint="0,0"
        EndPoint="0,1">

        <GradientStop Color="#90000000"
            Offset="0" />
        <GradientStop Color="#40000000"
            Offset="0.005" />
        <GradientStop Color="#10000000"
            Offset="0.04" />
        <GradientStop Color="#20000000"
            Offset="0.945" />
        <GradientStop Color="#60FFFFFF"
            Offset="1" />

    </LinearGradientBrush>
```

You're almost ready to run this puppy—you just have to tell the Application what your data source is. In *App.xaml*, add this code:

```
<Application x:Class="PhotoCooperative.App"
    xmlns="http://schemas.microsoft.com/winfx/2006/xaml/presentation"
    xmlns:x="http://schemas.microsoft.com/winfx/2006/xaml"
    xmlns:sbts="clr-namespace:PhotoCooperative"
    Startup="AppStartup">
    <Application.Resources>
        <ObjectDataProvider x:Name="PhotosODP" x:Key="Photos"
            ObjectType="{x:Type sbts:PhotoList}" />
    </Application.Resources>
</Application>
```

Then, in *App.xaml.cs*, add the following:

```
public partial class App : System.Windows.Application
{
    void AppStartup( object sender, StartupEventArgs args )
    {
        Window1 theWindow = new Window1( );
        theWindow.Show( );

        ObjectDataProvider dataProvider =
            this.Resources["Photos"] as ObjectDataProvider;

        PhotoList photoList = dataProvider.Data as PhotoList;
```

```
        theWindow.Photos = photoList;
        theWindow.Photos.Path = @"..\..\Photos";
    }
}
```

With all this wired together, you are ready to run your data-bound photo list (shown in Figure 4-6). The only thing left to do is create a *Photos* folder and put some GIF images in it. To add a new folder, right-click on the project and select Add → New Folder. Rename it *Photos*, then right-click on it and select Open in Windows Explorer. From there, you should be able to fill the folder with GIFs. If you need some GIFs in a hurry, you can download Alex's from *http://tinyurl.com/2jarve*.

Figure 4-6. Image slider

Displaying the Selected Image

You can add a display of the selected image with just a couple of small changes. To begin, just below the ListBox, add an Image control:

```
<Image Name="CurrentPhoto"
    Grid.Row="3"
    Grid.Column="1"
    Margin="10"
    MouseDown="OnMouseDown"/>
```

This depends on two things. The first is an OnMouseDown event handler, which you can stub out in *Window1.xaml.cs*:

```
private void OnMouseDown( object sender, MouseButtonEventArgs e )
{
}
```

The second is setting the CurrentPhoto when the user clicks in the image slider:

```
private void PhotoListSelection( object sender, RoutedEventArgs e )
{
    String path = ( ( sender as ListBox ).SelectedItem.ToString( ) );
    BitmapSource img = BitmapFrame.Create( new Uri( path ) );
    CurrentPhoto.Source = img;
}
```

Presto! When the user selects an image in the slider, a nice blow-up of the image is shown below it, in the Image control you placed in grid row 3, column 1. Figure 4-7 demonstrates the effect.

Figure 4-7. The Image control

Adding Cropping with the Adorner

There are two steps remaining to finish the first page. The first is to add the rubber-band adorner discussed earlier, using the code detailed in Example 4-1. (We'll deal with the second task—adding the shopping cart—in the next section.) Begin by adding a RubberbandAdorner class, which you'll place in a new file called *CropUtilities.cs*.

To tie this into the application, you need to make a few changes in *Window1.xaml*. First, add the Crop and Undo buttons to the Grid:

```
<ListBox Style="{DynamicResource PhotoListStyle}"
    Grid.Row="1"
    Grid.ColumnSpan="3"
    Name ="PhotoListBox"
    Margin="0,0,0,20"
    DataContext="{Binding Source={StaticResource Photos}}"
    SelectionChanged ="PhotoListSelection"
    ItemsSource="{Binding }"
    ItemContainerStyle="{DynamicResource PhotoListItem}"
    SelectedIndex="0" />
```

```
<StackPanel
    Grid.Row="3"
    Grid.Column="0">

    <Button
        Name="CropButton"
        VerticalAlignment="Bottom"
        HorizontalAlignment="Center"
        Click="Crop"
        Width="55"
        Margin="2">
      Crop
    </Button>

</StackPanel>

<Button Grid.Row="3"
    Grid.Column="0"
    Name="UndoButton"
    VerticalAlignment="Bottom"
    HorizontalAlignment="Center"
    Click="Undo"
    IsEnabled="False"
    Width="55"
    Margin="2">
  Undo
</Button>

<Image Name="CurrentPhoto"
    Grid.Row="3"
    Grid.Column="1"
    Margin="10"
    MouseDown="OnMouseDown" />
```

These buttons need gradients, which you should now add to the Window.Resources section:

```
<LinearGradientBrush x:Key="ButtonGradient"
    StartPoint="0,0"
    EndPoint="0,1">

    <GradientStop Color="#FDB6CADF"
        Offset="0" />
    <GradientStop Color="#FCC3C5FF"
        Offset="0.1" />
    <GradientStop Color="#FCC4D0EF"
        Offset="0.3" />
    <GradientStop Color="#FDB7C2DF"
        Offset="0.6" />
    <GradientStop Color="#FE95B3CF"
        Offset="0.8" />
    <GradientStop Color="#FE96AACF"
        Offset="1" />

</LinearGradientBrush>
```

```xml
<LinearGradientBrush x:Key="ButtonUpGradient"
    StartPoint="0,0"
    EndPoint="0,1">

    <GradientStop Color="Transparent"
        Offset="0" />
    <GradientStop Color="#33000000"
        Offset="1" />

</LinearGradientBrush>

<LinearGradientBrush x:Key="ButtonDownGradient"
    StartPoint="0,0"
    EndPoint="0,1">

    <GradientStop Color="#10000000"
        Offset="0" />
    <GradientStop Color="#20000000"
        Offset="1" />

</LinearGradientBrush>

<LinearGradientBrush x:Key="ButtonDisabledGradient"
    StartPoint="0,0"
    EndPoint="0,1">

    <GradientStop Color="#10302A90"
        Offset="0" />
    <GradientStop Color="#10201040"
        Offset="1" />

</LinearGradientBrush>
```

You'll also need to add some event handlers. One is obvious: you need to capture the OnMouseDown event to begin the rubberband. But you must also initialize the adorner. The best place to do this is in the Loaded event. To fire the Loaded event, add the following to the Window tag:

```xml
<Window x:Class="PhotoCooperative.Window1"
    xmlns="http://schemas.microsoft.com/winfx/2006/xaml/presentation"
    xmlns:x="http://schemas.microsoft.com/winfx/2006/xaml"
    Title="Photo Cooperative" Height="600" Width="800"
    xmlns:sbts="clr-namespace:PhotoCooperative"
    Loaded="WindowLoaded"
    >
```

This sets the event handler WindowLoaded( ) to handle the Loaded event. The event handlers, of course, go in *Window1.xaml.cs*. Make sure you reference the following namespaces:

```csharp
using System;
using System.Windows;
using System.Windows.Controls;
using System.Windows.Documents;
```

```
using System.Windows.Media;
using System.Windows.Media.Imaging;
using System.Windows.Media.Animation;
using System.Windows.Input;
using System.Collections;
```

Here's the top of that file:

```
public partial class Window1 : System.Windows.Window
{
    public PhotoList Photos;
    private Stack UndoStack;
    private RubberbandAdorner CropSelector;

    public Window1( )
    {
        InitializeComponent( );
        UndoStack = new Stack( );
    }

    private void WindowLoaded( object sender, EventArgs e )
    {
        AdornerLayer layer = AdornerLayer.GetAdornerLayer( CurrentPhoto );
        CropSelector = new RubberbandAdorner( CurrentPhoto );
        CropSelector.Window = this;
        layer.Add( CropSelector );
        CropSelector.Rubberband.Visibility = Visibility.Hidden;
    }
```

The constructor initializes the Undo stack, and then the WindowLoaded( ) event handler (which runs after the Window is, er, loaded) creates the rubberband. It does so by getting the AdornerLayer (the acetate layer that is placed "on top of" the element it adorns).

 The static method GetAdornerLayer( ) walks up the "visual tree," starting at CurrentPhoto, and returns the first adorner layer it finds.

CropSelector is a private member variable of type RubberbandAdorner (which itself is defined in *CropUtilities.cs*), and in WindowLoaded( ) you call its constructor, passing in the target element to be adorned (the current photo). You then set its Window property to the current window, add the RubberbandAdorner to the AdornerLayer, and set the RubberbandAdorner to invisible (awaiting the user's mouse-down).

MouseDown

When the user clicks in the current photo, the MouseDown event fires. Here, you remember the point where the mouse was clicked. You then capture the mouse through the CropSelector and call its StartSelection( ) method. You also enable the CropButton:

```
private void OnMouseDown( object sender, MouseButtonEventArgs e )
{
    Point anchor = e.GetPosition( CurrentPhoto );
    CropSelector.CaptureMouse();
    CropSelector.StartSelection( anchor );
    CropButton.IsEnabled = true;
}
```

Because the mouse has been captured, the MouseUp event is handled by the RubberbandAdorner (as you saw in Example 4-1, excerpted here):

```
public RubberbandAdorner( UIElement adornedElement ) : base( adornedElement )
{
    this.adornedElement = adornedElement;
    //...
    MouseMove += new MouseEventHandler( DrawSelection );
    MouseUp += new MouseButtonEventHandler( EndSelection );
}
```

With this in place, you can expand the PhotoListSelection() method to manage the Undo stack and the CropSelector:

```
private void PhotoListSelection( object sender, RoutedEventArgs e )
{
    String path = ( ( sender as ListBox ).SelectedItem.ToString() );
    BitmapSource img = BitmapFrame.Create( new Uri( path ) );
    CurrentPhoto.Source = img;
    ClearUndoStack();
    if ( CropSelector != null )
    {
        if ( Visibility.Visible == CropSelector.Rubberband.Visibility )
            CropSelector.Rubberband.Visibility = Visibility.Hidden;
    }
    CropButton.IsEnabled = false;
}
```

Handling the Crop button

You now need to implement the method to call when the Crop button is clicked, which will crop the current picture to the limits of the rubberband adorner:

```
private void Crop( object sender, RoutedEventArgs e )
{
    if ( CurrentPhoto.Source != null )
    {
        BitmapSource img = ( BitmapSource ) ( CurrentPhoto.Source );
        UndoStack.Push( img );
        Int32Rect rect = new Int32Rect();
        rect.X = ( int ) ( CropSelector.SelectRect.X *
            img.PixelWidth / CurrentPhoto.ActualWidth );
        rect.Y = ( int ) ( CropSelector.SelectRect.Y *
            img.PixelHeight / CurrentPhoto.ActualHeight );
        rect.Width = ( int ) ( CropSelector.SelectRect.Width *
            img.PixelWidth / CurrentPhoto.ActualWidth );
```

```
      rect.Height = ( int ) ( CropSelector.SelectRect.Height *
          img.PixelHeight / CurrentPhoto.ActualHeight );
      CurrentPhoto.Source = new CroppedBitmap( img, rect );

      CropSelector.Rubberband.Visibility = Visibility.Hidden;

      CropButton.IsEnabled = false;
      UndoButton.IsEnabled = true;
   }
}
```

You start by obtaining the `Source` property of the `CurrentPhoto`. `CurrentPhoto`, you will remember, is defined to be of type `Image`; its `Source` property returns the image source. You cast it to a `BitMapSource` and store it in the local variable `img`, which you push onto the `UndoStack` (to be restored if the user clicks the Undo button).

Next, you create a rectangle and obtain its size by asking the `CropSelector` for its proportions. You set the `CurrentPhoto`'s image source to a new `CroppedBitmap`, which you created by passing in the original `BitmapSource` and the rectangle you just sized.

That done, you hide the rubberband, disable the Crop button, and enable the Undo button.

The picture is now cropped, but pressing the Undo button will undo the cropping:

```
private void Undo( object sender, RoutedEventArgs e )
{
   if ( UndoStack.Count > 0 )
   {
      CurrentPhoto.Source = ( BitmapSource ) UndoStack.Pop( );
   }
   if ( UndoStack.Count == 0 )
   {
      UndoButton.IsEnabled = false;
   }
}
```

Adding the Shopping Cart

To finish the first page, you only need to add the shopping cart and the associated buttons. You want to offer the user the ability, having chosen a picture, to purchase a 5×7 photo, a sweatshirt, or a "holiday card."

Begin by adding the shopping cart template and triggers to `Window.Resources`:

```
<!-- SHOPPING CART TEMPLATE -->

<Style x:Key="ShoppingCartStyle"
    TargetType="{x:Type ListBox}">
    <Setter Property="Template">
       <Setter.Value>
          <ControlTemplate TargetType="{x:Type ListBox}" >
```

```
                <Border BorderBrush="Gray"
                    BorderThickness="1"
                    CornerRadius="6"
                    Background="{DynamicResource ShoppingCartGradient}" >
                    <ScrollViewer>
                        <WrapPanel ItemHeight="70"
                            ItemWidth="70"
                            Margin="0,25,0,0"
                            IsItemsHost="True"
                            Orientation="Horizontal"
                            HorizontalAlignment="Center" />
                    </ScrollViewer>
                </Border>
            </ControlTemplate>
        </Setter.Value>
    </Setter>
</Style>

<!-- SHOPPING CART TRIGGERS -->

<Style x:Key="ShoppingCartItem"
    TargetType="{x:Type ListBoxItem}">
    <Setter Property="BorderBrush"
        Value="Transparent" />
    <Setter Property="Template">
        <Setter.Value>
            <ControlTemplate TargetType="{x:Type ListBoxItem}">
                <Border x:Name="ContentBorder"
                    Opacity="0.85">
                    <ContentPresenter />
                </Border>
                <ControlTemplate.Triggers>
                    <Trigger Property="IsSelected"
                        Value="True">
                        <Setter TargetName="ContentBorder"
                            Property="Opacity"
                            Value="1.0" />
                    </Trigger>
                </ControlTemplate.Triggers>
            </ControlTemplate>
        </Setter.Value>
    </Setter>
</Style>
```

The ShoppingCart uses a ShoppingCartGradient, so of course you'll need to add that
to the Resources section with the other gradient brushes:

```
<LinearGradientBrush x:Key="ShoppingCartGradient" StartPoint="0,0" EndPoint="0,1">
    <GradientStop Color="#90000000" Offset="0" />
    <GradientStop Color="#40000000" Offset="0.002" />
    <GradientStop Color="#10000000" Offset="0.02" />
    <GradientStop Color="#20000000" Offset="0.98" />
    <GradientStop Color="#60FFFFFF" Offset="1" />
</LinearGradientBrush>
```

The trigger is set on the listbox, but the listbox it is set on is `ShoppingCartItem`, which we have not yet added. This is the drop-down from which the user selects an item to add to the cart. Add that combo box to your `Window`'s `Resources` section now:

```
<!-- COMBOBOX STYLE -->

<Style TargetType="{x:Type ComboBox}" >
    <Setter Property="Background"
        Value="{DynamicResource ComboBoxGradient}" />
    <Setter Property="BorderThickness"
        Value="0" />
    <Setter Property="Height"
        Value="18px" />
    <Setter Property="Foreground"
        Value="MidnightBlue" />
</Style>

<LinearGradientBrush x:Key="ComboBoxGradient" StartPoint="0,0" EndPoint="0,1">

    <GradientStop Color="#B2B6CAFF" Offset="0" />
    <GradientStop Color="#B0B3C5FF" Offset="0.1" />
    <GradientStop Color="#BEE4E0FF" Offset="0.3" />
    <GradientStop Color="#B0D7E2FF" Offset="0.6" />
    <GradientStop Color="#B0C5D3FF" Offset="0.8" />
    <GradientStop Color="#C4CBD8FF" Offset="1" />

</LinearGradientBrush>
```

With the styles in place, you only need to add the objects to the `Grid`. In this case, you'll use an inner `Grid`:

```
<Image Name="CurrentPhoto"
    Grid.Row="3"
    Grid.Column="1"
    Margin="10"
    MouseDown="OnMouseDown"/>

<Grid
    Grid.Row="5"
    Grid.Column="1"
    HorizontalAlignment="Center"
    Margin="0">
    <Grid.RowDefinitions>
        <RowDefinition Height="Auto"/>
        <RowDefinition Height="Auto"/>
    </Grid.RowDefinitions>
    <Grid.ColumnDefinitions>
        <ColumnDefinition/>
        <ColumnDefinition/>
    </Grid.ColumnDefinitions>
```

```xml
<ComboBox
    Grid.Row="0"
    Grid.Column="0"
    Margin="0,0,4,0"
    VerticalAlignment="Center"
    Name="PrintTypeComboBox"
    DataContext="{Binding Source={StaticResource PrintTypes}}"
    ItemsSource="{Binding}"
    Width="110"
    SelectedIndex="0" />

<Button
    Grid.Row="0"
    Grid.Column="1"
    Click="AddToShoppingCart"
    VerticalAlignment="Center"
    Width="100"
    IsDefault="True">
    Add To Cart
</Button>

<Button
    Grid.Row="1"
    Grid.Column="1"
    Name="RemoveButton"
    Click="RemoveShoppingCartItem"
    VerticalAlignment="Center"
    IsEnabled="False"
    Width="100"
    Margin="10" >
    Remove Item
</Button>

    </Grid>

</Grid>
```

Because you've declared event handlers, you'll have to stub them out in your code-behind:

```csharp
private void AddToShoppingCart( object sender, RoutedEventArgs e )
{
}

private void RemoveShoppingCartItem( object sender, RoutedEventArgs e )
{
}
```

You'll also need a few additional data templates for your visual shopping cart. Add them to the Resources section now:

```
<DataTemplate DataType="{x:Type sbts:Print}">
    <Grid Margin="3">
        <Image Source="baseImg/photoframe.gif" />
        <Image Source="{Binding Photo}"
            MaxWidth="50"
            MaxHeight="70"
            VerticalAlignment="Center"
            HorizontalAlignment="Center"/>
    </Grid>
</DataTemplate>

<DataTemplate DataType="{x:Type sbts:GreetingCard}">
    <Grid Margin="3" >
        <Border VerticalAlignment="Center"
            HorizontalAlignment="Center"
            Background="{DynamicResource GreetingCardGradient}"
            Width="40"
            Height="50"
            BorderBrush="#44000000"
            BorderThickness="1" >
            <Border.RenderTransform>
                <SkewTransform AngleY="-10" />
            </Border.RenderTransform>
        </Border>
        <Border VerticalAlignment="Center"
            HorizontalAlignment="Center"
            Background="White"
            Width="50"
            Height="50"
            BorderBrush="#66000000"
            BorderThickness="1" >
            <Image Margin="3"
                Source="{Binding Photo}" />
        </Border>
    </Grid>
</DataTemplate>

<DataTemplate DataType="{x:Type sbts:SShirt}">
    <Grid Margin="3">
        <Image Source="baseImg/sweatshirt-front.gif"/>
        <Image Source="{Binding Photo}"
            MaxWidth="20"
            MaxHeight="22.5"
            VerticalAlignment="Center"
            HorizontalAlignment="Center"/>
    </Grid>
</DataTemplate>
```

These new types need to be identified. Do that in the *App.xaml* file:

```
<Application x:Class="PhotoCooperative.App"
    xmlns="http://schemas.microsoft.com/winfx/2006/xaml/presentation"
    xmlns:x="http://schemas.microsoft.com/winfx/2006/xaml"
    xmlns:sbts="clr-namespace:PhotoCooperative"
    Startup="AppStartup"
    >
```

```
<Application.Resources>
    <ObjectDataProvider x:Name="PhotosODP"
        x:Key="Photos"
        ObjectType="{x:Type sbts:PhotoList}" />
    <ObjectDataProvider x:Name="ShoppingCartODP"
        x:Key="ShoppingCart"
        ObjectType="{x:Type sbts:PrintList}" />
    <ObjectDataProvider x:Name="PrintTypesODP"
        x:Key="PrintTypes"
        ObjectType="{x:Type sbts:PrintTypeList}" />
</Application.Resources>
</Application>
```

Then add the associated code to AppStartup( ) in *App.xaml.cs*:

```
dataProvider = this.Resources["ShoppingCart"] as ObjectDataProvider;
PrintList printList = dataProvider.Data as PrintList;
theWindow.ShoppingCart = printList;
```

And don't forget to add the ShoppingCart private member variable to *Window1.xaml.cs*:

```
public partial class Window1 : System.Windows.Window
{
    public PhotoList Photos;
    public PrintList ShoppingCart;
```

With this additional code, your first page is 80% complete. Figure 4-8 shows the result.

Figure 4-8. Combo box and buttons added

Adding scroll bars

To finalize the page, you need to add the shopping cart to it. You'll give the cart scroll bars so that users can scroll through the items they've added and, if desired, select items to remove from the cart.

As demonstrated earlier, you can begin by adding the resources you anticipate needing. Alternatively, you can add the widget and then add the resources it needs.

Let's begin by adding the shopping cart inside a Grid and the associated upload button and progress bar within a StackPanel:

```
<Grid Grid.Row="3"
    Grid.Column="2">
    <Grid.RowDefinitions>
        <RowDefinition Height="20" />
        <RowDefinition />
    </Grid.RowDefinitions>
    <TextBlock Grid.Row="0"
        Foreground="MidnightBlue"
        FontSize="13px"
        Margin="2"
        HorizontalAlignment="Center">
        Shopping Cart
    </TextBlock>
    <ListBox ScrollViewer.HorizontalScrollBarVisibility="Disabled"
        Style="{DynamicResource ShoppingCartStyle}"
        Name="ShoppingCartListBox"
        Grid.Row="1"
        Width="160"
        DataContext="{Binding Source={StaticResource ShoppingCart}}"
        ItemContainerStyle="{DynamicResource ShoppingCartItem}"
        ItemsSource="{Binding}" />
</Grid>

<StackPanel
    Grid.Row="5"
    Grid.Column="2" >
    <Button
        Name="UploadButton"
        Click="Checkout"
        VerticalAlignment="Bottom"
        HorizontalAlignment="Center"
        Width="100"
        Margin="2"
        IsEnabled="False">
        Checkout
    </Button>

    <ProgressBar
        Name="UploadProgressBar"
        Grid.Row="6"
        Grid.Column="2"
```

```
            VerticalAlignment="Top"
            Margin="0,10,0,0" />
    </StackPanel>
```

The shopping cart itself is the ListBox inside the Grid. You need a ShoppingCartStyle, a DataContext, and the ShoppingCartItem resource, all of which you've already created. What you need to create now are the scroll bar and progress bar resources:

```
<!-- PROGRESS BAR STYLE -->

<Style TargetType="{x:Type ProgressBar}" >
    <Setter Property="Background"
        Value="{DynamicResource ComboBoxGradient}" />
    <Setter Property="BorderThickness"
        Value="1" />
    <Setter Property="BorderBrush"
        Value="Gray" />
    <Setter Property="Foreground"
        Value="MidnightBlue" />
</Style>

<!--SCROLL BAR TEMPLATES -->

<Style x:Key="Scrollbar_LineButton"
    TargetType="{x:Type RepeatButton}">
    <Setter Property="Template">
        <Setter.Value>
            <ControlTemplate TargetType="{x:Type RepeatButton}">
                <Border BorderBrush="Transparent"
                    BorderThickness="1"
                    CornerRadius="6"
                    Background="{DynamicResource ButtonGradient}">
                    <ContentPresenter x:Name="ContentSite" />
                </Border>
            </ControlTemplate>
        </Setter.Value>
    </Setter>
    <Setter Property="MinHeight"
        Value="12" />
    <Setter Property="MinWidth"
        Value="12" />
    <Setter Property="Foreground"
        Value="Gray" />
    <Setter Property="FontSize"
        Value="6pt" />
    <Setter Property="FontWeight"
        Value="Bold" />
    <Setter Property="FontFamily"
        Value="Lucida Sans" />
    <Setter Property="VerticalAlignment"
        Value="Center" />
    <Setter Property="HorizontalAlignment"
        Value="Center" />
</Style>
```

```xml
<Style x:Key="ScrollBar_TrackRepeater"
    TargetType="{x:Type RepeatButton}">
    <Setter Property="IsTabStop"
        Value="false" />
    <Setter Property="Focusable"
        Value="false" />
    <Setter Property="Command"
        Value="ScrollBar.PageUpCommand" />
    <Setter Property="Template">
        <Setter.Value>
            <ControlTemplate TargetType="{x:Type RepeatButton}">
                <Rectangle Fill="Transparent" />
            </ControlTemplate>
        </Setter.Value>
    </Setter>
</Style>

<Style x:Key="ScrollBar_UpTrack"
    BasedOn="{StaticResource ScrollBar_TrackRepeater}"
    TargetType="{x:Type RepeatButton}">
    <Setter Property="Command"
        Value="ScrollBar.PageUpCommand" />
</Style>

<Style x:Key="ScrollBar_DownTrack"
    BasedOn="{StaticResource ScrollBar_TrackRepeater}"
    TargetType="{x:Type RepeatButton}">
    <Setter Property="Command"
        Value="ScrollBar.PageDownCommand" />
</Style>

<Style x:Key="ScrollBar_LeftTrack"
    BasedOn="{StaticResource ScrollBar_TrackRepeater}"
    TargetType="{x:Type RepeatButton}">
    <Setter Property="Command"
        Value="ScrollBar.PageLeftCommand" />
</Style>

<Style x:Key="ScrollBar_RightTrack"
    BasedOn="{StaticResource ScrollBar_TrackRepeater}"
    TargetType="{x:Type RepeatButton}">
    <Setter Property="Command"
        Value="ScrollBar.PageRightCommand" />
</Style>

<Style x:Key="ScrollBar_VerticalThumb"
    TargetType="{x:Type Thumb}">
    <Setter Property="Template">
        <Setter.Value>
            <ControlTemplate TargetType="{x:Type Thumb}">
                <Border CornerRadius="6"
                    BorderBrush="Transparent"
                    BorderThickness="1"
                    Background="{DynamicResource VerticalScrollGradient}" />
            </ControlTemplate>
```

```xml
            </Setter.Value>
        </Setter>
        <Setter Property="MinHeight"
            Value="10" />
        <Setter Property="MinWidth"
            Value="10" />
    </Style>

    <Style x:Key="ScrollBar_HorizontalThumb"
        TargetType="{x:Type Thumb}">
        <Setter Property="Template">
            <Setter.Value>
                <ControlTemplate TargetType="{x:Type Thumb}">
                    <Border CornerRadius="6"
                        BorderBrush="Transparent"
                        BorderThickness="1"
                        Background="{DynamicResource ButtonGradient}" />
                </ControlTemplate>
            </Setter.Value>
        </Setter>
        <Setter Property="MinHeight"
            Value="10" />
        <Setter Property="MinWidth"
            Value="10" />
    </Style>

    <Style TargetType="{x:Type ScrollBar}">
        <Setter Property="Background"
            Value="Transparent" />
        <Setter Property="MinWidth"
            Value="10" />
        <Setter Property="Template">
            <Setter.Value>
                <ControlTemplate TargetType="{x:Type ScrollBar}">
                    <Grid>
                        <Grid.ColumnDefinitions>
                            <ColumnDefinition Width="10"/>
                        </Grid.ColumnDefinitions>
                        <Grid.RowDefinitions>
                            <RowDefinition Height="10"/>
                            <RowDefinition Height="*"/>
                            <RowDefinition Height="10"/>
                        </Grid.RowDefinitions>
                        <Border Grid.Row="1"
                            BorderThickness="0"
                            Background="Transparent"
                            CornerRadius="4"/>
                        <RepeatButton Grid.Row="0"
                            Style="{DynamicResource Scrollbar_LineButton}"
                            Command="ScrollBar.LineUpCommand"
                            Content=" ^"/>
                        <Track Grid.Row="1"
                            Name="PART_Track"
                            IsDirectionReversed="True">
```

```xml
                    <Track.IncreaseRepeatButton>
                        <RepeatButton Style="{DynamicResource ScrollBar_DownTrack}"/>
                    </Track.IncreaseRepeatButton>
                    <Track.DecreaseRepeatButton>
                        <RepeatButton Style="{DynamicResource ScrollBar_UpTrack}"/>
                    </Track.DecreaseRepeatButton>
                    <Track.Thumb>
                        <Thumb Style="{DynamicResource ScrollBar_VerticalThumb}"/>
                    </Track.Thumb>
                </Track>
                <RepeatButton Grid.Row="2"
                    Style="{DynamicResource Scrollbar_LineButton}"
                    Command="ScrollBar.LineDownCommand"
                    Content=" v"/>
            </Grid>
        </ControlTemplate>
    </Setter.Value>
</Setter>
<Style.Triggers>
    <Trigger Property="Orientation"
        Value="Horizontal" >
        <Setter Property="Background"
            Value="Transparent" />
        <Setter Property="MinHeight"
            Value="10" />
        <Setter Property="Template">
            <Setter.Value>
                <ControlTemplate TargetType="{x:Type ScrollBar}">
                    <Grid>
                        <Grid.RowDefinitions>
                            <RowDefinition Height="12"/>
                        </Grid.RowDefinitions>
                        <Grid.ColumnDefinitions>
                            <ColumnDefinition Width="12" />
                            <ColumnDefinition Width="*"/>
                            <ColumnDefinition Width="12" />
                        </Grid.ColumnDefinitions>
                        <Border Grid.Column="1"
                            BorderThickness="0"
                            Background="Transparent"
                            CornerRadius="4"/>
                        <RepeatButton Grid.Column="0"
                            Style="{DynamicResource Scrollbar_LineButton}"
                            Command="ScrollBar.LineLeftCommand"
                            Content=" &lt;"/>
                        <Track Grid.Column="1"
                            Name="PART_Track">
                            <Track.IncreaseRepeatButton>
                                <RepeatButton Style=
                                    "{DynamicResource ScrollBar_RightTrack}"/>
                            </Track.IncreaseRepeatButton>
                            <Track.DecreaseRepeatButton>
                                <RepeatButton Style=
                                    "{DynamicResource ScrollBar_LeftTrack}"/>
                            </Track.DecreaseRepeatButton>
```

```xml
                    <Track.Thumb>
                       <Thumb Style=
                          "{DynamicResource ScrollBar_HorizontalThumb}"/>
                    </Track.Thumb>
                 </Track>
                 <RepeatButton Grid.Column="2"
                    Style="{DynamicResource Scrollbar_LineButton}"
                    Command="ScrollBar.LineRightCommand"
                    Content=" &gt;"/>

              </Grid>
           </ControlTemplate>
         </Setter.Value>
       </Setter>
     </Trigger>
   </Style.Triggers>
 </Style>
```

Now it's time to fill in the stubbed-out methods and add the CheckOut( ) method, shown in Example 4-3.

Example 4-3. Shopping cart methods for Window1.xaml.cs

```csharp
private void AddToShoppingCart( object sender, RoutedEventArgs e )
{
   if ( PrintTypeComboBox.SelectedItem != null )
   {
      PrintBase item;
      switch ( PrintTypeComboBox.SelectedIndex )
      {
         case 0:
            item = new Print( CurrentPhoto.Source as BitmapSource );
            break;
         case 1:
            item = new GreetingCard( CurrentPhoto.Source as BitmapSource );
            break;
         case 2:
            item = new SShirt( CurrentPhoto.Source as BitmapSource );
            break;
         default:
            return;
      }
      ShoppingCart.Add( item );
      ShoppingCartListBox.ScrollIntoView( item );
      ShoppingCartListBox.SelectedItem = item;
      if ( false == UploadButton.IsEnabled )
         UploadButton.IsEnabled = true;
      if ( false == RemoveButton.IsEnabled )
         RemoveButton.IsEnabled = true;
   }
}

private void RemoveShoppingCartItem( object sender, RoutedEventArgs e )
{
   if ( null != ShoppingCartListBox.SelectedItem )
```

Example 4-3. Shopping cart methods for Window1.xaml.cs (continued)

```
   {
      PrintBase item = ShoppingCartListBox.SelectedItem as PrintBase;
      ShoppingCart.Remove( item );
      ShoppingCartListBox.SelectedIndex = ShoppingCart.Count - 1;
   }
   if ( ShoppingCart.Count == 0 )
   {
      RemoveButton.IsEnabled = false;
      UploadButton.IsEnabled = false;
   }

private void Checkout( object sender, RoutedEventArgs e )
{
   if ( ShoppingCart.Count > 0 )
   {
      // go to checkout page
      // to be created later
   }
}
```

Finally, to finish off this page, you'll need to add a *baseImg* folder to your project, then download the *sweatshirt-front.gif* and *photoframe.gif* images from our web sites so as to be able to populate the shopping cart (go to *http://www.jliberty.com* and click on "Books," or go to *http://alexhorovitz.com/books/programming3.5/*).

If you look carefully, you'll see that the sweatshirts in the shopping cart have the appropriate photo imposed on them, as shown in Figure 4-9. This is accomplished in the AddToShoppingCart( ) event handler, where, for example, a new SShirt object is instantiated, passing in the current photo as a BitMapSource to the constructor. The SShirt constructor is in *StoreItems.cs*; it passes the bitmap to its base class, where it is assigned to the private member variable of type BitMapSource and rendered appropriately.

Page 2—Validating the Credit Card

The second page, shown in Figure 4-10, is pretty straightforward to lay out.

Start by creating the new page, *Checkout.xaml*. (Be sure to add a new Page, not a new Windows Form—Pages are used for WPF, and Windows Forms are used for .NET 2.x.)

Once again, let's start simple. You'll add the TextBlock for the header and a Grid to hold the radio buttons for the credit cards, all of which will be in a Viewbox so the user can resize the display.

Figure 4-9. Page 1 finished

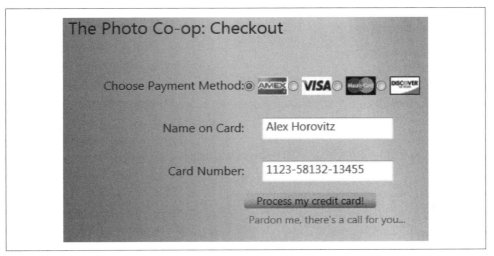

Figure 4-10. Page 2

```xaml
<Window x:Class="PhotoCooperative.Checkout"
    xmlns="http://schemas.microsoft.com/winfx/2006/xaml/presentation"
    xmlns:x="http://schemas.microsoft.com/winfx/2006/xaml"
    Title="Photo Cooperative: Checkout" Height="600" Width="800"
    xmlns:sbts="clr-namespace:PhotoCooperative"
    >
<Window.Resources>
    <LinearGradientBrush x:Key="WindowGradient"
        StartPoint="0,0.3" EndPoint="1,0">
      <GradientStop Color="#B2B6CAFF" Offset="0" />
      <GradientStop Color="#BFC3D5FF" Offset="0.1" />
      <GradientStop Color="#E0E4F0FF" Offset="0.3" />
      <GradientStop Color="#E6EAF5FF" Offset="0.5" />
      <GradientStop Color="#CFD7E2FF" Offset="0.6" />
      <GradientStop Color="#BFC5D3FF" Offset="0.8" />
      <GradientStop Color="#C4CBD8FF" Offset="1" />
    </LinearGradientBrush>

    <LinearGradientBrush x:Key="ButtonGradient"
        StartPoint="0,0" EndPoint="0,1">
      <GradientStop Color="#FDB6CADF" Offset="0" />
      <GradientStop Color="#FCC3C5FF" Offset="0.1" />
      <GradientStop Color="#FCC4D0EF" Offset="0.3" />
      <GradientStop Color="#FDB7C2DF" Offset="0.6" />
      <GradientStop Color="#FE95B3CF" Offset="0.8" />
      <GradientStop Color="#FE96AACF" Offset="1" />

    </LinearGradientBrush>

    <LinearGradientBrush x:Key="ButtonUpGradient"
        StartPoint="0,0" EndPoint="0,1">
      <GradientStop Color="Transparent" Offset="0" />
      <GradientStop Color="#33000000" Offset="1" />
    </LinearGradientBrush>

    <LinearGradientBrush x:Key="ButtonDownGradient"
        StartPoint="0,0" EndPoint="0,1">
      <GradientStop Color="#10000000" Offset="0" />
      <GradientStop Color="#20000000" Offset="1" />
    </LinearGradientBrush>

    <LinearGradientBrush x:Key="ButtonDisabledGradient"
        StartPoint="0,0" EndPoint="0,1">
      <GradientStop Color="#10302A90" Offset="0" />
      <GradientStop Color="#10201040" Offset="1" />
    </LinearGradientBrush>

<!-- STYLES -->
    <Style TargetType="{x:Type sbts:Checkout}">
      <Setter Property="Background"
          Value="{DynamicResource WindowGradient}" />
    </Style>
```

```xml
<Style x:Key="TitleText" TargetType="{x:Type TextBlock}" >
    <Setter Property="FontFamily" Value="Segoe Black" />
    <Setter Property="FontSize" Value="20px" />
    <Setter Property="Foreground" Value="MidnightBlue" />
</Style>

<Style x:Key="CheckoutText" TargetType="{x:Type TextBlock}" >
    <Setter Property="FontFamily" Value="Segoe Black" />
    <Setter Property="FontSize" Value="14px" />
    <Setter Property="Foreground" Value="MidnightBlue" />
</Style>

<Style x:Key="InputText" TargetType="{x:Type TextBox}">
    <Setter Property="Height" Value="25px" />
    <Setter Property="FontFamily" Value="Segoe Black" />
    <Setter Property="Foreground" Value="#0066CC" />
    <Setter Property="FontSize" Value="10pt" />
    <Setter Property="Margin" Value="10,10,20,10" />
    <Style.Triggers>
        <Trigger Property="Validation.HasError" Value="true">
            <Setter Property="ToolTip"
                Value="{Binding RelativeSource={RelativeSource Self},
                Path=(Validation.Errors)[0].ErrorContent}"/>
        </Trigger>
        <Trigger Property="Validation.HasError" Value="false">
            <Setter Property="ToolTip"
                Value="{Binding RelativeSource={RelativeSource Self},
                Path=ToolTip.Content}"/>
        </Trigger>
    </Style.Triggers>
</Style>
<!-- BUTTON TEMPLATE -->

<Style TargetType="{x:Type Button}">
    <Setter Property="Template">
        <Setter.Value>
            <ControlTemplate TargetType="{x:Type Button}">
                <Border x:Name="OuterBorder"
                    CornerRadius="3"
                    Background="{DynamicResource ButtonGradient}">
                    <Border x:Name="InnerBorder"
                        CornerRadius="3"
                        Background="{DynamicResource ButtonUpGradient}"
                        Padding="{TemplateBinding Padding}">
                        <ContentPresenter x:Name="ContentSite"
                            HorizontalAlignment="Center"
                            VerticalAlignment="Center" />
                    </Border>
                </Border>
                <ControlTemplate.Triggers>
                    <Trigger Property="IsPressed" Value="true">
```

```xml
                            <Setter TargetName="InnerBorder"
                                Property="Background"
                                Value="{DynamicResource ButtonDownGradient}" />
                        </Trigger>
                        <Trigger Property="IsEnabled" Value="false">
                            <Setter TargetName="InnerBorder"
                                Property="Background"
                                Value="{DynamicResource ButtonDisabledGradient}" />
                            <Setter Property="BorderBrush" Value="Silver" />
                            <Setter Property="Foreground" Value="SlateGray" />
                        </Trigger>
                    </ControlTemplate.Triggers>
                </ControlTemplate>
            </Setter.Value>
        </Setter>
        <Setter Property="Height" Value="18" />
        <Setter Property="Foreground" Value="MidnightBlue" />
    </Style>
</Window.Resources>
<Viewbox VerticalAlignment="Top" Stretch="Uniform">

    <Grid Margin="20" Width="650" ShowGridLines="False" >
        <Grid.RowDefinitions>
            <RowDefinition Height="Auto" />
            <RowDefinition Height="30" />
            <RowDefinition Height="50" />
            <RowDefinition Height="50" />
            <RowDefinition Height="50" />
            <RowDefinition Height="Auto" />
            <RowDefinition Height="*" />
        </Grid.RowDefinitions>
        <Grid.ColumnDefinitions>
            <ColumnDefinition Width="200" />
            <ColumnDefinition Width="50" />
            <ColumnDefinition Width="50" />
            <ColumnDefinition Width="50" />
            <ColumnDefinition Width="50" />
            <ColumnDefinition Width="50" />
        </Grid.ColumnDefinitions>

        <TextBlock Grid.Row="0" Grid.ColumnSpan="6"
            Style="{DynamicResource TitleText}">
            <Span>The Photo Co-op: Checkout</Span>
        </TextBlock>

        <TextBlock Grid.Row="2" Grid.Column="0"
            Style="{DynamicResource CheckoutText}"
            HorizontalAlignment="Right"
            VerticalAlignment="Center">
            <Span>Choose Payment Method:</Span>
        </TextBlock>

        <RadioButton Name="AmericanExpress" Grid.Row="2"
            Grid.Column="1" Click="OnCardSelected"
            VerticalAlignment="Center">
```

```
        <Image Source="baseImg/creditcardamex.gif"
            MaxWidth="38"
            MaxHeight="24"
            VerticalAlignment="Center"
            HorizontalAlignment="Center"/>
    </RadioButton>
    <RadioButton Name="Visa" Grid.Row="2"
        Grid.Column="2" Click="OnCardSelected"
        VerticalAlignment="Center">
        <Image Source="baseImg/creditcardvisa.gif"
            MaxWidth="38"
            MaxHeight="24"
            VerticalAlignment="Center"
            HorizontalAlignment="Center"/>
    </RadioButton>
    <RadioButton Name="MasterCard" Grid.Row="2"
        Grid.Column="3" Click="OnCardSelected"
        VerticalAlignment="Center">
        <Image Source="baseImg/creditcardmastercard.gif"
            MaxWidth="38"
            MaxHeight="24"
            VerticalAlignment="Center"
            HorizontalAlignment="Center"/>
    </RadioButton>
    <RadioButton Name="Discover" Grid.Row="2"
        Grid.Column="4" Click="OnCardSelected"
        VerticalAlignment="Center">
        <Image Source="baseImg/creditcarddiscover.gif"
            MaxWidth="38"
            MaxHeight="24"
            VerticalAlignment="Center"
            HorizontalAlignment="Center"/>
    </RadioButton>

    <TextBlock Grid.Row="3" Grid.Column="0"
        Style="{DynamicResource CheckoutText}"
        TextAlignment="Right" VerticalAlignment="Center">
        <Span>Name on Card:</Span>
    </TextBlock>

    <TextBox Style="{StaticResource InputText}"
        Grid.Column="1"
        Grid.Row="3"
        Grid.ColumnSpan="4"
        Name="nameOnCard"
        Width="150"
        VerticalAlignment="Center">
        <TextBox.ToolTip>Enter your name.</TextBox.ToolTip>
    </TextBox>

    <TextBlock Grid.Row="4" Grid.Column="0"
        Style="{DynamicResource CheckoutText}"
        TextAlignment="Right"
        VerticalAlignment="Center">
```

```
            <Span>Card Number:</Span>
        </TextBlock>
        <TextBox Style="{StaticResource InputText}"
            Grid.Column="1"
            Grid.Row="4"
            Grid.ColumnSpan="4"
            Name="ccNumber" Width="150"
            VerticalAlignment="Center">
            <TextBox.ToolTip>
                Enter valid credit card number.
            </TextBox.ToolTip>
        </TextBox>
        <Button Name="ProcessOrder" Grid.ColumnSpan="3"
            Grid.Column="1"
            Grid.Row="5"
            Click="ProcessOrderForCart">
            Process my credit card!
        </Button>
        <Label Name="ProcessResults"
            Grid.Column="1"
            Grid.Row ="6"
            Grid.ColumnSpan="4"
            TextBlock.Foreground="Red" />
    </Grid>
</Viewbox>
</Window>
```

 This code assumes that you downloaded the four *.gif* files for the four credit cards (*creditcardamex.gif*, *creditcardmastercard.gif*, *creditcardvisa. gif* and *creditcarddiscover.gif*) into the *baseImg* directory while you were downloading the *.gif* files required for the previous section.

You are probably already scanning this code to see what code-behind support you need, and what resources you'll want to add, and no doubt you've discovered these hints:

```
Click="OnCardSelected"
Style="{DynamicResource CheckoutText}"
Style="{DynamicResource TitleText}">
```

First add the two styles to the Resources section:

```
<Window.Resources>
    <!-- STYLES -->

    <Style x:Key="TitleText"
        TargetType="{x:Type TextBlock}" >
        <Setter Property="FontFamily"
            Value="Segoe Black" />
        <Setter Property="FontSize"
            Value="20px" />
        <Setter Property="Foreground"
            Value="MidnightBlue" />
    </Style>
```

```
<Style x:Key="CheckoutText"
    TargetType="{x:Type TextBlock}" >
    <Setter Property="FontFamily"
        Value="Segoe Black" />
    <Setter Property="FontSize"
        Value="14px" />
    <Setter Property="Foreground"
        Value="MidnightBlue" />
</Style>

</Window.Resources>
```

Then, in the code-behind, you can stub out the required event handler:

```
public void OnCardSelected( object sender, EventArgs e )
{

}
```

To see your shopping cart page, return to the first page and fill in the details in the Checkout event handler that you stubbed out earlier:

```
private void Checkout( object sender, RoutedEventArgs e )
{
    if ( ShoppingCart.Count > 0 )
    {
        Checkout co = new Checkout();
        co.ShoppingCart = ShoppingCart;
        co.Show();
        this.Hide();
    }
}
```

This code now makes an instance of your new (second) page and sets its ShoppingCart property to the ShoppingCart object created on the first page. It then shows the second page and hides the first.

Modify your ShoppingCart class to have a ShoppingCart property to match what the first page will set:

```
public partial class Checkout : System.Windows.Window
{
    private PrintList shoppingCart;
    public PrintList ShoppingCart { set { shoppingCart = value; } }
```

> The class PrintList, you will remember, is defined in your *StoreItems.cs* file, as an ObservableCollection of PrintBase. Print, GreetingCard, and SShirt (SweatShirt) all derive from PrintBase.

Layout

The rest of the layout is pretty straightforward. You need a place for the user's name and credit card number, and a button to submit the order:

```
<TextBlock Grid.Row="3"
    Grid.Column="0"
    Style="{DynamicResource CheckoutText}"
    TextAlignment="Right"
    VerticalAlignment="Center">
  <Span>Name on Card:</Span>
</TextBlock>

<TextBox Style="{StaticResource InputText}"
    Grid.Column="1"
    Grid.Row="3"
    Grid.ColumnSpan="4"
    Name="nameOnCard"
    Width="150"
    VerticalAlignment="Center">
  <TextBox.ToolTip>Enter your name.</TextBox.ToolTip>
</TextBox>

<TextBlock Grid.Row="4"
    Grid.Column="0"
    Style="{DynamicResource CheckoutText}"
    TextAlignment="Right"
    VerticalAlignment="Center">
  <Span>Card Number:</Span>
</TextBlock>
<TextBox Style="{StaticResource InputText}"
    Grid.Column="1"
    Grid.Row="4"
    Grid.ColumnSpan="4"
    Name="ccNumber"
    Width="150"
    VerticalAlignment="Center">
  <TextBox.ToolTip>Enter valid credit card number.</TextBox.ToolTip>
</TextBox>
<Button Name="ProcessOrder"
    Grid.ColumnSpan="3"
    Grid.Column="1"
    Grid.Row="5"
    Click="ProcessOrderForCart">Process my credit card!</Button>
<Label Name="ProcessResults"
    Grid.Column="1"
    Grid.Row ="6"
    Grid.ColumnSpan="4"
    TextBlock.Foreground="Red" />
```

Notice the use of tooltips attached to the TextBlocks. When the user hovers over the text entry block, a tooltip will provide additional information, as shown in Figure 4-11.

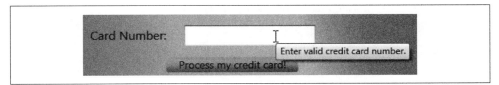

Figure 4-11. Tooltip

Validating the Credit Card

When the user clicks the "Process my credit card!" button, you'd like to validate the credit card number before submitting the information to the credit card company. You'll do so using the *Luhn algorithm* (also known as the modulus 10 algorithm), created by IBM scientist Hans Peter Luhn and described in U.S. Patent 2,950,048, filed on January 6, 1954 and granted on August 23, 1960 (according to Wikipedia).

To accomplish this, take the following steps:

1. Create a new business class, CreditCardValidator, as a C# class, and create a new enumerated constant, CardBrand.

2. When the user clicks on a credit card, you'll set the chosen CardBrand.

3. When the user clicks the "Process my credit card!" button, you'll call the static method Validate( ) in your new class.

Here's the listing for *CreditCardValidator.cs*:

```
using System;
using System.Collections.Generic;
using System.Text;

namespace PhotoCooperative
{
    public enum CardBrand
    {
        NotSelected,
        MasterCard,
        BankCard,
        Visa,
        AmericanExpress,
        Discover,
        DinersClub,
        JCB
    };

    public static class CreditCardValidator
    {
```

```csharp
public static bool Validate(CardBrand cardBrand,
    string cardNumber)
{

    byte[] number = new byte[16]; // card number to validate

        // Remove non-digits
        int length = 0;
        for (int i = 0; i < cardNumber.Length; i++)
        {
            if (char.IsDigit(cardNumber, i))
            {
                if (length == 16) return false; // card has too
                                                // many digits
                number[length++] = byte.Parse(cardNumber[i].ToString());
            }
        }

        // To validate a card, you need to
        // test length then prefix...
        switch (cardBrand)
        {
            case CardBrand.BankCard:
                if (length != 16)
                    return false;
                if (number[0] != 5 || number[1] != 6
                    || number[2] > 1)
                    return false;
                break;

            case CardBrand.MasterCard:
                if (length != 16)
                    return false;
                if (number[0] != 5 || number[1] == 0
                    || number[1] > 5)
                    return false;
                break;

            case CardBrand.Visa:
                if (length != 16 && length != 13)
                    return false;
                if (number[0] != 4)
                    return false;
                break;

            case CardBrand.AmericanExpress:
                if (length != 15)
                    return false;
                if (number[0] != 3 || (number[1] != 4
                    && number[1] != 7))
                    return false;
                break;
```

```
            case CardBrand.Discover:
                if (length != 16)
                    return false;
                if (number[0] != 6 || number[1] != 0
                    || number[2] != 1 || number[3] != 1)
                    return false;
                break;

            case CardBrand.DinersClub:
                if (length != 14)
                    return false;
                if (number[0] != 3 || (number[1] != 0
                    && number[1] != 6 && number[1] != 8)
                    || number[1] == 0 && number[2] > 5)
                    return false;
                break;

        }

        // Now we use the classic Luhn algorithm to validate
        int sum = 0;
        for (int i = length - 1; i >= 0; i--)
        {
            if (i % 2 == length % 2)
            {
                int n = number[i] * 2;
                sum += (n / 10) + (n % 10);
            }
            else
                sum += number[i];
        }
        return (sum % 10 == 0);

    }
    }
}
```

When the user clicks on a credit card, the OnCardSelected( ) event handler in *Checkout.xaml.cs* is called:

```
public void OnCardSelected( object sender, EventArgs e )
{
    RadioButton rb = sender as RadioButton;
    string rbName = rb.Name;
    switch ( rbName )
    {
        case "Visa":
            selectedCard = CardBrand.Visa;
            break;
        case "MasterCard":
            selectedCard = CardBrand.MasterCard;
            break;
```

```
        case "AmericanExpress":
            selectedCard = CardBrand.AmericanExpress;
            break;
        default:
            selectedCard = CardBrand.Discover;
            break;
    }
}
```

Finally, when the user clicks the "Process my credit card!" button, the ProcessOrderForCart( ) method in *Checkout.xaml.cs* is called:

```
public void ProcessOrderForCart( object sender, RoutedEventArgs e )
{
    String creditCardNumber = ccNumber.Text;

    if ( selectedCard == CardBrand.NotSelected )
    {
        MessageBox.Show( "Please select a credit card type", "Uh oh",
            MessageBoxButton.OK, MessageBoxImage.Error );
    }
    else
    {
        if ( CreditCardValidator.Validate( selectedCard, creditCardNumber ) )
        {
            ProcessResults.Content = "Validated";
        }
        else
        {
            ProcessResults.Content = "Excuse me sir, there's a call for you...";
        }
    }
}
```

That's it! A meaningful WPF application, with all the fixins.

Introducing AJAX: Moving Desktop UIs to the Web

One of the key features of .NET 3.5 is that it fosters separation of the user interface layer from the business and persistence layers. Since the UI layer is, by definition, the most visible layer and is often subject to the greatest scrutiny by customers, Microsoft has traditionally offered a spectrum of options to developers for this layer.

With .NET 3.5, developers have the ability to create multiple types of applications, including server-side-only (ASP.NET), thin-client (ASP.NET with AJAX), rich interactive (Silverlight), traditional desktop (WinForms), and rich desktop (WPF) applications.

While AJAX has not officially been put into the .NET 3.5 bucket, it is a key component of Microsoft's overall approach of offering a unified set of tools that foster well-designed programs that meet customers' needs. Thus, we have decided that any comprehensive coverage of the .NET 3.5 technologies must include Microsoft's AJAX libraries as well.

Web Applications Just Got a Whole Lot Faster

Get ready for ASP.NET applications that perform faster, from the user's point of view—*much* faster.

A key point that I have emphasized in every edition of my book *Programming ASP.NET* (O'Reilly) is that ASP.NET is a server-based technology. Traditionally, whatever you saw in your browser was (almost) exclusively produced on the server; (nearly) all the code was run on the server, and (just about) all the HTML that came to the browser came from the server via the Internet.

Feel free to tear out those pages and throw them through your office window. While server-based web applications have wonderful advantages, they have the obvious disadvantage that any time you want to run any code (or retrieve any data) you must endure the cost of a "round trip" from the browser to the server and back. Users tend to notice the delay. AJAX, however, changes all that.

AJAX is an acronym for *Asynchronous JavaScript And XML*—that is, it is a technique for combining well-established (some might say *old*) Internet technologies in new ways to greatly enhance the performance of web applications.

AJAX-enabled applications are very hot—they outperform server-based applications in ways that will make your eyeballs roll back in your head.

Microsoft, realizing that this was technology it couldn't ignore, and having learned well the lesson about making open-standards technology proprietary, took this very good idea and made it much, *much* better. Microsoft developers combined the power, speed, and flexibility of AJAX with the drag-and-drop simplicity of ASP.NET to make a library of AJAX controls that are as easy to use as the ASP controls you've been using all along.

AJAX Doesn't Exist

There really isn't any such thing as AJAX. It isn't a product; in fact, it isn't even a technology. It's just a way to refer to a set of existing technologies used together in new ways to do cool things.

The first use of the term as an acronym for "Asynchronous JavaScript and XML" was by Jesse James Garrett in February 2005.[a] He thought of it while in the shower (if you must know), when he realized the need for a shorthand term to represent the suite of technologies he was proposing to a client (who, we are assured, was not in the shower with him).

According to Garrett, "AJAX…is really several technologies, each flourishing in its own right, coming together in powerful new ways." AJAX incorporates:

- Standards-based presentation using XHTML and CSS
- Dynamic display and interaction using the Document Object Model (DOM)
- Data interchange and manipulation using XML and XSLT
- Asynchronous data retrieval using XMLHttpRequest
- JavaScript binding everything together

The key fact about AJAX is that it uses *asynchronous* data transfer to request units of information smaller than an entire page.

---

[a] The first recorded use of the term at all, on the other hand, may have been nearly 3,000 years earlier, by Homer, who wrote about Ajax the Great (and Ajax the Lesser) in the *Iliad* (Book 7, pp. 181–312). Ajax the Great was the tallest and strongest of the Achaeans, second only to Achilles in skill as a warrior. More recently there was that whole "Stronger than Dirt" thing, but we'll let that go.

With AJAX, you can eat your cake and have it, too: you can continue to create ASP.NET applications with the same incredible development environment, but add client-side scripts with asynchronous programming (especially asynchronous data retrieval!). What's more, you can do so with a library of tested, ready-to-use controls that fully encapsulate all the JavaScript for you.

 Don't panic; if you *like* JavaScript and you want to write your own controls, you're free to do so. Just like with custom controls, you can always extend or even reinvent the existing controls if you are so moved. We'll demonstrate how in this very chapter.

Getting Started

This section of the book depends on technology that is readily available from Microsoft. AJAX functionality is integrated into ASP.NET 3.5 and does not require any additional downloads. If, for some reason, you are not using ASP.NET 3.5, you can download the relevant parts from *http://asp.net/ajax/downloads/*.

Microsoft's announced intention is to split AJAX into three parts: a fully supported part; a Community Technology Preview that will have newly evolving parts; and the Control Toolkit, which will be an ever-expanding collection of samples and components, along with the tools you need to build your own custom AJAX controls.

ASP.NET and JavaScript

Microsoft's ASP.NET AJAX is a free framework for quickly creating the next generation of more efficient, more interactive, and highly personalized web experiences that work across most browsers.

To start, we'll look at an example that uses just client-side JavaScript to change the contents of a page, without the need to go back to a server.

Begin by creating a new ASP.NET Web Site named *JavaScriptExample*, as shown in Figure 5-1.

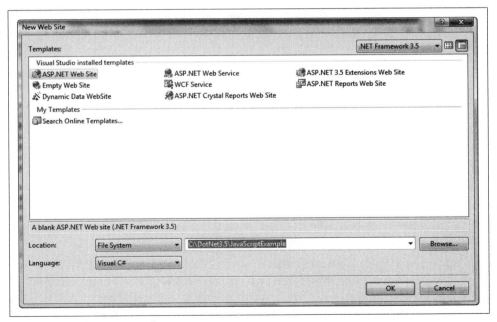

Figure 5-1. JavaScript example

Next, insert the following HTML and JavaScript at the top of the *default.aspx* page created for you by Visual Studio (or Visual Web Developer):

```
<%@ Page Language="C#" AutoEventWireup="true" CodeFile="Default.aspx.cs"
    Inherits="_Default" %>

<!DOCTYPE html PUBLIC "-//W3C//DTD XHTML 1.0 Transitional//EN"
    "http://www.w3.org/TR/xhtml1/DTD/xhtml1-transitional.dtd">

<html xmlns="http://www.w3.org/1999/xhtml">
<head runat="server">
    <title>Simple Partial AJAX example</title>

    <script language="javascript" type="text/javascript">
      function showText(str)
      {
          if (str.length==0)
          {
              document.getElementById("TextBoxContents").innerHTML=""
          }
          else
          {
              document.getElementById("TextBoxContents").innerHTML=str
          }
      }
    </script>

</head>
<body>
    <form id="form1" runat="server">
      <div>
          <b>What you type here:</b>
          <asp:TextBox
              ID="TextBox1"
              runat="server"
              onkeyup="showText(this.value)" />
          <p><b><i>Is what you see here: </i></b>
          <span id="TextBoxContents"></span>
          </p>
      </div>
    </form>
</body>
</html>
```

When you run this very simple example, everything you type is reflected in the text below the text entry box. Let's walk through how it works.

Just below the <title> element is a short script block (shown in bold). Within that block is a single function, showText( ), which takes a string as a parameter. Assuming the string length is greater than zero, the element in the document whose ID is TextBoxContents (in this case, a span) is retrieved, and its innerHTML property is set to the value of the string that was passed to the function. The net effect is that the string passed into the function is placed into the span.

To understand this bit of JavaScript you need some background in two technologies not familiar to every ASP.NET programmer: JavaScript itself, and DHTML for manipulating the Document Object Model.

We won't attempt a full tutorial on these topics. For those who like to "pick it up as you go," we'll annotate what we're doing in each example. For those who like a more structured approach, we highly recommend *JavaScript: The Definitive Guide* by David Flanagan and *Dynamic HTML: The Definitive Reference* by Danny Goodman (both from O'Reilly). If you're only going to buy one, buy the latter—but buy both!

Below the script is a fairly standard ASP.NET page that mixes an `<asp:TextBox>` with a `<span>` for the output. The `<asp:TextBox>` will be rendered in the browser as an HTML `<input>`. You want that `<input>` to have an event handler named onkeyup. The `<asp:TextBox>` does not have an attribute for such an event handler, but it's perfectly willing to pass along the event handler you designate to the HTML it will render.

Thus, you can write:

```
<asp:TextBox
    ID="TextBox1"
    runat="server"
    onkeyup="showText(this.value)" />
```

When the user types a character in the text box and then releases the key just pressed, the onkeyup event will fire. That event is a browser event and must be handled on the client; thus, it requires JavaScript.

Each time the user types a character, the JavaScript function is called; it evaluates the string in the text box and places the entire string into the inner HTML, creating immediate feedback to the user. All of this is handled on the client side, using the browser's built-in JavaScript interpreter and DHTML, without any involvement of the server (once the original page has been delivered).

Creating a "Word Wheel" with AJAX

One of the most-requested features in ASP.NET applications is a "word wheel" in which the user begins to type in a name (or other string) and the control shows all the names from our data source that begin with the letters entered; as the user types more, the provided list is narrowed.

This is painful to do with traditional ASP.NET, as you must make a round trip for each letter that's entered. Clearly, this is a place where AJAX can make all the difference. To provide some data to illustrate how blazingly fast this is, you'll borrow the first 65,535 names from the publicly available U.S. census list and put them in a SQL database table.

To begin, create a new Web Site called *LastNameLookup*.

 For now, you are not creating AJAX-enabled Web Sites, nor are you using ScriptManagers. You will do both shortly.

This Web Site uses two forms: *Default.aspx* and an AJAX Web Form that you will create called *LastNameLookup.aspx*. *Default.aspx* is presented in Example 5-1.

Example 5-1. Default.aspx

```
<%@ Page Language="C#" AutoEventWireup="true" CodeFile="Default.aspx.cs"
    Inherits="_Default" %>

<!DOCTYPE html PUBLIC "-//W3C//DTD XHTML 1.1//EN"
    "http://www.w3.org/TR/xhtml11/DTD/xhtml11.dtd">
<html xmlns="http://www.w3.org/1999/xhtml">

<head id="Head1" runat="server">
   <title>Word Wheel</title>
   <script language="javascript" type="text/javascript">
      var xmlHttp
      function showHint(str)
      {
         if (str.length==0)
         {
            document.getElementById("TextBoxHint").innerHTML=""
            return
         }
         xmlHttp=GetXmlHttpObject()
         if (!xmlHttp || xmlHttp==null)
         {
            alert ("Browser does not support HTTP Request")
            return
         }
         var url="LastNameLookup.aspx"
         url=url+"?q="+str
         xmlHttp.onreadystatechange=stateChanged
         xmlHttp.open("GET",url,true)
         xmlHttp.send(null)
      }

      function stateChanged( )
      {
         var OK = 200
         if (( xmlHttp.readyState == 4 ||
            xmlHttp.readyState == "complete" )
            && xmlHttp.status == OK )
         {
            document.getElementById("TextBoxHint").innerHTML =
               xmlHttp.responseText
         }
      }
```

Example 5-1. Default.aspx (continued)

```
    function GetXmlHttpObject(handler)
    {
       var objXMLHttp=null
       if (window.XMLHttpRequest)
       {
          try
          {
             objXMLHttp=new XMLHttpRequest( )
          }
          catch (e)
          {
             // Catch handler here
          }
       }
       else if (window.ActiveXObject)
       {
          try
          {
             objXMLHttp=new ActiveXObject("Microsoft.XMLHTTP")
          }
          catch(e)
          {
             // Catch handler here
          }
       }

       return objXMLHttp
    }
  </script>
</head>

<body>
  <form id="form1" runat="server">
     <div>
        <h1>US Census Last Name Lookup</h1><br />

        <b>Last name:</b> <asp:TextBox ID="TextBox1" runat="server"
           onkeyup="showHint(this.value)" />
        <p><b><i>Names in the US Census: </i></b>  
        <span id="TextBoxHint"></span>
        </p>
     </div>
  </form>
</body>

</html>
```

There is no code in the code-behind for *Default.aspx*.

Create the *LastNameLookup.aspx* AJAX Web Form, then replace everything in the file after the Page directive with this single line:

```
    <asp:literal runat="server" id="LastNames"/>
```

The entire page should look like this:

```
<%@ Page Language="C#" AutoEventWireup="true"
    CodeFile="LastNameLookup.aspx.cs" Inherits="LastNameLookup" %>

<asp:literal runat="server" id="LastNames"/>
```

The code-behind for *LastNameLookup.aspx* consists of two methods, Page_Load( )
and LastNamesForPartialName( ), as shown in Example 5-2.

Example 5-2. Code-behind for LastNameLookup.aspx

```
using System;
using System.Data;
using System.Data.SqlClient;
using System.Configuration;
using System.Collections;
using System.Web;
using System.Web.Security;
using System.Web.UI;
using System.Web.UI.WebControls;
using System.Web.UI.WebControls.WebParts;
using System.Web.UI.HtmlControls;

public partial class LastNameLookup : System.Web.UI.Page
{
    protected void Page_Load(object sender, EventArgs e)
    {
        if ( Request.QueryString.Count > 0 )
        {
            String queryLastName =
                Request.QueryString.Get( 0 ).ToString( );
            DataTable dt = LastNamesForPartialName( queryLastName );

            if ( dt == null || dt.Rows.Count == 0 )
            {
                LastNames.Text =
                    "Sorry no one found with that letter combination";
            }
            else
            {
                String returnString = "<select size=10 >";
                foreach ( DataRow row in dt.Rows )
                {
                    returnString += "<option>" +
                        row["lastName"].ToString( ) +
                        "</option>";
                }
                returnString += "</select>";
                LastNames.Text = returnString;
            }
        }
        else
```

Example 5-2. Code-behind for LastNameLookup.aspx (continued)

```
        {
            LastNames.Text = string.Empty;
        }
    }

    public DataTable LastNamesForPartialName(String aPartialName)
    {
        String connectionString =
            ConfigurationManager.AppSettings["Database"];
        SqlConnection connection = new SqlConnection(connectionString);

        string queryString =
            "select * from LastNames where lastName like '" +
            aPartialName+ "%'";
        DataSet ds = new DataSet( );

        try
        {
            SqlDataAdapter dataAdapter =
                new SqlDataAdapter(queryString, connection);
            dataAdapter.Fill(ds, "LastNames");
        }

        catch
        {
            // Handle exception
        }

        finally
        {
            connection.Close( );
        }
        return ds.Tables["LastNames"];
    }
}
```

The Data

This example will use a database of names (USLastNames) obtained from the U.S. Census Bureau. A backup can be found at *http://tinyurl.com/3dbtpm*. Download the backup and restore it to a database that you create with the same name locally. You'll need to add the appropriate connection string to *web.config* as well:

```
<appSettings>
    <add key="Database" value="Data Source=<<MACHINE_NAME_HERE>>;Initial
        Catalog=USLastNames;Integrated Security=True;" />
</appSettings>
```

The Pages

The division of responsibility among the pages is as follows.

Default.aspx has all the JavaScript, plus the UI. This consists of:

- A text box into which the user will type a last name
- A span, which is replaced by a listbox that is created dynamically as data is retrieved from the database

LastNameLookup.aspx has only an <asp:Literal> element, which will serve as a holder. The contents of that holder will be placed into the inner HTML of the span in *Default.aspx* at runtime, on the client side, using DHTML.

Where the Action Is

Before stepping through this example in detail, we need to focus on the XMLHttp object, as it is the core of AJAX's asynchronous client-side processing.

When *Default.aspx* loads, the user is presented with a text box and a prompt to enter the last name to search for. The user enters a letter (e.g., "L") and releases the key, and a keyup event is fired. The keyup event was registered in the declaration of the TextBox:

```
<asp:TextBox
    ID="TextBox1"
    runat="server"
    onkeyup="showHint(this.value)" />
```

The showHint( ) referred to is a JavaScript function:

```
function showHint(str)
    {
        if (str.length==0)
        {
            document.getElementById("TextBoxHint").innerHTML=""
            return
        }
        xmlHttp=GetXmlHttpObject( )
        if (!xmlHttp || xmlHttp==null)
        {
            alert ("Browser does not support HTTP Request")
            return
        }
        var url="LastNameLookup.aspx"
        url=url+"?q="+str
        xmlHttp.onreadystatechange=stateChanged
        xmlHttp.open("GET",url,true)
        xmlHttp.send(null)
    }
```

Examination of this function reveals that it receives the string passed in and, after ensuring that the string is not of zero length, attempts to get an XMLHttpRequest object through the helper function GetXmlHttpObject( ).

It does so by checking for the existence of window.XMLHttpRequest (an object made available by modern browsers) or window.ActiveXObject (an equivalent object made available by older versions of IE). Engineers on the Mozilla project implemented a compatible native version of XMLHttpRequest for Mozilla 1.0 (and Netscape 7), and Apple engineers added support for XMLHttpRequest to Safari 1.2. One of these objects must be available to proceed; any browser that is too old to return them cannot implement AJAX.

 Similar functionality is covered in a proposed W3C standard, the Document Object Model (DOM) Level 3 Load and Save Specification. In the meantime, growing support for the XMLHttpRequest object has made it a *de facto* standard that will likely be supported even after the W3C specification becomes final.

If the XMLHttpRequest object has been created, it is stored in the variable xmlHttp. With this in hand, you're ready to do the AJAX magic of updating the data asynchronously:

```
var url="LastNameLookup.aspx"
url=url+"?q="+str
xmlHttp.onreadystatechange=stateChanged
xmlHttp.open("GET",url,true)
xmlHttp.send(null)
```

url is declared as a var and is set to the URL of the page you'll use to get the values you need. To this you append the string ?q and whatever was passed in as a parameter (str). Thus, the *LastNameLookup.aspx* page would receive the query string ?q=Lib if the user entered "Lib" in the text box.

The onreadystatechange event handler, for asynchronous results, is set to the function stateChanged( ). stateChanged( ) will be called each time the ready state changes. This asynchronous mechanism allows you to proceed with calling open( ) and send( ), and then to respond to send( ) when it is complete:

```
function stateChanged( )
{
   var OK = 200
   if (( xmlHttp.readyState == 4 ||
       xmlHttp.readyState == "complete" )
       && xmlHttp.status == OK )
   {
      document.getElementById("TextBoxHint").innerHTML =
         xmlHttp.responseText
   }
}
```

The event handler sets the innerHTML property of the TextBoxHint span in *Default.aspx* if (and only if) the readyState is set to 4 (or "complete") and if xmlHttp.status is equal to 200 (indicating OK).

 You can find all the possible HTTP status codes in the MSDN Library under "HTTP status code."

There are five possible readyState values: uninitialized (0), loading (1), loaded (2), interactive (3), and complete (4). By waiting for complete, and for xmlHttp.status to be OK, you are assured that the data is fully ready to be displayed.

The call to open( ) initializes the request, specifies that you are doing a GET (that is, requesting the page), and passes in the URL (e.g., *LastNameLookup.aspx?q=Lib*). The value true indicates that you'd like the method to be handled asynchronously, returning immediately. This is fine, as you've already passed in the delegate (stateChanged) to be called when xmlHttp is ready. You then make it all go with a call to send( ). Common methods of the XMLHttpRequest object are explained in Table 5-1.

Table 5-1. Common XMLHttpRequest object methods

Method	Description
abort( )	Stops the current request
getAllResponseHeaders( )	Returns the complete set of headers (labels and values) as a string
getResponseHeader("headerLabel")	Returns the string value of a single header label
open("method", "URL"[, asyncFlag[, "userName"[, "password"]]])	Assigns the destination URL, method, and other attributes of a request
send(*content*)	Sends the request, optionally with a string or DOM object data
setRequestHeader("label", "value")	Assigns a key/value pair to the header that will be sent with the request

open( ) and send( ) are the most commonly used methods. You'll typically use open( ) with either GET (for operations that are primarily intended to retrieve data) or POST (for operations that are primarily intended to send data). If the length of the data exceeds 512 bytes, you'll want to use POST in both cases.

Some important properties of the XMLHttpRequest object are shown in Table 5-2. Note that with the exception of onreadystatechange, all properties are read-only.

Table 5-2. Common XMLHttpRequest object properties

Property	Description
onreadystatechange	Event handler for an event that fires at every state change
readyState	Object status integer, such as 4 for "complete"

Table 5-2. Common XMLHttpRequest object properties (continued)

Property	Description
responseText	String version of data returned from the server process
responseXML	DOM-compatible document object of data returned from the server process
status	Numeric code returned by server, such as 404 for "Not Found" or 200 for "OK"
statusText	String message accompanying the status code

All data is returned from the server via the responseText or responseXML properties. responseText provides a string, but the responseXML property returns an XML document object that can be parsed (and transformed) using the .NET XML manipulation classes.

Security issues

Because the XMLHttpRequest object operates within a browser, it adopts the same-domain security policies of typical JavaScript activity (sharing the same "sandbox"). This has important implications for your application.

On most browsers, any pages with scripts that access document objects need to be retrieved via the http: protocol, meaning that you won't be able to test the pages from a local hard disk (using the file: protocol) without security issues cropping up, especially in Mozilla and Internet Explorer on Windows. In fact, Mozilla requires that you wrap access to the object inside UniversalBrowserRead security privileges. IE, on the other hand, simply displays an alert to the user that a potentially unsafe activity may be going on and offers a chance to cancel.

Note that the domain of the URL request destination must be the same as the one that serves up the page containing the script. This means, unfortunately, that client-side scripts cannot fetch web service data from other sources and blend that data into a page. All the data must come from the same domain.

Asynchronous updates

One of the most powerful features implied by this new model is that data can be retrieved asynchronously and pages can be updated *in part*. That is, you can update only those aspects of a page that have changed (rather than refetching the entire page), avoiding needless flicker and greatly speeding up the updating process.

Step-by-Step Walkthrough

With an understanding of the XMLHttp object in hand, let's walk through this example step by step. A full understanding of it will serve as the foundation for all of the material to come.

The user begins, as noted previously, by typing a letter into the text box displayed by *Default.aspx*. The onkeyup event handler is called, and it checks to make sure the string has at least one letter, obtains the XMLHttp object, and sets the URL with the query string. It then sets the event handler for asynchronous events with the onreadystatechange property, calls open( ) for the GET request, and calls send( ) to start the asynchronous call.

The call to open( ) causes the GET request to be sent to *LastNameLookup.aspx*, which in turn causes Page_Load to fire on that page. If the QueryString count is greater than zero—that is, if you've entered one or more letters—you extract those letters into a string and call a helper method to find all the names that begin with those letters:

```
if ( Request.QueryString.Count > 0 )
{
    String queryLastName = Request.QueryString.Get( 0 ).ToString( );
    DataTable dt = LastNamesForPartialName( queryLastName );
```

Assuming you get back some names, you create a listbox and populate it with each name retrieved. You do this by initializing the listbox with a <select> element and then bracketing the contents of each row's "last name" column with <option> tags:

```
String returnString = "<select size=10 >";
foreach ( DataRow row in dt.Rows )
{
    returnString += "<option>" +
        row["lastName"].ToString( ) +
        "</option>";
}
returnString += "</select>";
```

All of this is bundled up into the Text property of the literal control on the page (LastNames):

```
LastNames.Text = returnString;
```

The call to GET returns the *LastNameLookup.aspx* page (i.e., the contents of the literal the page consists of) as a string. In other words, what is returned to the XMLHttp object in its responseText property is whatever you put into the literal.

You may need to stop and think about this for a moment. Because the page is so simple, containing nothing but a literal, no other text is returned. If you were to open *LastNameLookup.aspx* and examine its HTML, you'd see that it contains nothing but the select box with its options filled with names. To prove this to myself, I created a virtual directory (*LastNameLookup*) in IIS and pointed it to my development directory. I then opened a browser with the following URL: *http://localhost/ LastNameLookup/LastNameLookup.aspx?q=Lib*. Once the listbox was displayed, I right-clicked and selected View Source; sure enough, the entire source for that page was the select box and its contents, as shown in Figure 5-2.

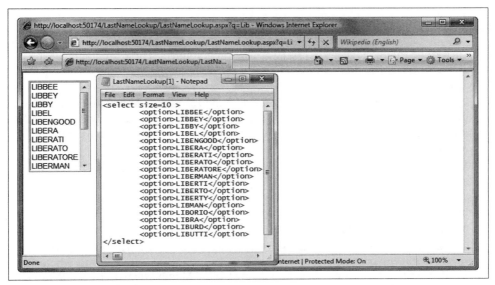

Figure 5-2. LastNameLookup source

Inserting this text, which is returned via the XMLHttp object, into the innerHTML property of the span in *Default.aspx* causes it to be displayed as a listbox.

The key thing to note is that at no time does the web server handle the keyup event. There is no round trip to the web server to fetch the data. If the database is local (or the data is cached), there is no round trip at all!

 Each time the user enters a character, the program must interact with the database server and must loop through all the rows in the data table to construct the HTML output. This can cause a human-noticeable delay. Solving that problem—e.g., by waiting for the user to enter a few characters before checking for matches—is left as an exercise for the ambitious reader.

ScriptManager

The ScriptManager control is central to integrating AJAX with ASP.NET. The ScriptManager manages the components on a page and is responsible for handling partial page updates. It takes care of loading the ASP.NET AJAX client script libraries into the browser, and it's responsible for using proxy objects so that you can access web service methods from JavaScript.

\<Rant>

AJAX came to ASP.NET by way of JavaScript programmers. These programmers' primary concern is with how they can improve the performance of, or the users' experience with, client-side scripting.

ASP.NET programmers, however, are (or, I would argue, should be) concerned with how they can leverage existing tools Microsoft (or others) have already created and tested, so they can focus on design and high-level implementation rather than on building the plumbing.

When we build ASP.NET programs, we drag and drop controls such as listboxes, text boxes, and even calendars with little thought about how they work or how they emit standard HTML to browsers. When we use validation controls, we may be aware that they will emit client-side validation script, but few of us bother to examine that script. We trust that Microsoft got it right.

The goal of using the Microsoft Atlas library, and especially the AJAX Control Toolkit, should be (in my opinion) to enable developers to drag and drop controls wherever possible, writing JavaScript and manipulating the DOM only when necessary. Writing JavaScript is analogous to writing custom ASP controls: you should do so only when needed, and even then only when the cost/benefit ratio is clear and you can't buy a control that is already tested and ready for less than it would cost to build one yourself.

This may be considered a bold statement today, because AJAX is still young. The theory is that if something goes wrong, it's important to understand the underlying technology. I remember this kind of talk from when I was learning Assembler (you have to know the machine language), when I was learning C (you have to be able to examine Assembly), and so forth. But the truth is that I haven't dropped into a non-symbolic debugger in longer than I care to think about, and if I'm totally honest, I haven't really used ILDASM for anything other than demonstration purposes in at least five years.

That said, AJAX *is* still young, and unlike with other aspects of ASP.NET development, there is not yet a complete library of tools available for it. So, at times, you will have to create custom AJAX controls (or, more accurately, put together some AJAX code) to accomplish what you want. For example, there is no well-tested word wheel, so we wrote our own, and along the way we were able to demonstrate how things fit together. That's all fine and dandy, but don't let it scare you into thinking that in order to use AJAX you'll have to spend six months learning JavaScript and DHTML. There is a lot you can do right out of the box, and I would argue that you'll be able to achieve the vast majority of what you want just by dragging and dropping the controls already provided, without ever writing a line of JavaScript yourself.

\</Rant>

Partial Page Rendering

To implement partial page rendering on your page, you must set the ScriptManager's EnablePartialRendering property to true (the default), either declaratively or programmatically, in or before the page's init event handler. You then place UpdatePanel objects on your page, and each UpdatePanel can be updated individually, without updating other panels and without a postback of the entire page.

From a practical programming point of view, this is very simple; you drag a ScriptManager onto the page (it is not visible), and then you drag one or more UpdatePanels onto the page. You update each UpdatePanel only when needed, resulting in your data being updated asynchronously and without flicker. The performance boost is immediate, unmistakable, and nearly effortless.

A Better Calendar Control

While the Calendar control provided with ASP.NET is very powerful, it is also painful to use, as each date change causes a postback. An AJAX-based solution using the CalendarExtender is a great alternative; with this approach, you can refresh only the TextBox control (not the entire page) when the date in the CalendarExtender changes.

To see this at work, create a new ASP.NET Web Site and name it *AJAXCalendar*. Open the Toolbox and make sure you have access to all the Toolkit controls, as shown in Figure 5-3. If not, you can download the ASP.NET AJAX Control Toolkit that targets .NET 3.5 from *http://tinyurl.com/2j9pjy*. You can then drag and drop the *AJAXControlToolkit.dll* assembly (found in the *bin* folder inside the *Sample Website* folder) to the VS 2008 Toolbox to have its control extenders show up as controls that you can add to any ASP.NET Web Site or Project.

 At the time of this writing, there is a known issue involving the use of Microsoft's wireless mouse and keyboard with the AJAX Control Toolkit and Visual Studio 2008. If you are using wireless input devices and your controls are grayed out (meaning you cannot use them) or you were unable to add the AJAX Control Toolkit to your Tools pane, switch to a wired keyboard and mouse and follow the instructions at *http://tinyurl.com/2uxvrd*.

Each AJAX application must have exactly one ScriptManager control. To get started, change to the design view and drag a ScriptManager control from the ASP.NET 3.5 Extensions toolset onto your *Default.aspx* component. Next, drag a label onto the form from the standard tools and set its text to "Date Selection." Right below that, drag on a TextBox. Immediately, you should have the ability to add an extender (as you can see in Figure 5-4).

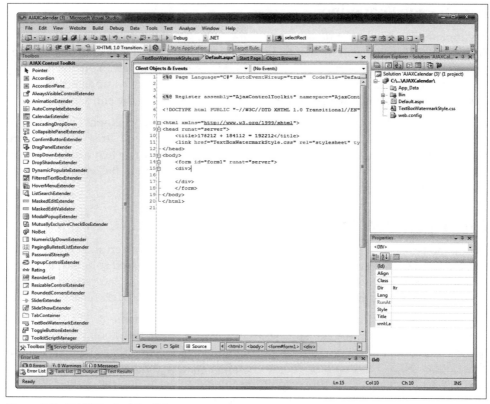

Figure 5-3. AJAX Control Toolkit

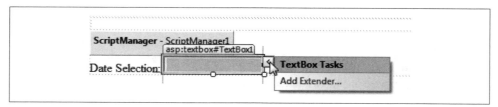

Figure 5-4. The Add Extender option

Click Add Extender and then select `CalendarExtender` from the choices provided in the dialog window, as seen in Figure 5-5.

The `CalendarExtender` is an ASP.NET AJAX extender that can be attached to any ASP.NET `TextBox` control. The user interacts with the calendar by clicking on a day to set the date (or the "Today" link to set the current date).

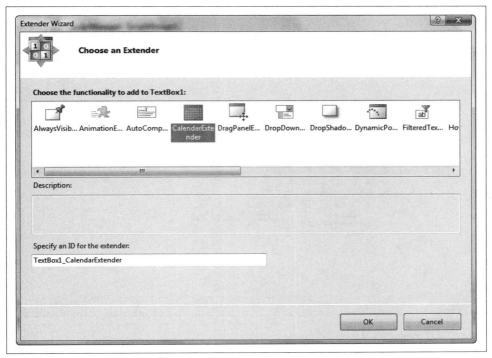

Figure 5-5. Adding a CalendarExtender

The CalendarExtender has a number of properties that can be configured to create custom behavior. These include:

CssClass
    The name of the CSS class used to style the calendar.

Format
    The *format string* used to display the selected date.

PopupButtonID
    The ID of a control to show the calendar pop up when clicked. If this value is not set, the calendar will pop up when the textbox receives focus.

PopupPosition
    Indicates whether the calendar pop up should appear at the BottomLeft (the default), BottomRight, TopLeft, or TopRight of the TextBox.

SelectedDate
    Indicates the date with which the Calendar extender is initialized.

If you run your application at this point you will get the default behavior shown in Figure 5-6.

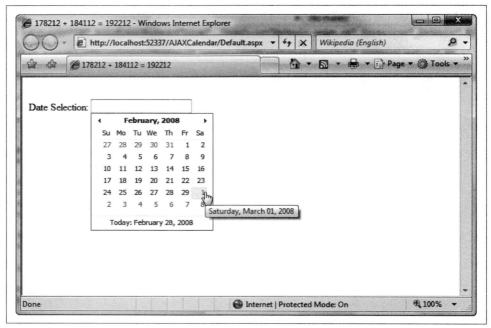

Figure 5-6. Running the default behavior

If you pick a date—say, the 1st of the month—the TextBox will display the date in the "d" format (m/d/yyyy) by default. Change the format for the control to MMMM d, yyyy. When you run the application now, when you select a date (in this case, July 4, 2010) the TextBox will display it in the format shown in Figure 5-7.

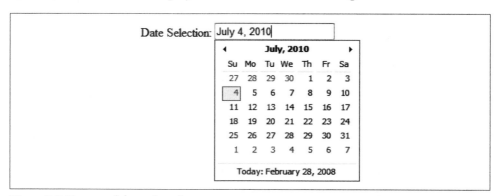

Figure 5-7. Formatted date selected

Returning to the design view, you should see a result that closely resembles Figure 5-8.

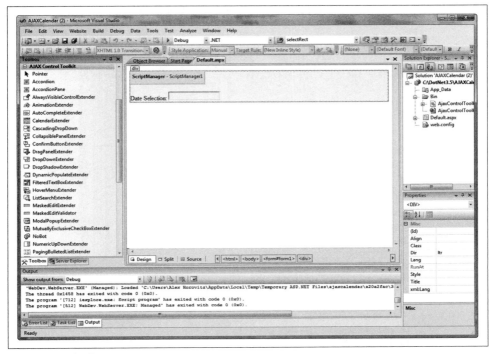

Figure 5-8. The design view

Adding a Watermark

You can improve the user experience by not wasting screen real estate with the Label. Instead, you can add another nifty little widget called the TextBoxWatermarkExtender.

Return to the design view, take out the Label, and click on the arrow to the right of the TextBox. Click Add Extender, as you did before, and choose TextBoxWatermarkExtender in the Extender wizard. Then go to the properties window and select the TextBox1_ TextBoxWatermarkExtender control. Set the WatermarkText property to "Click here to enter date" and run the page to see the results.

You've done a lot of work with the visual designer at this point (which is great, mind you!), and you may be curious about what's been happening under the hood. Looking at *Default.aspx* now, you will find the following:

```
<%@ Page Language="C#" AutoEventWireup="true"
    CodeFile="Default.aspx.cs"
    Inherits="_Default" %>

<%@ Register assembly="AjaxControlToolkit"
    namespace="AjaxControlToolkit" tagprefix="cc1" %>
```

```
<!DOCTYPE html PUBLIC "-//W3C//DTD XHTML 1.0 Transitional//EN"
    "http://www.w3.org/TR/xhtml1/DTD/xhtml1-transitional.dtd">

<html xmlns="http://www.w3.org/1999/xhtml">
<head runat="server">
    <title>178212 + 184112 = 192212</title>
</head>
<body>
    <form id="form1" runat="server">
    <div>

        <asp:ScriptManager ID="ScriptManager1" runat="server">
        </asp:ScriptManager>
        <br />

        <asp:TextBox ID="TextBox1" runat="server">
        </asp:TextBox>
        <cc1:TextBoxWatermarkExtender
            ID="TextBox1_TextBoxWatermarkExtender"
            runat="server"
            Enabled="True"
            TargetControlID="TextBox1"
            WatermarkText="Click here to enter date">
        </cc1:TextBoxWatermarkExtender>
        <cc1:CalendarExtender ID="TextBox1_
            CalendarExtender"
            runat="server"
            Enabled="True"
            TargetControlID="TextBox1"
            Format="MMMM d, yyyy">
        </cc1:CalendarExtender>

    </div>
    </form>
</body>
</html>
```

This is all fairly straightforward and easy to understand. Considerng all the functionality you've added, there is surprisingly little complexity to the underlying source view. This speaks volumes to the level of effort that Microsoft has made in .NET 3.5 to hide the implementation details, making life much more pleasant for developers.

Adding Stylesheets to Extender Controls

To distinguish the instructional text from text entered by the user, you can add a stylesheet to format the watermark text. You do so by adding the WatermarkCssClass attribute.

Begin by adding to your project a stylesheet called *TextBoxWatermarkStyle.css*:

```
/*Watermark off/on*/

.unwatermarked {
    height:18px;
    width:148px;
    font-weight:bold;
    background-color:#FFFFFF;
    color:#000000;
}

.watermarked {
    height:20px;
    width:150px;
    padding:2px 0 0 2px;
    border:1px solid #BEBEBE;
    background-color:#FFFFCC;
    color:#666666;
}
```

To add this stylesheet to your page, simply open the *Default.aspx* page in the design view and drag *TextBoxWatermarkStyle.css* onto the main div.

To get the experience you want, set the `WatermarkCssClass` of the `TextBoxWatermarkExtender` to `watermarked`, but set the `CssClass` attribute of the `TextBox` to `unwatermarked`. This ensures that when the user selects a date, the text in the text box will look correct, in its unwatermarked format.

Looking at the web site now, you should see a text box with the watermark "Click here to enter date," as shown in Figure 5-9.

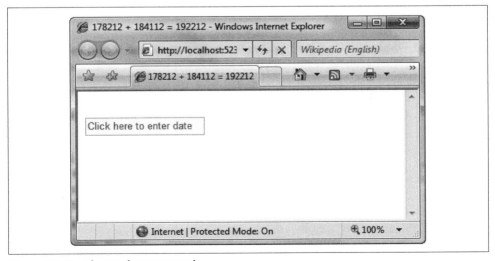

Figure 5-9. Text box with a watermark

When the user clicks in the text box, the watermark disappears and the calendar appears, as shown in Figure 5-10.

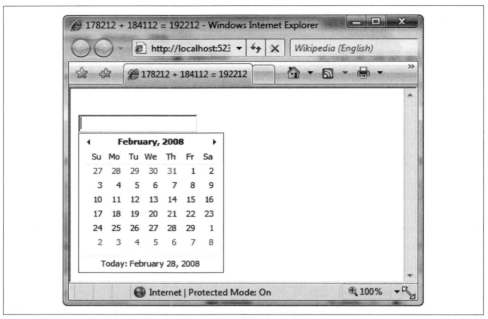

Figure 5-10. After clicking in the text box

When the user clicks on a date, the calendar instantly disappears, and the date is placed in the text box. Zow! Is this really a web application?

What's Next?

You've seen how AJAX can be used to enable asynchronous communication and client-side processing in your ASP.NET applications. In large measure, this is accomplished with the same kind of drag-and-drop, set parameters, and let 'er rip ease offered by other ASP.NET controls. In the next chapter, you'll put these tools together to build a meaningful application.

Applying AJAX: ListMania

This chapter will walk you through a significant AJAX-enhanced ASP.NET application to demonstrate how the various AJAX tools can enrich a real-world application.

The application you'll build is a To-Do List Manager, which will consist of two *.aspx* pages. The first is the login page shown in Figure 6-1. This page allows users to access their personal to-do lists by entering an email address and a password, then clicking the sign-in button. New users can create to-do lists by clicking the Need To Register? button, completing the form that appears, and clicking the Register button.

The login page uses an AJAX `CollapsiblePanelExtender` control that expands and contracts when the user clicks on the Need To Register? button. It also includes an AJAX `WaterMark` control (as described in the previous chapter) and an AJAX `PasswordStrength` control to assist the user in choosing a strong password. We will examine the `PasswordStrength` control in detail later in the chapter.

The second page you'll create is the page for the To-Do List Manager itself, shown in Figure 6-2.

On this page, users can maintain the enormous lists of things they need to do. They will be able to add items to their lists and prioritize those items.

This page uses an AJAX `ReorderList` control to allow the user to change the order of the to-do items using drag handles. Each to-do item has an item name, a full description, and a hidden priority value (an integer).

Creating the To-Do List Manager

Begin by creating a new C# web application, as you did in the previous chapter. Choose New Web Site from the File menu, and select "ASP.NET Web Site" from the Templates section. Name the application *ListMania*.

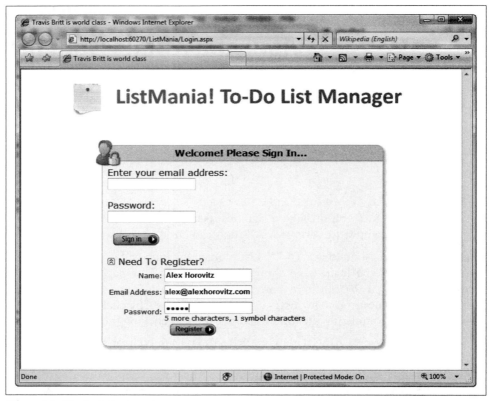

Figure 6-1. The login/registration page

We'll build this application in stages: you'll get parts of it working and then add on more parts, successively approximating the final product shown in the preceding figures.

 To save you a bit of work upfront, you can download the images and CSS files for this application from *http://tinyurl.com/2s6oqh*.

Create the Application Master Page

First, create the Application Master Page. This will be used to hold the `ScriptManager`, as well as the CSS information for the application. Think of it as a donut—the request/response loop will insert the content from the other pages into the donut-hole in the middle of this master page. To do this, click on your web site's

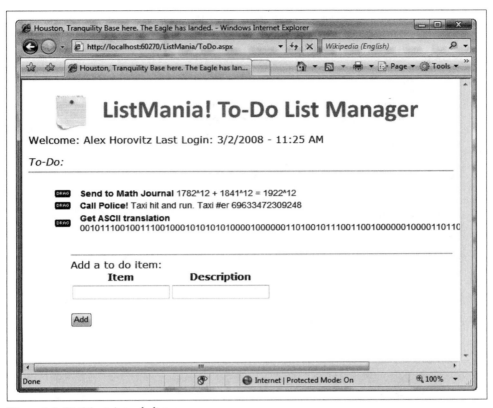

Figure 6-2. ListMania's to-do list page

icon in the Solution Explorer and select Add → New Item. Add a new Master Page template called *ListManager.master*, as seen in Figure 6-3.

Bring up *ListManager.master* in the design view and set the Properties inspector to the DOCUMENT view. Then set the Title property to "Oh the things I need to do…," as seen in Figure 6-4.

Take the time now to add an *Images* folder and fill it with the images in the downloadable *listmania_media.zip* file. Also, add a new CSS file to the project, using the default name *StyleSheet.css*. Cut and paste the contents of the *StyleSheet.css* file that was also in the *.zip* file into this new file.

There are three more general housekeeping items to do. First, add the CSS file to the master. Second, make sure you have a ScriptManager embedded in the master. In the next section you will take care of the third item, configuring the database.

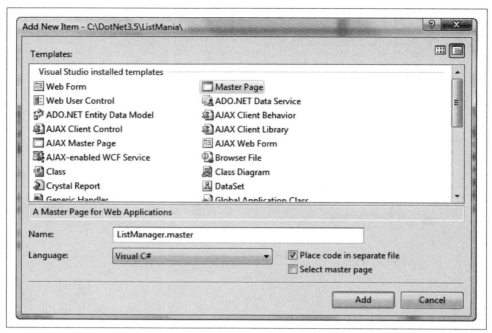

Figure 6-3. Adding a Master Page template

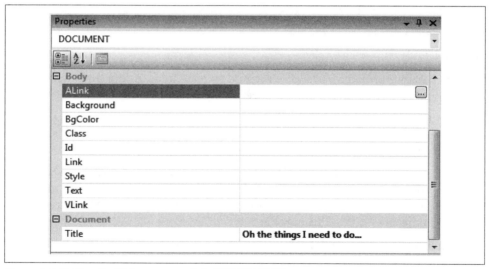

Figure 6-4. Setting the Title property of the DOCUMENT

To add the CSS file to the master, simply drag it onto *ListManager.master* while it is in the design view. Adding the ScriptManager is just as easy: from the AJAX Extensions toolbox, drag and drop a ScriptManager control onto the master. With that done, you can switch to the source view. Your *ListManager.master* should look like this:

```
<%@ Master Language="C#" AutoEventWireup="true"
    CodeFile="ListManager.master.cs" Inherits="ListManager" %>

<!DOCTYPE html PUBLIC "-//W3C//DTD XHTML 1.0 Transitional//EN"
    "http://www.w3.org/TR/xhtml1/DTD/xhtml1-transitional.dtd">

<html xmlns="http://www.w3.org/1999/xhtml">
<head runat="server">
    <title>Oh the things I need to do...</title>
    <asp:ContentPlaceHolder id="head" runat="server">
    </asp:ContentPlaceHolder>
    <link href="StyleSheet.css" rel="stylesheet" type="text/css" />
</head>
<body>
    <form id="form1" runat="server">
    <div>
        <asp:ContentPlaceHolder id="ContentPlaceHolder1" runat="server">
        </asp:ContentPlaceHolder>
    </div>
    <asp:ScriptManager ID="ScriptManager1" runat="server">
    </asp:ScriptManager>
    </form>
</body>
</html>
```

Create the Database

Next, you need to create a place to store the items in your users' to-do lists. This example assumes you are using SQL Server Express. First create a database called ToDo, then create the table shown in Figure 6-5 in the ToDo database.

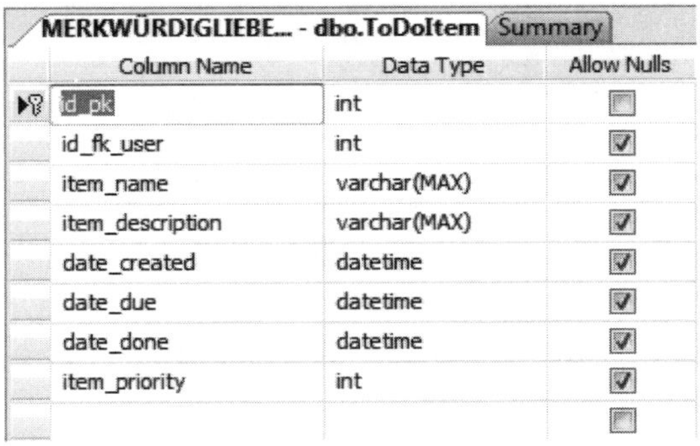

Figure 6-5. The ToDoItem table

If you want to take a faster route, you can download a backup of this database from *http://tinyurl.com/2puxew* and then create a new database called ToDo and restore it from the file. Make sure you select the "overwrite" option, or you will get complaints about tables not existing (they don't yet, of course!).

Create the To-Do List Page

Now you're ready to get cracking on the to-do list that will display the items in the database and allow the user to add new items. Start by creating a new page named it *ToDo.aspx*. To ensure that it uses the Master Page you created earlier (*ListManager. master*), check the "Select master page" option, as seen in Figure 6-6.

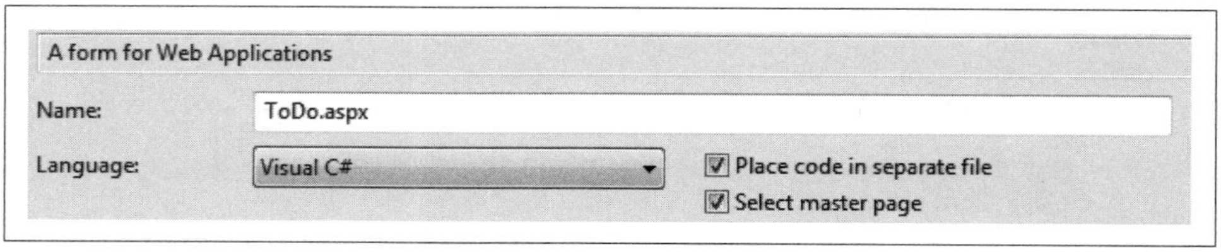

Figure 6-6. Be sure to check "Select master page"

Drag and drop a ReorderList control into the content placeholder section of the design view for the page. When you do this, you will be presented with the now-familiar dialog box that asks you to identify a data source (Figure 6-7). In this case, you will choose a new data source.

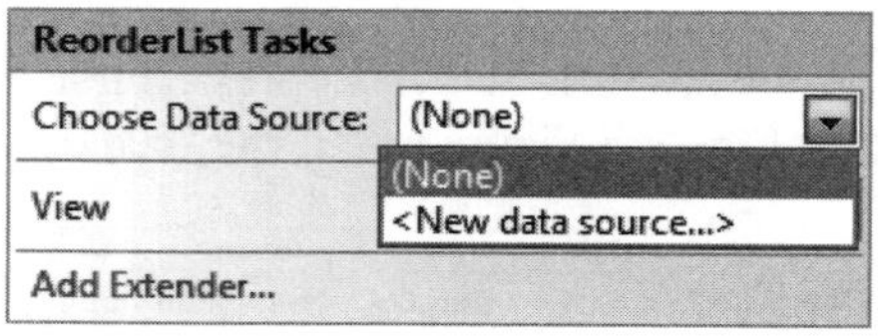

Figure 6-7. Selecting a data source for ReorderList

At this point, you have several options. For the purposes of this example, you should pick the Database type and specify "SqlDataSourceToDo" as the ID for the data source. Next, you will configure this data source using the configuration wizard that appears. Make sure you save the connection string as "ToDoConnectionString."

The wizard will go on to ask you about retrieving data from the database. Specify ToDoItem as the table and select * (all columns) as the columns you wish to select by. You should also specify an ORDER BY so that your SELECT statement looks like this:

```
SELECT * FROM [ToDoItem] ORDER BY [item_priority]
```

Be sure to configure the advanced settings as well. Check the "Generate INSERT, UPDATE, and DELETE" and "Use optimistic concurrency" options, as seen in

Figure 6-8. This will allow users to update the database when they change the order of items in the list or insert new items.

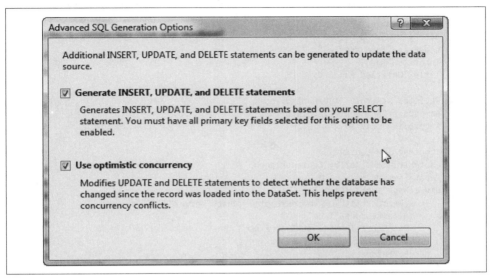

Figure 6-8. Advanced configuration

Testing the query in the next step should produce a result like Figure 6-9.

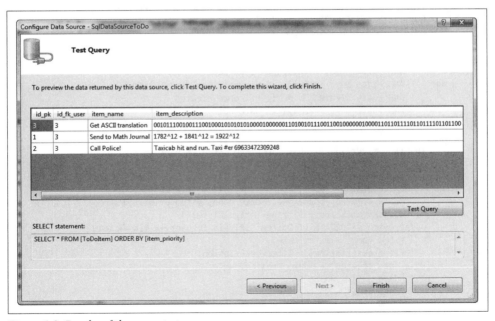

Figure 6-9. Results of the query test

Open up the source view of *ToDo.aspx* and insert a div with class = "reorderList" around the ReorderList control. This will apply the reorderList CSS style to your list when you preview it. Your *ToDo.aspx* file should contain the following source:

```
<%@ Page Language="C#" MasterPageFile="~/ListManager.master"
    AutoEventWireup="true"
    CodeFile="ToDo.aspx.cs"
    Inherits="ToDo"
    Title="Untitled Page" %>

<%@ Register assembly="AjaxControlToolkit"
    namespace="AjaxControlToolkit"
    tagprefix="cc1" %>

<asp:Content ID="Content1"
    ContentPlaceHolderID="ContentPlaceHolder1"
    Runat="Server">
    <div class="reorderList">
        <cc1:ReorderList ID="ReorderList1" runat="server"
            AllowReorder="True"
            DataSourceID="SqlDataSourceToDo"
            PostBackOnReorder="False">
        </cc1:ReorderList>
    </div>

    <asp:SqlDataSource ID="SqlDataSourceToDo"
        runat="server"
        ConnectionString="<%$ ConnectionStrings:ToDoConnectionString %>"
        SelectCommand="SELECT * FROM [ToDoItem] ORDER BY [item_priority]"
        ConflictDetection="CompareAllValues"
        DeleteCommand="DELETE FROM [ToDoItem]
            WHERE [id_pk] = @original_id_pk
            AND [id_fk_user] = @original_id_fk_user
            AND [item_name] = @original_item_name
            AND [item_description] = @original_item_description
            AND [date_created] = @original_date_created
            AND [date_due] = @original_date_due
            AND [date_done] = @original_date_done
            AND [item_priority] = @original_item_priority"
        InsertCommand="INSERT INTO [ToDoItem] ([id_fk_user],
            [item_name], [item_description], [date_created],
            [date_due], [date_done], [item_priority])
            VALUES (@id_fk_user, @item_name, @item_description,
            @date_created, @date_due, @date_done, @item_priority)"
        OldValuesParameterFormatString="original_{0}"
        UpdateCommand="UPDATE [ToDoItem] SET [id_fk_user] = @id_fk_user,
            [item_name] = @item_name,
            [item_description] = @item_description,
            [date_created] = @date_created,
            [date_due] = @date_due,
            [date_done] = @date_done,
            [item_priority] = @item_priority
            WHERE [id_pk] = @original_id_pk
```

```
                AND [id_fk_user] = @original_id_fk_user
                AND [item_name] = @original_item_name
                AND [item_description] = @original_item_description
                AND [date_created] = @original_date_created
                AND [date_due] = @original_date_due
                AND [date_done] = @original_date_done
                AND [item_priority] = @original_item_priority">
        <DeleteParameters>
            <asp:Parameter Name="original_id_pk" Type="Int32" />
            <asp:Parameter Name="original_id_fk_user" Type="Int32" />
            <asp:Parameter Name="original_item_name" Type="String" />
            <asp:Parameter Name="original_item_description" Type="String" />
            <asp:Parameter Name="original_date_created" Type="DateTime" />
            <asp:Parameter Name="original_date_due" Type="DateTime" />
            <asp:Parameter Name="original_date_done" Type="DateTime" />
            <asp:Parameter Name="original_item_priority" Type="Int32" />
        </DeleteParameters>
        <UpdateParameters>
            <asp:Parameter Name="id_fk_user" Type="Int32" />
            <asp:Parameter Name="item_name" Type="String" />
            <asp:Parameter Name="item_description" Type="String" />
            <asp:Parameter Name="date_created" Type="DateTime" />
            <asp:Parameter Name="date_due" Type="DateTime" />
            <asp:Parameter Name="date_done" Type="DateTime" />
            <asp:Parameter Name="item_priority" Type="Int32" />
            <asp:Parameter Name="original_id_pk" Type="Int32" />
            <asp:Parameter Name="original_id_fk_user" Type="Int32" />
            <asp:Parameter Name="original_item_name" Type="String" />
            <asp:Parameter Name="original_item_description" Type="String" />
            <asp:Parameter Name="original_date_created" Type="DateTime" />
            <asp:Parameter Name="original_date_due" Type="DateTime" />
            <asp:Parameter Name="original_date_done" Type="DateTime" />
            <asp:Parameter Name="original_item_priority" Type="Int32" />
        </UpdateParameters>
        <InsertParameters>
            <asp:Parameter Name="id_fk_user" Type="Int32" />
            <asp:Parameter Name="item_name" Type="String" />
            <asp:Parameter Name="item_description" Type="String" />
            <asp:Parameter Name="date_created" Type="DateTime" />
            <asp:Parameter Name="date_due" Type="DateTime" />
            <asp:Parameter Name="date_done" Type="DateTime" />
            <asp:Parameter Name="item_priority" Type="Int32" />
        </InsertParameters>
    </asp:SqlDataSource>

    </div>
</asp:Content>
```

You could run the application at this point, but with nothing in the ReorderList, you would just get a blank page.

Returning to the design view, set your view of the ReorderList to ItemTemplate (see Figure 6-10).

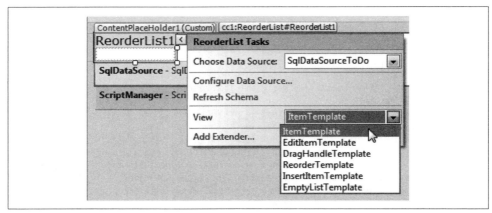

Figure 6-10. Setting the view for the ReorderList

Once this is done, drop a <DIV> inside the ReorderList and set its class to "itemArea" using the Properties inspector. Now drag, drop, and configure a couple of Label controls. After you drag in a Label control, you will have the opportunity to edit its DataBindings. Set the first Label's binding properties to be Text bound to item_name with the format set to "none" (Figure 6-11).

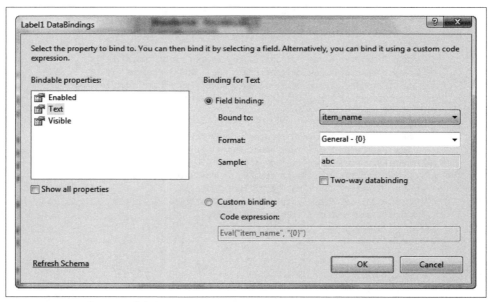

Figure 6-11. Binding your label

Now run the application. Depending on what you have in the database, you should wind up with a short list of items in on a plain white background.

To improve the UI, add this to the source:

```
<i>To-Do:</i>
<hr />
```

Switch to the source view and drop it in just below the following line:

```
<asp:Content ID="Content1"
    ContentPlaceHolderID="ContentPlaceHolder1"
    Runat="Server">
```

Back in the design view, return to your ReorderList and switch the view to DragHandleTemplate. Insert a `<DIV>` from the HTML toolbox and set the class to "dragHandle". Now switch back to the Item Template view and select the first Label you inserted earlier. Using the Properties inspector, set the font bold property to True.

Now, when you run the application, it should look like Figure 6-12.

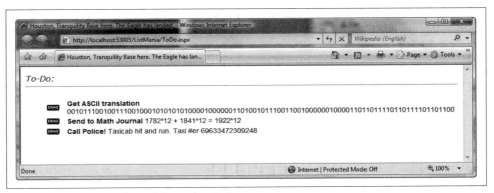

Figure 6-12. The start of a well-formed to-do list

You should be able to drag list items around, but as of yet these changes will not persist. To test this, move some items around using the drag handle and make a mental note of where they are. Then quit and restart the application. You will note that the items have returned to their original order. The next step takes care of this problem.

Persist the List

To ensure that changes to the list order persist, you need to create two methods and bind an action to the OnItemReorder property of the ReorderList. First, open up the *ToDo.aspx.cs* file and make sure you have referenced the following namespaces:

```
using System;
using System.Collections;
using System.Configuration;
using System.Data;
using System.Data.SqlClient;
using System.Linq;
```

```
using System.Web;
using System.Web.Security;
using System.Web.UI;
using System.Web.UI.HtmlControls;
using System.Web.UI.WebControls;
using System.Web.UI.WebControls.WebParts;
using System.Xml.Linq;
```

Now, add a method that will take care of writing updates to your database:

```
public void TalkToDatabaseUsingSQLConnectionAndSQLStatement(
    SqlConnection connection,
    String updateStatement)
{
    try
    {
        connection.Open();
        SqlCommand cmd = new SqlCommand(updateStatement, connection);
        cmd.CommandType = CommandType.Text;
        int rowsAffected = cmd.ExecuteNonQuery();
        if (rowsAffected == 0)
        {
            // Do something here to call attention to the fact
            // that your update has failed...
        }
        connection.Close();
    }

    catch (Exception ex_set_aside)
    {

        // Do something here to call attention to the fact
        // that something went wrong...
    }

    finally
    {
        connection.Close();
    }

}
```

The reason you are creating this method is that for each movement of a list item, you need to make several updates to the database. In other words, the same bit of logic will be used over and over in the method that you will call from OnItemReorder. You could use the "Cut-and-Paste" design pattern, but (while it may be handy) this is not considered good form. With this method in place, you are ready to code the next step.

Moving an item from one spot to another in the list using the drag handle sets off a chain of events. To handle this action correctly, bind a new event to OnItemReorder on your ReorderList. You can do this by going to the Properties inspector in the design view and viewing the available actions. From there, double-click on the

OnItemReorder action. You should be transported back to *ToDo.apsx.cs*, where a new empty method like this should be staring you in the face:

```
protected void ReorderList1_ItemReorder(object sender,
    AjaxControlToolkit.ReorderListItemReorderEventArgs e)
{

}
```

Change this method to make it look like the following:

```
protected void ReorderList1_ItemReorder(object sender,
    AjaxControlToolkit.ReorderListItemReorderEventArgs e)
{

    // We've been given the new and old index information
    // as part of the event args (e).
    int newIndex = e.NewIndex;
    int oldIndex = e.OldIndex;

    // So now we'll find the appropriate rows in the
    // database and update them.
    string connectionString =
        "Data Source=MERKWÜRDIGLIEBE\\SQLEXPRESS;
        Initial Catalog=ToDo;Integrated Security=True";
    SqlConnection connection = new SqlConnection(connectionString);

    try
    {
        connection.Open();

        // Get all the rows for this user and sort by item_priority.
        String fetchStatement = "SELECT * FROM ToDoItem WHERE
            id_fk_user = 3 ORDER BY item_priority";
        DataSet ds = new DataSet();
        SqlDataAdapter dataAdapter =
            new SqlDataAdapter(fetchStatement, connection);
        dataAdapter.Fill(ds, "CURRENT_TODOS");
        DataTable dataTable = ds.Tables["CURRENT_TODOS"];

        connection.Close();

        // Clone the stucture of the dataTable so we can
        // keep the current keys to access data with...
        DataTable reorderedDataTable = dataTable.Clone();
        DataTable dataTableWithSelectedItemRemoved =
            dataTable.Clone();

        // Smash through the data set and grab everything
        // that is not at the old index.
        int counter1 = dataTable.Rows.Count;
        for (int i = 0; i < counter1; i++)
        {
            if (i < oldIndex)
                dataTableWithSelectedItemRemoved.ImportRow(dataTable.Rows[i]);
```

```
        if (i > oldIndex)
            dataTableWithSelectedItemRemoved.ImportRow(dataTable.Rows[i]);
    }

    // Smash through the data set and put it all
    // back together again in the right order.
    int counter2 = dataTableWithSelectedItemRemoved.Rows.Count;
    for (int j = 0; j < counter2 + 1; j++)
    {
        if (j < newIndex) reorderedDataTable.ImportRow(
            dataTableWithSelectedItemRemoved.Rows[j]);
        if (j == newIndex) reorderedDataTable.ImportRow(
            dataTable.Rows[oldIndex]);
        if (j > newIndex) reorderedDataTable.ImportRow(
            dataTableWithSelectedItemRemoved.Rows[j - 1]);
    }

    // Now change the item_priority for each row based
    // on the new order of the rows in the DataTable.
    int counter3 = reorderedDataTable.Rows.Count;
    for (int k = 0; k < counter3; k++)
    {
        DataRow dr = reorderedDataTable.Rows[k];
        int idPK = Convert.ToInt32(dr["id_pk"]);

        String updateStatement =
            "UPDATE ToDoItem SET item_priority = " +
            k + " WHERE id_pk = " + idPK;
        TalkToDatabaseUsingSQLConnectionAndSQLStatement(
            connection, updateStatement);
    }

    // Et voila! Persistent database storage for
    // the items as reordered.
}
catch (Exception ex)
{
    // Do something here to call attention to the
    // fact that something went very wrong...
}

}
```

This listing is pretty straightforward. The first two lines are where you grab the old and new indexes of the item that was moved from the ReorderList:

```
// We've been given the new and old index information
// as part of the event args (e).
int newIndex = e.NewIndex;
int oldIndex = e.OldIndex;
```

The next lines deal with the fact that you need to have a database connection to read from and write to the database. This is handled for you:

```
string connectionString =
    "Data Source=MERKWÜRDIGLIEBE\\SQLEXPRESS;Initial Catalog=ToDo;
    Integrated Security=True";
SqlConnection connection = new SqlConnection(connectionString);
```

Change this connection string to one that makes sense for your environment.

With the SqlConnection in place, your goal is to grab the to-do items for the current user. For now, we'll assume this is the user with an id_fk_user of 3. Later, you will change the code to enable the application to grab the user's ID dynamically from the session, but for the moment, if you are using a restored copy of the database, this will work just fine. Otherwise, for each of the items you entered, make sure that id_fk_user is set to 3.

Once you have gotten back a DataSet and processed that into a DataTable, you are ready to walk through the rows and apply our update algorithm. Here's the section of code that gets you there:

```
// Hardcoded for "3" right now, we'll change this later.
string fetchStatement =
    "SELECT * FROM ToDoItem WHERE id_fk_user = 3";

DataRow returnValue = null;

DataSet ds = new DataSet();

try
{
    connection.Open();
    SqlDataAdapter dataAdapter =
        new SqlDataAdapter(fetchStatement, connection);
    dataAdapter.Fill(ds, "CURRENT_TODOS");
    DataTable dataTable = ds.Tables["CURRENT_TODOS"];
    connection.Close();
    int counter = dataTable.Rows.Count;
    int idOfRowThatMoved = -1;
```

The persistence algorithm sets aside the row that moved by giving it a new item_priority value of -1. Then, for each other row, a decision must be made about whether its item_priority value needs to be changed. Note that each time you update the list by dragging something to a new location, you're updating the row in question; you ensure that with the AND id_pk = "+idPK; at the end of each SQL statement. You work through all the rows, then circle back and update the row where the item_priority is -1 to its new value based on where you dragged it in the list.

The complete listing for *Default.aspx.cs* is now:

```
using System;
using System.Collections;
using System.Configuration;
using System.Data;
using System.Data.SqlClient;
using System.Linq;
```

```csharp
using System.Web;
using System.Web.Security;
using System.Web.UI;
using System.Web.UI.HtmlControls;
using System.Web.UI.WebControls;
using System.Web.UI.WebControls.WebParts;
using System.Xml.Linq;

public partial class ToDo : System.Web.UI.Page
{
    protected void Page_Load(object sender, EventArgs e)
    {

    }

    protected void ReorderList1_ItemReorder(object sender,
        AjaxControlToolkit.ReorderListItemReorderEventArgs e)
    {
        // We've been given the new and old index information
        // as part of the event args (e)
        int newIndex = e.NewIndex + 1;
        int oldIndex = e.OldIndex + 1;

        // So now we'll find the appropriate rows in the
        // database and update them in three steps.
        string connectionString =
            "Data Source=MERKWÜRDIGLIEBE\\SQLEXPRESS;
            Initial Catalog=ToDo;Integrated Security=True";

        SqlConnection connection = new SqlConnection(connectionString);

        // Get all the rows for this user.
        // Hardcoded for "3" right now, we'll change this later.
        string fetchStatement =
            "SELECT * FROM ToDoItem WHERE id_fk_user = 3";

        DataRow returnValue = null;

        DataSet ds = new DataSet();

        try
        {
            connection.Open();
            SqlDataAdapter dataAdapter =
                new SqlDataAdapter(fetchStatement, connection);
            dataAdapter.Fill(ds, "CURRENT_TODOS");
            DataTable dataTable = ds.Tables["CURRENT_TODOS"];
            connection.Close();
            int counter = dataTable.Rows.Count;
            int idOfRowThatMoved = -1;

            foreach ( DataRow dr in dataTable.Rows)
```

```csharp
{
    string updateStatement = "";
    int currentIndexOfDataRow =
        Convert.ToInt32(dr["item_priority"]);
    int idPK = Convert.ToInt32(dr["id_pk"]);

    if ( currentIndexOfDataRow == oldIndex )
    {
        // Set this aside for later treatment
        updateStatement = "UPDATE ToDoItem SET
            item_priority = -1
            WHERE id_pk = "+idPK;

        // We need to "remember" this row's ID
        idOfRowThatMoved = idPK;
    }
    else if (currentIndexOfDataRow != oldIndex)
    {
        if (oldIndex > newIndex)
        {
            if (currentIndexOfDataRow >= newIndex)
            {
                updateStatement =
                    "UPDATE ToDoItem SET item_priority = "
                    + (currentIndexOfDataRow + 1) +
                    " WHERE id_pk = "+idPK;
            }
        }
        else
        {
            if (currentIndexOfDataRow <= newIndex
                && currentIndexOfDataRow >= oldIndex )
            {
                updateStatement = "UPDATE ToDoItem
                    SET item_priority = "
                    + (currentIndexOfDataRow - 1) +
                    " WHERE id_pk = "+idPK;
            }
        }
    }
    else
    {
        // Do nothing here
    }

    UpdateDatabaseUsingSQLConnectionWithUpdateString(
        connection, updateStatement);

}

// Now come back and deal with the set-aside row
UpdateDatabaseUsingSQLConnectionWithUpdateString(
    connection, "UPDATE ToDoItem SET item_priority = "
    + newIndex + " WHERE id_pk = "+idOfRowThatMoved);
```

```
        }
        catch (Exception ex)
        {
            // Do something here to call attention to the fact
            // that something went very wrong...
        }
    }

    public void UpdateDatabaseUsingSQLConnectionWithUpdateString(
        SqlConnection connection,
        String updateStatement)
    {
        try
        {
            connection.Open( );
            SqlCommand cmd = new SqlCommand(updateStatement, connection);
            cmd.CommandType = CommandType.Text;
            int rowsAffected = cmd.ExecuteNonQuery( );
            if (rowsAffected == 0)
            {
                // Do something here to call attention to the fact
                // that your update has failed...
            }
            connection.Close( );
        }

        catch (Exception ex_set_aside)
        {

            // Do something here to call attention to the fact
            // that something went wrong...
        }

        finally
        {
            connection.Close( );
        }

    }
}
```

At this point, when you run your application any changes you make should persist. That is, you should be able to change the order of the list and see the results in the database, and you should be able to stop your application and have the list present itself in the same order it was last in when you restart it (Figure 6-13).

But what if you want to add items to your list? The ReorderList has an InsertItemTemplate. You'll add to this template a Panel, a couple of divs, and an HTML table, and bind in some TextBoxes. You'll top it all off with an asp:Button that will be bound to the ReorderList's built-in Insert statement.

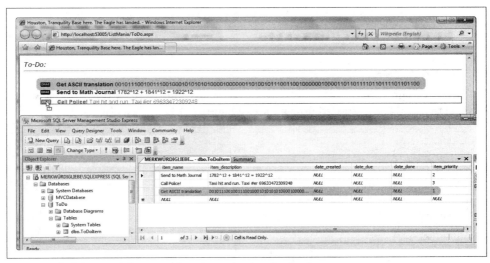

Figure 6-13. Position of the moved item is persisted to the database

In the source view, type the following snippet into the ReorderList element just before the </cc1:ReorderList> tag (the closing of the ReorderList element):

```
<InsertItemTemplate>
<div style="padding-left: 25px;border-bottom: thin solid transparent;">
    <asp:Panel ID="panel1" runat="server" DefaultButton="Button1">
    <hr />
        <div style="font-family: Verdana; color:Black;">
            Add a to do item:<br />
            <table>
                <tr>
                    <th>Item</th>
                    <th>Description</th>
                </tr>
                <tr>
                    <td>
                        <asp:TextBox ID="TextBox1" runat="server"
                            Text='<%# Bind("item_name") %>'>
                        </asp:TextBox>
                    </td>
                    <td>
                        <asp:TextBox ID="TextBox2" runat="server"
                            Text='<%# Bind("item_description") %>'>
                        </asp:TextBox>
                    </td>
                </tr>
            </table>
        </div>
        <br />
```

```
      <asp:Button ID="Button1" runat="server"
         CommandName="Insert" Text="Add">
      </asp:Button>
   </asp:Panel>
</div>
</InsertItemTemplate>
```

In the design view of *ToDo.aspx*, toggle the ReorderList's view to InsertItemTemplate. It should now look like Figure 6-14.

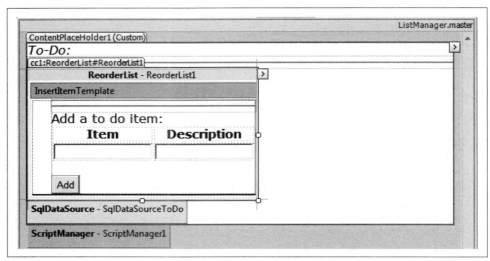

Figure 6-14. ReorderList with view of InsertItemTemplate

Run the application now. You should be able to add to-do items, change the order of the list items, and have your changes persist. The application should now look like Figure 6-15.

Personalizing the To-Do List

It would be nice to allow various members of your family (or office) to keep to-do lists, and to separate the lists based on the users' IDs. So next, you'll create a login form to ask the user to provide an email address and a password. We (the authors) hate being shunted off to a separate page to register, so we'll put the registration form right on the login page. Of course, you don't want the user to see the registration form unless it's needed, so you'll hide it in a collapsible panel that will swing open only if it's needed.

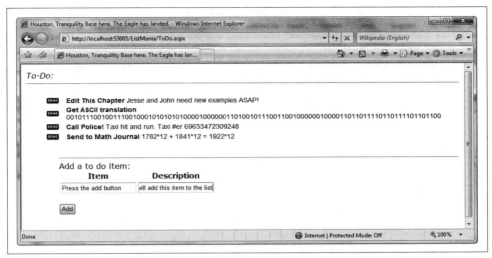

Figure 6-15. Application with the ability to add items

Confirm the Database Table

Make sure that your database contains the table shown in Figure 6-16. If this isn't the case, please create it now (normally we'd suggest that you use the forms-based security tables for ASP.NET, but for the purposes of this example this is faster).

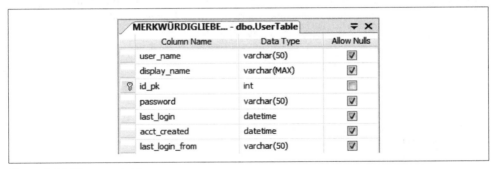

Figure 6-16. The users table

Create a DataHelper Class

In this section, you are going to talk the database more. The code that you used earlier in TalkToDatabaseUsingSQLConnectionAndSQLStatement( ) will turn out to be very handy here. Rather than cutting and pasting, you need to refactor!

Right-click on your web site in the Solution Explorer and select Add ASP.NET Folder → App_Code, as seen in Figure 6-17.

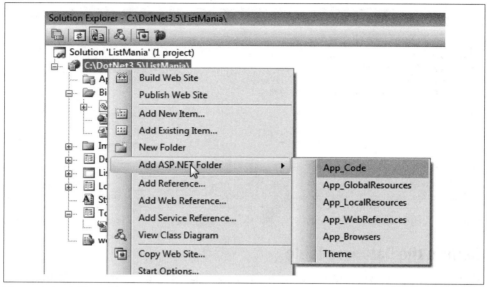

Figure 6-17. Adding the ASP.NET App_Code folder

Now, add a C# class to it called *DataHelper.cs* to the *App_Code* folder you just added to your project. The preliminary listing for this class is as follows:

```csharp
using System;
using System.Data;
using System.Data.SqlClient;
using System.Configuration;
using System.Text;

/// <summary>
/// Summary description for DataHelper
/// </summary>
public class DataHelper
{
    // Change your connection string as appropriate...
    private string connectionString = "Data
        Source=MERKWÜRDIGLIEBE\\SQLEXPRESS;
        Initial Catalog=ToDo;Integrated Security=True";
    private SqlConnection connection = new SqlConnection(connectionString);

    public DataHelper()
    {
        //
        // TODO: Add constructor logic here
        //
    }
```

```
public static void TalkToDatabaseUsingSQLConnectionAndSQLStatement(
    SqlConnection connection, String sqlStatement )
{
  try
  {
    connection.Open( );
    SqlCommand cmd = new SqlCommand(sqlStatement, connection);
    cmd.CommandType = CommandType.Text;
    int rowsAffected = cmd.ExecuteNonQuery( );
    if (rowsAffected == 0)
    {
        // Do something here to call attention to the fact
        // that your SQL statement has failed...
    }
    connection.Close( );
  }

  catch (Exception ex_set_aside)
  {

      // Do something here to call attention to
      // the fact that something went wrong...
  }

  finally
  {
      connection.Close( );
  }
 }
}
```

If this looks very familiar, it should—it is almost the same method you wrote in your *ToDo.aspx.cs* class. The only difference is that this method is static, which means you can use it without instantiating the class. This is where you refactor.

Return to your *ToDo.aspx.cs* class and rip out the version of this method that is there. Change the line of code inside ReorderList1_ItemReorder that currently says:

```
TalkToDatabaseUsingSQLConnectionAndSQLStatement(connection,
    updateStatement);
```

to this:

```
DataHelper.TalkToDatabaseUsingSQLConnectionAndSQLStatement(connection,
    updateStatement);
```

Build the application and watch it work as before. Now you will be able to use this method for the other methods you are going to write in your DataHelper class.

Add the following three methods to *DataHelper.cs*. You will use this first method to grab user data out of the database for the purposes of authorizing the user, as well as setting the user information held in the session:

```
public static SqlDataReader GetUserInfo(string userName, string pw)
{
```

```
      string cleanName = CleanText(userName);
      string cleanPW = CleanText(pw);

      string queryString = "Select * from UserTable where user_name = '" +
          cleanName + "' and password = '" + cleanPW + "'";
      SqlDataReader rdr = null;


      try
      {
         connection.Open( );
         SqlCommand cmd = new SqlCommand(queryString, connection);
         cmd.CommandType = CommandType.Text;
         rdr = cmd.ExecuteReader(CommandBehavior.CloseConnection);
      }
      catch (Exception ex)
      {
         // Exception! Probably a good idea to send yourself a copy of the insert
         // statement along with ex.message via email and figure out why.
      }
      // do not close connection until reader is done!
      return rdr;
   }
```

You will use this second method to create new users and insert them into the database:

```
   public static void InsertNewUser(
      string name,
      string email,
      string pw,
      DateTime accountCreated)
   {
      string cleanName = CleanText(name);
      string cleanEmail = CleanText(email);
      string cleanPW = CleanText(pw);

      string insertStatement = "Insert into UserTable ( user_name,
         display_name, password, acct_created, last_login ) " +
         " values ( '" + cleanEmail + "', '" + cleanName + "', '" +
         cleanPW + "', '" + accountCreated + "', '" + accountCreated + "')";
      DataHelper.TalkToDatabaseUsingSQLConnectionAndSQLStatement(connection,
         insertStatement);
   }
```

The last method will allow you to update the user's audit trail information with a timestamp after a successful login:

```
   public static void UpdateLastLogin(int userID, DateTime last_login)
   {
      string updateStatement = "Update UserTable set last_login =  '" +
         last_login.ToString() + "' where id_pk = " + userID;
      DataHelper.TalkToDatabaseUsingSQLConnectionAndSQLStatement(connection,
         updateStatement);
   }
```

Note that all three of these methods are static.

Create the Login Page

Create a new page, remembering to hook it to the Master Page as described earlier in this chapter. Name the new page *Login.aspx*. You'll define the layout of the new page with HTML tables rather than CSS.

 It is usually preferable to use CSS in web interface development these days, but in this case we feel it will be easier for you to visualize how all the parts come together if you use tables.

Insert the following snippet of code into *Login.aspx*, placing it inside the content placeholder tag with the ContentPlaceHolderID of "ContentPlaceHolder1":

```
<br /><br />
<center>
<table border="0" cellpadding="0" cellspacing="0" width="520">
   <tr>
      <td>
         <table border="0" cellpadding="0"
            cellspacing="0" width="100%">
            <tr>
               <td>
                  <img alt="border" src="images/table_left_login.gif" />
               </td>
               <td align="center"
                  style="background:
                  url(images/table_top.gif);
                  width:100%">
                  <b>Welcome! Please Sign In...</b>
               </td>
               <td>
                  <img alt="border" src="images/top_right.gif" />
               </td>
            </tr>
         </table>
      </td>
   </tr>
   <tr>
      <td align="left">
         <table border="0" cellpadding="0"
            cellspacing="0" width="100%">
            <tr>
               <td style="background:
                  url(images/background.gif)" >
                  <img alt="border" src="images/dot.gif" width="25" />
               </td>
               <td style="background-color:#F2FEE9;
                  width:100%" class="text10_search" >
                  <!-- We'll be inserting everything into the table below -->
                  <table style="background-color:#F2FEE9;
                     border:0"
                     cellpadding="0"
                     cellspacing="0">
```

```
            <tr>
                <td>

                <td>
            </tr>
        </table>
        <!-- End of Content Table -->
        </td>
        <td style="background:url(images/right.gif)">
            <img alt="border" src="images/dot.gif" width="22" />
        </td>
    </tr>
    </table>
    </td>
</tr>
<tr>
    <td colspan="3">
        <table border="0" cellpadding="0"
            cellspacing="0" width="100%">
        <tr>
            <td>
                <img alt="border" src="images/bottom_left.gif" />
            </td>
            <td style="background:url(images/bottom.gif);
                width:100%">
                 
            </td>
            <td>
                <img src="images/bottom_right.gif" alt="border" />
            </td>
        </tr>
        </table>
    </td>
</tr>
</table>
</center>
```

Notice the HTML comments. They are intended to guide your insertion of future code snippets:

```
<!-- We'll be inserting everything into the table below -->
<table style="background-color:#F2FEE9;
    border:0" cellpadding="0" cellspacing="0">
    <tr>
        <td>

        <td>
    </tr>
</table>
<!-- End of Content Table -->
```

The rest of the page will remain largely unmodified. If you view this page in a web browser now, you should see something that looks like Figure 6-18.

Figure 6-18. The Login page before we really get going

As you can see, we have an attractive starting point. Switch to the design view in Visual Studio. You will now be able to drag and drop the appropriate controls to continue development. Start by placing your cursor in the first column of the content table, as seen in Figure 6-19.

Figure 6-19. Cursor in the column of the content table

Type in "Enter your email address:" and hit the Tab key. Another table row should be created for you.

Next, drag and drop in a TextBox and set its ID property to UserNameTextBox. Hit Tab twice to insert a spacer row between the username and the next block of text you are going to enter. Type in the text "Password:" and hit Tab one more time.

Drag and drop in another TextBox, and add the PasswordStrength extender right away. Set the ID property to PasswordBox and the TextMode property to Password.

The PasswordStrength extender is used to extend a text box to indicate to the users the strength of the passwords they enter. That is, it gives users an indication of what your system expects from a password by providing instant feedback. If a user enters the string "abc" as the password, for example, the extender might indicate that the password chosen is "weak." View the page in a web browser to see how it works (Figure 6-20).

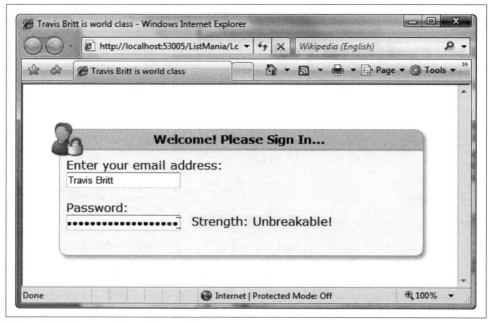

Figure 6-20. PasswordStrength extender in action

Hit the Tab key two more times, then drag and drop in an asp:ImageButton with the properties set as follows:

```
ID="LoginButton"
runat="server"
ImageUrl="~/images/signIn.gif"
OnClick="LoginButton_Click"
```

Hit Tab twice more.

With the OnClick property set, you will need to make sure the code-behind has a corresponding method. Add the following to your *Login.aspx.cs* file:

```
protected void LoginButton_Click( object sender, ImageClickEventArgs e )
{
    SqlDataReader rdr = null;
    int userID = -1;
    DateTime lastLogin = DateTime.Now;
    try
    {
        rdr = DataHelper.GetUserInfo(
            UserNameTextBox.Text, PasswordBox.Text );
        while ( rdr.Read( ) )
```

```
        {
            if ( rdr["user_name"] != null )
            {
                Session["user_name"] = rdr["user_name"].ToString( );
                Session["display_name"] = rdr["display_name"].ToString( );
                Session["id_pk"] = rdr["id_pk"].ToString( );

                if ( rdr["last_login"] != null )
                {
                    lastLogin = Convert.ToDateTime( rdr["last_login"] );
                    Session["last_login"] = lastLogin.ToShortDateString( )
                        + " - " +
                        lastLogin.ToShortTimeString( );

                }
                else
                {
                    lastLogin = DateTime.Now;
                    Session["last_login"] = lastLogin.ToShortDateString( )
                        + " - " + lastLogin.ToShortTimeString( );
                }
                userID = Convert.ToInt32( rdr["id_pk"] );
            }   // end if we have a user
        }       // end while
    }
    catch
    {
        // handle exception
    }
    finally
    {
        if ( rdr != null )
        {
            rdr.Close( );
            DataHelper.UpdateLastLogin( userID, DateTime.Now );
        }
    }

    if ( Session["display_name"] != null &&
         Session["display_name"].ToString( ).Length > 0 )
    {
        Response.Redirect( "ToDo.aspx" );
    }
}
```

You are now leveraging both the DataHelper class you wrote earlier and the Session to set up a personalized To-Do list on the *ToDo.aspx* page. But at this point you are in a bit of a bind (sorry, we put you here!), because you do not have any user accounts.

The CollapsiblePanelExtender Control

As noted earlier, if a user needs to create an account, you do not want to dispatch her to a new page to do so. Instead, your login page will have a button the user can press to display the registration form. You'll accomplish this by dragging and dropping in a Panel from the Standard toolbox. Set its ID property to Register_ContentPanel. Next, add an extender called CollapsiblePanelExtender.

Switch to the source view and make sure the extender's properties are configured like this:

```
<ajaxToolkit:
CollapsiblePanelExtender
    ID="cpeRegister"
    runat="Server"
    CollapseControlID="Register_HeaderPanel"
    Collapsed="True"
    CollapsedImage="images/expand.jpg"
    CollapsedText="Need To Register?"
    ExpandControlID="Register_HeaderPanel"
    ExpandDirection="Vertical"
    ExpandedImage="images/collapse.jpg"
    ExpandedText="All Done"
    ImageControlID="Register_ToggleImage"
    SuppressPostBack="true"
    TargetControlID="Register_ContentPanel"
>                                               </ajaxToolkit:
CollapsiblePanelExtender>
```

Make sure you change the contents of Register_HeaderPanel to:

```
<asp:Panel
    ID="Register_HeaderPanel"
    runat="server"
    Style="cursor: pointer;">
    <div class="heading">
        <asp:Image
            ID="Register_ToggleImage"
            runat="server"
            ImageUrl="images/collapse.jpg" />
        Need To Register?
    </div>
</asp:Panel>
```

Then add an additional Panel just below the Register_HeaderPanel panel and set it up like this:

```
<asp:Panel
    ID="Register_ContentPanel"
    runat="server"
    Style="overflow: hidden;">
    Registration content goes here...
</asp:Panel>
```

These are the two `Panels` that will be hidden and revealed (alternately) when your users interact with the toggle buttons. Return to the design view and run your application to see this in action.

Unfortunately, at the time of this writing, the design view does not afford you a quick and easy way of adding the registration content. You'll have to insert the following HTML in place of the text "Registration content goes here…":

```
<table id="Table1" runat="server" class="registerText">
    <tr>
        <td align="right">Name:</td>
        <td>
            <asp:TextBox ID="NameTextBox"
                runat="server"
                CssClass="unwatermarked" />
            <cc1:TextBoxWatermarkExtender
                ID="NameTBWME"
                runat="server"
                TargetControlID="NameTextBox"
                WatermarkCssClass="watermarked"
                WatermarkText="Your full name" />
            <br />
        </td>
    </tr>
    <tr>
        <td align="right">Email Address:</td>
        <td>
            <asp:TextBox ID="EmailAddressTextBox"
                runat="server"
                CssClass="unwatermarked" />
            <cc1:TextBoxWatermarkExtender
                ID="TextBoxWatermarkExtender1"
                runat="server"
                TargetControlID="EmailAddressTextBox"
                WatermarkCssClass="watermarked"
                WatermarkText="Your email address" />
            <br />
        </td>
    </tr>
    <tr>
        <td align="right">Password:</td>
        <td style="width: 360px">
            <asp:TextBox ID="PasswordTextBox"
                runat="server"
                TextMode="Password" />
            <br />
            <asp:Label ID="PasswordTextBox_HelpLabel"
                runat="server"></asp:Label>
            <cc1:PasswordStrength
                ID="PasswordStrengthControl"
                runat="server"
                DisplayPosition="RightSide"
                HelpStatusLabelID="PasswordTextBox_HelpLabel"
```

```
                    MinimumNumericCharacters="1"
                    MinimumSymbolCharacters="1"
                    PreferredPasswordLength="10"
                    PrefixText="Strength:"
                    RequiresUpperAndLowerCaseCharacters="false"
                    StrengthIndicatorType="Text"
                    TargetControlID="PasswordTextBox"
                    TextCssClass="StrengthIndicator"
                    TextStrengthDescriptions=
                        "Very Poor;Weak;Average;Strong;Excellent" />
            </td>
        </tr>
        <tr>
            <td></td>
            <td  align="Left">
                <asp:ImageButton
                    ID="RegisterImageButton"
                    runat="server"
                  ImageUrl="images/register.gif"
                    OnClick="RegisterImageButton_Click" />
            </td>
        </tr>
    </table>
```

Switching back to the design view should reveal something that looks like Figure 6-21.

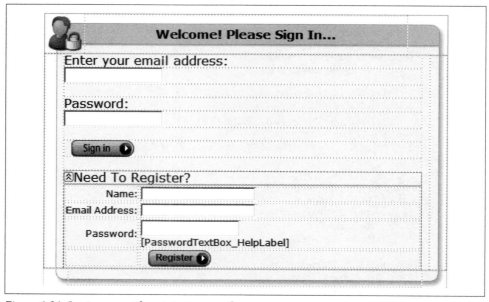

Figure 6-21. Login page with registration panel

To support the registration behavior, you have attached a `RegisterImageButton_`
`Click()` method to the `OnClick` event of the registration image button. You now need
to add this to your *Login.apsx.cs* file to get your application to run.

Here is the implementation:

```
protected void RegisterImageButton_Click( object sender,
    ImageClickEventArgs e )
{

    DataHelper.InsertNewUser(
        NameTextBox.Text,
        EmailAddressTextBox.Text,
        PasswordTextBox.Text,
        DateTime.Now );

    cpeRegister.Collapsed.Equals( true );   // close the accordion

    Response.Redirect( "Login.aspx" );

}
```

If you run your application now, it should handle registration for new users. You will
need to take care of a couple of housekeeping items before the application is fully
functional, though.

In *ListManager.master*, add the following lines just above `ContentPlaceHolder1`:

```
<center>
    <img src="http://alexhorovitz.com/images/list-mania.gif"
        alt="List Mania!" />
</center>
```

Then, in *ToDo.aspx.cs*, add the following to `Page_Load()`:

```
WelcomeUserName.Text = Session["display_name"].ToString();
LastLogin.Text = Session["last_login"].ToString();
SqlDataSourceToDo.SelectCommand = "SELECT * FROM [ToDoItem]
    WHERE id_fk_user = "+ Session["id_pk"].ToString() +
    " ORDER BY [item_priority]"
```

Next, turn to the source view of *ToDo.aspx* and add some HTML to take advantage
of these personalizing variables retrieved from the `Session`. In the main content area
just above `<i>To-Do:</i>`, add this:

```
Welcome: <asp:Label ID="WelcomeUserName" runat="server" Text="" />
Last Login:  <asp:Label ID="LastLogin" runat="server" Text="" />
<br /> <br />
```

Now find the `SqlDataSourceToDo` and remove the `SelectCommand` from the properties.

Returning to *ToDo.aspx.cs*, find the line inside ReorderList1_ItemReorder( ) that reads:

```
String fetchStatement =
    "SELECT * FROM ToDoItem WHERE id_fk_user = 3
    ORDER BY item_priority";
```

and change it to:

```
String fetchStatement =
    "SELECT * FROM ToDoItem WHERE id_fk_user = "
    + Session["id_pk"].ToString( )+
    " ORDER BY item_priority";
```

What you have done here is make sure that the data that gets loaded into this page will be for the logged-in user only. This means you can no longer run the *ToDo.aspx* page on its own; you must start at the *Login.aspx* page. You should set this to be the Start Page for this web site.

When you run the code now, you should have a fully functional multiuser list manager web application. Enjoy!

Introducing Silverlight: A Richer Web UI Platform

Microsoft has recently added another option in the spectrum running from ASP.NET (server-only) through AJAX (client code running JavaScript) to WPF (Windows-only). This new option is Silverlight, which offers two important improvements:

- Rich client-side controls running in a browser
- Cross-platform and cross-browser operation

Silverlight also incorporates a subset of the CLR and thus is able to run managed code and a carefully chosen subset of the .NET 3.5 Framework.

Silverlight leverages many of the advantages of .NET 3.5. However, it provides this power through the browser, allowing for all the deployment and platform-agnostic benefits that come with a browser-deployed application without giving up the rich interactivity of WPF.

In fact, Silverlight 2 (in beta at the time of this writing) is built on a subset of the WPF control model and uses the same markup language as WPF and WF (XAML).

Silverlight in One Chapter

Silverlight cannot be fully covered in one chapter; a comprehensive discussion would take a whole book. (In fact, it does—see the forthcoming book *Programming Silverlight 2* by Jesse Liberty and Tim Heuer, also from O'Reilly.) There are two possible approaches to providing an introduction in a single chapter: we can give you an overview of its myriad features, or we can show you how to code the most fundamental features. Neither is entirely satisfactory, so we'll do a bit of both.

The next section lists, extremely briefly, what is in Silverlight. The rest of this chapter introduces what it is like to use the basic controls to write a simple Silverlight data application.

The Breadth of Silverlight

Silverlight 2 offers a lot of features to support very rich interactive Internet applications. Some of the more important areas include:

Controls, events, and data
> These three topics make up the heart of this chapter, so we'll defer discussion of them for now.

Media
> Silverlight provides extensive support for both audio and video, including out-of-the-box media players. It also gives you the ability to use media, both interactively and combined with controls, to create new forms of compelling user interfaces.

Graphics
> Silverlight 2's graphics capabilities are quite advanced. The use of vector graphics allows for significant scaling, the engines provided are high-performance, and the ability to integrate transformations with animation allows for the creation of unprecedented browser-hosted graphics.

Text and fonts
> Silverlight enables the control and manipulation of fonts developed to allow WPF to provide a rich and rewarding interactive user interface. All of the transformation and animation effects available for graphic elements apply to text as well; taken together, Silverlight's manipulation and display of text are unprecedented for a cross-platform browser technology.

Streaming, syndication, and web services
> Silverlight applications can be provided on the client, or they can be streamed to the browser from a Microsoft or other server. Silverlight also supports syndication (e.g., via RSS) and exports data that web services can consume easily.

Advanced programming services
> Among the advanced services baked into Silverlight and available out of the box are Cryptography, Threading, Reflection, and Isolated Storage, the latter two of which are most often used either for maintaining state on the user's machine or for caching to improve performance.

Diving Deep: Building an Application

As developers, we like to sink our teeth into a new technology like Silverlight 2 by building a basic application. For us, that means a form that interacts with the user, with some business objects that represent data. The rest of this chapter will be devoted to exploring those aspects of Silverlight in a bit more depth.

To create this first example, open Visual Studio 2008 and click on Create Project. In the New Project window, create a C# project using the Silverlight Application template.

Pick a location for your application and give it a meaningful name. Be sure that you are building against the 3.5 Framework, as shown in Figure 7-1.

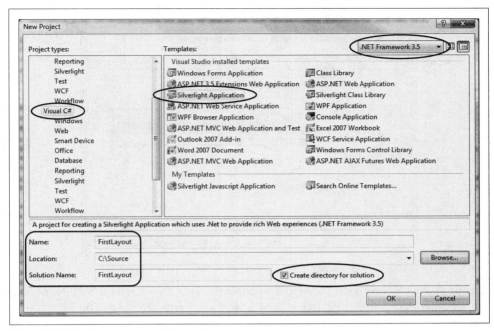

Figure 7-1. Creating a new project

When you click OK, you'll be asked if you'd like to generate a Web Site/Web Application (using the top radio button) or just a test page (using the bottom radio button), as shown in Figure 7-2.

If you create just a test page, the project remains very simple. If, however, you choose to generate a Web Site or Web Application Project, Visual Studio creates two projects in your new solution: the Silverlight Application and a test application. This is excellent for test-based programming, but it's more than we need right now, so stick with the test page.

Regardless of which option you select, Visual Studio sets up your development environment and guesses (incorrectly, this time) that you'd like to wrap your application in a Grid.

Controls

Silverlight 2 had more than two dozen user interface controls in beta, as shown in Figure 7-3.

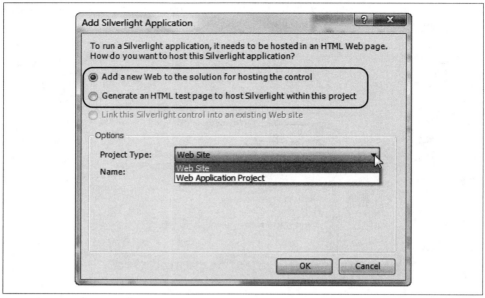

Figure 7-2. Choosing the application type

Layout of the UI controls is facilitated by three panel controls, which we'll explore in the sections that follow: the Canvas, the StackPanel, and the Grid. The final layout control is the Border control, which can be used to draw a border around one or more controls.

Canvases

The Canvas enables absolute positioning of controls. The default background color for a Canvas is transparent, and the default width and height are 0.

Every visible UI control will describe its position on the Canvas by referring to the Canvas's Left and Top properties (as you'll recall from Chapter 3, these are called *attached properties*). For example, the Button object might use the attached property Canvas.Left to position itself with respect to the left border of its surrounding Canvas:

```
<Canvas>
    <Button Canvas.Left="150" Canvas.Top="50"
        Content="I'm Indented!" />
</Canvas>
```

This will place the button 150 pixels to the right of the left border and 50 pixels down from the top border of the immediately surrounding Canvas, as shown in Figure 7-4.

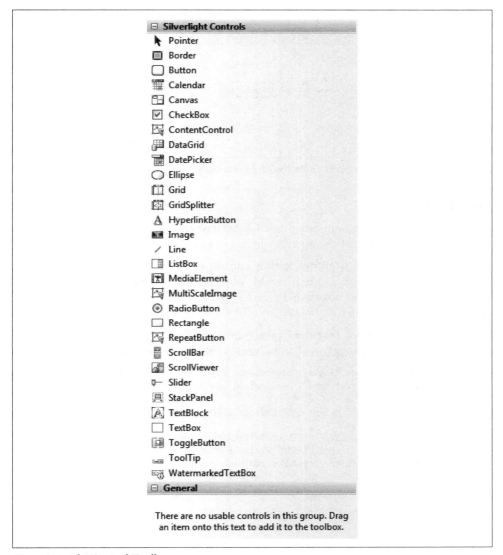

Figure 7-3. The Control Toolbox

 You may have noticed the apparent paradox that the Canvas defaults to a width and height of 0×0 pixels, yet you often position an object "in" the canvas (e.g., at Canvas.Left="150" Canvas.Top="50"). This works *as if* the canvas had a height and width large enough to encompass all its controls. In other words, you will get the expected behavior even if the canvas is technically too small.

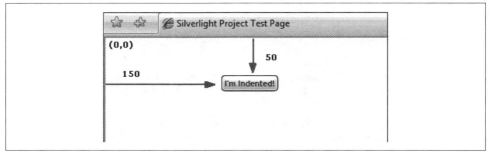

Figure 7-4. *Using attached properties for absolute positioning*

StackPanels

StackPanels are typically combined with other layout controls. They allow you to stack objects one on top of the other, or next to each other (like books on a shelf).

One convenience of a StackPanel is that you do not have to provide the absolute positions of the objects it holds; the first object is positioned relative to the container, and all others are positioned relative to the previous object declared in the StackPanel.

This code snippet stacks a TextBlock on top of a TextBox, which in turn sits on top of a Button, which itself sits on top of a CheckBox (shades of Yertle the Turtle!):

```
<StackPanel Background="Bisque" Orientation="Vertical" >
    <TextBlock Text="First Name?" HorizontalAlignment="Left"
        Margin="10,2,0,1" />
    <TextBox Width="150" Height="30" HorizontalAlignment="Left"
        Margin="10,2,0,1" />
    <Button Content="Submit!" HorizontalAlignment="Left"
        Margin="10,2,0,1" Height="30" Width="150" />
    <CheckBox Content="With Zing!" HorizontalAlignment="Left"
        Margin="10,2,0,1" />
</StackPanel>
```

There's quite a bit of information in this code snippet, so let's unpack it piece by piece.

The top and bottom lines are the open and close element tags for the StackPanel. This StackPanel is declared with two attributes: a BackgroundColor and an Orientation (which must be either Vertical or Horizontal).

As with most controls, there are numerous attributes you can set. All the properties and methods are conveniently listed in the documentation, as shown in Figure 7-5.

By setting the Orientation to Vertical, you indicate that the contents should be stacked one on top of another rather than side by side.

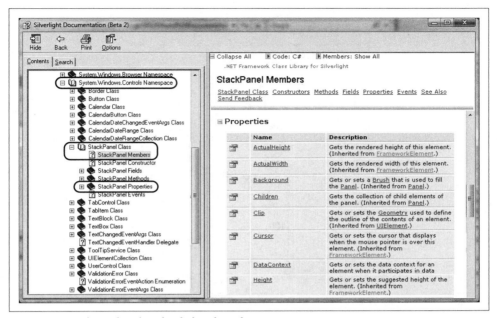

Figure 7-5. *StackPanel in the Silverlight 2 beta documentation*

The four objects are declared within the StackPanel, and the order of their declaration determines the order in which they are stacked. The TextAlignment property of each is set to Left so that they will align along the left side, and each has its Margin property set.

The Margin property is actually an object of type Thickness. The documentation states that when you declare a Thickness object in XAML, you may do so in one of three ways.

The first option is to provide a double that will be the value for the margin on all four sides (left, top, right, and bottom) uniformly around the object. Thus, you might write:

```
<Button Content="Submit!" HorizontalAlignment="Left"
    Margin="100" Height="30" Width="150" />
```

This isolates the button with a margin of 100 pixels on either side and above and below, as shown in Figure 7-6.

Notice that to accommodate the oversized margin, the width of the button was compromised!

The second way to declare a Thickness (and, in this case, a Margin) is to provide the sum of the sides and the sum of the top and bottom:

```
<Button Content="Submit!" HorizontalAlignment="Left"
    Margin="50,20" Height="30" Width="150" />
```

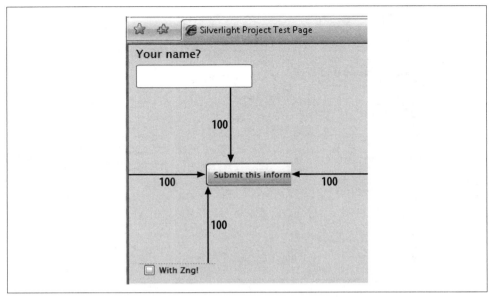

Figure 7-6. Using a margin of 100

The sides must be equal and the top and bottom must be equal, so the effect of this declaration is that the left and right margins are each 25 pixels and the top and bottom margins are each 10 pixels.

Finally, you may declare each margin independently, as long as you do so in the required order (shown in Figure 7-7).

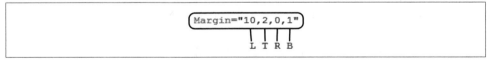

Figure 7-7. Margin values

That is, you must declare first the left margin, then the top, right, and bottom margins in that order. In this case, the left margin is 10 pixels, the top margin is 2, the right margin is 0, and the bottom margin is 1.

Once you've aligned the four controls in the StackPanel, the StackPanel is responsible for their placement, as shown in Figure 7-8.

Notice that the StackPanel is responsible for its own background color and for stacking its contents (the four controls), but each control is responsible for its own alignment and margins.

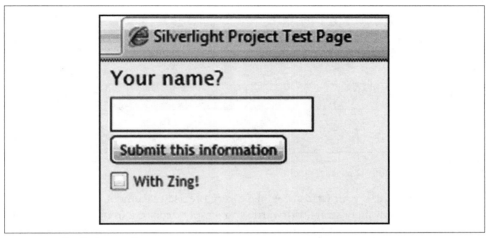

Figure 7-8. Stacked controls

Horizontal StackPanels

If you want the StackPanel to align all the controls into a single row rather than one on top of another, you'll need to make a few changes. Not all controls default to aligning in the same way (top, center, or bottom), so in this example you'll explicitly set the vertical alignment of the controls to Center, just as you previously set their horizontal alignment to Left. You'll also set the margins to provide a bit of space between each object, as the default is for them to abut one another:

```
<StackPanel Background="Bisque" Orientation="Horizontal" >
    <TextBlock Text="First Name?" VerticalAlignment="Center"
        Margin="10,2,0,1" />
    <TextBox Width="150" Height="30" VerticalAlignment="Center"
        Margin="5,2,0,1" />
    <Button Content="Submit!" VerticalAlignment="Center"
        Margin="10,2,0,1" Height="30" Width="150" />
    <CheckBox Content="With Zing!" VerticalAlignment="Center"
        Margin="10,2,0,1" />
</StackPanel>
```

Note that the left margin on the TextBox is set to 5 (rather than 10) pixels. This brings it a bit closer to the TextBlock that serves as its label, as shown in Figure 7-9.

Grids

Grids enable easy placement of controls by providing a table-like structure. You declare rows and columns, then place controls into specific row/column locations using attached properties.

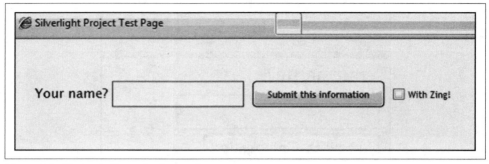

Figure 7-9. Horizontally stacked controls

While you can tweak your Grids to achieve very precise placement, the fundamental use of Grids is extremely straightforward: you simply declare a Grid, declare its rows and columns, and then start placing controls into cells.

To see this at work, start a new Silverlight project called *SimpleGrid*. Note that Visual Studio automatically creates a Grid for you. The code that follows names the Grid and defines the rows and columns. Notice that you can also designate the minimum, maximum, and/or exact size for each row and column:

```
<Grid x:Name="LayoutRoot" Background="Beige" ShowGridLines="True">
    <Grid.RowDefinitions>
        <RowDefinition Height="15" /> <!--Margin-->
        <RowDefinition MinHeight="10" MaxHeight="50" />
        <RowDefinition MinHeight="10" MaxHeight="50" />
        <RowDefinition MinHeight="10" MaxHeight="50" />
        <RowDefinition MinHeight="10" MaxHeight="50" />
        <RowDefinition Height="*" />
        <RowDefinition Height="15" />  <!--Margin-->
    </Grid.RowDefinitions>

    <Grid.ColumnDefinitions>
        <ColumnDefinition Width="10" />        <!--0 Margin-->
        <ColumnDefinition Width="200" />       <!--1 Left -->
        <ColumnDefinition Width="15" />        <!--2 Padding-->
        <ColumnDefinition Width="*" />         <!--3 Right-->
        <ColumnDefinition Width="10" />        <!--4 Margin-->
    </Grid.ColumnDefinitions>
```

The declaration of this Grid sets ShowGridLines to True. This causes the gridlines to be visible, which can be very handy when you're laying out your Grid (see Figure 7-10).

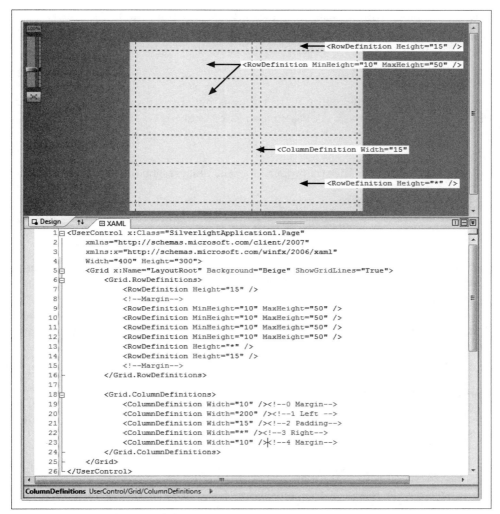

Figure 7-10. Row and column definitions

The first block within the Grid defines the rows. The first and last rows each have a fixed height of 15 pixels and define the top and bottom margins. All the other rows (except the penultimate) define their minimum and maximum heights and are set by the Grid based on the available room within those parameters. The next-to-last row has its height set to *, meaning it will take all the remaining room (this is why it's larger).

The second block within the Grid defines the sizes for the columns. In this case, all the columns except the next-to-last have fixed widths. Numbering the columns, as is done here in the comments, makes placing objects in their cells trivial.

Sizing rows and columns

To provide the most flexibility, Grid columns and rows are sized by GridLength objects. Each GridLength object has an associated GridUnitType, which in turn allows you to choose among:

Auto
> The size is based on the size properties of the object being placed in the Grid.

Pixel
> An exact size in pixels is specified.

Star
> The size is based on a weighted proportion of the available space.

In proportional sizing, the size value of a column or row is expressed in XAML as *. However, you can assign twice the available space to one column or row as another by using 2* (similarly, you could give two columns or rows a 5:7 ratio by using the values 5* and 7*). If you combine this with HorizontalAlignment and VerticalAlignment, which default to a value of Stretch (indicating that the cell will fill the available area), you can assign the available space in whatever proportions you choose without assigning absolute values.

Placing controls into cells

The first four controls you'll add will prompt for and accept the user's first and last names. You'll also give the TextBoxes a background color:

```
<TextBlock Text="First Name" HorizontalAlignment="Right"
    Grid.Column="1" Grid.Row="1" VerticalAlignment="Bottom"/>
<TextBox x:Name="First" Width="150" Height="30"
    HorizontalAlignment="Left" Grid.Column="3" Grid.Row="1"
    VerticalAlignment="Bottom" Background="Bisque"/>

<TextBlock Text="Last Name" HorizontalAlignment="Right"
    Grid.Column="1" Grid.Row="2" VerticalAlignment="Bottom"/>
<TextBox x:Name="Last" Width="150" Height="30"
    HorizontalAlignment="Left" Grid.Column="3" Grid.Row="2"
    VerticalAlignment="Bottom" Background="Bisque"/>
```

The TextBlocks each serve as prompts to the TextBoxes. Since you'll need to access the TextBoxes programmatically, they are each named. To ensure correct alignment, all the controls have their VerticalAlignment properties set to Bottom.

In addition, all the controls in the left column are aligned to the right, and all the controls in the right column are aligned to the left, so they abut the padding columns. Running the partially complete program (leaving the gridlines on) gives you the screen shown in Figure 7-11.

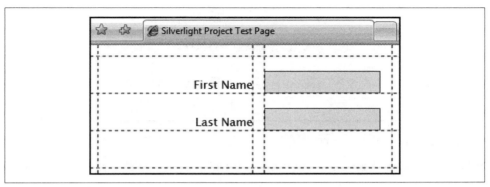

Figure 7-11. Grid alignment

Now let's add two checkboxes after a prompt. If you just put the two checkboxes into the same cell in the Grid they'd be placed one on top of the other, so instead you'll put them into a StackPanel, which will be responsible for setting them next to one another:

```
<TextBlock Text="Technical Skills " HorizontalAlignment="Right"
    Grid.Column="1" Grid.Row="3" VerticalAlignment="Bottom"/>

<StackPanel Orientation="Horizontal" VerticalAlignment="Bottom"
    HorizontalAlignment="Right" Grid.Column="3" Grid.Row="3" >
  <CheckBox x:Name="DotNet" Content=".NET" Width="50" Height="30" />
  <CheckBox x:Name="CSharp" Content="C#" Width="50"
      Height="30" Margin="5,0,0,0" />
  <CheckBox x:Name="Silverlight" Content="VB" Width="50"
      Height="30" Margin="5,0,0,0" />
</StackPanel>
```

Now set the ShowGridLines property of the Grid to False and run the program again. The effect is shown in Figure 7-12.

Events and Event Handlers

There are two ways to declare event handlers in Silverlight 2. The first is directly in the XAML:

```
<Button x:Name="myPushyButton" Content="Click Me Please" Height="30"
    Width="100" Grid.Column="1" Grid.Row="4" Click="myPushyButton_Click"
/>
```

Figure 7-12. The completed Grid

When you declare a button in the XAML, IntelliSense is available to help you create the event handler name (as shown in Figure 7-13).

```
<Button x:Name="myPushyButton" Content="Click Me Please" Height="30"
    Grid.Column="1" Grid.Row="4" Click="|    />
                                    <New Event Handler>
```

Figure 7-13. Inline event handler

If you use IntelliSense to wire the event handler, a skeleton event handler method is created in the code-behind (*Page.xaml.cs*):

```
private void myPushyButton_Click(object sender, RoutedEventArgs e
{
    myPushyButton.Width *= 1.25;
    myPushyButton.Content = "Thanks, I needed that!";
}
```

The first thing to notice is that the name of the method is identical to that declared in the XAML.

The second is that this method follows the pattern of all .NET event handlers: it returns void and takes two parameters. The first is of type object and contains a reference to the object that raised the event. The second is of type EventArgs, or a type that derives from EventArgs (in this case, RoutedEventArgs). Also notice that nowhere in the code-behind do you see anything like this:

```
Button myPushyButton = GetTheButtonIDeclaredinTheXAML
```

Any object declared in the XAML is available in the code-behind (and fully type-safe) as soon as you save the XAML file. This is wonderfully convenient.

In this case, the actual event handler grows the width of the button by 125% and then changes its contents, as shown in Figure 7-14.

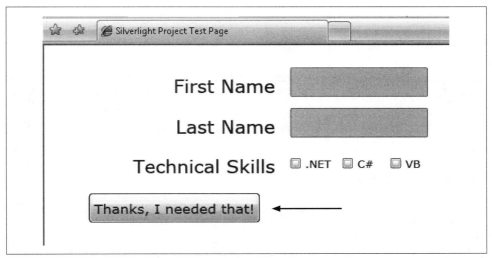

Figure 7-14. After clicking MyPushyButton

Declaring Event Handlers in Code

We admit it: we have a strong preference for declaring all event handlers in code. We believe it provides better encapsulation, making for more scalable and more maintainable code. However, this is a personal opinion.

We've settled into a pattern of wiring up the Loaded event in the Page's constructor and all the other events in the OnLoaded event handler. Thus, we strip out the event from the Button's XAML and modify the code-behind as shown in Example 7-1.

Example 7-1. Code-behind for event handlers

```
public partial class Page : UserControl
{
    public Page( )
    {
        InitializeComponent( );
        Loaded += new RoutedEventHandler(Page_Loaded);
    }

    void Page_Loaded(object sender, RoutedEventArgs e)
    {
        myPushyButton.Click +=new RoutedEventHandler(myPushyButton_Click);

    }
```

Example 7-1. Code-behind for event handlers (continued)

```
private void myPushyButton_Click(object sender, RoutedEventArgs e)
{
    myPushyButton.Width *= 1.25;
    myPushyButton.Content = "Thanks, I needed that!";
}
}
```

In this example the constructor adds the handler for the Loaded event, which fires when the page is loaded. That event handler in turn adds the handler for when the button is clicked. Putting all the event handler code in the code-behind makes it easier to locate and maintain, and it means only one file is affected if your event-handling logic needs to change.

The Content Property

Have you noticed that where you might expect Button to have a Text property, instead it has a Content property? This allows a Button to contain more than just text: in fact, it can contain almost anything, including other controls. We'll leave a discussion of *why* you might want to do this—and of the fact that doing so can make for ugly, unusable controls—for another time. The fact is you can, and there is no doubt that at times this will be a good thing.

As a quick illustration, take a look at Example 7-2. This example is called *Bubbling* (the reason for its name will be made clear in the next section).

Example 7-2. Button with CheckBoxes in its contents

```
<Grid x:Name="LayoutRoot" Background="White">
    <Grid.RowDefinitions>
        <RowDefinition Height="10" />
        <RowDefinition Height="50" />
        <RowDefinition Height="10" />
    </Grid.RowDefinitions>
    <Grid.ColumnDefinitions>
        <ColumnDefinition Width="10" />
        <ColumnDefinition Width="250" />
        <ColumnDefinition Width="15" />
        <ColumnDefinition Width="*" />
        <ColumnDefinition Width="10" />
    </Grid.ColumnDefinitions>

    <Button x:Name="SetFeatures" Height="40" Width="250"
        Background="Blue" Grid.Row="1" Grid.Column="1">
        <Button.Content>
            <StackPanel x:Name="Features" Orientation="Horizontal"
                VerticalAlignment="Bottom" >
```

Example 7-2. Button with CheckBoxes in its contents (continued)

```
            <CheckBox x:Name="Soft2" Content="Soft" Width="50"
                Height="40" Margin="5,0,0,0" />
            <CheckBox x:Name="Cozy" Content="Cozy" Width="50"
                Height="40" />
            <CheckBox x:Name="Warm" Content="Warm" Width="60"
                Height="40" />
            <CheckBox x:Name="Happy" Content="Happy" Width="60"
                Height="40" />
        </StackPanel>
    </Button.Content>
  </Button>
  <TextBlock x:Name="FeaturesEffects" Grid.Row="1" Grid.Column="3"
      Text="Waiting...." VerticalAlignment="Center"
      HorizontalAlignment="Left" />

</Grid>
```

The result is a button that contains four checkboxes. The checkboxes can be checked and the button can be pressed, as shown in Figure 7-15.

Figure 7-15. Button with checkboxes

Property elements

Take a careful look at the declaration of the Button. Note that the Content property is called out explicitly (Button.Content). This is called a *property element*. Content is often marked as an inline property of Button, but you can use this alternative syntax if you wish to explicitly fill the content with its own elements.

Thus, you can write code like this:

```
<Button Content="hello" />
```

Or like this:

```
<Button>
    <Button.Content>
        <TextBlock Text="Hello" />
    </Button.Content>
</Button>
```

In Example 7-2, within the Content property element a StackPanel is created, and within the StackPanel are the four CheckBox declarations (the first has a margin set to keep it from abutting the left edge of the StackPanel).

Creating Controls Dynamically

In Silverlight 2, anything you can create in XAML you can create in code.

Thus, where you might write this in XAML:

```
<Button x:Name="myButton" Content="Hello" />
```

You can also write this in code:

```
Button myButton = new Button( );
myButton.Content = "Hello";
```

You *could* create all of your objects in code, but even though it takes some getting used to, writing them in XAML has tremendous advantages. The most significant is that XAML is highly toolable. A toolable language lends itself to being manipulated and maintained by tools such as Expression Blend and Visual Studio 2008, and that makes for programs that are much easier to maintain.

That said, you will still need to create objects dynamically when you can't know at design time which objects, or how many, are required. This is especially true with data-driven applications, where the design of the form or the user interface will be dictated by user interactions and lookups in a database.

In the next example, you'll ask the user which platform he is building for ("Web" or "Desktop") and then dynamically create checkboxes based on the user's choice, as shown in Figure 7-16.

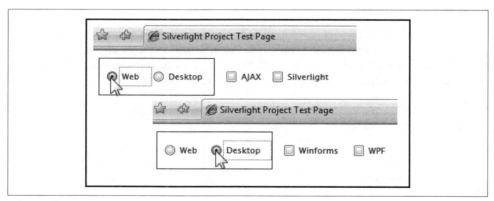

Figure 7-16. Dynamic creation of controls

If the user clicks on "Web," you dynamically create two checkboxes in a StackPanel and add them to the righthand column of the Grid. If the user clicks on "Desktop," you clear that column and fill the StackPanel with two new checkboxes.

The XAML lays out the controls that are not dynamic:

```xml
<Grid x:Name="LayoutRoot" Background="White">
   <Grid.RowDefinitions>
      <RowDefinition Height="10" />
      <RowDefinition Height="50" />
      <RowDefinition Height="10" />
   </Grid.RowDefinitions>
   <Grid.ColumnDefinitions>
      <ColumnDefinition Width="10" />
      <ColumnDefinition Width="150" />
      <ColumnDefinition Width="15" />
      <ColumnDefinition Width="*" />
      <ColumnDefinition Width="10" />
   </Grid.ColumnDefinitions>
   <Border BorderBrush="Black" BorderThickness="1"
       Grid.Column="1" Grid.Row="1" >
       <StackPanel x:Name="Choice" Orientation="Horizontal"  >
          <RadioButton x:Name="Web" Content="Web"
              Width="60" Height="30" Margin="10,0,0,0" />
          <RadioButton x:Name="Desk" Content="Desktop"
              Width="80" Height="30" />
       </StackPanel>
   </Border>
</Grid>
```

Notice that the only controls created are the two radio buttons in the lefthand column.

All the action is in the event handlers for these radio buttons. To keep things simple, you'll give each radio button its own event handler and declare an enumerated constant as a flag to indicate which is pressed:

```csharp
private enum Platform { Web, Desktop } ;
private StackPanel dynamicStackPanel = null;
public Page( )
{
   InitializeComponent( );
   Loaded += new RoutedEventHandler(Page_Loaded);
}

void Page_Loaded(object sender, RoutedEventArgs e)
{
   Web.Checked += new RoutedEventHandler(Web_Checked);
   Desk.Checked += new RoutedEventHandler(Desk_Checked);
}

void Desk_Checked(object sender, RoutedEventArgs e)
{
   SetChoices(Platform.Desktop);
}

void Web_Checked(object sender, RoutedEventArgs e)
{
   SetChoices(Platform.Web);
}
```

Here is the code for the SetChoices( ) method:

```
private void SetChoices(Platform platform)
{
    if ( dynamicStackPanel != null )
        dynamicStackPanel.Children.Clear( );

    dynamicStackPanel = new StackPanel( );
    dynamicStackPanel.Orientation = Orientation.Horizontal;
    dynamicStackPanel.SetValue(Grid.RowProperty, 1);
    dynamicStackPanel.SetValue(Grid.ColumnProperty, 3);
    if (platform == Platform.Desktop)
    {
        CheckBox cb = new CheckBox( );
        cb.Content = "Winforms";
        cb.Height = 30;
        cb.Width = 90;
        dynamicStackPanel.Children.Add(cb);
        cb = new CheckBox( );
        cb.Content = "WPF";
        cb.Height = 30;
        cb.Width = 50;
        dynamicStackPanel.Children.Add(cb);
    }
    else
    {
        CheckBox cb = new CheckBox( );
        cb.Content = "AJAX";
        cb.Height = 30;
        cb.Width = 60;
        dynamicStackPanel.Children.Add(cb);
        cb = new CheckBox( );
        cb.Content = "Silverlight";
        cb.Height = 30;
        cb.Width = 90;
        dynamicStackPanel.Children.Add(cb);
    }
    LayoutRoot.Children.Add(dynamicStackPanel);
}
```

Making the StackPanel a member variable makes it trivial to clear out its children as we switch between "Desktop" and "Web":

```
if ( dynamicStackPanel != null )
    dynamicStackPanel.Children.Clear( );
```

The StackPanel is then set up for either case, "Web" or "Desktop":

```
dynamicStackPanel = new StackPanel( );
dynamicStackPanel.Orientation = Orientation.Horizontal;
dynamicStackPanel.SetValue(Grid.RowProperty, 1);
dynamicStackPanel.SetValue(Grid.ColumnProperty, 3);
```

Notice how the attached properties are handled in code, using the SetValue( ) method of the StackPanel and passing in the attached property (Grid.RowProperty) and the value to which it should be set.

Once that is done, you create the controls based on which button was chosen, dynamically creating the checkboxes, setting their properties, and adding them to the Children collection of the StackPanel:

```
cb = new CheckBox( );
cb.Content = "WPF";
cb.Height = 30;cb.Width = 50;
dynamicStackPanel.Children.Add(cb);
```

Once all the children are added to the StackPanel, you must add the StackPanel to the Grid:

```
LayoutRoot.Children.Add(dynamicStackPanel);
```

That's all it takes; adding the CheckBox controls to the StackPanel and then the StackPanel to the Grid makes the checkboxes instantly visible and usable.

Data Binding

A *data binding* is a connection between the user interface and a business object or other data provider. The user interface object is called the *target*, and the provider of the data is called the *source*.

Data binding assists with the separation of the user-interface layer of your application from its other layers (business objects, data, and so forth).

Separation of the UI layer from the underlying layers is accomplished through a Binding object, which has two modes: one-way and two-way. One-way binding displays data from the source in the target; two-way binding also updates the source in response to changes made in the user interface.

Binding to a Business Object

To see one-way and two-way binding at work, create a new Silverlight Application named *BookDisplay*. Add to the application a *Book.cs* file, which will represent the business layer.

What separates a Silverlight business object from one created for a platform like ASP.NET is that you want the business object to participate in one-way or two-way binding with the UI layer. If you want the UI to be updated every time the business object changes (for example, if the quantity on hand changes), the business object must implement the INotifyPropertyChanged interface. This interface requires the class to have an event of the type PropertyChangedEventHandler (named

PropertyChanged by convention). Implicit in supporting binding, however, is that your business object must, by convention, fire the PropertyChanged event when any property that is tied to a UI control is set or cleared.

Place the code in Example 7-3 in the *Book.cs* file.

Example 7-3. Book class

```csharp
using System.ComponentModel;
using System.Collections;
using System.Collections.Generic;

namespace BookDisplay
{
    public class Book : INotifyPropertyChanged
    {
        private string bookTitle;
        private string bookAuthor;
        private int quantityOnHand;
        private bool multipleAuthor;
        private string authorURL;
        private string authorWebPage;
        private List<string> myChapters;

        // implement the required event for the interface
        public event PropertyChangedEventHandler PropertyChanged;

        public string Title
        {
            get { return bookTitle; }
            set
            {
                bookTitle = value;
                NotifyPropertyChanged("Title");
            }
        }
        public string Author
        {
            get { return bookAuthor; }
            set
            {
                bookAuthor = value;
                NotifyPropertyChanged("Author");
            }
        }

        public List<string> Chapters
        {
            get { return myChapters; }
            set
            {
                myChapters = value;
```

Example 7-3. Book class (continued)

```
            NotifyPropertyChanged("Chapters");
        }
    }

    public bool MultipleAuthor
    {
        get { return multipleAuthor; }
        set
        {
            multipleAuthor = value;
            NotifyPropertyChanged("MultipleAuthor");
        }
    }

    public int QuantityOnHand
    {
        get { return quantityOnHand; }
        set
        {
            quantityOnHand = value;
            NotifyPropertyChanged("QuantityOnHand");
        }
    }

    // factoring out the call to the event
    public void NotifyPropertyChanged(string propertyName)
    {
        if (PropertyChanged != null)
        {
            PropertyChanged(this,
                new PropertyChangedEventArgs(propertyName));
        }
    }
  }
}
```

Note that each of the properties must use its full form and have a backing variable because you do work in the Setter; specifically, you call NotifyPropertyChanged, which checks whether the PropertyChanged event is registered (presumably by the UI). If it is, it fires the event with a new PropertyChangedEventArgs object that contains the name of the property.

The user interface for this application doesn't contain anything new: it consists of two columns, with TextBlocks for prompts and a ListBox, a CheckBox, a TextBox, and a Button for interacting with the user. We'll take a closer look at the Button after the listing, presented in Example 7-4 (I've left out the row and column definitions to save space).

Example 7-4. XAML for binding data

```
<Grid x:Name="LayoutRoot" Background="White">

    <TextBlock x:Name="TitlePrompt" Text="Title:   "
        VerticalAlignment="Bottom"
        HorizontalAlignment="Right"
        Grid.Row="0" Grid.Column="0" />
    <TextBlock x:Name="Title"
        Text="{Binding Title, Mode=OneWay }"
        VerticalAlignment="Bottom"
        HorizontalAlignment="Left"
        Grid.Row="0" Grid.Column="1" />

    <TextBlock x:Name="AuthorPrompt" Text="Author: "
        VerticalAlignment="Bottom"
        HorizontalAlignment="Right"
        Grid.Row="1" Grid.Column="0" />
    <TextBlock x:Name="Author"
        Text="{Binding Author, Mode=OneWay }"
        VerticalAlignment="Bottom"
        HorizontalAlignment="Left"
        Grid.Row="1" Grid.Column="1" />

    <TextBlock x:Name="ChapterPrompt" Text="Chapters:   "
        VerticalAlignment="Bottom"
        HorizontalAlignment="Right"
        Grid.Row="2" Grid.Column="0" />

    <ListBox x:Name="Chapters"
        ItemsSource="{Binding  Chapters, Mode=OneWay}"
        VerticalAlignment="Bottom"
        HorizontalAlignment="Left"
        Height="80" Width="200"
        Grid.Row="2" Grid.Column="1" />

    <TextBlock x:Name="MultipleAuthorPrompt"
        Text="Multiple authors?:   "
        VerticalAlignment="Bottom"
        HorizontalAlignment="Right"
        Grid.Row="3" Grid.Column="0" />

    <CheckBox x:Name="MultipleAuthor"
        IsChecked="{Binding MultipleAuthor, Mode=TwoWay}"
        VerticalAlignment="Bottom"
        HorizontalAlignment="Left"
        Grid.Row="3" Grid.Column="1" />
```

Example 7-4. XAML for binding data (continued)

```
<TextBlock x:Name="QOHPrompt"
    Text="Quantity On Hand:  "
    VerticalAlignment="Bottom"
    HorizontalAlignment="Right"
    Grid.Row="4" Grid.Column="0" />

<TextBox x:Name="QuantityOnHand"
    Text="{Binding QuantityOnHand, Mode=TwoWay}"
    VerticalAlignment="Bottom"
    HorizontalAlignment="Left"
    Height="30" Width="90"
    Grid.Row="4" Grid.Column="1" />
```

```
</Grid>
```

Each of the bound fields uses the new `Binding` syntax: within curly braces, you use the keyword `Binding`, followed by the name of the public property to which the control will be bound and the `Mode` setting (which defaults to `OneWay`). For example:

```
<TextBlock x:Name="Title"
    Text="{Binding Title, Mode=OneWay }"
```

You do not, at this point in the design, know what object will supply the value; you know only that in the case of this `TextBlock` it will have a `Title` property. That allows you to work your way through a collection of objects that have the bound property and display each.

For an object with two-way binding, the only difference is in the `Mode` setting:

```
<TextBox x:Name="QuantityOnHand"
    Text="{Binding QuantityOnHand, Mode=TwoWay}"
    VerticalAlignment="Bottom"
    HorizontalAlignment="Left"
    Height="30" Width="90"
    Grid.Row="4" Grid.Column="1" />
```

Recall that when the user changes a control set to two-way binding, the source object is updated.

Finally, some controls are populated from a collection:

```
<ListBox x:Name="Chapters"
    ItemsSource="{Binding Chapters, Mode=OneWay}"
    VerticalAlignment="Bottom"
    HorizontalAlignment="Left"
    Height="80" Width="200"
    Grid.Row="2" Grid.Column="1" />
```

Here, you are going to bind the `ListBox`'s `ItemSource` to a specific property in the `DataSource` (in this case, `Chapters`).

DataContext

At this point, you've told the "Title" control that it will bind to the Title property, but you haven't told it which object to bind to. The DataContext object is the specific book, which is chosen at runtime and assigned to the DataContext property of the framework element (in this case, the TextBlock) so that it knows "I get the Title from *this* book."

DataContext objects can be inherited down the UI tree. Thus, you can set the DataContext for a Grid, and all the controls in that Grid will have access to it (unless they set their own). You're going to set the DataContext on the Grid and not on each of the controls, though you could of course assign a specific DataContext to any given control or set of controls.

The Event Handlers

The Page_Loaded event handler takes three actions: it creates an instance of a Book, initializes that Book with data (as if it retrieved it from a database or a web service), and then binds that Book to the Grid as its DataContext. Once that is done, the data will be displayed by the Bindings, matching the properties in the Book to the properties named in the Bindings:

```
void Page_Loaded(object sender,
    RoutedEventArgs e)
{
    Book book = new Book( );
    InitializeProgramming(book);
    LayoutRoot.DataContext = book;
}

private void InitializeProgramming(Book b)
{
    b.Title = "Programming Silverlight";
    b.Author = "Jesse Liberty, Tim Heuer";
    b.MultipleAuthor = true;
    b.QuantityOnHand = 20;
    b.Chapters = new List<string>( )
        {
        "Introduction", "Controls",
        "Events", "Data", "Styles and Templates",
        "Media", "Graphics", "Text", "Animation", "Custom Controls",
        "Network", "Web Services", "App Model"
        };
}
```

InitializeProgramming( ) is a helper (hack!) method to mimic retrieving this information from the database. The result is that the data in the Book object is bound to the controls as shown in Figure 7-17.

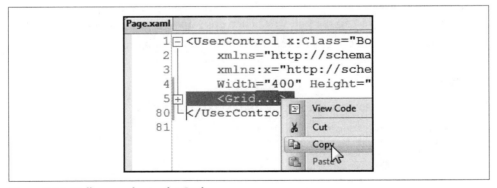

Figure 7-17. The bound Book displayed

Styling Controls

Programmers like to tinker with the look of controls. There are two ways to do so in Silverlight: minor adjustments can be made with styles, and wholesale redesigns with templates.

To illustrate how to use styles, we'll start with the program you just wrote. You can just make a copy, but the safest way is to create a new project and copy the XAML and the classes into the new namespace. Here are the steps:

1. Create a new project (let's call it *BookStyles*).
2. In the original *Page.xaml*, collapse the Grid as shown in Figure 7-18 and copy it.

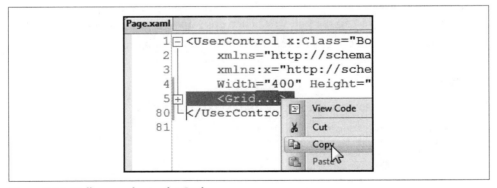

Figure 7-18. Collapse and copy the Grid

3. In the new *Page.xaml*, collapse the Grid and paste the old Grid over it.

4. Back in the original *Page.xaml.cs*, collapse and copy the Page class (as Figure 7-19 shows) and paste it into the new project. Then copy and paste the using statements.

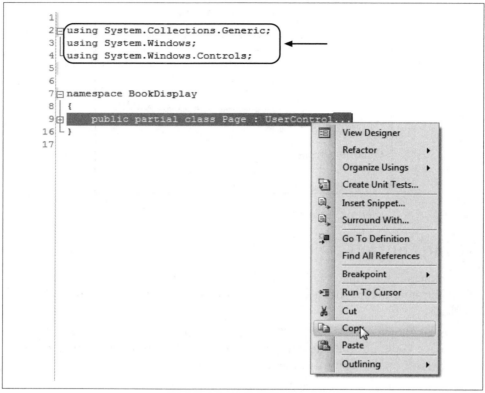

Figure 7-19. Collapse and copy the Page class

5. In the new project, create a *Book.cs* file and then collapse and copy the Book class from the old project to the new one. Then copy and paste the using statements.

6. Run the new project to ensure that everything is working properly.

Applying Styles Inline

Let's start by adding some inline styling to the TextBlock for the "Title" prompt:

```
<TextBlock x:Name="TitlePrompt"
    Text="Title:  "
    VerticalAlignment="Bottom"
    HorizontalAlignment="Right"
    Grid.Row="0"  Grid.Column="0"
    FontFamily="Comic Sans MS"
    FontSize="16"
    FontWeight="Bold"
    Foreground="Red" />
```

Barnes & Noble Booksellers #2592
591 South University Drive
Plantation, FL 33924
954-723-0489

STR:2592 REG:007 TRN:6241 CSHR:Melissa L

BARNES & NOBLE MEMBER   EXP: 11/30/2009

Myth-Chief
  9780441016877
  (1 @ 7.99) Member Card 10% (0.80)
  (1 @ 7.19)   7.19
Year's Best SF 13
  9780061252099
  (1 @ 7.99) Member Card 10% (0.80)
  (1 @ 7.19)   7.19
Programming NET 3 5
  9780596527563
  (1 @ 44.99) Member Card 10% (4.50)
  (1 @ 40.49)   40.49

Subtotal   54.87
Sales Tax (6.000%)   3.29
TOTAL   58.16
DISCOVER   58.16
  Card#: XXXXXXXXXXXX3287
  Expdate: XX/XX
  Auth: 023553
  Entry Method: Swiped

MEMBER SAVINGS   6.10

Thanks for shopping at
Barnes & Noble

V101 16   03/23/2009 06:00PM

CUSTOMER COPY

through Barnes & Noble.com via PayPal). Opened music/DVDs/audio may not be returned, but can be exchanged only for the same title if defective.

After 14 days or without a sales receipt, returns or exchanges will not be permitted.

Magazines, newspapers, and used books are not returnable.
Product not carried by Barnes & Noble or Barnes & Noble.com will not be accepted for return.

Policy on receipt may appear in two sections.

Return Policy

With a sales receipt, a full refund in the original form of payment will be issued from any Barnes & Noble store for returns of new and unread books (except textbooks) and unopened music/DVDs/audio made within (i) 14 days of purchase from a Barnes & Noble retail store (except for purchases made by check less than 7 days prior to the date of return) or (ii) 14 days of delivery date for Barnes & Noble.com purchases (except for purchases made via PayPal). A store credit for the purchase price will be issued for (i) purchases made by check less than 7 days prior to the date of return, (ii) when a gift receipt is presented within 60 days of purchase, (iii) textbooks returned with a receipt within 14 days of purchase, or (iv) original purchase was made through Barnes & Noble.com via PayPal). Opened music/DVDs/audio may not be returned, but can be exchanged only for the same title if defective.

After 14 days or without a sales receipt, returns or exchanges will not be permitted.

Magazines, newspapers, and used books are not returnable.
Product not carried by Barnes & Noble or Barnes & Noble.com will not be accepted for return.

Policy on receipt may appear in two sections.

Return Policy

With a sales receipt, a full refund in the original form of payment will be issued from any Barnes & Noble store for returns of new and unread books (except textbooks) and unopened music/DVDs/audio made within (i) 14 days of purchase from a Barnes & Noble retail store (except for purchases made by check less than 7 days prior to the date of return) or (ii) 14 days of delivery date for Barnes & Noble.com purchases (except for purchases made via PayPal). A store credit for the purchase price will be issued for (i) purchases made by check less than 7 days prior to the date of return, (ii) when a gift receipt is presented within 60 days of purchase, (iii) textbooks returned with a receipt within 14 days of purchase, or (iv) original purchase was made through Barnes & Noble.com via PayPal). Opened music/DVDs/audio may not be returned, but can be exchanged only for the same title if defective.

After 14 days or without a sales receipt, returns or exchanges will not be permitted.

Magazines, newspapers, and used books are not returnable.
Product not carried by Barnes & Noble or Barnes & Noble.com will not be accepted for return.

The effect is shown in Figure 7-20. This is a very simple example, but rest assured that the capabilities of the platform are extensive.

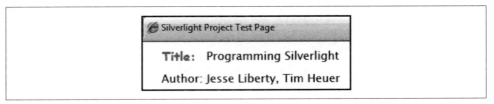

Figure 7-20. Adding inline style attributes

Assuming you like the look of the "Title" prompt, you may want to add the same styling to "Author" and the other prompts. That could lead to quite a bit of work, and if you later decide to change the font, for example, you'll have to change it everywhere. Applying styles inline does not scale well, but fortunately, there's an alternative.

Creating and Using Style Objects

Style objects are reusable resources. You can attach them to any container, or you can apply them to a whole project by placing them in the Resources section of *App.xaml*. Each Style object consists of a Style element with attributes for:

- The target type (the element type to which you'll apply the style)
- A Key (the name that you'll use to refer to the style)
- Zero or more Setters

A Setter object represents a style attribute. Each Setter consists of a Setter element with Property/Value pairs, where the Property is the style property you are setting and the Value is the value to be set for that property.

You can see how you can move from inline styles to Style objects quite clearly in Figure 7-21, where there is a 1:1 correspondence between the inline styles and the Setter properties contained in the global Style objects.

Once the global style is set, you can replace all the inline styles in the TextBlocks with references to the Style object, making for code that is far easier to scale and maintain:

```
<TextBlock x:Name="TitlePrompt"
    Text="Title:   "
    Grid.Row="0" Grid.Column="0"
    Style="{StaticResource TextBlockStyle}" />
<TextBlock x:Name="AuthorPrompt" Text="Author: "
    Grid.Row="1" Grid.Column="0"
    Style="{StaticResource TextBlockStyle}" />
```

Of course, you would rarely do this by hand, as Expression Blend makes this work fast, easy, and reliable.

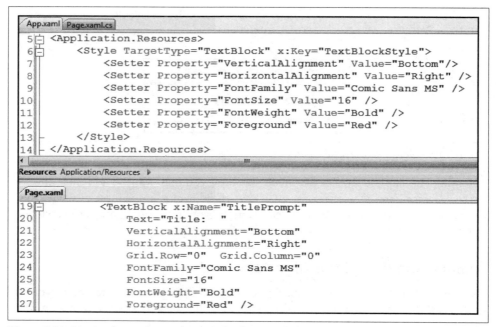

```
  App.xaml  Page.xaml.cs
 5    <Application.Resources>
 6        <Style TargetType="TextBlock" x:Key="TextBlockStyle">
 7            <Setter Property="VerticalAlignment" Value="Bottom"/>
 8            <Setter Property="HorizontalAlignment" Value="Right" />
 9            <Setter Property="FontFamily" Value="Comic Sans MS" />
10            <Setter Property="FontSize" Value="16" />
11            <Setter Property="FontWeight" Value="Bold" />
12            <Setter Property="Foreground" Value="Red" />
13        </Style>
14    </Application.Resources>
```

Resources Application/Resources ▶

```
  Page.xaml
19            <TextBlock x:Name="TitlePrompt"
20                Text="Title:   "
21                VerticalAlignment="Bottom"
22                HorizontalAlignment="Right"
23                Grid.Row="0"  Grid.Column="0"
24                FontFamily="Comic Sans MS"
25                FontSize="16"
26                FontWeight="Bold"
27                Foreground="Red" />
```

Figure 7-21. Moving from inline styles to Style objects

Interlude on Design Patterns

Chapter 8, *Implementing Design Patterns with .NET 3.5*

Implementing Design Patterns with .NET 3.5

Though you may not realize it, you are actually holding two books in your hand. (Don't panic, you only have to pay for one!) They exist in the same space, at the same time; not side by side but in the same words, the same pages, and the same illustrations; separated not by chapters, headings, or content, but only by perspective.

One book is a programmer's guide to a set of new technologies. The second book describes how .NET 3.5 can be viewed as an integrated set of technologies that facilitates the key architectural patterns we've all been trying to implement for the past decade.

You don't have to accept the latter premise to read this book, but it may give you some new options. In the long run, incorporating these architectural patterns into your programming may be as revolutionary as the move from procedural to object-oriented programming.

Here is the primary theory behind this book, in a nutshell: you can approach .NET 3.5 as a set of new, individual technologies for presentation, communication, and workflow that includes dramatic client-side performance enhancements for web development; additionally, you can approach .NET 3.5 as an integrated framework designed to help you move beyond object-oriented programming and step up to object-oriented *design* based on high-level industry-standard architectural patterns.

These perspectives are not mutually exclusive; you can (and we hope you will) move between them. However, you may choose to ignore the patterns, which is also perfectly reasonable. It's up to you—it's your book!

.NET 3.5 Fosters Good Design

We believe that .NET 3.5 fosters the creation of high-quality applications by enabling easy implementation of industry-standard architectural design patterns. The most important of these are:

- The *n-tier pattern*, which encourages separation of the user interface from the business objects and the persistence (data) layer
- The *Model-View-Controller (MVC) pattern*, which has recently been integrated into the ASP.NET Framework as an optional set of classes enabling you to implement MVC design through Visual Studio
- The *Observer pattern*, also known as *Publish and Subscribe*
- The *Factory Method pattern*, based on abstracting out the creation of objects
- The *Chain-of-Command pattern*, which separates command objects from processing objects
- The *Singleton pattern*, which ensures that at most one instance of a class can ever exist

A key premise of this book is that the NET 3.5 class libraries represent Microsoft's first .NET release to truly foster usage of the design patterns and best practices that Microsoft and the software development community have collectively agreed make for the most robust applications.

Undermining Good Design?

A case can be made that previous versions of .NET, and the Microsoft Foundation Class Library (MFC) before them, actually undermined the best practices and architectural patterns we all claimed to be implementing.

For example, an early architectural pattern that many programmers found valuable was the MVC pattern, which separates the model (the software-based representation of the problem you are trying to solve) from the view (the presentation to the user) and the controller (which responds to events such as button presses and system events).

.NET has generally made this pattern nearly impossible to implement, because it spreads traditional controller responsibilities among the operating system, the framework, the control classes, and the event handlers. Furthermore, many .NET programs didn't really have much of a model; they just had a view and some data to store.

A second popular approach was to build "n-tier" (most commonly three-tier) applications. The three tiers were supposed to be presentation, business logic, and persistence (data). Once again, however, it was easy for the business logic layer to get lost and to end up with just two tiers: presentation and data.

For many .NET programmers, it isn't even clear what the business layer *does*. Business objects seem to have more value in theory than in practice, and they may seem redundant with the information held in the controls or in the data objects. ("We don't need no stinkin' business objects!")

To anticipate a fuller discussion later in this chapter, however, ask yourself this: when a user logs in, if you have code to decide which page that user should be directed to based on her "role" (e.g., Employee versus Supervisor), where should that code reside? Three-tier design argues that it does not belong in the presentation layer (though that is where it often ends up), and it can't reside in the data layer (though that is where it will be stored). Rather, it should reside in a class that encapsulates that knowledge. Such a class is part of the model—i.e., the business layer.

.NET seemed to foster web (and even Windows) applications in which the presentation layer (the controls) was connected directly to the persistence layer (the database) through ADO.NET objects (especially with the advent of data source controls).

However, the direct connection many programmers built between the presentation layer and the data layer led to tight coupling between controls such as DataGrids and data objects such as DataSets, and as one layer changed, the other layer would break. This was exactly the problem the n-tier pattern was designed to solve, and it represented a major obstacle to creating enterprise-level applications.

Please do not misread this; many .NET (and MFC, and even C) programmers have managed to create very well-designed n-tier or MVC applications in the past. However, the tools they were using were not *facilitating* this design; these programmers were succeeding *in spite of* the framework.

Perhaps one of the most egregious examples of the framework fighting industry-standard best design practices was seen in the implementation of web services. With the very best of intentions, Microsoft decided to "ease" programmers into web services, "hiding" the SOAP and XML aspects by creating a Remote Procedure Call (RPC) metaphor in which programmers were encouraged to think of the web service as a set of methods represented by a proxy on the client. The client called the methods through the proxy, and presto, the results of the method were passed to the client. At no time did the developer have XML under his fingernails.

Unfortunately, web services were designed for data exchange, and as every programmer knows, the first job in creating data exchange is to work out the contract—in this case, to agree on the Web Services Description Language (WSDL) document. Microsoft's tools did not facilitate this; in fact, just the opposite was true. There was no easy way for the provider and the consumer to start with WSDL design and then implement the classes from that design. The illusion of RPCs made the transition to web services easy, but like all illusions, it soon got in the way of developers truly understanding the technology and accomplishing more complex business goals.

Standing on the Shoulders of Giants

As World War II raged, the Blue Funnel Shipping Company transported goods across the Atlantic from the United States to England. It soon became a prime target for German U-boats. To the dismay of Blue Funnel's management, many of the company's younger sailors fared poorly under the duress and rigors of ship life, war, and lifeboat rescues. They quickly came to understand that youth and technical training were no match for experience.

Blue Funnel's management recognized that they needed to do something to increase the survival rates of their younger sailors. In the end, they hired a man named Kurt Hahn and helped to fund the creation of an organization that still exists today. That organization, Outward Bound, created a 28-day course designed to deliver experiential education to supplement the technical training the young sailors were getting at the academies.

What was true in the past for sailors facing German U-boats is true today for programmers facing new technologies: *experience matters*.

In software development, the experience of an industry veteran still counts for more than youth and technical know-how. Consider the task of building an online banking system. The first time you tackle such a project, you have no real appreciation of the number of things that can, and do, and *will* go wrong. In fact, you won't even know to ask the right questions about the project, because there is no textbook or technical manual that covers the pitfalls and unexpected problems that can arise when working with multiple legacy systems all at once.

Software Design Patterns

Software design patterns attempt to deliver the experience acquired through years of work on software development projects in a compressed time frame (usually the length of time required to read and digest a design patterns book). They enable developers to leverage the experience of others while avoiding the pain of failed software projects.

Software design patterns originated in the world of architecture. In the late 1970s, an architect and civil engineer named Christopher Alexander (from Alex's hometown of Berkeley, California) came to the conclusion that people knew way more about the buildings they needed than architects did. Alexander felt that certain design constructs, when used time and time again, led to the desired effects. He documented and published the wisdom and experience he gained so that others could benefit.

Fortunately for us in the software world, Kent Beck and Ward Cunningham began experimenting with the idea of applying patterns to programming and presented their results at the OOPSLA conference in 1987. After this conference, Beck, Cunningham, and others continued with this work.

Design patterns gained popularity among working programmers after the book *Design Patterns: Elements of Reusable Object-Oriented Software*, by Erich Gamma et al. (Addison-Wesley), was published in 1994.

In many companies that were doing cutting-edge software development, this book quickly rose to the top of employees' reading lists. That same year, the first Pattern Languages of Programs (PLOP) conference was held; the following year, the Portland Pattern Repository was set up for documentation of design patterns.

Since then, design patterns have languished somewhat, often observed more in spirit than in practice. In part this was because few development environments were "pattern friendly." With the release of .NET 3.5, however, we now have a framework that supports and, to a degree, encourages and integrates many of the core design patterns documented by the Design Patterns community.

In this chapter we're going to describe a few key patterns and provide you with C# implementations that you can carry forward in your software development projects.

The N-Tier Pattern

Microsoft has been committed to n-tier development for a very long time. It was the heart of the now-deprecated Distributed interNet Architecture (DNA) introduced in 1999, and it remains the heart of .NET today.

As noted earlier, n-tier really means "three or more" tiers. The "required" three are the presentation (user interface), business logic, and persistence (data) layers (see Figure 8-1).

It is possible, of course, to have many more than three tiers. For example, some developers find it useful to break up the application layer into a workflow and a rules layer, and to break up the persistence layer into a data layer that exists in the application and a data layer that is implemented in stored procedures and thus exists on the database server. Such an architecture is illustrated in Figure 8-2.

The key to solid n-tier development is clean separation between the layers. The presentation-layer objects should know as little as possible about the internals of the business objects, and they certainly should know nothing about how the data they represent is persisted.

The arguments for this decoupling between the layers only grow stronger as we face a rapidly changing and evolving development environment. The presentation options are proliferating more quickly than we can learn how to code for them, and the kinds of data (and the volume of data) that we must present are expanding exponentially.

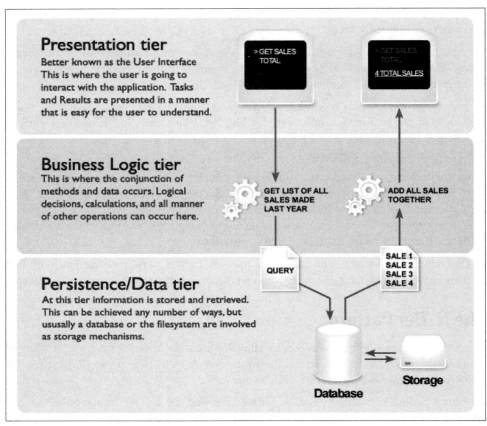

Presentation tier

Better known as the User Interface
This is where the user is going to
interact with the application. Tasks
and Results are presented in a manner
that is easy for the user to understand.

> GET SALES
TOTAL

> GET SALES
TOTAL
4 TOTAL SALES

Business Logic tier

This is where the conjunction of
methods and data occurs. Logical
decisions, calculations, and all manner
of other operations can occur here.

GET LIST OF ALL
SALES MADE
LAST YEAR

ADD ALL SALES
TOGETHER

Persistence/Data tier

At this tier information is stored and retrieved.
This can be achieved any number of ways, but
ususally a database or the filesystem are involved
as storage mechanisms.

QUERY

SALE 1
SALE 2
SALE 3
SALE 4

Storage

Database

Figure 8-1. Typical three-tier architecture

We are no longer in the position of just extracting data from a database and present-ing it as a simple web form. Now, we are just as likely to be aggregating data from mail messages, spreadsheets, XML documents, queries from various databases, and values retrieved from web services, and presenting them both over the Web and on mobile devices. Furthermore, all of this is mediated by business rules that determine which users have access, editing, and manipulation rights and takes place in an envi-ronment in which the tools and the specifications are in a near-constant state of flux.

The MVC Pattern

Wikipedia attributes the Model-View-Controller architectural pattern to Trygve Mikkjel Heyerdahl Reenskaug, who developed it in 1979 while working on Small-talk at Xerox PARC.

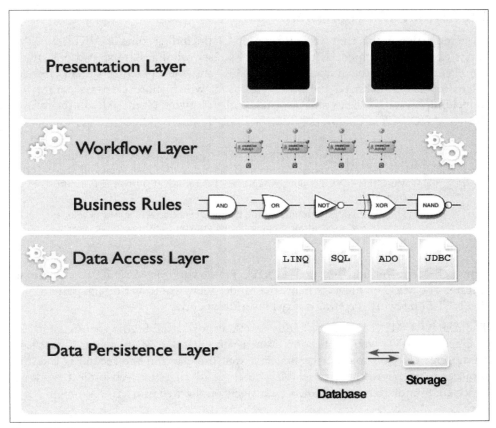

Figure 8-2. Possible n-tier architecture

The key concept in this pattern is that you start with a *model*—that is, a representation of the problem domain. The model includes the state of the application and its data; it focuses on the structure of the data and how it will be manipulated.

The second key concept in the MVC pattern is the *view*, which is how the model is presented to the user (i.e., the user interface). The view typically includes controls with which the user interacts (drop-down lists, buttons, etc.).

The third and final key concept is (you guessed it!) the *controller*, which responds to user actions (and other events) and mediates the interaction between the model and the view, possibly modifying one and/or the other. For example, pressing a button may cause the controller to send a message to the model, thereby changing the state of the model. This may in turn cause the controller to send another message, this time back to the view, updating the view to represent the new state of the model.

The ASP.NET MVC Framework

As stated earlier in this chapter, in most of .NET (including some of .NET 3.5), MVC is not easily implemented, as the controller's responsibilities are spread out among the event handlers, the framework, the CLR, and the operating system. Instead, Microsoft has emphasized the n-tier approach, which more clearly separates the model into business objects and persistence objects (which it provides in the form of the new ADO.NET class libraries, like the Entity Framework).

 Be sure you have the ASP.NET 3.5 Extensions Preview (or better) installed. You can get it from *http://tinyurl.com/393boh*. You will also want the MVCToolkit, which can be found at *http://tinyurl.com/2mmzdq*.

The MVCToolkit provides some nice widgets that will speed development of the application. Remember where you put this project, as you are going to import it.

However, Microsoft now provides an MVC Framework for ASP.NET as an optional feature. The MVC Framework maps the Model-View-Controller design pattern onto the .NET Framework, creating a very powerful synergy.

The ASP.NET MVC Framework adds templates for Visual Studio that make it easy to create an MVC web application. When you create an MVC application, Visual Studio creates two projects: the first is a web project, and the second is a testing project specifically created to enable you to verify that the web project works as expected. Our discussion will focus exclusively on the web project.

 Wikipedia verifies our memory that test-driven programming first came to prominence as an integral aspect of eXtreme Programming, an "agile" technique invented by Kent Beck in the late 1990s. XP is marked by pair programming and extremely short development cycles.

Within the web project, Visual Studio creates three folders, conveniently named */Controllers*, */Models*, and */Views*.

Controller classes and action methods

The MVC Framework maps URL requests directly to controller classes, by default. Controllers are responsible for handling incoming page requests, managing user input, and executing the underlying logic.

A controller class can respond to URL requests by overriding the Execute( ) method of its base class and examining the incoming URL to see what is being requested. An easier option, however, is to define *action methods* on the subclassed controller. The base class will then automatically route the requests to the correct method, based on the rules of your application.

Incoming URL parameters are typically accessed as parameter arguments to the action methods.

Model classes

In traditional MVC, the model is the component responsible for maintaining state. With ASP.NET, state is typically persisted in a database. The model classes of the ASP.NET MVC Framework work well with ADO.NET, LINQ, or any other implementation you may choose.

View classes

The application logic is encapsulated in the controller classes and the persistence logic in the model classes. This leaves the view classes free to focus on the presentation logic.

Typically, controller action methods will handle incoming web requests, use the incoming parameter values to execute the application logic code, talk to the model to retrieve data as needed, and then select view objects to render results to the requester.

An MVC Example

To give you some experience with the MVC Framework in its simplest form, in this section we'll walk you through creating an excerpt from an ASP.NET MVC shopping application that can be used to gather a user's shipping preference. You will prompt the user with a drop-down list to indicate her preferred carrier. For the purposes of this demonstration, you can assume that you already know the user's ID.

Creating the database

To support the application fragment, create a two-table (half-caf, low-fat, extra-dry, SQL Server) database called MVCDatabase, as illustrated in Figure 8-3.

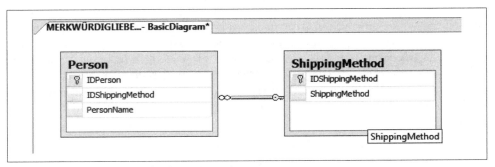

Figure 8-3. Sample database for the MVC application

Be sure that the Identity Specification for the primary key on each table (Person.IDPerson, ShippingMethod.IDShippingMethod) is set to Yes. If you are unsure about exactly how to do this, please feel free to download a backup of this database from *http://tinyurl.com/2sbvs3*. Restore the backup in that *.zip* file into MVCDatabase.

Creating the MVC application

Open Visual Studio and create a new ASP.NET MVC Web Application called (creatively) *ASPMVCApplication*, as pictured in Figure 8-4.

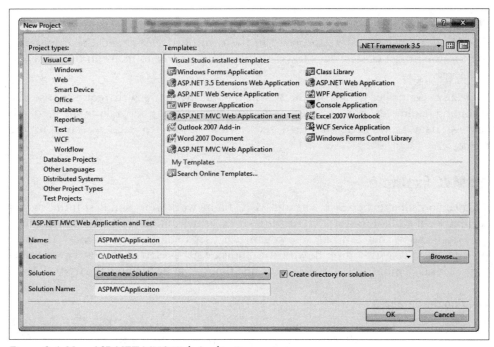

Figure 8-4. New ASP.NET MVC Web Application project

As mentioned previously, the structure of this application will be a little different from that of other ASP.NET applications you have created in the past. In addition to the *MVCApplication* and *MVCApplicationTest* projects, you're going to add the *MVCToolkit* project you downloaded earlier. To do this, right-click on the Solution icon in your Solution Explorer pane and select Add → Existing Project. Navigate to the directory where your *MVCToolkit* project is located and select *MVCToolkit.csproj*, as shown in Figure 8-5.

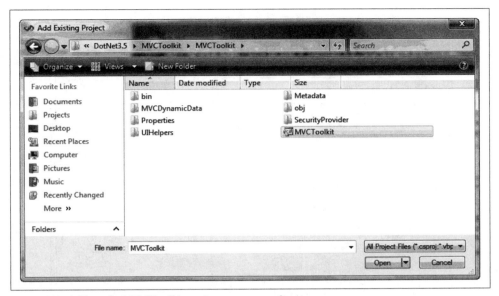

Figure 8-5. Adding the MVCToolkit project to your application

At this point, the Solution Explorer should report that your solution has three projects. It's not strictly necessary to add the *MVCToolkit* project at this point, but later it will provide you with a convenient place to rummage through if you get curious about the implementation of the UIHelpers you're going to leverage in your application.

Next, add a reference to *MVCToolkit.dll* to the primary Web Application. Open up *MVCApplication* and right-click on the *References* folder. Select Add Reference, then select the Browse tab and navigate to the *bin/debug* folder inside the *MVCToolkit* project. Select *MVCToolkit.dll*, as seen in Figure 8-6, and click OK to add the reference.

Next, click on the *ASPMVCApplication* solution and rebuild it. If you've done everything correctly, you should be able to go to *Views/Home*, open up the *Index.aspx* file in Visual Studio, and type <%=Html. %> just below the level-2 header (<h2>) that says "Welcome to my ASP.NET MVC Application!" IntelliSense should display a list like the one in Figure 8-7.

At the time of writing, there was an issue with the MVCToolkit and wireless keyboards and mice. If you cannot see the IntelliSense display, you are strongly encouraged to unplug your wireless keyboard and mouse, replace them with wired ones, and reboot. (Sad, but true.)

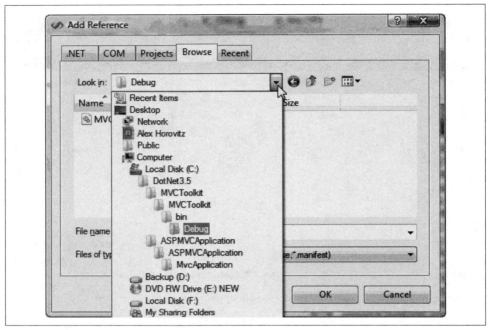

Figure 8-6. Finding the MVCToolkit DLL

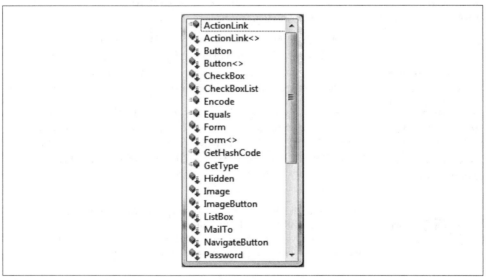

Figure 8-7. Correctly installed MVCToolkit.dll view of the <%=Html. %> IntelliSense completion dialog

The final step is to add a data connection between your application and the database you created. To do so, select "Connect to Database" from the Visual Studio Tools menu and enter the name of the database you created at the start of the exercise (MVCDatabase). Your dialog box should look something like the one in Figure 8-8.

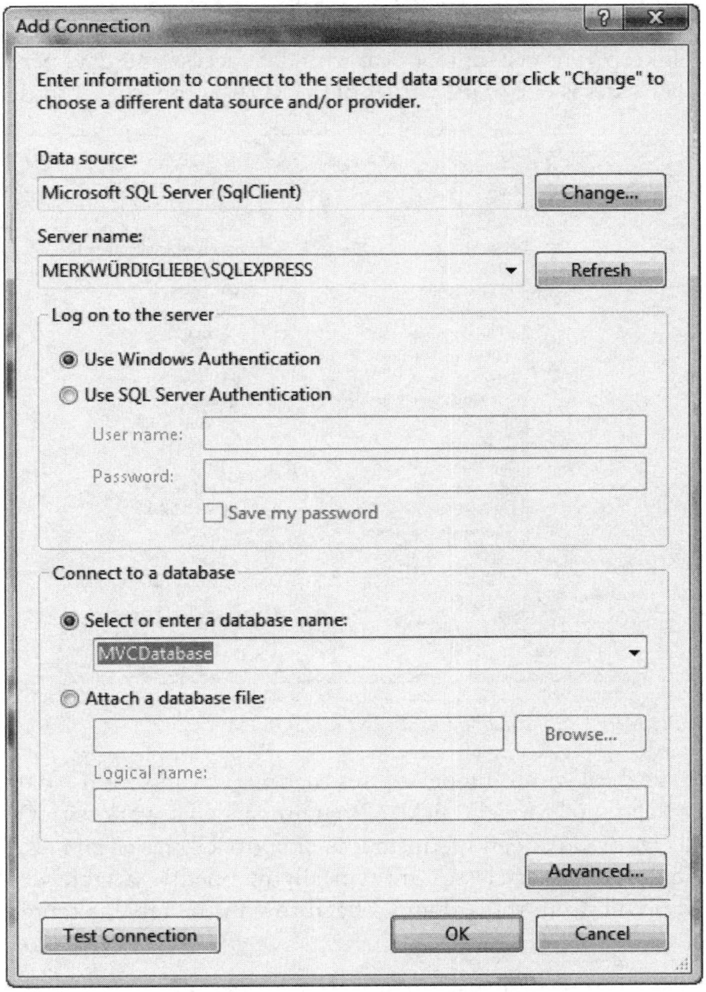

Figure 8-8. Adding a connection to the database

The model

The ASP.NET MVC Framework lets you use any data-access pattern or framework you prefer. In this case, you'll use the LINQ to SQL classes that ship with .NET 3.5.

For a full exploration of LINQ, see Chapter 9.

Right-click on the *Models* subdirectory of the MVC web project and choose Add → New Item to add a LINQ to SQL class, as seen in Figure 8-9. The *Models* directory is where you will keep your classes that deal with data access and data persistence. This organization of classes is one of the virtues of the MVC approach, for those who like it.

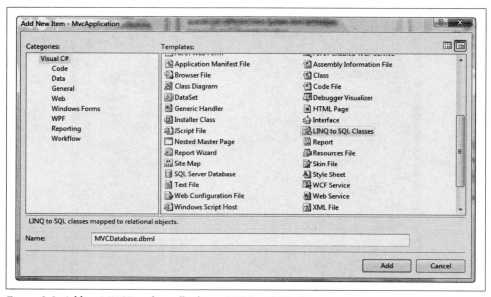

Figure 8-9. Adding MVCDatabase.dbml as a LINQ to SQL class

LINQ to SQL enables you to model classes that map to and from a database, creating an Object Relational Model (ORM). Programmers who work with ORMs refer to such classes as *entity classes* and to instances of entity classes as *entities*. The properties and attributes of entity classes are typically mapped to a table's columns, and that's what you will do in this example. Each row in the table is represented by an entity.

Unlike with the DataSet/TableAdapter feature provided in VS 2005, when using the LINQ to SQL designer you do not have to specify the SQL queries to use when creating your data model and access layer. Because you already have a database schema defined, you can use it to quickly create LINQ to SQL entity classes modeled from it. The easiest way to accomplish this is to open up your database in the Visual Studio Server Explorer, select the tables and views you want to model, then drag and drop them onto the LINQ to SQL designer surface, as shown in Figure 8-10.

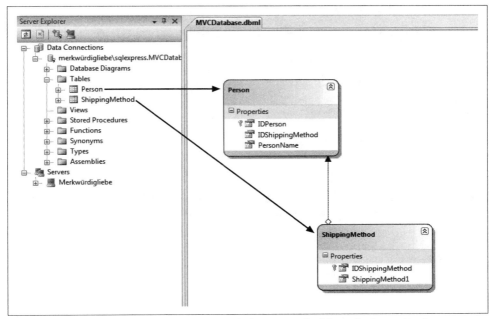

Figure 8-10. Dragging and dropping Person and ShippingMethod from the Server Explorer

The design surface infers the relationship between ShippingMethod and Person from the database schema.

MVC is a lot easier to implement with a couple of helper classes. For more on when and where to use these helper classes, check out Scott Guthrie's in-depth four-part series on MVC that begins here: *http://tinyurl.com/2qcoh8*.

In the *Models* folder, add a C# class and name it *MVCDatabaseDataContext.cs*. Here's the complete listing:

```csharp
using System;
using System.Collections.Generic;
using System.Linq;

namespace MvcApplication.Models
{
    public partial class MVCDatabaseDataContext
    {

        // Retrieve all Person objects

        public List<Person> GetPeople()
        {
            return Persons.ToList();
        }
```

```
        // Add a new Person

        public void AddPerson(Person p)
        {
            Persons.InsertOnSubmit(p);
        }
        // Retrieve all Shippers

        public List<ShippingMethod> GetShippers()
        {
            return ShippingMethods.ToList();
        }
    }
}
```

Then add a second helper class, *PersonViewData.cs*, to the *Models* folder. This class passes lists of people to a view. The complete listing follows:

```
using System;
using System.Collections.Generic;
using MvcApplication.Models;

namespace MvcApplication.Models
{
    public class PersonViewData
    {
        public List<Person> People { get; set; }
    }
    public class NewPersonViewData
    {
        public List<ShippingMethod> Shippers { get; set; }
    }
}
```

The controller

With your model classes complete, you are ready to build your controller. You'll need only one class, *PersonController.cs*, which you'll add to the *Controllers* folder:

```
using System;
using System.Web;
using System.Web.Mvc;
using System.Web.Mvc.BindingHelpers;
using MvcApplication.Models;

namespace MvcApplication.Controllers
{
    public class PersonController : Controller
    {
        MVCDatabaseDataContext db = new MVCDatabaseDataContext();

        [ControllerAction]
        public void PeopleList()
```

```
        {
            PersonViewData pvd = new PersonViewData();
            pvd.People = db.GetPeople();
            RenderView("PeopleList", pvd);
        }

        // Person/New

        [ControllerAction]
        public void New()
        {
            NewPersonViewData npvd = new NewPersonViewData();
            npvd.Shippers = db.GetShippers();
            RenderView("New",npvd);
        }

        // Person/NewInsert

        [ControllerAction]
        public void NewInsert()
        {
            Person p = new Person();
            p.UpdateFrom(Request.Form);

            db.AddPerson(p);
            db.SubmitChanges();

            RedirectToAction(new { Controller="Person",
                Action="PeopleList"});
        }
    }
}
```

This controller class is the mechanism by which data is passed between the model and the view(s).

The view(s)

Create a *Person* folder inside the *Views* folder. Then, inside the *Person* folder, create two MVC View Pages: one named *PeopleList.aspx* and one named *New.aspx*.

The contents of *PeopleList.aspx* are shown in Example 8-1.

Example 8-1. PeopleList.aspx

```
<%@ Page Language="C#" MasterPageFile="~/Views/Shared/Site.Master"
    AutoEventWireup="true" CodeBehind="PeopleList.aspx"
    Inherits="MvcApplication.Views.Person.PeopleList"%>

<asp:Content ID="Content2" ContentPlaceHolderID="MainContentPlaceHolder"
    runat="server">
```

Example 8-1. PeopleList.aspx (continued)

```
<h2>People In Our Database</h2>

<ul>

    <% foreach (var person in ViewData.People) { %>

        <li>
            <%=person.PersonName%>
        </li>

    <% } %>

</ul>
<%= Html.ActionLink("Add New Person", new { Action="New" }) %>
</asp:Content>
```

The Controller base class has a ViewData dictionary property that can be used to populate data that you want to pass to a view. You add and read objects into the ViewData dictionary using key/value pairs. This inline code iterates through the PeopleList dictionary that is part of the ViewData dictionary and displays each person's name inline.

You must be specific when passing in ViewData. Modify *PeopleList.aspx.cs* as follows:

```
using System;
using System.Web;
using System.Web.Mvc;
using MvcApplication.Models;

namespace MvcApplication.Views.Person
{
    public partial class PeopleList : ViewPage<PersonViewData>
    {
    }
}
```

To test your applicaton, add some data to your database. Then add the following to the *Site.Master* file (found in *Views/Shared*), in the "menu" div right below the "About us" HTML action link:

```
<li>
    <%= Html.ActionLink("People", new { Controller = "Person",
        Action = "PeopleList"})%>
</li>
```

When you run the application and click on "People," you should see the data retrieved from the database, similar to what you see in Figure 8-11.

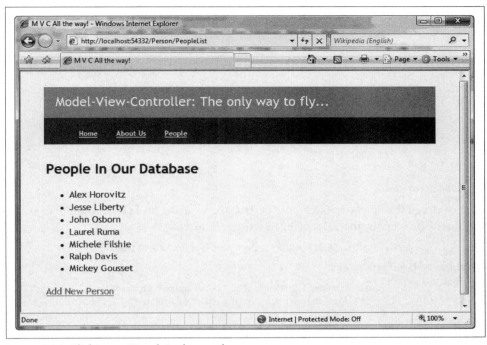

Figure 8-11. Clicking on "People" takes you here

Adding new people to the database

The next step is to implement the Add New Person functionality. The first task is to modify *New.aspx* so it reads as follows:

```
<%@ Page Language="C#" MasterPageFile="~/Views/Shared/Site.Master"
    AutoEventWireup="true" CodeBehind="New.aspx.cs"
    Inherits="MvcApplication.Views.Person.New" %>

<asp:Content ID="PageContent"
    ContentPlaceHolderID="MainContentPlaceHolder" runat="server">

    <h2>Add a Person to our Database</h2>

    <form action="/Person/NewInsert" method="post">

        <table>
            <tr>
                <td>Name:</td>
                <td>
                    <input id="PersonName" type="text" name="PersonName" />
                </td>
            </tr>
```

```
        <tr>
           <td>Shipping Preference:</td>
           <td>
              <%=Html.Select("IDShippingMethod", ViewData.Shippers)%>
           </td>
        </tr>
     </table>

     <p></p>

     <input type="submit" value="Save" />

  </form>

</asp:Content>
```

One of the first things to notice here is that you're using an HTML UIHelper. Without the MVCToolkit, the Select( ) call written here as:

```
<%=Html.Select("IDShippingMethod", ViewData.Shippers)%>
```

would have been written as:

```
<select name="ShippingPrefs" id="ShippingPrefsDropDown">
   <% foreach (var option in ViewData.Shippers)
   { %>
      <option value='<%= option.IDShippingMethod %>'>
      <%= option.shippingMethod%></option>
   <% } %>
</select>
```

As, you can see, HTML UIHelpers allow you to wire together objects without having to worry about the implementation details, so you can write much more concise code. In the long run, this will make writing and maintaining ASP.NET applications a great deal simpler.

Make sure you edit the *New.aspx.cs* file to reflect the fact that you are passing an object in to the ViewData dictionary:

```
using System;
using System.Web;
using System.Web.Mvc;
using System.Web.Mvc.BindingHelpers;
using MvcApplication.Models;

namespace MvcApplication.Views.Person
{
   public partial class New : ViewPage<NewPersonViewData>
   {
   }
}
```

Note that with the addition of MVC.BindingHelpers the data now flows two ways. Ultimately, this allows you to do things like this:

```
Person p = new Person();
p.UpdateFrom(Request.Form);

db.AddPerson(p);
db.SubmitChanges();
```

Here, the Person object is automagically updated with the values from the Form. This also applies in a situation where the user is editing a Person object and you have pushed the values to the edit form; on submit, the values will return with the user's modifications.

Run the application now. Click on "Add New Person," and you should get something that looks like Figure 8-12.

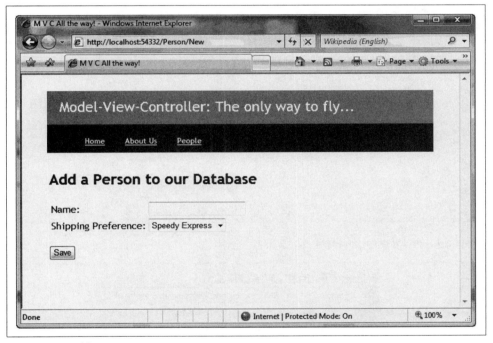

Figure 8-12. Adding a Person

Enter the name Barack Obama, pick the second shipping method, and click Save. The resulting screen should look like the one in Figure 8-13.

One of the more amazing things about wiring objects in the presentation and business tiers to columns in a row of the database is that you don't have to write SQL statements, yet you still manage to get Barack and his preferred shipping method (option 2) into the database correctly (Figure 8-14).

That wraps up this sample application. The MVC Web Application should only get better with each release.

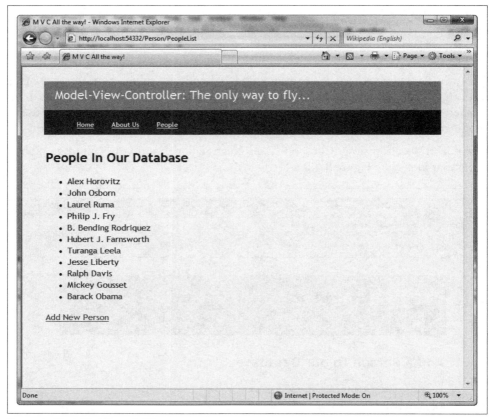

Figure 8-13. Added Barack Obama

IDPerson	IDShippingMethod	PersonName
2	1	Alex Horovitz
4	3	John Osborn
5	1	Laurel Ruma
13	2	Philip J. Fry
14	3	B. Bending Rodriquez
15	2	Hubert J. Farnsworth
16	2	Turanga Leela
17	1	Jesse Liberty
18	1	Ralph Davis
19	1	Mickey Gousset
20	2	Barack Obama
NULL	NULL	NULL

Figure 8-14. Automagic! The database reflects the addition

The Observer Pattern/Publish and Subscribe

As you might guess from its name, the Observer pattern is used to observe the state of an object. A variant on this pattern is Publish and Subscribe, where the observed object "publishes" some event or events (e.g., a clock says "I announce every second") and other objects (the observers) "subscribe" to those events.

To keep things simple, we'll refer to the two patterns together as the Observer pattern; it really is just a matter of perspective (are you observing me, or am I publishing my events for you to subscribe to?).

The Observer pattern defines a one-to-many dependency between objects, so that when one object changes state, all its dependents are notified and have a chance to respond to the change.

Fundamental to this pattern is the notion that objects (known as observers or listeners) are registered (or self-register) to observe an event that may be raised by the observed object (known as the subject), as seen in Figure 8-15.

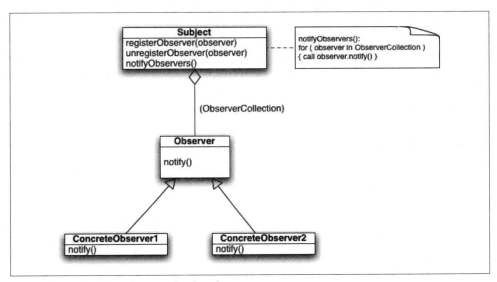

Figure 8-15. UML class diagram for the Observer pattern

To make this a bit more concrete, we'll borrow an example from the real world. Many of you probably read the blog Slashdot.org, pictured in Figure 8-16. (If you don't already, you'll probably start now.) Some of you might even subscribe to Slashdot's daily digest. This site illustrates almost everything there is to know about the Observer pattern: Slashdot publishes and you subscribe, or, from the inverse perspective, you observe and Slashdot is observed.

Figure 8-16. The subject of your observations

An Observer Example

Let's build a little observer application for dealing with flight departures and air traffic control. There will be four pattern participants in this example:

Subject
> The subject knows its observers and provides an interface for attaching and detaching observers. Any number of observer objects may observe a subject.

Concrete subject
> The concrete subject stores the state of interest to concrete observer objects and sends appropriate notifications based on state changes.

Observer
> The observer defines the updating interface for objects that should be notified of changes in a subject.

Concrete observer
> The concrete observer maintains the reference to a concrete subject object. Additionally, it stores the state that should stay consistent with the subject's state and provides the implementation of the observer updating interface.

You'll start with the subject, which in this example will be the `AirlineSchedule` class. The constructor is fairly straightforward. You have the name of an airline, a departure city, an arrival city, and a departure time:

```
abstract class AirlineSchedule
{
    public string Name              { get; set; }
    public string DepartureAirport  { get; set; }
    public string ArrivalAirport    { get; set; }

    private DateTime departureDateTime;
    public DateTime DepartureDateTime
    {
        get { return departureDateTime; }
        set
        {
            departureDateTime = value;
            OnChange(new ChangeEventArgs(
                this.Name,
                this.DepartureAirport,
                this.ArrivalAirport,
                this.departureDateTime));
            Console.WriteLine("");
        }
    }

    public AirlineSchedule(
        string airline,
        string outAirport,
        string inAirport,
        DateTime leaves)
    {
        this.Name = airline;
        this.DepartureAirport = outAirport;
        this.ArrivalAirport = inAirport;
        this.DepartureDateTime = leaves;
    }
}
```

The class declares four properties, only one of which is unusual: the `DepartureDateTime` set method not only sets a member variable but also fires an event, `OnChange( )`.

You set up the event like this:

```
public event ChangeEventHandler<AirlineSchedule, ChangeEventArgs> Change;

// Invoke the Change event
public virtual void OnChange(ChangeEventArgs e)
{
    if (Change != null)
    {
        Change(this, e);
    }
}
```

A key aspect of the subject is that it provides the interface for attaching and detaching observers. The two methods that accomplish this are Attach( ) and Detach( ):

```
public void Attach(AirTrafficControl airTrafficControl)
{
    Change += new ChangeEventHandler<AirlineSchedule,
        ChangeEventArgs>(airTrafficControl.Update);
}

public void Detach(AirTrafficControl airTrafficControl)
{
    Change -= new ChangeEventHandler<AirlineSchedule, ChangeEventArgs>
        (airTrafficControl.Update);
}
```

Your concrete subject class provides the state of interest to observers. It also sends a notification to all observers, by calling the Notify( ) method in its base class (i.e., the subject class). We'll keep things fairly simple here:

```
// A concrete subject
class CarrierSchedule : AirlineSchedule
{
    // Jesse and Alex only really ever need to fly to one place...
    public CarrierSchedule(
        string name,
        DateTime departing):
        base(name,"Boston", "Seattle", departing)
    {
    }
}
```

The observer class defines an updating interface for all observers. This allows them to receive update notifications from the subject(s). Every interested observer will implement the observer interface. The interface requires implementation of a single method, Update( ):

```
interface IATC
{
    void Update(AirlineSchedule sender, ChangeEventArgs e);
}
```

Each concrete observer maintains a reference to a concrete subject so that it may receive notifications of changes to the state of the subject.

As you can see, you override Update( ) in the concrete observer class. When the subject calls the Update( ) method, the concrete observer asks the subject to update the information it has about the subject's state. Each concrete observer implements Update( ) and, as a consequence, defines its own behavior when the notification occurs:

```
// The concrete observer
class AirTrafficControl : IATC
{
    public string Name { get; set; }
    public CarrierSchedule CarrierSchedule { get; set; }
```

```
    // Constructor
    public AirTrafficControl(string name)
    {
        this.Name = name;
    }

    public void Update(AirlineSchedule sender, ChangeEventArgs e)
    {

        Console.WriteLine(
            "{0} Air Traffic Control Notified:\n {1}'s flight 497 from {2} " +
            "to {3} new departure time: {4:hh:mmtt}",
            Name,
            e.Airline,
            e.DepartureAirport,
            e.ArrivalAirport,
            e.DepartureDateTime);
        Console.WriteLine("---------");
    }
}
```

Running the Code

To exercise this Observer pattern, you'll need some code that uses all of your classes. Here is the simple Console Application code:

```
class Program
{
    static void Main( )
    {
        DateTime now = DateTime.Now;
        // Create new flights with a departure time and
        // add from and to destinations
        CarrierSchedule jetBlue =
            new CarrierSchedule("JetBlue", now);
        jetBlue.Attach(new AirTrafficControl("Boston"));
        jetBlue.Attach(new AirTrafficControl("Seattle"));

        // ATCs will be notified of delays in departure time
        jetBlue.DepartureDateTime =
            now.AddHours(1.25); // weather delay
        jetBlue.DepartureDateTime =
            now.AddHours(2.75); // weather got worse
        jetBlue.DepartureDateTime =
            now.AddHours(3.5);  // security delay
        jetBlue.DepartureDateTime =
            now.AddHours(3.75); // Seattle ground stop

        // Wait for user
        Console.Read( );
    }
}
```

Go ahead and create a new C# Console Application project called *Observer*, as shown in Figure 8-17.

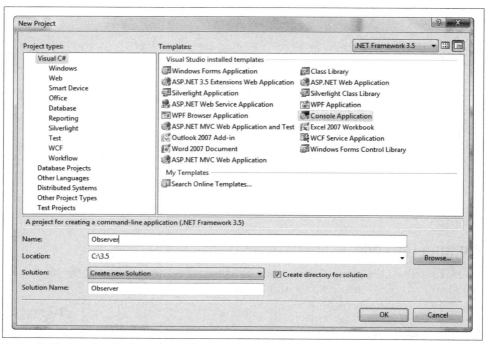

Figure 8-17. Creating the Console Application

The complete code listing for the application is presented in Example 8-2.

Example 8-2. Complete code listing for C# Console Application project Observer

```
using System;

namespace Observer
{
    class Program
    {
        static void Main( )
        {
            DateTime now = DateTime.Now;

            // Create new flights with a departure time
            // and add from and to destinations

            CarrierSchedule jetBlue = new CarrierSchedule("JetBlue", now);
            jetBlue.Attach(new AirTrafficControl("Boston"));
            jetBlue.Attach(new AirTrafficControl("Seattle"));
```

```
        // ATCs will be notified of delays in departure time
        jetBlue.DepartureDateTime =
            now.AddHours(1.25); // weather delay

        jetBlue.DepartureDateTime =
            now.AddHours(1.75); // weather got worse

        jetBlue.DepartureDateTime =
            now.AddHours(0.5);  // security delay

        jetBlue.DepartureDateTime =
            now.AddHours(0.75); // Seattle puts a ground stop in place

        // Wait for user
        Console.Read();
    }
}

// Generic delegate type for hooking up flight schedule requests
public delegate void ChangeEventHandler<T,U>
    (T sender, U eventArgs);

// Customize event arguments to fit the activity
public class ChangeEventArgs : EventArgs
{
    public ChangeEventArgs(
        string name,
        string outAirport,
        string inAirport,
        DateTime leaves)
    {
        this.Airline = name;
        this.DepartureAirport = outAirport;
        this.ArrivalAirport = inAirport;
        this.DepartureDateTime = leaves;
    }

    // Our properties
    public string Airline            { get; set; }
    public string DepartureAirport   { get; set; }
    public string ArrivalAirport     { get; set; }
    public DateTime DepartureDateTime { get; set; }

}

// Subject: This is the thing being watched by Air Traffic Control centers
abstract class AirlineSchedule
{

    // Properties
    public string Name               { get; set; }
    public string DepartureAirport   { get; set; }
```

```
        public string ArrivalAirport        { get; set; }
        private DateTime departureDateTime;

        public AirlineSchedule(
            string airline,
            string outAirport,
            string inAirport,
            DateTime leaves)
        {
            this.Name = airline;
            this.DepartureAirport = outAirport;
            this.ArrivalAirport = inAirport;
            this.DepartureDateTime = leaves;
        }
        // Event
        public event ChangeEventHandler<AirlineSchedule, ChangeEventArgs> Change;

        // Invoke the Change event
        public virtual void OnChange(ChangeEventArgs e)
        {
            if (Change != null)
            {
                Change(this, e);
            }
        }


        // Here is where we actually attach our observers (ATCs)
        public void Attach(AirTrafficControl airTrafficControl)
        {
            Change +=
                new ChangeEventHandler<AirlineSchedule, ChangeEventArgs>
                (airTrafficControl.Update);
        }

        public void Detach(AirTrafficControl airTrafficControl)
        {
            Change -= new ChangeEventHandler<AirlineSchedule, ChangeEventArgs>
                (airTrafficControl.Update);
        }

        public DateTime DepartureDateTime
        {
            get { return departureDateTime; }
            set
            {
                departureDateTime = value;
                OnChange(new ChangeEventArgs(
                    this.Name,
                    this.DepartureAirport,
                    this.ArrivalAirport,
                    this.departureDateTime));
                Console.WriteLine("");
```

```
        }
    }

}

// A concrete subject
class CarrierSchedule : AirlineSchedule
{
    // Jesse and Alex only really ever need to fly to one place...
    public CarrierSchedule(string name, DateTime departing):
        base(name,"Boston", "Seattle", departing)
    {
    }
}

// An observer
interface IATC
{
    void Update(AirlineSchedule sender, ChangeEventArgs e);
}

// The concrete observer
class AirTrafficControl : IATC
{
    public string Name { get; set; }

    // Constructor
    public AirTrafficControl(string name)
    {
        this.Name = name;
    }

    public void Update(AirlineSchedule sender, ChangeEventArgs e)
    {

        Console.WriteLine(
            "{0} Air Traffic Control Notified:\n {1}'s flight 497 from {2} " +
            "to {3} new departure time: {4:hh:mmtt}",
            Name,
            e.Airline,
            e.DepartureAirport,
            e.ArrivalAirport,
            e.DepartureDateTime);
        Console.WriteLine("---------");
    }
    public CarrierSchedule CarrierSchedule { get; set; }
    }
}
```

When you compile and run the application you should get a console window like the one shown in Figure 8-18.

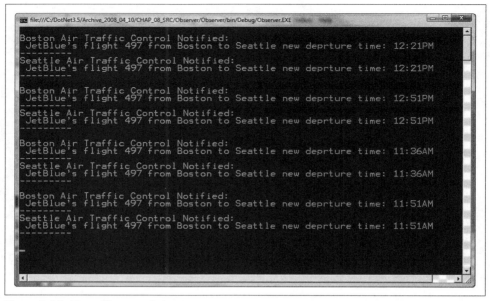

Figure 8-18. Air traffic control observations

The Factory Method Pattern

The Factory Method pattern allows you to abstract the creation of objects, specifying the class of the object at runtime rather than at design time. It accomplishes this by defining a separate method for creating objects (see Figure 8-19). Subclasses can then override the creation method to specify the type of derived object to create, as needed (you can think of it as a "just-in-time inventory" for software). The term "factory" is loosely used to refer to any method whose main purpose is the creation of objects.

Factory methods are most commonly found in toolkits and frameworks, where library code needs to create objects of types that applications using the framework may subclass. It is common in parallel class hierarchies to require objects from one hierarchy to be able to create appropriate objects from another.

Although the primary motivation behind the Factory Method pattern is to allow subclasses to choose which types of objects to create, there are other benefits to using factory methods, some of which do not depend on subclassing. Therefore, it is common to define "factory methods" that are not polymorphic in order to gain these other benefits.

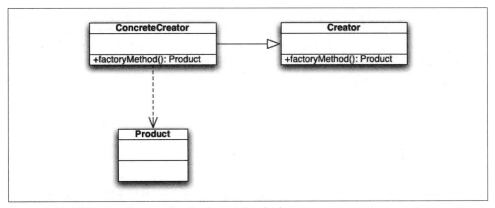

Figure 8-19. UML class diagram for the Factory Method pattern

A Factory Method Example

The ultimate goal of this pattern is to encapsulate the creation of objects. For illustration purposes, you'll build a very pedestrian 20th-century car factory. Each Car class will use an overridden factory method to assign itself the features of its particular subclass.

To start with, consider an abstract Car class:

```
abstract class Car
{
    private List<Feature> features = new List<Feature>();

    // Constructor invokes factory method
    public Car()
    {
        this.CreateFeatures();
    }

    // Property
    public List<Feature> Features
    {
        get { return features; }
    }

    // The Money Method: Factory Method
    public abstract void CreateFeatures();

    // Override
    public override string ToString()
    {
        return this.GetType().Name;
    }
}
```

As you can see, the car has a property that is a list of features (the products). Because the features are very simple, you can focus on the concepts here rather than on the implementation of getters and setters. For display purposes, a feature will just print its class name:

```
abstract class Feature
{
    // Override. Display class name.
    public override string ToString()
    {
        return this.GetType().Name;
    }
}
```

As you can see, you have the basic car features that one would expect from a car factory in a programming book:

```
// ConcreteProduct(s)

class FourWheels : Feature
{
}

class V6Engine : Feature
{
}

class V8Engine : Feature
{
}

class FourDoors : Feature
{
}

class TwoDoors : Feature
{
}

class SunRoof : Feature
{
}

class AirBags : Feature
{
}

class HybridEngine : Feature
{
}
```

Now you're in a position to make concrete subclasses of Car. Each subclass will override the CreateFeatures() method. In this manner, the subclasses will be customized to their types in conformance with the Factory Method pattern:

```
// ConcreteCreator(s)

class CooperMini : Car
{
    // Factory Method implementation (a requirement of the pattern)
    public override void CreateFeatures()
    {
        Features.Add(new FourWheels());
        Features.Add(new TwoDoors());
        Features.Add(new AirBags());
        Features.Add(new V6Engine());
        Features.Add(new SunRoof());
    }
}


class BMWSedan : Car
{
    // Factory Method implementation (a requirement of the pattern)
    public override void CreateFeatures()
    {
        Features.Add(new FourDoors());
        Features.Add(new FourWheels());
        Features.Add(new AirBags());
        Features.Add(new V8Engine());
        Features.Add(new SunRoof());
    }
}

class Prius : Car
{
    // Factory Method implementation (a requirement of the pattern)
    public override void CreateFeatures()
    {
        Features.Add(new TwoDoors());
        Features.Add(new FourWheels());
        Features.Add(new HybridEngine());
        Features.Add(new AirBags());
        Features.Add(new SunRoof());
    }
}

class FordExpedition : Car
{
    // Factory Method implementation (a requirement of the pattern)
    public override void CreateFeatures()
```

```
        {
            Features.Add(new FourDoors());
            Features.Add(new FourWheels());
            Features.Add(new V8Engine());
            Features.Add(new AirBags());
        }
    }
```

Once again, you'll need some code that uses all of these creations and outputs the
results to the console:

```
class Program
{
    static void Main()
    {
        // Note: document constructors call factory method
        List<Car> cars = new List<Car>();
        cars.Add(new CooperMini());
        cars.Add(new BMWSedan());
        cars.Add(new Prius());
        cars.Add(new FordExpedition());

        // Display document pages
        foreach (Car car in cars)
        {
            Console.WriteLine(car +
                " fully loaded with these features:");
            foreach (Feature feature in car.Features)
            {
                Console.WriteLine(" " + feature);
            }
            Console.WriteLine();
        }

        // Wait for user
        Console.Read();
    }
}
```

Go ahead and create a new C# Console Application project, and add the complete
listing for the Factory Method pattern example (shown in Example 8-3).

Example 8-3. Old-fashioned newfangled car factory

```
using System;
using System.Collections.Generic;
using System.Linq;
using System.Text;

namespace FactoryMethod
{
    class Program
    {
        static void Main()
```

Example 8-3. Old-fashioned newfangled car factory (continued)

```
    {
        // Note: car constructors call factory method
        List<Car> cars = new List<Car>();
        cars.Add(new CooperMini());
        cars.Add(new BMWSedan());
        cars.Add(new Prius());
        cars.Add(new FordExpedition());

        // Display car pages
        foreach (Car car in cars)
        {
            Console.WriteLine(car + " fully loaded with these features:");
            foreach (Feature feature in car.Features)
            {
                Console.WriteLine(" " + feature);
            }
            Console.WriteLine();
        }

        // Wait for user
        Console.Read();
    }
}

// Product - in our case our products consist of car features

abstract class Feature
{
    // Override. Display class name.
    public override string ToString()
    {
        return this.GetType().Name;
    }
}

// ConcreteProduct(s)

class FourWheels : Feature
{
}

class V6Engine : Feature
{
}

class V8Engine : Feature
{
}

class FourDoors : Feature
{
}
```

Example 8-3. Old-fashioned newfangled car factory (continued)

```
class TwoDoors : Feature
{
}

class SunRoof : Feature
{
}

class AirBags : Feature
{
}

class HybridEngine : Feature
{
}

// The creator

abstract class Car
{
    private List<Feature> features = new List<Feature>();

    // Constructor invokes factory method
    public Car()
    {
        this.CreateFeatures();
    }

    // Property
    public List<Feature> Features
    {
        get { return features; }
    }

    // The Money Method: Factory Method
    public abstract void CreateFeatures();

    // Override
    public override string ToString()
    {
        return this.GetType().Name;
    }
}

// ConcreteCreator(s)

class CooperMini : Car
{
    // Factory Method implementation (a requirement of the pattern)
    public override void CreateFeatures()
```

Example 8-3. Old-fashioned newfangled car factory (continued)

```
        {
            Features.Add(new FourWheels());
            Features.Add(new TwoDoors());
            Features.Add(new AirBags());
            Features.Add(new V6Engine());
            Features.Add(new SunRoof());
        }
    }

    class BMWSedan : Car
    {
        // Factory Method implementation (a requirement of the pattern)
        public override void CreateFeatures()
        {
            Features.Add(new FourDoors());
            Features.Add(new FourWheels());
            Features.Add(new AirBags());
            Features.Add(new V8Engine());
            Features.Add(new SunRoof());
        }
    }

    class Prius : Car
    {
        // Factory Method implementation (a requirement of the pattern)
        public override void CreateFeatures()
        {
            Features.Add(new TwoDoors());
            Features.Add(new FourWheels());
            Features.Add(new HybridEngine());
            Features.Add(new AirBags());
            Features.Add(new SunRoof());
        }
    }

    class FordExpedition : Car
    {
        // Factory Method implementation (a requirement of the pattern)
        public override void CreateFeatures()
        {
            Features.Add(new FourDoors());
            Features.Add(new FourWheels());
            Features.Add(new V8Engine());
            Features.Add(new AirBags());
        }
    }
}
```

Your fully functioning car factory should run and look something like Figure 8-20.

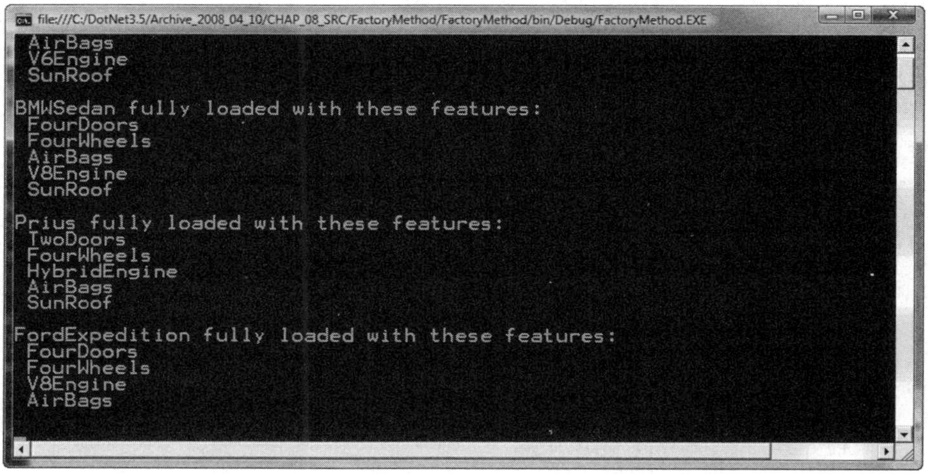

Figure 8-20. Car factory in action

The Chain-of-Command Pattern

This very powerful design pattern allows you to separate command objects from helper (processing) objects, and to create objects that have both responsibilities and a place in a sequence of actions. This is very useful in workflow or other sequential situations.

The Chain-of-Command pattern must be used with caution, however, because programmers moving from procedural programming to object-oriented programming are wont to create a single master commander object and zillions of little processing objects, recreating the procedural pattern that object-oriented programming replaces!

Each processing object contains logic that describes the types of command objects that it can handle, and how to pass off those that it cannot to the next processing object in the chain. Thus, each object is neatly encapsulated and has a single, well-defined set of responsibilities.

For this pattern to work, it must be extensible. That is, a mechanism must exist for adding new processing objects to the end of the chain.

A well-implemented Chain-of-Command pattern (Figure 8-21) can promote loose coupling, which is integral to the kind of n-tier programming that .NET 3.5 fosters and that makes for sustainable software.

A Chain-of-Command Example

To illustrate this pattern, we're going to (grossly) simplify the chain-of-command requirements to allow liftoff of a space shuttle.

Trees of Responsibility

There is an advanced variation of this pattern in which handlers are divided into two subtypes: those that handle the required actions themselves and those that "dispatch" the requirements to other handlers. This variation creates less of a chain than a "tree" of responsibility, which can get quite complex in a large application.

If dispatcher classes can dispatch to themselves, or if object A can dispatch to other objects that can eventually dispatch back to object A, the tree can become recursive. This is not necessarily problematic, as long as the recursion is carefully controlled (i.e., it has an endpoint and the recursion is limited sufficiently so as not to overload the stack). An example of a very successful recursive tree is an XML parser.

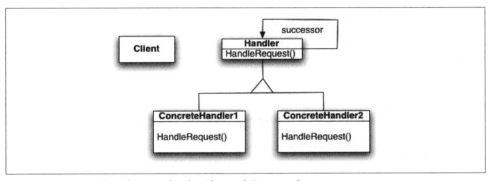

Figure 8-21. UML class diagram for the Chain-of-Command pattern

The requirements for allowing liftoff in this example are:

- There must be three crew members.
- There must be one million pounds of fuel on board.
- All three launch commanders must give a "Go" order in the correct sequence.

In this example, you will create a LaunchRequestEventArgs object to pass into each event. It will contain all the information needed to handle the events (the number of crew members, the amount of fuel on board, and the launchCommandRequest as a string):

```
public class LaunchRequestEventArgs : EventArgs
{

    // Properties
    public int Crew                 { get; set; }
    public string LaunchCommand     { get; set; }
    public double FuelOnBoardInLbs  { get; set; }

    // Constructor
    public LaunchRequestEventArgs(
```

```
      int crewCount,
      double fuelOnBoard,
      string launchCommandRequest)
   {
      this.Crew = crewCount;
      this.FuelOnBoardInLbs = fuelOnBoard;
      this.LaunchCommand = launchCommandRequest;
   }
}
```

This allows you to create a generic delegate that takes an Approver (to be defined in a moment) and an object of type LaunchRequestEventArgs:

```
public delegate void LaunchRequestEventHandler<T, U>(
   T sender, U eventArgs);
```

You will use this delegate to create type-specific events (e.g., one LaunchRequestEventHandler for Pilots and another for Commanders). To do so, you'll take advantage of polymorphism by creating a common (and abstract) base class, Approver:

```
abstract class Approver
{
   public Approver Successor { get;  set; }

   // Event
   public event
      LaunchRequestEventHandler<Approver, LaunchRequestEventArgs> Request;

   // Invoke the launch Request event
   public virtual void OnRequest(LaunchRequestEventArgs e)
   {
      if (Request != null)
      {
         Request(this, e);
      }
   }

   public void ProcessRequest(Request request)
   {
      OnRequest(new LaunchRequestEventArgs(
         request.Crew, request.FuelOnBoardInLbs, request.LaunchCommand));
   }
}
```

You're now ready to create the derived Approver types, each with its own specialized event:

```
class Pilot : Approver
{

   public Pilot()
   {
      this.Request +=
         new LaunchRequestEventHandler<
         Approver, LaunchRequestEventArgs>(PilotRequest);
   }
```

```
public void PilotRequest(Approver approver,
    LaunchRequestEventArgs e)
{
    if (e.Crew < 3)
    {
        Console.WriteLine(
            "{0}, you are only reporting {1} crew on board.",
            this.GetType( ).Name,
            e.Crew);
        Console.WriteLine("We need at least 3. {0} denied.\n\n",
            e.LaunchCommand);
    }
    else if (Successor != null)
    {
        Console.WriteLine("{0}: Commander says: {1} Go.\n\n",
            e.LaunchCommand,
            this.GetType( ).Name);
        Successor.OnRequest(e);
    }
}
}
```

The logic of the PilotRequest is this: if there are fewer than three crew members, the
pilot will deny the request. Otherwise, if there is a successor (another approver in
line after this one), the pilot will give the "Go" order.

The Commander class is very much the same, except that the condition checked for is
sufficient fuel:

```
class Commander : Approver
{
    public Commander( )
    {
        // Hook up delegate to event
        this.Request +=
            new LaunchRequestEventHandler<
            Approver, LaunchRequestEventArgs>(CommanderRequest);
    }

    public void CommanderRequest(Approver approver,
        LaunchRequestEventArgs e)
    {
        if (e.FuelOnBoardInLbs < 1000000.0)
        {
            // Report error
        }
        else if (Successor != null)
        {
            // Report Go and chain to Successor
        }
    }
}
```

The complete program is shown in Example 8-4.

Example 8-4. Complete chain-of-command program

```
using System;

namespace ChainOfCommand
{
    class Program
    {

        static void Main( )
        {
            Request request;

            // Set up chain of responsibility
            Approver Buzz = new Pilot( );
            Approver Neil = new Commander( );
            Approver Gene = new FlightDirector( );

            Buzz.Successor = Neil;
            Neil.Successor = Gene;

            // Generate and process launch requests
            request = new Request(2, 35000.00, "Launch 1");
            Buzz.ProcessRequest(request);

            request = new Request(3, 35000.00, "Launch 2");
            Buzz.ProcessRequest(request);

            request = new Request(3, 1221000.50, "Launch 3");
            Buzz.ProcessRequest(request);

            // Wait for user
            Console.Read( );
        }
    }

    public class LaunchRequestEventArgs : EventArgs
    {

        // Properties
        public int Crew             { get; set; }
        public string LaunchCommand    { get; set; }
        public double FuelOnBoardInLbs  { get; set; }

        // Constructor
        public LaunchRequestEventArgs(
            int crewCount,
            double fuelOnBoard,
            string launchCommandRequest)
        {
            this.Crew = crewCount;
            this.FuelOnBoardInLbs = fuelOnBoard;
            this.LaunchCommand = launchCommandRequest;
        }
```

Example 8-4. Complete chain-of-command program (continued)

```
    }

    // Generic delegate for hooking up launch requests
    public delegate void LaunchRequestEventHandler<T, U>(
        T sender, U eventArgs);

    // "Handler"
    abstract class Approver
    {
        public Approver Successor { get;  set; }

        // Event
        public event LaunchRequestEventHandler<
            Approver, LaunchRequestEventArgs> Request;

        // Invoke the launch request event
        public virtual void OnRequest(LaunchRequestEventArgs e)
        {
            if (Request != null)
            {
                Request(this, e);
            }
        }

        public void ProcessRequest(Request request)
        {
            OnRequest(new LaunchRequestEventArgs(
                request.Crew,
                request.FuelOnBoardInLbs,
                request.LaunchCommand));
        }

    }

    // "ConcreteHandler"

    class Pilot : Approver
    {
        // Constructor
        public Pilot()
        {
            // Hook up delegate to event
            this.Request += new LaunchRequestEventHandler<
                Approver, LaunchRequestEventArgs>(PilotRequest);
        }

        public void PilotRequest(Approver approver,
            LaunchRequestEventArgs e)
        {
            if (e.Crew < 3)
            {
                Console.WriteLine(
```

Example 8-4. Complete chain-of-command program (continued)

```
                "{0}, you are only reporting {1} crew on board.",
                this.GetType( ).Name, e.Crew);
            Console.WriteLine(
                "We need at least 3. {0} denied.\n\n",
                e.LaunchCommand);
        }
        else if (Successor != null)
        {
            Console.WriteLine(
                "{0}: Commander says: {1} Go.\n\n",
                e.LaunchCommand, this.GetType( ).Name);
            Successor.OnRequest(e);
        }
    }
}

// "ConcreteHandler"
class Commander : Approver
{
    // Constructor
    public Commander( )
    {
        // Hook up delegate to event
        this.Request +=
            new LaunchRequestEventHandler<
            Approver, LaunchRequestEventArgs>(CommanderRequest);
    }

    public void CommanderRequest(Approver approver,
        LaunchRequestEventArgs e)
    {
        if (e.FuelOnBoardInLbs < 1000000.0)
        {
            Console.WriteLine(
                "{0}, you are only reporting {1}
                lbs of fuel on board.",
                this.GetType( ).Name, e.FuelOnBoardInLbs);
            Console.WriteLine(
                "You need at least 1 Million. {0} denied.\n\n",
                e.LaunchCommand);
        }
        else if (Successor != null)
        {
            Console.WriteLine(
                "{0}: Flight Director says: {1} Go.\n\n",
                e.LaunchCommand, this.GetType( ).Name);
            Successor.OnRequest(e);
        }

    }
}
```

Example 8-4. Complete chain-of-command program (continued)

```
// "ConcreteHandler"
class FlightDirector : Approver
{
    // Constructor
    public FlightDirector( )
    {
        // Hook up delegate to event
        this.Request +=
            new LaunchRequestEventHandler<
            Approver, LaunchRequestEventArgs>(FlightDirectorRequest);
    }

    public void FlightDirectorRequest(Approver approver,
        LaunchRequestEventArgs e)
    {
        if (e.FuelOnBoardInLbs < 1000000.0)
        {
            Console.WriteLine(
                "{0}, you are only reporting {1}
                lbs of fuel on board.",
                this.GetType( ).Name, e.FuelOnBoardInLbs);
            Console.WriteLine(
                "You need at least 1 Million. {0} Denied.\n\n",
                e.LaunchCommand);
        }
        else
        {
            Console.WriteLine(
                "{0}: All Systems Go! Launch Control,
                launch is a Go!",
                this.GetType( ).Name);
        }
    }
}

// Request details

class Request
{
    private int crew;
    private double fuelOnBoardInLbs;
    private string launchCommand;

    public Request(
        int crewCount,
        double fuelOnBoard,
        string launchCommandRequest)
    {
        this.crew = crewCount;
        this.fuelOnBoardInLbs = fuelOnBoard;
        this.launchCommand = launchCommandRequest;
    }
```

Example 8-4. Complete chain-of-command program (continued)

```
      // Properties
      public int Crew
      {
         get { return crew; }
         set { crew = value; }
      }

      public string LaunchCommand
      {
         get { return launchCommand; }
         set { launchCommand = value; }
      }

      public double FuelOnBoardInLbs
      {
         get { return fuelOnBoardInLbs; }
         set { fuelOnBoardInLbs = value; }
      }
   }
}
```

Its output is as follows:

```
Pilot, you are only reporting 2 crew on board.
We need at least 3. Launch 1 denied.

Launch 2: Commander says: Pilot Go.

Commander, you are only reporting 35000 lbs of fuel on board.
You need at least 1 Million. Launch 2 denied.

Launch 3: Commander says: Pilot Go.
Launch 3: Flight Director says: Commander Go.

FlightDirector: All Systems Go! Launch Control, launch is a Go!
```

The flight can launch only once the required conditions are met (all three crew members are on board and there's enough fuel) and the three commanders (Launch 1, 2, and 3) give the "Go" command in order, followed by the "Go" from the FlightDirector.

The Singleton Pattern

One of the simplest (yet perhaps most useful) patterns is the Singleton pattern. The entire purpose of this pattern is to ensure that only one instance of an object is ever created during the lifetime of an application.

The typical implementation of the Singleton pattern is to create a private constructor (not accessible to other classes), and then a public method that poses as a constructor but has the job of, when called, serving up the existing instance if there is one, or creating an instance if none exists.

Singletons and Multithreading

The Singleton pattern's implementation can get a bit tricky in multithreaded applications, so programmers often turn to well-tested code rather than reinventing Singleton implementations. If two threads are to execute the creation method at the same time when a singleton does not yet exist, they both must check for an instance of the singleton, and only one may create the new instance. Also note that if the programming language has concurrent processing capabilities (as .NET languages do), the method must be constructed to execute as a mutually exclusive operation.

The classic solution to these problems is to use mutual exclusion on the class that indicates that the object is being instantiated, most often through a mutex or other thread-locking device. The Singleton pattern (Figure 8-22) is often used in conjunction with the Factory Method pattern to create a system-wide resource whose specific type is not known to the code that uses it.

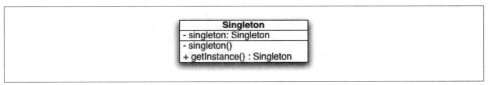

Figure 8-22. UML class diagram for the Singleton pattern

A Singleton Example

To see how the Singleton pattern works, create a new Console Application and add a simple SMTPHost object:

```
class SMTPHost
{
    private string name;
    private string ip;

    public SMTPHost(string name, string ip)
    {
        this.name = name;
        this.ip = ip;
    }
    public string Name
    {
        get { return name; }
    }
    public string IP
    {
        get { return ip; }
    }
}
```

You have to create the backing variable for the properties because you are not creating a setter.

Now create a `MailDelivery` class containing a list of `SMTPHost` objects named (appropriately) `smtpServers`. The `MailDelivery` constructor will populate its list with 10 `SMTPHost` objects:

```
private MailDelivery( )
{
    // List of available smtp servers
    smtpServers.Add(new SMTPHost("Mail 1","192.168.0.100"));
    smtpServers.Add(new SMTPHost("Mail 2","192.168.0.101"));
    smtpServers.Add(new SMTPHost("Mail 3","192.168.0.102"));
    smtpServers.Add(new SMTPHost("Mail 4","192.168.0.103"));
    smtpServers.Add(new SMTPHost("Mail 5","192.168.0.104"));
    smtpServers.Add(new SMTPHost("Mail 6","192.168.0.105"));
    smtpServers.Add(new SMTPHost("Mail 7","192.168.0.106"));
    smtpServers.Add(new SMTPHost("Mail 8","192.168.0.107"));
    smtpServers.Add(new SMTPHost("Mail 9","192.168.0.108"));
    smtpServers.Add(new SMTPHost("Mail 10","192.168.0.109"));
}
```

Note that the constructor is private. As stated previously, that's because this application will only ever have zero or one instances of a `MailDelivery` object: when clients ask for a `MailDelivery` object, they will get the singleton. They ask for the `MailDelivery` object by calling the public property `SMTPServer`, which will load balance by randomly delivering one of the SMTP servers in the `MailDelivery`'s list of `SMTPServer` objects:

```
public SMTPHost SmtpServer
{
    get
    {
        int r = random.Next(smtpServers.Count);
        return smtpServers[r];
    }
}
```

Let C# take care of the threading issues for you by declaring the one instance of `MailDelivery` to be static; .NET guarantees thread safety for static initialization (thank you very much!). The complete application is shown in Example 8-5.

Example 8-5. Singleton pattern example

```
using System;
using System.Collections.Generic;

namespace Singleton
{
    class Program
```

Example 8-5. Singleton pattern example (continued)

```
{
    /// Entry point into console application
    /// </summary>
    static void Main()
    {
        // What happens when we ask for the load distributor 10 times?
        MailDelivery m1 = MailDelivery.GetSMTPLoadDistributor();
        MailDelivery m2 = MailDelivery.GetSMTPLoadDistributor();
        MailDelivery m3 = MailDelivery.GetSMTPLoadDistributor();
        MailDelivery m4 = MailDelivery.GetSMTPLoadDistributor();
        MailDelivery m5 = MailDelivery.GetSMTPLoadDistributor();
        MailDelivery m6 = MailDelivery.GetSMTPLoadDistributor();
        MailDelivery m7 = MailDelivery.GetSMTPLoadDistributor();
        MailDelivery m8 = MailDelivery.GetSMTPLoadDistributor();
        MailDelivery m9 = MailDelivery.GetSMTPLoadDistributor();
        MailDelivery m10 = MailDelivery.GetSMTPLoadDistributor();

        // Because we are creating a singleton, each
        // instance should be the same

        // Trust but verify!

        if (m1 == m2 && m2 == m3 && m3 == m4 && m4 == m5 &&
            m5 == m6 && m6 == m7 && m7 == m8 && m8 == m9 && m9 == m10)
        {
            Console.WriteLine("Verified. Just one instance ever created.\n");
        }

        // Distribute 100 outbound email requests for an SMTP server
        MailDelivery md = MailDelivery.GetSMTPLoadDistributor();
        for (int i = 0; i < 100; i++)
        {
            Console.WriteLine(md.SmtpServer.Name+" @ "+md.SmtpServer.IP);
        }

        // When the user hits Enter the console will quit...
        Console.Read();
    }
}

// Singleton
sealed class MailDelivery
{
    // Static members are initialized immediately when the class is
    // loaded for the first time. You should note that .NET guarantees
    // thread safety for static initialization. This is a great thing,
    // because thread safety can be a hard thing to do on your own.

    private static readonly MailDelivery instance =
        new MailDelivery();
```

Example 8-5. Singleton pattern example (continued)

```
        private List<SMTPHost> smtpServers = new List<SMTPHost>();

        private Random random = new Random();

        public SMTPHost SmtpServer
        {
            get
            {
                int r = random.Next(smtpServers.Count);
                return smtpServers[r];
            }
        }

        // Private constructor -- no going around making your own, thank you
        private MailDelivery()
        {
            // List of available smtp servers
            smtpServers.Add(new SMTPHost("Mail 1","192.168.0.100"));
            smtpServers.Add(new SMTPHost("Mail 2","192.168.0.101"));
            smtpServers.Add(new SMTPHost("Mail 3","192.168.0.102"));
            smtpServers.Add(new SMTPHost("Mail 4","192.168.0.103"));
            smtpServers.Add(new SMTPHost("Mail 5","192.168.0.104"));
            smtpServers.Add(new SMTPHost("Mail 6","192.168.0.105"));
            smtpServers.Add(new SMTPHost("Mail 7","192.168.0.106"));
            smtpServers.Add(new SMTPHost("Mail 8","192.168.0.107"));
            smtpServers.Add(new SMTPHost("Mail 9","192.168.0.108"));
            smtpServers.Add(new SMTPHost("Mail 10","192.168.0.109"));
        }

        public static MailDelivery GetSMTPLoadDistributor()
        {
            return instance;
        }

    }

    // Simple server machine
    class SMTPHost
    {
        private string name;
        private string ip;

        public SMTPHost(string name, string ip)
        {
            this.name = name;
            this.ip = ip;
        }
        public string Name
        {
            get { return name; }
        }
```

Example 8-5. Singleton pattern example (continued)

```
    public string IP
    {
        get { return ip; }
    }
  }
}
```

Figure 8-23 shows the output from running this program.

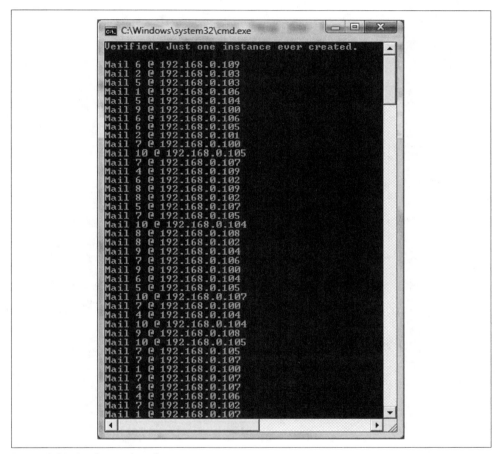

Figure 8-23. Singleton example output

There you have it—a brief interlude into the wonderful world of design patterns. Now back to your regularly scheduled book.

The Business Layer

Understanding LINQ:
Queries As First-Class Language
Constructs

One of the tasks programmers typically perform every day is finding and retrieving objects in memory, a database, or an XML file. For example, you may be developing an application to allow your customers to keep track of all their music purchases from various sources (e.g., online, brick and mortar shops, or one another) and where their music is stored. To accomplish this, you'll need to retrieve data from multiple sources (e.g., iTunes, various online sites, and computers on your network), and to filter that information by numerous and changing criteria (name, month, cost, artist, last-listened-to date, etc.).

In the past, you might have implemented all of this by uploading all your data into a relational database and then querying that database using Transact-SQL. Unfortunately, the data is likely to change frequently (in some families, hourly!). Also, much of it will already be available to you, though not natively in a database; it will be available through web services and other data sources.

The traditional .NET Framework approach using ADO.NET does not lend itself to easily aggregating and searching disparate data sources. In-memory searches lack the powerful and flexible query capabilities of SQL, while ADO.NET is not integrated into C#, and SQL itself is not object-oriented (in fact, the point of ADO.NET was to bridge the gap between the object and relational models).

To solve these and other issues, the designers of .NET 3.x introduced *Language INtegrated Query* (LINQ) syntax. LINQ is a first-class part of all .NET 3.x languages. It provides (at long last) an object-oriented language feature that fully bridges the so-called impedance mismatch between object-oriented languages and relational databases—namely, the differences between objects and the way data is actually stored in a database—while allowing you to search, filter, and aggregate disparate data sources.

Defining and Executing a LINQ Query

In previous versions of the Common Language Syntax, you queried a database through the Framework using ADO.NET outside your specific programming language. With LINQ, you can stay within your language and within a fully class-based perspective.

Let's start with a simple use case: searching a collection for objects that match a given criterion, as demonstrated in Example 9-1 using C# 3.0. The LINQ-specific code is highlighted and is explained after the listing.

Example 9-1. A simple LINQ query

```
using System;
using System.Collections.Generic;
using System.Linq;
using System.Text;

namespace SimpleLINQ
{
    // Simple customer class
    public class Customer
    {
        public string FirstName { get; set; }
        public string LastName { get; set; }
        public string EmailAddress { get; set; }

        // Overrides the Object.ToString() to provide a
        // string representation of the object properties.
        public override string ToString()
        {
            return string.Format("{0} {1}\nEmail:   {2}",
                FirstName, LastName, EmailAddress);
        }
    }

    // Main program
    public class Tester
    {
        static void Main()
        {
            List<Customer> customers = CreateCustomerList();

            // Find customer by first name
            IEnumerable<Customer> result =
                from customer in customers
                where customer.FirstName == "Donna"
                select customer;
            Console.WriteLine("FirstName == \"Donna\"");
            foreach (Customer customer in result)
                Console.WriteLine(customer.ToString());
```

Example 9-1. A simple LINQ query (continued)

```
        customers[3].FirstName = "Donna";
        Console.WriteLine("FirstName == \"Donna\" (take two)");
        foreach (Customer customer in result)
            Console.WriteLine(customer.ToString());
        Console.Read();
    }

    // Create a customer list with sample data
    private static List<Customer> CreateCustomerList()
    {
        List<Customer> customers = new List<Customer>
        {
            new Customer { FirstName = "Orlando",
                LastName = "Gee",
                EmailAddress = "orlando0@adventure-works.com"},
            new Customer { FirstName = "Keith",
                LastName = "Harris",
                EmailAddress = "keith0@adventure-works.com" },
            new Customer { FirstName = "Donna",
                LastName = "Carreras",
                EmailAddress = "donna0@adventure-works.com" },
            new Customer { FirstName = "Janet",
                LastName = "Gates",
                EmailAddress = "janet1@adventure-works.com" },
            new Customer { FirstName = "Lucy",
                LastName = "Harrington",
                EmailAddress = "lucy0@adventure-works.com" }
        };
        return customers;
    }
  }
}
```

Example 9-1 defines a very simple Customer class with three properties: FirstName, LastName, and EmailAddress. It overrides the Object.ToString() method to provide a custom string representation of its instances, thereby simplifying the output of this sample program (see Figure 9-1).

Creating the Query

The main program starts by creating a customer list with some sample data, taking advantage of object initialization. Once the list of customers is created, Example 9-1 defines a LINQ query:

```
IEnumerable<Customer> result =
    from    customer in customers
    where   customer.FirstName == "Donna"
    select  customer;
```

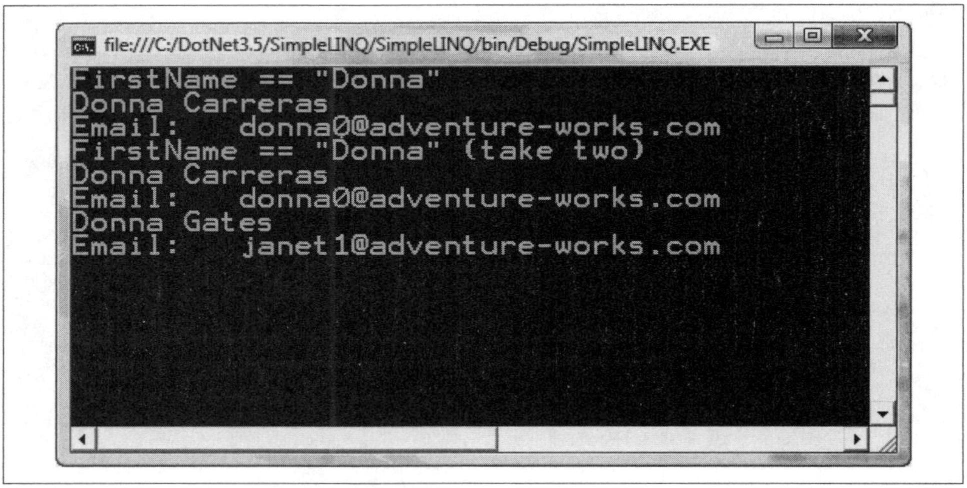

Figure 9-1. Output from the SimpleLINQ console

The result variable is initialized with a query expression. In this example, the query will retrieve from the customers list all Customer objects with a FirstName property value of Donna. The result of such a query is a collection that implements IEnumerable<T>, where T is the type of the result object. In this example, since the query result is a set of Customer objects, the type of the result variable is IEnumerable<Customer>. Now let's dissect the query and look at each part in a little more detail.

The from clause

The first part of a LINQ query is the from clause:

```
from    customer in customers
```

The generator of a LINQ query specifies the data source and a range variable. A LINQ data source can be any collection that implements the System.Collections.Generic.IEnumerable<T> interface. In this example, the data source is customers, an instance of List<Customer> that implements IEnumerable<T>.

A LINQ range variable acts like an iteration variable in a foreach loop, iterating over the data source. Because the data source implements IEnumerable<T>, the C# compiler can infer the type of the range variable from the data source. In this example, since the type of the data source is List<Customer>, the range variable customer is of type Customer.

Filtering

The second part of this LINQ query is the where clause, which is also called a *filter*:

```
where   customer.FirstName == "Donna"
```

The filter is a Boolean expression that returns either true or false. It is common to use the range variable in the where clause to filter the objects in the data source. In this example, because customer is of type Customer, you use one of its properties (FirstName) to apply the filter for the query.

You can, however, use any expression that evaluates to either true or false. For instance, you can invoke the String.StartsWith() method to filter customers by the first letter of their last names:

```
where  customer.LastName.StartsWith("G")
```

You can also use composite expressions to construct more complex queries, or even nested queries, where the result of one query (the inner query) is used to filter another query (the outer query).

Projection

The last part of a LINQ query is the select clause (known to database geeks as a "projection"), which defines (or projects) the results. In this example, the query returns the customer objects that satisfy the query condition:

```
select customer;
```

However, the result can be anything. For instance, you can return the qualified customers' email addresses only:

```
select customer.EmailAddress;
```

That's all there is to a simple LINQ query.

 You may notice a striking similarity between the syntax of LINQ and SQL. The one outstanding difference is the select (projection) clause. C# requires that variables be declared before they are used; since the from clause defines the range variable, it must be stated first in a LINQ query.

Deferred Query Evaluation

LINQ implements *deferred query evaluation*, meaning that the declaration and initialization of a query expression do not actually cause the query to be executed. Instead, a LINQ query is executed, or evaluated, when you iterate through the query result:

```
foreach (Customer customer in result)
    Console.WriteLine(customer.ToString());
```

Because this query returns a collection of Customer objects, the iteration variable is an instance of the Customer class that you can use as you would any Customer object. This example simply calls each Customer object's ToString() method to output its property values to the console.

You can iterate through the query many times. The query will be re-evaluated each time, and if the data source has changed between executions, the result will be different. This is demonstrated in the next section of Example 9-1:

```
customers[3].FirstName = "Donna";
```

This statement modifies the first name of the customer "Janet Gates" to "Donna," and the following lines iterate through the result again:

```
Console.WriteLine("FirstName == \"Donna\" (take two)");
foreach (Customer customer in result)
    Console.WriteLine(customer.ToString( ));

Console.Read( );  // This forces the console to wait for your input
```

As you can see in the sample output (shown earlier in Figure 9-1), in "take two" the result includes Donna Gates as well as Donna Carreras.

In most situations, deferred query evaluation is desired because you want to obtain the most recent data from the data source each time you run the query. However, if you want to cache the result so it can be processed later without having to re-execute the query, you can call either the ToList( ) or the ToArray( ) method to save a copy of the result. Example 9-2 demonstrates this technique. As in Example 9-1 and all subsequent examples, the LINQ-specific code is highlighted.

Example 9-2. A simple LINQ query with cached results

```
using System;
using System.Collections.Generic;
using System.Linq;

namespace LinqChapter
{
    // Simple customer class
    public class Customer
    {
        // Same as in Example 9-1
    }

    // Main program
    public class Tester
    {
        static void Main( )
        {
            List<Customer> customers = CreateCustomerList( );

            // Find customer by first name
            IEnumerable<Customer> result =
                from customer in customers
                where customer.FirstName == "Donna"
                select customer;
            List<Customer> cachedResult = result.ToList<Customer>( );
```

Example 9-2. A simple LINQ query with cached results (continued)

```
        Console.WriteLine("FirstName == \"Donna\"");
        foreach (Customer customer in cachedResult)
            Console.WriteLine(customer.ToString());

        customers[3].FirstName = "Donna";
        Console.WriteLine("FirstName == \"Donna\" (take two)");
        foreach (Customer customer in cachedResult)
            Console.WriteLine(customer.ToString());
        Console.Read();
    }

    // Create a customer list with sample data
    private static List<Customer> CreateCustomerList()
    {
        // Same as in Example 9-1
    }
  }
}
```

Figure 9-2 shows the results.

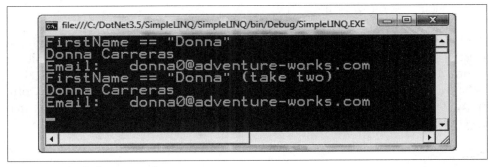

Figure 9-2. Cached query results

In this example, you call the ToList<T>( ) method of the result collection to cache the result. Note that calling this method causes the query to be evaluated immediately. If the data source is subsequently changed, the change will not be reflected in the cached result: as you can see in the output, this time "take two" does not include Donna Gates.

One interesting point here is that the ToList<T>( ) and ToArray<T>( ) methods are not actually methods of IEnumerable; rather, they are extension methods provided by LINQ. Extension methods are discussed later in this chapter.

Joining

Often, you'll want to search for objects from more than one data source. LINQ provides a join clause that offers you the ability to join many data sources. Suppose, for example, you have a list of customers containing customer names and email addresses, and a list of customer home addresses. You can use LINQ to combine both lists to produce a list of customers and both their email and home addresses:

```
from customer in customers
    join address in addresses on
        customer.Name equals address.Name
...
```

Like in SQL, the join condition is specified in the on subclause. The join class syntax is:

```
[data source 1] join [data source 2] on [join condition]
```

In the preceding example we joined two data sources, customers and addresses, based on the Name properties in each customer object. In fact, you can join more than two data sources using a combination of join clauses. For example:

```
from customer in customers
    join address in addresses on
        customer.Name equals address.Name
    join invoice in invoices  on
        customer.Id    equals invoice.CustomerId
    join invoiceItem in invoiceItems on
        invoice.Id    equals invoiceItem.invoiceId
```

A LINQ join clause returns a result only when objects satisfying the join condition exist in all data sources. For instance, if a customer has no invoice, the query will not return anything for that customer (not even her name and email address). This behavior is the equivalent of the SQL inner join clause. LINQ does not perform outer joins, which return results if *either* of the data sources contains objects that meet the join condition.

Ordering

You can sort a LINQ query's results by specifying the sort order with the orderby clause:

```
from customer in customers
    orderby customer.LastName
    select customer;
```

This sorts the results by customer last name, in ascending order. You can sort in descending order as well. Example 9-3 shows how you can sort the results of a join query.

Example 9-3. A sorted join query

```
using System;
using System.Collections.Generic;
using System.Linq;
```

Example 9-3. A sorted join query (continued)

```
namespace LinqChapter
{
    // Simple customer class
    public class Customer
    {
        // Same as in Example 9-1
    }

    // Customer Address class
    public class Address
    {
        public string Name   { get; set; }
        public string Street { get; set; }
        public string City   { get; set; }

        // Overrides the Object.ToString( ) to provide a
        // string representation of the object properties.
        public override string ToString( )
        {
            return string.Format("{0}, {1}", Street, City);
        }
    }

    // Main program
    public class Tester
    {
        static void Main( )
        {
            List<Customer> customers = CreateCustomerList( );
            List<Address>  addresses = CreateAddressList( );

            // Find all addresses of a customer
            var result =
                from customer in customers
                    join address in addresses on
                        string.Format("{0} {1}", customer.FirstName,
                            customer.LastName)
                        equals address.Name
                orderby customer.LastName, address.Street descending
                select new { Customer = customer, Address = address };
            foreach (var ca in result)
            {
                Console.WriteLine(string.Format("{0}\nAddress: {1}",
                    ca.Customer, ca.Address));
            }

            Console.Read( );
        }

        // Create a customer list with sample data
        private static List<Customer> CreateCustomerList( )
```

Example 9-3. A sorted join query (continued)

```
    {
        // Same as in Example 9-1
    }

    // Create a customer list with sample data
    private static List<Address> CreateAddressList()
    {
        List<Address> addresses = new List<Address>
        {
            new Address { Name   = "Janet Gates",
                Street = "165 North Main",
                City = "Austin" },
            new Address { Name   = "Keith Harris",
                Street = "3207 S Grady Way",
                City = "Renton" },
            new Address { Name   = "Janet Gates",
                Street = "800 Interchange Blvd.",
                City = "Austin" },
            new Address { Name   = "Keith Harris",
                Street = "7943 Walnut Ave",
                City = "Renton" },
            new Address { Name   = "Orlando Gee",
                Street = "2251 Elliot Avenue",
                City = "Seattle" }
        };
        return addresses;
    }
  }
}
```

The output from this example is shown in Figure 9-3.

The `Customer` class in Example 9-3 is identical to the one used in Example 9-1. The `Address` class is also very simple, with a customer name field containing names in the `<first name> <last name>` form, and fields for the street and city.

The `CreateCustomerList()` and `CreateAddressList()` methods are just helper functions to create sample data for this example. They also use the new C# object and collection initializers.

The query definition, however, looks quite different from the one in the last example:

```
var result =
    from customer in customers
        join address in addresses on
            string.Format("{0} {1}", customer.FirstName,
                customer.LastName)
            equals address.Name
    orderby customer.LastName, address.Street descending
    select new { Customer = customer, Address = address.Street };
```

The first difference is the declaration of the result. Instead of declaring the result as an explicitly typed `IEnumerable<Customer>` instance, this example declares the result

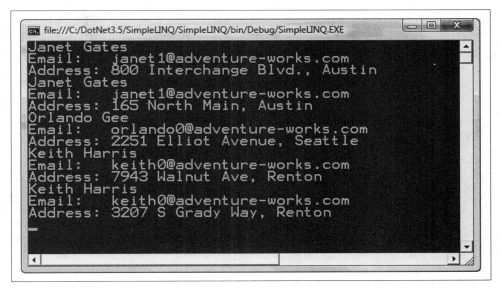

Figure 9-3. Sorted join query output

as an implicitly typed variable using the new var keyword. We'll return to this topic in the next section; for now, we'll stick with the query definition itself.

The generator now contains a join clause to signify that the query is to be operated on two data sources, customers and addresses. Because the customer name property in the Address class is a concatenation of the customers' first and last names, you construct the names in Customer objects using the same format:

```
string.Format("{0} {1}", customer.FirstName,
    customer.LastName)
```

The dynamically constructed full name is then compared with the customer name properties in the Address objects using the equals operator:

```
equals address.Name
```

The orderby clause indicates the order in which the results should be sorted. In this example, they will be sorted first by customer last name in ascending order, then by street address in descending order:

```
orderby customer.LastName, address.Street descending
```

The combined customer name, email address, and home address are returned. But here you have a problem—LINQ can return a collection of objects of any type, but it can't return multiple objects of different types in the same query unless they are encapsulated in one type. For instance, you can select either an instance of the Customer class, or an instance of the Address class, but you cannot select both like this:

```
select customer, address
```

One solution is to define a new type containing both objects. An obvious choice is to define a `CustomerAddress` class:

```
public class CustomerAddress
{
    public Customer Customer { get; set; }
    public Address Address   { get; set; }
}
```

You can then return customers and their addresses from the query in a collection of `CustomerAddress` objects:

```
var result =
    from customer in customers
        join address in addresses on
            string.Format("{0} {1}", customer.FirstName,
                customer.LastName)
            equals address.Name
    orderby customer.LastName, address.Street descending
    select new CustomerAddress { Customer = customer, Address = address };
```

Implicitly Typed Local Variables

Now let's go back to the declaration of query results, where you declare the result as type var:

```
var result = ...
```

Because the `select` clause returns an instance of an anonymous type, you cannot define an explicit type `IEnumerable<T>`. Fortunately, C# 3.0 provides another feature, *implicitly typed local variables*, that solves this problem.

You can declare an implicitly typed local variable by specifying its type as var:

```
var id = 1;
var name = "Keith";
var customers = new List<Customer>();
var person = new {FirstName = "Donna",
    LastName = "Gates",
    Phone="123-456-7890" };
```

The C# compiler infers the type of an implicitly typed local variable from its initialized value. Therefore, you must initialize such a variable when you declare it. In the preceding code snippet, the type of `id` will be set as an `integer` and the type of `name` as a `string`, while `customers` will be set as a strongly typed `List<T>` of `Customer` objects. The type of the last variable, `person`, is an anonymous type containing three properties: `FirstName`, `LastName`, and `Phone`. Although this type has no name in your code, the C# compiler secretly assigns it one and keeps track of its instances. In fact, Visual Studio's IntelliSense is also aware of anonymous types, as shown in Figure 9-4.

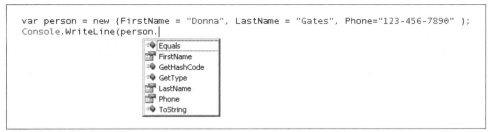

Figure 9-4. Visual Studio IntelliSense on anonymous types

Back in Example 9-3, result is an instance of the constructed IEnumerable<T> that contains query results, where the type of the argument T is an anonymous type that contains two properties: Customer and Address.

Now that the query is defined, the next statement executes it using the foreach loop:

```
foreach (var ca in result)
{
    Console.WriteLine(string.Format("{0}\nAddress: {1}",
        ca.Customer, ca.Address));
}
```

As the result is an implicitly typed IEnumerable<T> of the anonymous class {Customer, Address}, the iteration variable is also implicitly typed to the same class. For each object in the result list, this example simply prints its properties.

Anonymous Types

Often, you won't want to create a new class just for storing the result of a query. The .NET 3.x languages provide *anonymous types*, which allow you to declare both an anonymous class and an instance of that class using object initializers. For instance, you can initialize an anonymous customer Address object as follows:

```
new { Customer = customer, Address = address }
```

This declares an anonymous class with two properties, Customer and Address, and initializes it with an instance of the Customer class and an instance of the Address class. The C# compiler can infer the property types from the types of the assigned values, so here the Customer property type is the Customer class, and the Address property type is the Address class. Just like normal, named classes, anonymous classes can have properties of any type.

Behind the scenes, the C# compiler generates a unique name for the new type. Because this name cannot be referenced in application code, however, the type is considered nameless.

Grouping

Another powerful feature of LINQ, commonly used by SQL programmers but now integrated into the language itself, is grouping. Grouping allows you to organize the results into logical "groups," such as "all the clients grouped together by address," as demonstrated in Example 9-4.

Example 9-4. A group query

```
using System;
using System.Collections.Generic;
using System.Linq;

namespace LinqChapter
{
    // Customer Address class
    public class Address
    {
        // Same as in Example 9-3
    }

    // Main program
    public class Tester
    {
        static void Main()
        {
            List<Address> addresses = CreateAddressList();

            // Find addresses of customers grouped by customer name
            var result =
                from address in addresses
                group address by address.Name;
            foreach (var group in result)
            {
                Console.WriteLine("{0}", group.Key);
                foreach (var a in group)
                    Console.WriteLine("\t{0}", a);
            }
            Console.Read();
        }

        // Create a customer list with sample data
        private static List<Address> CreateAddressList()
        {
        // Same as in Example 9-3
        }
    }
}
```

The output of this example is shown in Figure 9-5. The result is a collection of groups, and you'll need to enumerate each group to get the objects belonging to it.

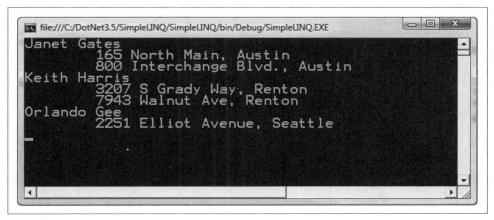

Figure 9-5. Group query output

Extension Methods

LINQ is similar to SQL, so if you already know a little SQL the query expressions introduced in the previous sections should seem quite intuitive and easy to understand. However, as C# code is ultimately executed by the .NET CLR, the C# compiler has to translate the query expressions to a format that the .NET runtime understands. In other words, the LINQ query expressions written in C# must be translated into a series of method calls. The methods called are known as *extension methods*, and they are defined in a slightly different way than normal methods.

Example 9-5 is identical to Example 9-1, except it uses query operator extension methods instead of query expressions. The parts of the code that have not changed are omitted for brevity.

Example 9-5. Using query operator extension methods

```
using System;
using System.Collections.Generic;
using System.Linq;

namespace Programming_CSharp
{
    // Simple customer class
    public class Customer
    {
        // Same as in Example 9-1
    }

    // Main program
    public class Tester
```

Example 9-5. Using query operator extension methods (continued)

```
{
    static void Main( )
    {
        List<Customer> customers = CreateCustomerList( );

        // Find customer by first name
        IEnumerable<Customer> result =
            customers.Where(
                customer => customer.FirstName == "Donna");
        Console.WriteLine("FirstName == \"Donna\"");
        foreach (Customer customer in result)
            Console.WriteLine(customer.ToString( ));
        Console.Read( );
    }

    // Create a customer list with sample data
    private static List<Customer> CreateCustomerList( )
    {
        // Same as in Example 9-1
    }
}
}
```

Figure 9-6 shows the output from this example.

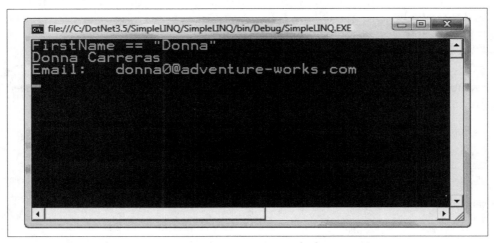

Figure 9-6. Output from using query operator extension methods

Example 9-5 searches for customers whose first name is Donna using a query expression with a where clause. Here's the original from Example 9-1:

```
IEnumerable<Customer> result =
    from   customer in customers
    where  customer.FirstName == "Donna"
    select customer;
```

And here is the extension `Where()` method:

```
IEnumerable<Customer> result =
    customers.Where(customer => customer.FirstName == "Donna");
```

You may have noticed that the select clause seems to have vanished from this example. For details on this, please see the upcoming sidebar "Whither the select Clause?" (and try to remember, as Chico Marx reminded us, "there ain't no such thing as a Sanity clause").

Whither the select Clause?

The reason the select clause is omitted is that you simply use the resulting `Customer` object, without projecting it into a different form. Therefore, this statement:

```
IEnumerable<Customer> result =
    customers.Where(customer => customer.FirstName ==
    "Donna");
```

is the same as this:

```
IEnumerable<Customer> result =
    customers.Where(customer => customer.FirstName ==
    "Donna").Select(customer => customer);
```

If a projection of results is required, you will need to use the `Select()` method. For instance, if you want to retrieve the email address of anyone called Donna instead of the whole `Customer` object, you can use the following statement:

```
IEnumerable<string> result =
    customers.Where(customer => customer.FirstName ==
    "Donna").Select(customer => customer.EmailAddress);
```

Recall that the data source `customers` is of the type `List<Customer>`. This might lead you to think that `List<T>` must implement the `Where()` method to support LINQ. However, it does not: the `Where()` method is called an "extension method" because it extends an existing type. Before we go into more details of this example, let's take a closer look at extension methods.

Defining and Using Extension Methods

The extension methods introduced in the .NET 3.x languages enable programmers to add methods to existing types. For instance, `System.String` does not provide a `Right()` function that returns the rightmost *n* characters of a string. If you use this functionality a lot in your application, you may have considered building such a function and adding it to your library. However, `System.String` is defined as sealed, so you can't subclass it. It is not a partial class, so you can't extend it using that feature either, and of course you can't modify the .NET core library directly.

Therefore, prior to .NET 3.x you would have had to define your own helper method outside of System.String and call it with syntax like this:

```
MyHelperClass.GetRight(aString, n)
```

This is not exactly intuitive. With the .NET 3.x languages, however, there is a more elegant solution: you can actually add a method to the System.String class. In other words, you can extend the System.String class without having to modify the class itself. Example 9-6 demonstrates how to define and use such an extension method.

Example 9-6. Defining and using extension methods

```
using System;

namespace LinqChapter
{
    // Container class for extension methods
    public static class ExtensionMethods
    {
        // Returns the a substring containing the rightmost
        // n characters in a specific string
        public static string Right(this string s, int n)
        {
            if (n < 0 || n > s.Length)
                return s;
            else
                return s.Substring(s.Length - n);
        }
    }

    public class Tester
    {
        public static void Main()
        {
            string hello = "Hello";
            Console.WriteLine("hello.Right(-1) = {0}", hello.Right(-1));
            Console.WriteLine("hello.Right(0) = {0}", hello.Right(0));
            Console.WriteLine("hello.Right(3) = {0}", hello.Right(3));
            Console.WriteLine("hello.Right(5) = {0}", hello.Right(5));
            Console.WriteLine("hello.Right(6) = {0}", hello.Right(6));
            Console.Read();
        }
    }
}
```

Figure 9-7 shows the output from this example.

The first parameter of an extension method is always the target type, which is string in this example. Thus, this example effectively defines a Right() function for the String class. You want to be able to call this method on any string, just like calling a normal System.String member method:

```
aString.Right(n)
```

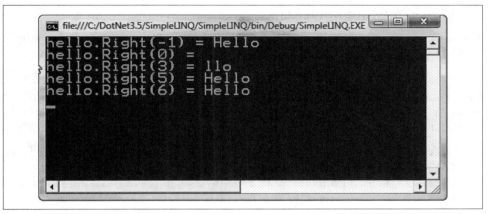

Figure 9-7. Output from designing and using extension methods

In C#, an extension method must be defined as a static method in a static class. Therefore, this example defines a static class, ExtensionMethods, and a static method in this class:

```
public static string Right(this string s, int n)
{
    if (n < 0 || n > s.Length)
        return s;
    else
        return s.Substring(s.Length - n);
}
```

Compared to a regular method, the only notable difference is that the first parameter of an extension method always consists of the this keyword, followed by the target type and an instance of the target type:

```
this string s
```

The subsequent parameters are just normal parameters of the extension method, and the method body is just like that of a regular method. This function simply returns either the desired substring or, if the length argument n is invalid, the original string.

For an extension method to be used, it must be in the same scope as the client code. If the extension method is defined in another namespace, you must add a using directive to import the namespace where the extension method is defined. You can't use fully qualified extension method names, as you can with a normal method. The use of extension methods is otherwise identical to any built-in methods of the target type. In this example, you simply call Right( ) like a regular System.String method:

```
hello.Right(3)
```

It is worth mentioning, however, that extension methods are somewhat more restrictive than regular member methods: extension methods can only access public members of target types, which prevents breaches of the encapsulation of the target types.

Lambda Expressions in LINQ

Lambda expressions can be used to define inline delegates. In the following expression:

```
customer => customer.FirstName == "Donna"
```

the lefthand operand, customer, is the input parameter, and the righthand operand is the lambda expression. In this case, it checks whether the customer's FirstName property is equal to Donna. This lambda expression is passed into the Where() method to perform this comparison operation on each customer in the customer list.

Queries defined using extension methods are called *method-based queries*. While the ordinary and method-based query syntaxes are different, they are semantically identical and are translated into the same IL code by the compiler. You can use either of them, based on your preference.

Looking at how a complex query is expressed in method syntax will help you gain a better understanding of LINQ, because the method syntax is close to how the C# compiler processes queries. Example 9-7 shows what Example 9-3 looks like translated into a method-based query.

Example 9-7. Complex query in method syntax

```
using System;
using System.Collections.Generic;
using System.Linq;

namespace LinqChapter
{
    // Simple Customer class
    public class Customer
    {
        // Same as in Example 9-2
    }

    // Customer Address class
    public class Address
    {
        // Same as in Example 9-3
    }

    // Main program
    public class Tester
    {
        static void Main()
        {
            List<Customer> customers = CreateCustomerList();
            List<Address> addresses = CreateAddressList();

            var result = customers.Join(addresses,
                customer => string.Format("{0} {1}", customer.FirstName,
                    customer.LastName),
                address => address.Name,
```

Example 9-7. Complex query in method syntax (continued)

```
        (customer, address) => new { Customer = customer,
            Address =  address })
        .OrderBy(ca => ca.Customer.LastName)
        .ThenByDescending(ca => ca.Address.Street);

    foreach (var ca in result)
    {
        Console.WriteLine(string.Format("{0}\nAddress: {1}",
            ca.Customer, ca.Address));
    }

    Console.Read( );
}

// Create a customer list with sample data
private static List<Customer> CreateCustomerList( )
{
    // Same as in Example 9-2
}

// Create a customer list with sample data
private static List<Address> CreateAddressList( )
{
    // Same as in Example 9-2
}
}
}
```

As you can see in Figure 9-8, the result is the same.

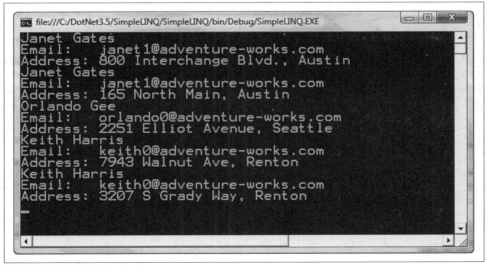

Figure 9-8. Complex query in method syntax

The query is written in query syntax as follows:

```
var result =
    from customer in customers
        join address in addresses on
            string.Format("{0} {1}", customer.FirstName,
                customer.LastName)
            equals address.Name
    orderby customer.LastName, address.Street descending
    select new { Customer = customer, Address = address.Street };
```

And here it is translated into method syntax:

```
var result = customers.Join(addresses,
    customer => string.Format("{0} {1}", customer.FirstName,
        customer.LastName),
    address => address.Name,
    (customer, address) => new { Customer = customer,
        Address = address })
    .OrderBy(ca => ca.Customer.LastName)
    .ThenByDescending(ca => ca.Address.Street);
```

The main data source, the customers collection, is still the main target object. The extension method, Join(), is applied to it to perform the join operation. Its first argument is the second data source, addresses. The next two arguments are join condition fields in each data source. The final argument is the result of the join condition, which is in fact the select clause in the query.

The orderby clauses in the query expression indicate that you want to order the results by customer's last name in ascending order, and then by street address in descending order. In the method syntax, you must specify this preference by using the OrderBy() and ThenBy() (or ThenByDescending()) methods.

You can just call OrderBy() methods in sequence, but the calls must be in reverse order. That is, you must invoke the method to order the last field in the query orderby list first and the method to order the first field in the query orderby list last. Thus, in this example you would need to invoke the "order by street" method first, followed by the "order by name" method:

```
var result = customers.Join(addresses,
    customer => string.Format("{0} {1}", customer.FirstName,
        customer.LastName),
    address => address.Name,
    (customer, address) => new { Customer = customer,
        Address = address })
    .OrderByDescending(ca => ca.Address.Street)
    .OrderBy(ca => ca.Customer.LastName);
```

As you can see from Figures 9-3 and 9-8, the results for these examples are identical. Therefore, you can choose either style, based on your preference.

 Ian Griffiths (one of the smarter programmers on Earth) makes the following point: "You can use exactly these same two syntaxes on a variety of different sources, but the behavior *isn't always the same*." The meaning of a lambda expression varies according to the signature of the function to which it is passed. In these examples, it's a succinct syntax for a delegate. But if you were to use *exactly the same form of query* against a SQL data source, the lambda expression would be turned into something else.

All these extension methods—Join( ), Select( ), Where( ), and so on— have multiple implementations with different target types. Here we're looking at the ones that operate over IEnumerable. The ones that operate over IQueryable are subtly different: rather than taking delegates for the join, projection, where, and other clauses, they take expressions. Those wonderful and magical things enable C# source code to be transformed into equivalent SQL queries.

Adding the AdventureWorksLT Database

The rest of the examples in this chapter use the SQL Server 2005 AdventureWorksLT sample database, which you can download from *http://tinyurl.com/2xzkf7*.

 Please note that while this database is a simplified version of the more comprehensive AdventureWorks, the two are quite different. The examples in this chapter will *not* work with the full AdventureWorks database. Please select the AdventureWorksLT *.msi* package applicable for your platform (32-bit, x64, or IA64). If SQL Server is installed in the default directory, install the sample database to *C:\Program Files\ Microsoft SQL Server\MSSQL.1\MSSQL\Data*. Otherwise, install the database to the *Data* subdirectory under its installation directory.

If you are using SQL Server Express (included in Visual Studio 2008), you will need to enable the Named Pipes protocol:

1. Open the SQL Server Configuration Manager (Start → All Programs → Microsoft SQL Server 2005 → Configuration Tools → SQL Server Configuration Manager).

2. In the left pane, select SQL Server Configuration Manager (Local) → SQL Server 2005 Network Configuration → Protocols for SQLEXPRESS.

3. In the right pane, right-click the Named Pipes protocol and select Enable, as shown in Figure 9-9.

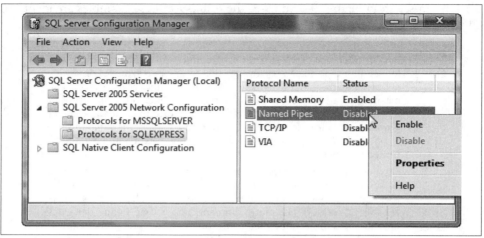

Figure 9-9. Enabling the Named Pipes protocol in SQL Server 2005 Express

4. In the left pane, select SQL Server 2005 Services, then right-click SQL Server (SQLEXPRESS) and select Restart to restart SQL Server, as shown in Figure 9-10.

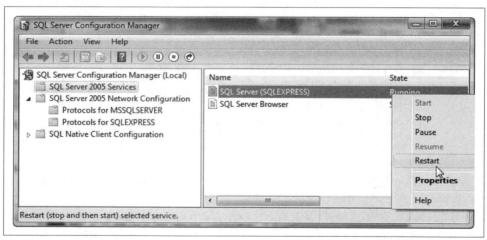

Figure 9-10. Restarting SQL Server 2005 Express

5. Attach the sample database to SQL Server Express using one of the following methods:

   a. If you already have the SQL Server client tools installed, open the SQL Server Management Studio (Start → All Programs → Microsoft SQL Server 2005 → SQL Server Management Studio) and connect to the local SQL Server Express database.

   b. Otherwise, download the SQL Server Express Management Studio from the Microsoft SQL Server Express page (*http://msdn2.microsoft.com/en-us/express/bb410792.aspx*) and install it on your machine. Then open it and connect to the local SQL Server Express database.

6. In the left pane, right-click on *Databases* and select Attach, as shown in Figure 9-11.

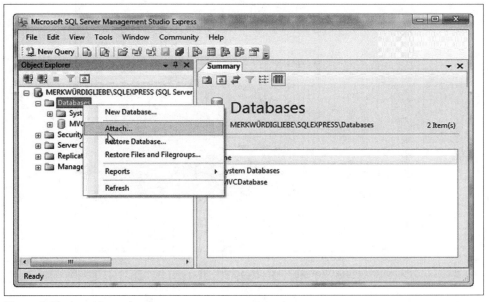

Figure 9-11. Attaching a database

7. In the Attach Database dialog, click Add. Select the AdventureWorksLT database, as shown in Figure 9-12.

8. Click OK to close this dialog and OK again to close the Attach Database dialog.

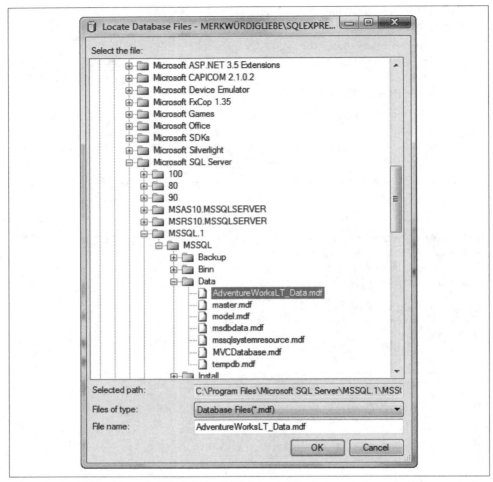

Figure 9-12. Adding AdventureWorksLT to SQL Server 2005 Express

LINQ to SQL Fundamentals

To get started with LINQ to SQL, open Visual Studio 2008 and create a new Console Application named *Simple LINQ to SQL*. Once the IDE is open, click View and open the Server Explorer. Make a connection to the AdventureWorksLT database and test that connection, as shown in Figure 9-13.

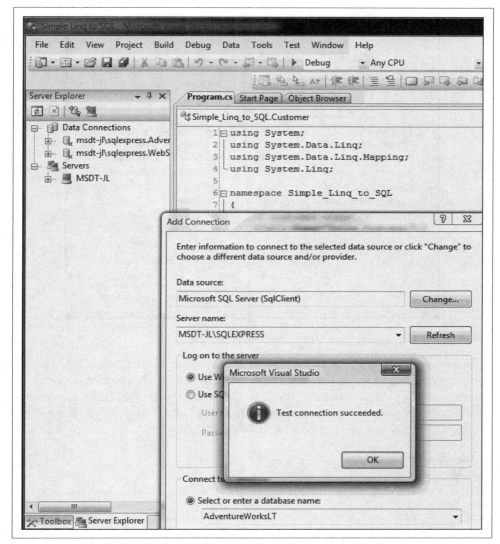

Figure 9-13. Testing the connection to AdventureWorksLT

The next example illustrates using LINQ. For it to compile, you will need to add a reference to the LINQ components. To do so, click on References in your project and add a reference. This opens the dialog shown in Figure 9-14.

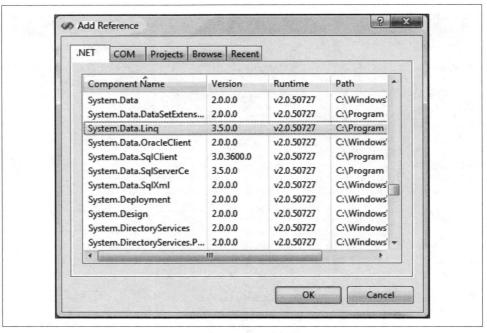

Figure 9-14. Adding System.Data.Linq to the project's references

Click on the .NET tab, then scroll down to and select System.Data.Linq. You are now ready to test Example 9-8, which illustrates an extremely stripped-down LINQ connection to a SQL database (in this case, AdventureWorksLT). The mapping between a class property and a database column is accomplished, as you'll see in the listing, by using the column attribute. A full analysis follows.

Example 9-8. Simple LINQ to SQL

```
using System;
using System.Data.Linq;
using System.Data.Linq.Mapping;
using System.Linq;

namespace Simple_Linq_to_SQL
{
   // Customer class
   [Table(Name="SalesLT.Customer")]
   public class Customer
   {
      [Column] public string FirstName    { get; set; }
      [Column] public string LastName     { get; set; }
      [Column] public string EmailAddress { get; set; }
```

Example 9-8. Simple LINQ to SQL (continued)

```
    // Overrides the Object.ToString() to provide a
    // string representation of the object properties
    public override string ToString()
    {
       return string.Format("{0} {1}\nEmail:    {2}",
          FirstName, LastName, EmailAddress);
    }
  }

  public class Tester
  {
    static void Main()
    {
       DataContext db = new DataContext(
          @"Data Source=.\SqlExpress;
       Initial Catalog=AdventureWorksLT;
       Integrated Security=True");

       Table<Customer> customers = db.GetTable<Customer>();
       var query =
          from customer in customers
          where customer.FirstName == "Donna"
          select customer;

       foreach(var c in query)
          Console.WriteLine(c.ToString());

       Console.ReadKey();
    }
  }
}
```

```
Output:
Donna Carreras
Email:   donna0@adventure-works.com
```

The key to this program is in the first line of Main( ), where you define db to be of type DataContext. A DataContext object is the entry point for the LINQ to SQL Framework, providing a bridge between the application code and database-specific commands. Its job is to translate high-level C# LINQ to SQL code into corresponding database commands and execute them behind the scenes. It maintains a connection to the underlying database, fetches data from the database when requested, tracks changes made to every entity retrieved from the database, and updates the database as needed. It maintains an "identity cache" to guarantee that if you retrieve an entity more than once, all duplicate retrievals will be represented by the same object instance (thereby preventing database corruption).

Database Corruption

There are many ways in which the data in a large database can be "corrupted"—that is, inadvertently come to misrepresent the information you hoped to keep accurate.

A typical scenario would be this: you have data representing the books in your store and how many are available. When you make a query about a book, the data is retrieved from the database into a temporary record (or object) that is no longer connected to the database until you "write it back." Thus, any changes to the database are not reflected in the record you are looking at unless you refresh the data (this is necessary to keep a busy database responsive).

Suppose that Joe takes a call asking how many copies of *Programming C#* are on hand. He calls up the record in his database and finds, to his horror, that the shop is down to a single copy. While he is talking with his customer, a second seller (Jane) takes a call from someone looking for the same book. She sees one copy available and sells it to her customer, while Joe is discussing the merits of the book with his customer. Joe's customer decides to make the purchase, but by the time he does it's too late; Jane has already sold the last copy. Joe tries to put through the sale, but the book that is quite clearly showing as available no longer is. You now have one very unhappy customer and a salesman who has been made to look like an idiot. Oops.

We mentioned in the text that LINQ ensures that multiple retrievals of a database record are all represented by the same object instance. This makes it much harder for the scenario just described to occur, as both Joe and Jane are working on the same record in memory. Thus, if Jane were to change the "number on hand," that change would immediately be reflected in Joe's representation of the object because they'd both be looking at the same data, not at independent snapshots.

Once the `DataContext` object has been instantiated, you can access the objects contained in the underlying database. This example uses the `Customer` table in the `AdventureWorksLT` database, which it accesses via the `DataContext`'s `GetTable()` function:

```
Table<Customer> customers = db.GetTable<Customer>();
```

`GetTable()` is a generic function, so you can specify that the table should be mapped to a collection of `Customer` objects. The `DataContext` has many methods and properties, one of which is `Log`. This property lets you specify the destination where the `DataContext` logs the executed SQL queries and commands. If you redirect the log to somewhere you can access it, you can see how LINQ does its magic. For instance, you can redirect the `Log` property to `Console.Out` so that you can see the output on the system console:

```
Output:
SELECT [t0].[FirstName], [t0].[LastName], [t0].[EmailAddress]
FROM [SalesLT].[Customer] AS [t0]
WHERE [t0].[FirstName] = @p0
-- @p0: Input String (Size = 5; Prec = 0; Scale = 0) [Donna]
-- Context: SqlProvider(Sql2005) Model: AttributedMetaModel
Build: 3.5.20706.1
```

Using the Visual Studio LINQ to SQL Designer

Rather than working out the data relationships in the underlying database and mapping them in the DataContext manually, you can use the designer built into Visual Studio. This is a very powerful mechanism that makes working with LINQ incredibly simple. To see how it works, first open the AdventureWorksLT database in SQL Server Management Studio Express and examine the Customer, CustomerAddress, and Address tables. Make sure you understand their relationship, which is illustrated in the entity-relationship diagram in Figure 9-15.

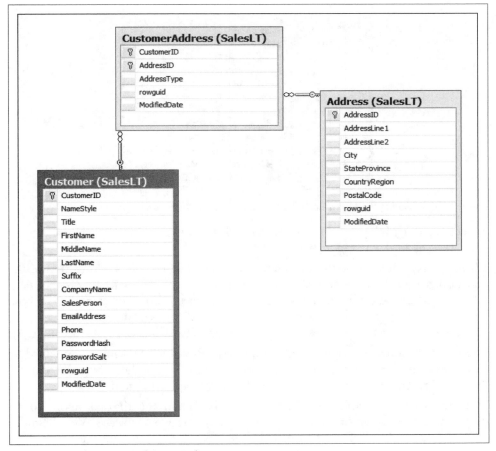

Figure 9-15. AdventureWorksLT DB diagram

Create a new Visual Studio Console Application called *AdventureWorksDBML*. Make sure that the Server Explorer is visible and that you have a connection to AdventureWorksLT, as shown in Figure 9-16. If the connection is not available, follow the instructions outlined earlier to create it.

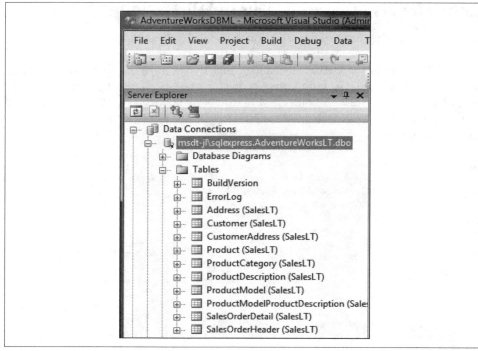

Figure 9-16. Checking the AdventureWorksLT connection in the Server Explorer

To create your LINQ to SQL classes, right-click on the project and choose Add → New Item, as shown in Figure 9-17.

When the New Item dialog opens, choose "LINQ to SQL Classes." You can use the default name for the class (probably DataClasses1), or replace it with a more meaningful one—we'll use AdventureWorksAddress. Now click Add. The name you chose becomes the name of your DataContext object (with the word DataContext appended). Thus, the DataContext object's name here will be AdventureWorksAddressDataContext.

The center window will now display the Object Relational Designer. You can drag tables from the Server Explorer or the Toolbox onto the designer. Drag the Address, Customer, and CustomerAddress tables from the Server Explorer onto this space.

In Figure 9-18, two tables have been dragged on and the third is about to be dropped. Once you've dropped your tables onto the work surface, Visual Studio 2008 automatically retrieves and displays the relationships among the tables. You can arrange them to ensure that the table relationships are displayed clearly.

When you've finished, you'll find that two new files have been created: *AdventureWorksAddress.dbml.layout* and *AdventureWorksAddress.designer.cs*. The former contains the XML representation of the tables you've put on the design surface, a short segment of which is shown here:

```
<?xml version="1.0" encoding="utf-8"?>
<ordesignerObjectsDiagram dslVersion="1.0.0.0"
```

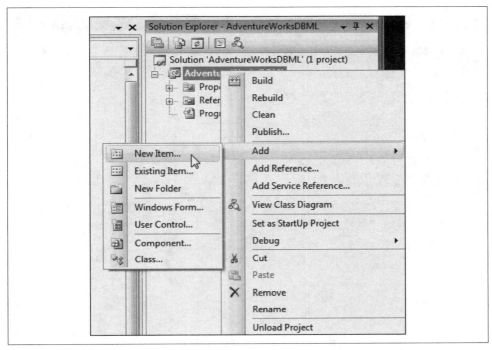

Figure 9-17. Adding a new item to the project

```
absoluteBounds="0, 0, 11, 8.5"
name="AdventureWorksAddress">
<DataContextMoniker Name="/AdventureWorksAddressDataContext" />
<nestedChildShapes>
    <classShape Id="4a893188-c5cd-44db-a114-0444cced4057"
        absoluteBounds="1.125,
        1.375, 2, 2.5401025390625">
        <DataClassMoniker
            Name="/AdventureWorksAddressDataContext/Address" />
        <nestedChildShapes>
            <elementListCompartment Id="d59f1bc4-752e-41db-a940-4a9938014ca7"
                absoluteBounds="1.1400000000000001, 1.835, 1.9700000000000002,
                1.9801025390625" name="DataPropertiesCompartment"
                titleTextColor="Black" itemTextColor="Black" />
        </nestedChildShapes>
    </classShape>
    <classShape Id="c432968b-f644-4ca3-b26b-61dfe4292884"
        absoluteBounds="5.875, 1, 2, 3.6939111328124996">
        <DataClassMoniker Name="/AdventureWorksAddressDataContext/Customer" />
        <nestedChildShapes>
            <elementListCompartment Id="c240ad98-f162-4921-927a-c87781db6ac4"
                absoluteBounds="5.8900000000000006, 1.46, 1.9700000000000002,
                3.1339111328125" name="DataPropertiesCompartment"
                titleTextColor="Black" itemTextColor="Black" />
        </nestedChildShapes>
    </classShape>
```

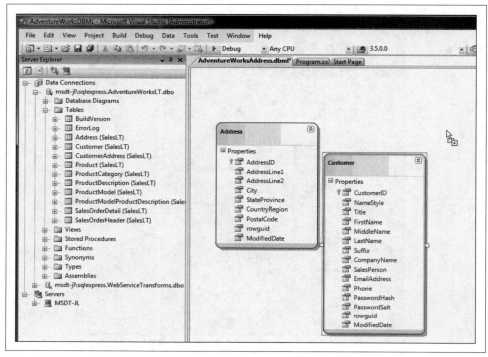

Figure 9-18. Dragging tables onto the work surface

The *.cs* file contains the code to handle all the LINQ to SQL calls that you otherwise would have to write by hand. Like all machine-generated code, it is terribly verbose. Here is a very brief excerpt:

```
public Address()
{
  OnCreated();
  this._CustomerAddresses = new EntitySet<CustomerAddress>(new
      Action<CustomerAddress>(this.attach_CustomerAddresses),
      new Action<CustomerAddress>(this.detach_CustomerAddresses));
}

[Column(Storage="_AddressID", AutoSync=AutoSync.OnInsert,
DbType="Int NOT NULL IDENTITY", IsPrimaryKey=true, IsDbGenerated=true)]
public int AddressID
{
  get
  {
    return this._AddressID;
  }
  set
  {
    if ((this._AddressID != value))
```

```
        {
            this.OnAddressIDChanging(value);
            this.SendPropertyChanging( );
            this._AddressID = value;
            this.SendPropertyChanged("AddressID");
            this.OnAddressIDChanged( );
        }
    }
}
```

The classes that are generated are strongly typed, and a class is generated for each table you place in the designer.

The DataContext class exposes each table as a property, and the relationships among the tables are represented by properties of the classes representing data records. For example, the CustomerAddress table is mapped to the CustomerAddresses property, which is a strongly typed collection (LINQ table) of CustomerAddress objects. You can access the parent Customer and Address objects of a CustomerAddress object through its Customer and Address properties, respectively. The next section discusses this in more detail.

Retrieving Data

Replace the contents of *Program.cs* with the code in Example 9-9, which uses the generated LINQ to SQL code to retrieve data from the three tables you've mapped using the designer.

Example 9-9. Using LINQ to SQL Designer-generated classes

```
using System;
using System.Linq;
using System.Text;

namespace AdventureWorksDBML
{
    // Main program
    public class Tester
    {
        static void Main( )
        {
            AdventureWorksAddressDataContext dc = new
                AdventureWorksAddressDataContext( );
            // Uncomment the statement below to show the
            // SQL statement generated by LINQ to SQL.
            // dc.Log = Console.Out;

            // Find one customer record.
            Customer donna = dc.Customers.Single(
                c => c.FirstName == "Donna");
            Console.WriteLine(donna);
```

Example 9-9. Using LINQ to SQL Designer-generated classes (continued)

```
        // Find a list of customer records.
        var customerDs =
            from customer in dc.Customers
            where customer.FirstName.StartsWith("D")
            orderby customer.FirstName, customer.LastName
            select customer;

        foreach (Customer customer in customerDs)
        {
            Console.WriteLine(customer);
        }
    }
}

// Add a method to the generated Customer class to
// show formatted customer properties.
public partial class Customer
{
    public override string ToString()
    {
        StringBuilder sb = new StringBuilder();
        sb.AppendFormat("{0} {1} {2}",
            FirstName, LastName, EmailAddress);
        foreach (CustomerAddress ca in CustomerAddresses)
        {
            sb.AppendFormat("\n\t{0}, {1}",
                ca.Address.AddressLine1,
                ca.Address.City);
        }
        sb.AppendLine();
        return sb.ToString();
    }
}
```

```
Output:
Donna Carreras donna0@adventure-works.com
        12345 Sterling Avenue, Irving

(only showing the first 5 customers):
Daniel Blanco daniel0@adventure-works.com
        Suite 800 2530 Slater Street, Ottawa
Daniel Thompson daniel2@adventure-works.com
        755 Nw Grandstand, Issaquah
Danielle Johnson danielle1@adventure-works.com
        955 Green Valley Crescent, Ottawa
Darrell Banks darrell0@adventure-works.com
        Norwalk Square, Norwalk
Darren Gehring darren0@adventure-works.com
        509 Nafta Boulevard, Laredo
```

Creating Properties for Each Table

As you can see, you begin by creating an instance of the DataContext object you asked the tool to generate:

```
AdventureWorksAddressDataContext dc =
    new AdventureWorksAddressDataContext();
```

When you use the designer, one of the things it does (besides creating the DataContext class) is define a property for each table you've placed in the designer—in this case, Customer, Address, and CustomerAddress. It names those properties by making the table names plural. Therefore, the properties of AdventureWorksAddressDataContext include Customers, Addresses, and CustomerAddresses.

 Because of this convention, it's a good idea to name your database tables in singular form (to avoid potential confusion in your code). By default, the LINQ to SQL Designer names the generated data classes the same as the table names. If you use plural table names, the class names will be the same as the DataContext property names, and you will need to manually modify the generated class names to avoid name conflicts.

You can access these properties through the DataContext instance:

```
dc.Customers
```

The properties are themselves table objects that implement the IQueryable interface, which has a number of very useful methods that allow you to perform filtering, traversal, and projection operations over the data in a LINQ table.

Most of these methods are extension methods of the LINQ types, which means they can be called just as if they were instance methods of objects that implement IQueryable<T> (in this case, the tables in the DataContext). Therefore, since Single() is a method of IQueryable that returns the only element in a collection that meets a given set of criteria, you can use it to find the customer whose first name is Donna (if there is more than one customer with that first name, only the first customer record is returned):

```
Customer donna = dc.Customers.Single(c => c.FirstName == "Donna");
```

Let's unpack this line of code. You begin by getting the Customers property of the DataContext instance, dc:

```
dc.Customers
```

What you get back is a Customer table object, which implements IQueryable. You can, therefore, call the method Single() on this object:

```
dc.Customers.Single(condition);
```

The result will be a Customer object, which you can assign to a local variable of type Customer:

```
Customer donna = dc.Customers.Single(condition);
```

Notice that everything we are doing here is strongly typed. This is good.

Inside the parentheses, you must place the expression that will filter for the one record you need. This is a *great* opportunity to use a lambda expression, as discussed in the previous chapter:

```
c => c.FirstName == "Donna"
```

You read this as "c goes to c.FirstName where c.FirstName equals Donna." In this notation, c is an implicitly typed variable (of type Customer). LINQ to SQL translates this expression into a SQL statement similar to this:

```
Select * from Customer where FirstName = 'Donna';
```

You can see the exact SQL as generated by LINQ to SQL by redirecting the DataContext log and examining the output as described earlier in this chapter.

The SQL statement is fired when the Single( ) method is executed:

```
Customer donna = dc.Customers.Single(c => c.FirstName == "Donna");
```

This Customer object (donna) is then printed to the console:

```
Console.WriteLine(donna);
```

The output is:

```
Donna Carreras donna0@adventure-works.com
        12345 Sterling Avenue, Irving,
```

Note that although you searched only by first name, what you retrieved was a complete record, including the address information. Also note that the output is created just by passing in the object, using the overridden method you created for the tool-generated class (see the upcoming sidebar "Appending a Method to a Generated Class").

A LINQ Query

The next block of code in Example 9-9 uses the keyword var (new to C# 3.0) to declare a variable called customerDs, which is implicitly typed by the compiler based on the information returned by the LINQ query:

```
var customerDs =
    from customer in dc.Customers
    where customer.FirstName.StartsWith("D")
    orderby customer.FirstName, customer.LastName
    select customer;
```

Appending a Method to a Generated Class

One of the wonderful things about the partial class keyword added in C# 2.0 is that you can add a method to the classes generated by the designer. In this case, we are overriding the ToString method of the Customer class to have it display all its members in a relatively easy-to-read manner:

```
public partial class Customer
{
    public override string ToString( )
    {
        StringBuilder sb = new StringBuilder( );
        sb.AppendFormat("{0} {1} {2}",
                FirstName, LastName, EmailAddress);
        foreach (CustomerAddress ca in CustomerAddresses)
        {
            sb.AppendFormat("\n\t{0}, {1}",
                ca.Address.AddressLine1,
                ca.Address.City);
        }
        sb.AppendLine( );
        return sb.ToString( );
    }
}
```

This query is similar to a SQL query, as noted earlier in this chapter. As you can see, you select each Customer object whose FirstName property (i.e., the value in the FirstName column) begins with "D" from the DataContext Customers property (i.e., the Customer table). You order the records by FirstName and LastName and return all of the results into customerDs, whose implicit type is a TypedCollection of Customers.

With that in hand, you can iterate through the collection and print the data about these customers to the console, treating them as Customer objects rather than as data records:

```
foreach (Customer customer in customerDs)
{
    Console.WriteLine(customer);
}
```

This is reflected in this excerpt of the output:

```
Delia Toone delia0@adventure-works.com
        755 Columbia Ctr Blvd, Kennewick

Della Demott Jr della0@adventure-works.com
        25575 The Queensway, Etobicoke
```

```
Denean Ison denean0@adventure-works.com
        586 Fulham Road, London

Denise Maccietto denise1@adventure-works.com
        Port Huron, Port Huron

Derek Graham derek0@adventure-works.com
        655-4th Ave S.W., Calgary

Derik Stenerson derik0@adventure-works.com
        Factory Merchants, Branson

Diane Glimp diane3@adventure-works.com
        4400 March Road, Kanata
```

LINQ to XML

If you would like the output of your work to go to an XML document rather than to a SQL database, all you need to do is create a new XML element for each object in the Customer table and a new XML attribute for each property representing a column in the table. To do this, you use the LINQ to XML API.

Note that this code takes advantage of the new LINQ to XML classes, such as XAttribute, XElement, and XDocument. Working with XAttributes is very similar to working with standard XML elements. However, note that XAttributes are *not* nodes in an XML tree; rather, they are name/value pairs, each of which is associated with an actual XML element. This is also quite different from what programmers are used to when working with the DOM.

The XElement object represents an actual XML element and can be used to create elements. It interoperates cleanly with System.XML and makes for a terrific transition class between LINQ to XML and XML itself.

Finally, the XDocument class derives from XContainer and has exactly one child node (you guessed it: an XElement). It can also have an XDeclaration, zero or more XProcessingInstructions and XComments, and one XDocumentType (for the DTD), but that's more detail than you need.

In Example 9-10, you're going to create some XElements and assign some XAttributes. This should be very familiar to anyone comfortable with XML, and a relatively easy first glimpse for those who are totally new to raw XML.

Example 9-10. Constructing an XML document using LINQ to XML

```
using System;
using System.Data.Linq;
using System.Linq;
using System.Xml.Linq;
```

Example 9-10. Constructing an XML document using LINQ to XML (continued)

```
namespace LinqToXML
{
    // Main program
    public class Tester
    {
        static void Main( )
        {
            XElement customerXml = CreateCustomerListXml( );
            Console.WriteLine(customerXml);
        }

        /// <summary>
        /// Create an XML document containing a list of customers.
        /// </summary>
        /// <returns>XML document containing a list of customers.
        /// </returns>
        private static XElement CreateCustomerListXml( )
        {
            AdventureWorksAddressDataContext dc =
                new AdventureAddressWorksDataContext( );
            // Uncomment the statement below to show the
            // SQL statement generated by LINQ to SQL.
            // dc.Log = Console.Out;

            // Find a list of customer records.
            var customerDs =
                from customer in dc.Customers
                where customer.FirstName.StartsWith("D")
                orderby customer.FirstName, customer.LastName
                select customer;

            XElement customerXml = new XElement("Customers");
            foreach (Customer customer in customerDs)
            {
                customerXml.Add(new XElement("Customer",
                    new XAttribute("FirstName", customer.FirstName),
                    new XAttribute("LastName", customer.LastName),
                    new XElement("EmailAddress",
                                customer.EmailAddress)));
            }
            return customerXml;
        }
    }
}
```

In this example, rather than simply writing out the values of the customerDs that you've retrieved from the database, you convert the customerDs object to an XML file by using the LINQ to XML API. It's remarkably straightforward.

Let's unpack this example a bit. You start by calling CreateCustomerListXml( ) and assigning the results to an XElement named customerXml. CreateCustomerListXml( ) begins by creating a LINQ statement (it will take those of us who grew up with SQL a long time to get used to having the select statement come at the end!):

```
var customerDs =
from customer in dc.Customers
where customer.FirstName.StartsWith("D")
orderby customer.FirstName, customer.LastName
select customer;
```

Let me remind you that even though you use the keyword var here, which in Java-Script is not type-safe, in C# this is entirely type-safe; the compiler imputes the type based on the query.

The next step is to create an XElement named customerXml:

```
XElement customerXml = new XElement("Customers");
```

This is also potentially confusing. You've given the C# XElement an identifier, customerXml, so that you can refer to it in C# code, but when you instantiated the XElement, you passed a name to the constructor (Customers). It is that name (Customers) that will appear in the XML file. This distinction is shown in Figure 9-19.

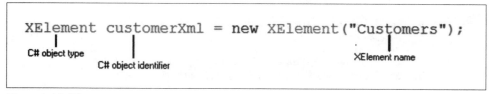

Figure 9-19. Element names

Moving on, you iterate through the customerDs collection that you retrieved in the first step, pulling out each Customer object in turn. You create a new XElement based on each Customer object, adding an XAttribute for the FirstName, LastName, and EmailAddress "columns":

```
foreach (Customer customer in customerDs)
{
    XElement cust = new XElement("Customer",
        new XAttribute("FirstName", customer.FirstName),
        new XAttribute("LastName", customer.LastName),
        new XElement("EmailAddress", customer.EmailAddress));
```

As you iterate through the Customers, you also iterate through each Customer's associated CustomerAddress collection (customer.Addresses). Each of its elements is an object of type Customer.Address. You add the attributes for the address to the XElement cust, beginning with a new XElement Address. This gives the Customer element an Address subelement, with attributes for AddressLine1, AddressLine2, City, etc.

Thus, a single Address object in the XML will look like this:

```
<Customer FirstName="Dora" LastName="Verdad">
  <EmailAddress>dora0@adventure-works.com</EmailAddress>
  <Address AddressLine1="Suite 2502 410 Albert Street" AddressLine2=""
      City="Waterloo" StateProvince="Ontario" PostalCode="N2V" />
</Customer>
```

You want each of these Customer elements (with their child Address elements) to be child elements of the Customers (plural) element that you created earlier. You accomplish this by opening the C# object and adding the new Customer to the element after each iteration of the loop:

```
customerXml.Add(cust);
```

Notice that because you're doing this in C# you access the element through its C# identifier, not its XML identifier (refer back to Figure 9-19). In the resulting XML document, the name of the outer element will be Customers. Within Customers will be a series of Customer elements, each of which will contain Address elements:

```
<Customers>
  <Customer ...
    <Address ... </Address>
    <EmailAddress ... </EmailAddress>
  </Customer>
  <Customer ...
    <Address ... </Address>
    <EmailAddress ... </EmailAddress>
  </Customer>
</Customers>
```

Once you've iterated through the lot, you return the customerXml XElement (the Customers element) that contains all the Customer elements, which in turn contain all the Address elements (that is, the entire tree):

```
return customerXml;
```

Piece of pie. Easy as cake.

Here is an excerpt from the complete output (slightly reformatted to fit the page):

```
<Customers>
  <Customer FirstName="Daniel" LastName="Blanco">
    <EmailAddress>daniel0@adventure-works.com</EmailAddress>
    <Address AddressLine1="Suite 800 2530 Slater Street" AddressLine2=""
        City="Ottawa" StateProvince="Ontario" PostalCode="K4B 1T7" />
  </Customer>
  <Customer FirstName="Daniel" LastName="Thompson">
    <EmailAddress>daniel2@adventure-works.com</EmailAddress>
    <Address AddressLine1="755 Nw Grandstand" AddressLine2=""
        City="Issaquah" StateProvince="Washington" PostalCode="98027" />
  </Customer>
  <Customer FirstName="Danielle" LastName="Johnson">
    <EmailAddress>danielle1@adventure-works.com</EmailAddress>
    <Address AddressLine1="955 Green Valley Crescent" AddressLine2=""
        City="Ottawa" StateProvince="Ontario" PostalCode="K4B 1S1" />
  </Customer>
```

```
<Customer FirstName="Darrell" LastName="Banks">
    <EmailAddress>darrell0@adventure-works.com</EmailAddress>
    <Address AddressLine1="Norwalk Square" AddressLine2=""
        City="Norwalk" StateProvince="California" PostalCode="90650" />
</Customer>
<Customer FirstName="Darren" LastName="Gehring">
    <EmailAddress>darren0@adventure-works.com</EmailAddress>
    <Address AddressLine1="509 Nafta Boulevard" AddressLine2=""
        City="Laredo" StateProvince="Texas" PostalCode="78040" />
</Customer>
<Customer FirstName="David" LastName="Givens">
    <EmailAddress>david15@adventure-works.com</EmailAddress>
    <Address AddressLine1="#500-75 O'Connor Street" AddressLine2=""
        City="Ottawa" StateProvince="Ontario" PostalCode="K4B 1S2" />
</Customer>
</Customers>
```

So, there you have it! LINQ in all its newfangled glory.

Introducing
Windows Communication Foundation:
Accessible Service-Oriented Architecture

There is a great deal of buzz around the concept of Service-Oriented Architecture (SOA), and with good reason. People engaged in the world of enterprise computing spend a great deal of time and energy getting systems to talk to one another and interoperate. In an ideal world, we would like to be able to connect systems arbitrarily, and without the need for proprietary software, in order to create an open, interoperable computing environment. SOA (often pronounced SO-ah) is a big step in the right direction.

SOA Defined

A Service-Oriented Architecture is based on four key abstractions:

- An application frontend
- A service
- A service repository
- A service bus

The application frontend is decoupled from the services. Each service has a "contract" that defines what it will do, and one or more interfaces to implement that contract.

The service repository provides a home for the services, and the service bus provides an industry-standard mechanism for connecting to and interacting with the services.

Because all the services are decoupled from one another and from the application frontend, SOA provides the desired level of interoperability in a nonproprietary open-systems environment.

Enterprise architects look at SOA (Figure 10-1) as a means of helping businesses respond more quickly and cost-effectively to changing market conditions.

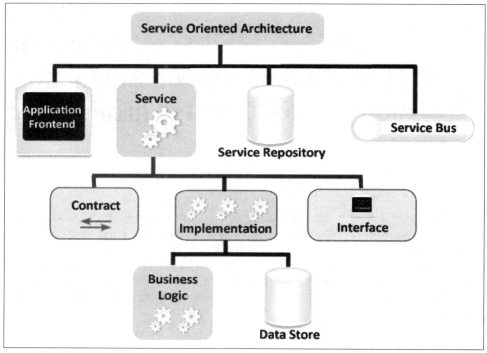

Figure 10-1. SOA overview

Windows Communication Foundation (WCF) provides a SOA technology that offers the ability to link resources with an eye on promoting reuse. Reuse is enabled at the macro (service) level rather than the micro (object) level. The SOA approach coupled with WCF also simplifies interconnection among (and usage of) existing IT assets.

Defining a Service More Precisely

It is important to be clear about what we mean when we use the word "service" in the SOA context. Typically we are thinking about a business service, such as making a hotel reservation or buying a computer online, but keep in mind that these services do not include a visible element. Services do not have a frontend—they expose either functionality or data with which other programs can interact through web browsers, desktop applications, or even other services.

These services might implement business functions like `searchForAvailability` or `setShippingMethod`. In this respect they are distinctly different from technical services, which might provide messaging or transactional functions such as updating data or monitoring transactions. By design, SOA deliberately decouples business services from technical services so that your implementation does not require a specific underlying infrastructure or system. In short, *a SOA service is the encapsulation of a high-level business concept.*

A SOA service is composed of three parts:

- A service class that implements the service to be provided
- A host environment to host the service
- One or more endpoints to which clients will connect

All communication with a service happens through the endpoints. Each endpoint specifies a contract (which we will discuss in greater detail later in this chapter) that defines which methods of the service class will be accessible to the client through that specific endpoint.

Because the endpoints have their own contracts, they may expose different (and perhaps overlapping) sets of methods. Each endpoint also defines a binding that specifies how a client will communicate with the service and the address where the endpoint is hosted.

You can think of SOA services in terms of four basic tenets:

- Boundaries are explicit.
- Services are autonomous.
- Schemas and contracts are shared, but not classes.
- Compatibility is based on policy.

These fundamental tenets help drive the design of the services you'll create, so it's worth exploring each in detail.

Boundaries Are Explicit

If you want to get somewhere in the physical world, it is crucial to know where you are and where you need to go, as well as any considerations that need to be accounted for on your way (which is why GPS systems are one of the fastest-selling technologies in the consumer market).

This also applies to services. There will be boundaries between each interaction, and crossing these boundaries involves a cost for which you must account.

As a concrete example, when driving from Boston to Manhattan, you can take a faster toll route (that costs money) or a slower free route (that costs time). A similar tradeoff applies with service operations that cross process or machine boundaries. You face decisions about resource marshaling, physical location and network hops, security constraints, and so forth. Among the "best practices" for minimizing the cost of crossing these boundaries are the following considerations:

- Make sure your entry-point interface is well defined, comprehensive, and public. This will encourage consumers to utilize your service as opposed to doing end runs around it.

- Consumption is your primary reason for existence, so make that easy. Don't make the developers who consume your service *think* (with apologies to Steve Krug).

- Be explicit! Use messages, *not* Remote Procedure Calls. The RPC model was an interim (crutch) analogy used by Microsoft for web services in earlier versions of .NET to smooth the transition; due to its synchronous implementation, the modern WCF style eschews RPC in the interest of building strong SOA decoupling through asynchronous messaging.

- Hide implementation details to avoid tight coupling.

- Keep it simple—send well-defined messages in both directions with as small an interface as possible to get the job done. To quote Albert Einstein (Figure 10-2), "As simple as possible, but not simpler."

Figure 10-2. Albert Einstein Sticking Out His Tongue ©Bettmann/CORBIS

Services Are Autonomous

SOA services are expected to run in the wild world of decoupled systems. A well-designed service should stand alone and be totally independent and relatively fail-safe. As the service topology is almost guaranteed to evolve over time, and there is no presiding authority, you should plan to meet this goal through autonomous design.

Here are some points to keep in mind:

- If Murphy ("Anything that can go wrong will go wrong") designed a service, he would do everything he could to isolate that service from all other services, to prevent dependencies and reduce the risk of failure.
- Your service deployments and versions will be independent of the system on which they are deployed.
- Keep your word—once you publish a contract, never change it!
- There is no presiding authority, so plan accordingly.

Schemas and Contracts Are Shared, But Not Classes

As the creator of a service, it is your responsibility to provide a well-formed contract. Your service contract will contain the message formats, the message exchange patterns, BPEL scripts that might be required, and any WS-Policy requirements. After publication, stability becomes your biggest responsibility. Make no changes, and ensure that any changes you do make (paradox intentional) have a minimal impact on your consumers. Key considerations include:

- Stability is job one! Don't publish a contract for others until you are sure the service is stable and not likely to change.
- Say what you mean and mean what you say. Be explicit in your contracts to ensure that people understand both the explicit and intended usages.
- Make sure the public data schema is abstract; don't expose internal representations.
- If you break it, you version it. Even the best-designed service might need to change; use versioning to help insulate your consumers from these changes.

WS-Policy

WS-Policy provides a syntax and a general-purpose model to describe and communicate the policies of a web service. WS-Policy assertions express the capabilities and constraints of your particular web service. WS-PolicyAttachments tell your consumers which of the several methods for associating the WS-Policy expressions with web services (e.g., WSDL) your web service implements.

Compatibility Is Based on Policy

There may come a time when you will not be able to capture all the requirements of a service interaction via the Web Services Description Language (WSDL) alone. This is where *policies* come in. Policies allow you to separate the *what* from the *how* and the *whom* when it comes to a communicated message. If you have policy assertions, you need to make sure you are very explicit with respect to expectations and compatibility. Keep these points in mind:

- Say what your service can do, not how it does it—separate interactions from constraints on these interactions.
- Express capabilities in terms of policies.
- Assertions should be identified by stable and unique names.

Implementing Web Services

It is important to recognize that a web service is just one of many service implementations. That said, the increasing ease with which one can create a web service has been a catalyst for the explosion of SOA implementations in recent years. It is the basic nature of the web service, "a programmable application component accessible via standard web protocols," that is helping deliver on the promise of SOA. In a nutshell, you can think of SOA as having three components:

- Standard protocols—HTTP, SMTP, FTP with HTTP
- Service description—WSDL and XSD
- Service discovery—UDDI and other "yellow pages"

The protocol stack for WCF's implementation of web services is outlined in Figure 10-3. Web services typically flow from top to bottom (discovery, then description, then messaging).

To consume a web service, you need to know that it exists, what it does, what kind of interface it offers, and so on. You should also note that with WCF, you are strongly encouraged to use UDDI for publishing your web service's metadata exchange endpoints, and to query the service directly for the WSDL document and policies. After all of this has been accomplished, your client can invoke the web service via SOAP.

We'll start at the bottom of the stack and work our way back up.

SOAP: More Than Just a Cleanser

SOAP is the preferred protocol for exchanging XML-based messages over computer networks using the standard transport mechanisms outlined in the preceding section. SOAP is the top end of the foundation layer of the web services stack. As such, it provides a basic messaging framework that is used to construct more abstract layers.

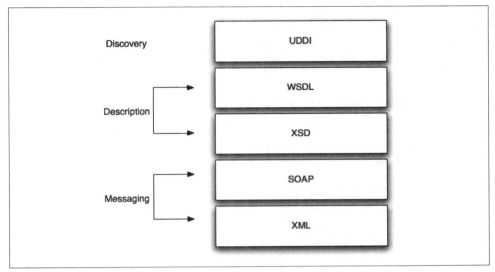

Figure 10-3. The web services protocol stack

 Trivia question: What does SOAP stand for?

Old answer: Simple Object Access Protocol.

New answer (by dictate of the World Wide Web Consortium as of June 2003): Nothing at all.

While there are several different types of messaging patterns in SOAP, up to this point the most common for .NET programmers has been the RPC pattern, in which one side of the messaging relationship is designated the server and one side the client. The client pretends to make a method call on the server through a proxy, and the server pretends to respond by running a method and returning a value (Figure 10-4). What is actually happening, however, is that XML documents are being exchanged "under the covers," hidden by the framework so that the developer need not be exposed to the details of XML syntax.

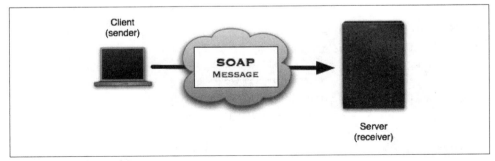

Figure 10-4. Bare-bones, one-way SOAP communication

Here is an example of how a client might format a SOAP message requesting product information from a computer seller's warehouse web service. The client needs to know which product corresponds with the ID MA450LL/A:

```
<soap:Envelope xmlns:soap="http://schemas.xmlsoap.org/soap/envelope/">
  <soap:Body>
    <getProductDetails xmlns="http://computer.seller.com/ws">
      <productID>MA450LL/A</productID>
    </getProductDetails>
  </soap:Body>
</soap:Envelope>
```

And here is a possible response to the client request:

```
<soap:Envelope xmlns:soap="http://schemas.xmlsoap.org/soap/envelope/">
  <soap:Body>
    <getProductDetailsResponse xmlns="http:// computer.seller.com/ws">
      <getProductDetailsResult>
        <productName>iPod </productName>
        <productID>MA450LL/A</productID>
        <description>iPod, 80GB - Black</description>
        <price currency="NIS">349.00</price>
        <inStock>true</inStock>
      </getProductDetailsResult>
    </getProductDetailsResponse>
  </soap:Body>
</soap:Envelope>
```

If you break down a SOAP message you'll see that it contains distinct parts, which are represented in Figure 10-5.

SOAP messages come in three flavors: requests, responses, and faults. The only required element of a SOAP message is the envelope, which encapsulates the message that is being communicated and specifies the protocol the message uses for communication. As you can see, the SOAP envelope can have two subsections, a header and a body. The header contains metadata about the message that is used for specific processing (this is the place for authentication tokens or timestamps and the like). Inside the body, you have the guts of the message, or a SOAP fault.

SOAP messages are rather simple in their syntax, but there are a few rules of the road that the good service provider will follow when handcrafting a message:

- Use XML as the encoding mechanism.
- Use the SOAP envelope namespace:

```
<soap:Envelope
    xmlns:soap="http://schemas.xmlsoap.org/soap/envelope/">
```

- Use the SOAP encoding namespace, by adding it to your envelope:

```
<soap:Envelope xmlns:soap="http://schemas.xmlsoap.org/soap/envelope/"
    soap:encodingStyle="http://schemas.xmlsoap.org/soap/encoding/">
```

- You cannot use Document Type Definition (DTD) references.
- You cannot use XML processing directives.

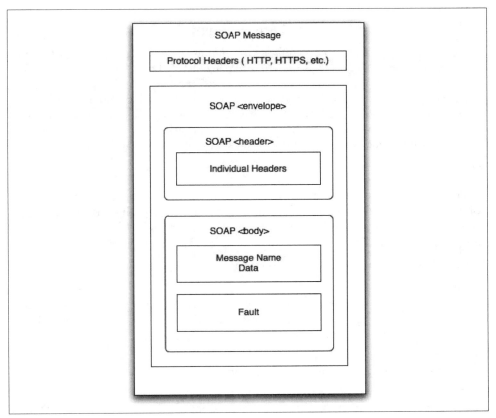

Figure 10-5. The structure of a SOAP message

Faulty Service

If you want to provide a nice experience for consumers of your service, you will need to take the time to make sure you understand the `fault` element. Fault messages need to be in the body, and they can appear only once. A fault message will contain details about the exception (as appropriate) and one of the fault codes defined by the SOAP specification.

WSDL Documents: Describing the Service Endpoints

Once you've created a service, what's next? You need a way of describing this service and its endpoints to potential consumers. Fortunately, there's a convenient way to do this.

WSDL is an XML format for publishing network services. It describes a set of endpoints that operate on messages, which are abstract descriptions of the data being exchanged. Operations are likewise described abstractly and bound to a concrete network protocol and message format, which constitutes an endpoint.

The WSDL document itself has three parts:

Definitions
> Definitions can be about data types as well as messages. They are expressed in XML using a mutually agreed-upon vocabulary. This allows you to adopt industry-based vocabularies for greater interoperability in a specific industry segment.

Operations
> Web services support four basic operation types:

> *One-way request*
>> Only the service endpoint receives a message.

> *Request/response*
>> The endpoint receives a message and responds to the sender accordingly.

> *Solicit response*
>> The endpoint initiates a message and expects a response.

> *Notification*
>> The endpoint sends out a message without expecting a response.

Service bindings
> The service bindings allow for the connection of a port type to an actual port. In other words, they tie the protocol and message format to a specific port. These bindings are typically created using SOAP.

> A service binding might look something like this:

```
<service name="MyService" interface="tns:MyInterface">
    <endpoint name="MyServiceRestEndpoint"
        binding="tns:MyInterfaceHttpBinding"
        address="http://my.example.com/rest/"/>
    <endpoint name="MyServiceSoapEndpoint"
        binding="tns:MyInterfaceSoapBinding"
        address="http://my.example.com/soap/"/>
</service>
```

UDDI: Who Is Out There, and What Can They Do for Me?

The Universal Description, Discovery, and Integration (UDDI) registry has made the process of finding web services infinitely easier. UDDI is a platform-independent, XML-based registry that allows service vendors to list themselves on the Internet. As an open industry initiative, UDDI is sponsored by the Organization for the Advancement of Structured Information Standards (OASIS). UDDI enables businesses to publish service listings, discover one another's services, and define how the services or software applications interact over the Internet.

A UDDI business registration consists of three components:

White pages
> Contain addresses, contacts, and known identifiers

Yellow pages
> Provide industrial categorizations based on standard taxonomies

Green pages
> Hold technical information about services exposed by the business

UDDI is designed to be interrogated by SOAP messages. It provides access to WSDL documents describing the protocol bindings and message formats required to interact with the web services listed in its directory.

UDDI Data Types

UDDI defines four essential data types:

BusinessEntity
> The top-level structure. It describes a business or other entity for which information is being registered.

BusinessService
> A structure that represents a logical service classification. The element name includes the term "business" in an attempt to describe the purpose of this level in the service-description hierarchy. It can contain one or more bindingTemplates.

bindingTemplate
> A structure that contains the information necessary to invoke specific services, which may require bindings to one or more protocols (such as HTTP or SMTP).

tModel
> A technical "fingerprint" for a given service, which may also function as a namespace to identify other entities, including other tModels.

How It All Works

How do all these pieces—UDDI, WSDL, and SOAP—actually work together to get the work of web services done? Take a look at Figure 10-6.

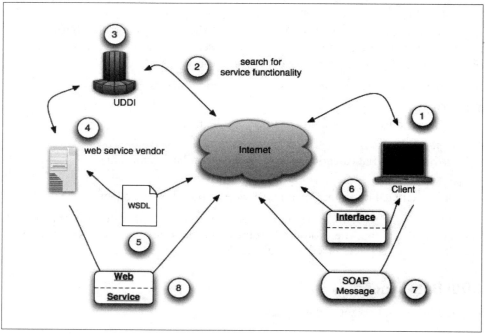

Figure 10-6. The web service lifecycle

The eight steps in the web service lifecycle are:

1. Somewhere in the world a client wants to use a web service, so it seeks out a directory service.
2. The client connects to the directory to discover a relevant service.
3. By asking the directory service about the services available, the client is able to determine the presence of a service that meets the client's criteria.
4. The directory contacts the service vendor to check on availability and validity.
5. The service vendor sends the client a WSDL document.
6. A proxy class is used to create a new instance of the web service.
7. SOAP messages originating from the client are sent over the network.
8. Return values are sent as a result of executing the SOAP message.

This isn't that bad, is it? What's more, Microsoft's WCF and Visual Studio tools make implementing a Service-Oriented Architecture very easy. Let's roll up our sleeves and see how WCF helps you get SOA implementations done fast.

WCF's SOA Implementation

The WCF team at Microsoft has been trying to deliver three big items to the development community. The design goals include:

- Interoperability across platforms
- Unification of existing technologies
- Enabling service-oriented development

With the release of .NET 3.5, Microsoft is delivering on all fronts.

To maximize interoperability across platforms, WCF's architects chose SOAP as the native messaging protocol. This makes it possible for WCF applications running on Windows to reliably communicate with legacy applications, Mac OS X machines, Linux machines, Windows clients, Solaris machines, and anyone else out there who abides by the Web Services Interoperability Organization (WS-I) specification. (The WS-I is an industry consortium chartered to promote interoperability among the stack of web services specifications.)

To unify existing technologies, WCF takes all the capabilities of the distributed systems' technology stacks and overlays a simplified clean API in System.ServiceModel. Thus, you are able to accomplish the same things that previously required ASMX, WSE, System.Messaging, .NET remoting, and other enterprise solutions, all from within WCF. This helps cut down a developer's time to implementation and reduces the complexity of dealing with distributed technologies.

The WCF team has faced up to the future in a big way. Designed from the ground up to facilitate the business orientation of modern software projects, WCF enables rather than hinders the design and implementation of SOA. WCF allows you to build on object orientation and take on the service orientation required of today's distributed systems.

.NET 3.5 allows a very flexible approach to programming, providing a great set of mix-and-match ways to tackle most programming challenges you'll face. You can use configuration files, you can tap into the object model programmatically, and you can use declarative programming. Odds are that in most cases you will utilize all of these approaches, leveraging the strengths of each while minimizing your exposure to their respective weaknesses.

The ABCs of WCF

Every client needs to know the ABCs of a contract in order to consume a service: the *address* indicates where messages can be sent, the *binding* tells you how to send the messages, and the *contract* specifies what the messages should contain.

Addresses

As you might imagine, addressing is an essential component of being able to utilize a web service. An address is comprised of the following specifications:

Transport mechanism
> The transport protocol to employ

Machine name
> A fully qualified domain name for the service provider

Port
> The port to use for the connection (as the default port is 80, specifying the port is not necessary when using HTTP)

Path
> The specific path to a service

The format of a correctly specified service address is as follows:

```
protocol://<machinename>[:port]/<pathToService>
```

WCF supports a number of protocols, so we'll take the time to outline the addressing formats of each:

HTTP
> HTTP is by far the most common way you will address your service.
>
> ```
> http://silverlightconsulting.info/OrderStatus/GetShippingInfo
> ```
>
> ```
> <endpoint
>     address="http://silverlightconsulting.info/OrderStatus/GetShippingInfo"
>     bindingSectionName="BasicHttpBinding"
>     contract="IGetShippingInfo" />
> ```
>
> For secure communication you only need to substitute https for http, and you're good to go.

Named pipes
> When you need to do inter-process or in-process communication, named pipes are probably your best choice. The WCF implementation supports only local communication, as follows:
>
> ```
> net.pipe://silverlightconsulting.info/OrderStatus/GetShippingInfo
> ```
>
> ```
> <endpoint
>     address="net.pipe://silverlightconsulting.info/OrderStatus/GetShippingInfo"
>     bindingSectionName="NetNamedPipeBinding"
>     contract="IGetShippingInfo" />
> ```

TCP

This protocol is very similar to HTTP:

```
net.tcp://silverlightconsulting.info/OrderStatus/GetShippingInfo
```

```
<endpoint
    Address="net.tcp://silverlightconsulting.info/OrderStatus/GetShippingInfo"
    bindingSectionName="NetTcpBinding"
    contract="IGetShippingInfo" />
```

MSMQ

Finally, if you need asynchronous messaging patterns, you will want to use a message queue. Microsoft's Message Queue (MSMQ) can typically be accessed through Active Directory. In an MSMQ message, port numbers don't have any meaning:

```
net.msmq://my.info/OrderStatus/GetShippingInfo
```

```
<endpoint
    Address="net.msmq://my.info/OrderStatus/GetShippingInfo"
    bindingSectionName="NetMsmqBinding"
    contract="IGetShippingInfo" />Binding
```

Bindings

Bindings are the primary driver of the programming model of WCF. The binding you choose will determine the following:

- The transport mechanism
- The nature of the channel (duplex versus request/response, etc.)
- The type of encoding (XML, binary, etc.)
- The supported WS-* protocols

 Web service specifications are occasionally referred to collectively as "WS-*," though there is not a single managed set of specifications that this consistently refers to, nor a recognized owning body across them all.

WCF gives you a default set of bindings that should cover the bulk of what you will need to do. If you come across something that falls outside the bounds of coverage, you can extend CustomBinding to cover your custom needs. Just remember, a binding needs to be unique in its name and namespace for identification purposes.

If you are looking for complete interoperability, your first (and obvious) choice of bindings will be anything in the WS-prefixed set. If you need to bind to pre-WCF service stacks, you'll likely want to use the BasicHttpBinding. If you are only really servicing a Windows-centric environment without interoperability requirements, you can utilize the Net-prefixed bindings. Just remember that your choice of binding determines the transport mechanism you will be able to use.

Contracts

As we discussed earlier, one of the four tenets of service orientation is the notion of explicit boundaries. Contracts allow you to decide up front what you will expose to the outside world (the folks across the boundary). This frees you to work on the implementation without worry—as long as you uphold the contract, you are free to change the underlying implementation as needed. Therefore, contracts are one of the keys to interoperability among the many platforms from which your service might be called.

A WCF contract is essentially a collection of operations that specify how the endpoint in question communicates with the outside world. Every operation is a simple message exchange like the one-way, request/response, and duplex message exchanges.

Like a binding, each contract has a name and namespace that uniquely identify it. You will find these attributes in the service's metadata.

The class `ContractDescription` describes WCF contracts and their operations. Within a `ContractDescription`, every contract operation will have a related `OperationDescription` that will describe the aspects of the operation, such as whether the operation is one-way, request/response, or duplex. The messages that make up the operation are described in the `OperationDescription` using a collection of `MessageDescriptions`.

A `ContractDescription` is usually created from a .NET interface or class that defines the contract using the WCF programming model. This type is annotated with `ServiceContractAttribute`, and its methods that correspond to endpoint operations are annotated with `OperationContractAttribute`.

Talk Amongst Yourselves

The default pattern of message exchange is (surprise) the request/response pattern. Again, for those of you who have been making a living writing web-based software, this pattern should be very familiar. It is outlined in Figure 10-7.

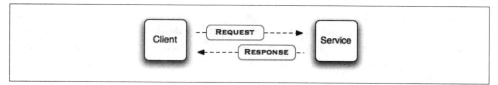

Figure 10-7. The default request/response message exchange

A duplex contract is more complex. It defines two logical sets of operations: a set that the service exposes for the client to call and a set that the client exposes for the service to call. When creating a duplex contract programmatically, you split each set into separate types (each type must be a class or an interface). You also need to annotate the contract that represents the service's operations with `ServiceContractAttribute`, referencing the contract that defines the client (or callback) operations. In addition, `ContractDescription` will contain a reference to each of the types, thereby grouping them into one duplex contract. This is really a peer-to-peer pattern, as illustrated by Figure 10-8.

Figure 10-8. Duplex messaging

The last type of message pattern is the set-it-and-forget-it one-way messaging style. In this scenario, as seen in Figure 10-9, you send a message as a client, but you do not expect any sort of return message. This is often the behavior you engage in when dealing with message queues.

Figure 10-9. One-way messaging

Putting It All Together

Now that you understand the basic nature of a WCF service, let's roll up our sleeves and create a service contract from scratch. This example will be based on our favorite fictional stock-quoting service, YahooQuotes. YahooQuotes provides stock quotes via the exposed behavior of the service. To make this a fully functional WCF service contract, you'll have to annotate the interface with both the `ServiceContract` and `OperationContract` attributes. You will also need to make sure you include the `System.ServiceModel` namespace, as shown here:

```
using System;
using System.ServiceModel;
```

A WCF service class implements a service as a set of methods. The class must implement *at least one* `ServiceContract` to define the operational contracts (i.e., methods) that the service will provide to the end user. Optionally, you can also implement data contracts that define what sort of data the exposed operations can utilize. You'll do that second.

Start by defining the interface of the service contract that defines a single operation contract for the YahooQuotes service:

```
namespace YahooQuotes.TradeEngine.ServiceContracts
{
    [ServiceContract(Namespace = "http://my.info/YahooQuotes")]
    public interface IYahooQuotes
    {
        [OperationContract]
        BadQuote GetLastTradePriceInUSD(string StockSymbol);
    }
}
```

That was simple enough. Now you need to implement the data contract for the BadQuote class:

```
namespace YahooQuotes.TradeEngine.DataContracts
{
    [DataContract(Namespace = "http://my.info/YahooQuotes")]
    public class BadQuote
    {
        [DataMember(Name="StockSymbol"]
        public  string StockSymbol;

        [DataMember(Name="Last"]
        public  decimal Last;

        [DataMember(Name="Bid"]
        public  decimal Bid;

        [DataMember(Name="Ask"]
        public  decimal Ask;

        [DataMember(Name="TransactionTimestamp"]
        private  DateTime TransactionTimestamp;

        [DataMember(Name="InformationSource"]
        public  decimal InformationSource;
    }
}
```

There may come a time when you decide you want more control over the SOAP envelope that WCF generates. When that time comes, you can annotate your class with the MessageContract attribute and then direct the output to either the SOAP body or the SOAP header by utilizing the MessageBody and MessageHeader attributes:

```
namespace YahooQuotes.TradeEngine.MessageContracts
{
    [MessageContract]
    Public class YahooQuotesMessage
    {
        [MessageBody]
        public string StockSymbol;
```

```
    [MessageBody]
    public decimal Last;

    [MessageBody]
    public decimal Bid;

    [MessageBody]
    public decimal Ask;

    [MessageBody]
    private DateTime TransactionTimestamp;

    [MessageHeader]
    public string InformationSource;
  }
}
```

In this case, you've specified that the InformationSource should be in the SOAP header by annotating it with the MessageHeader attribute. It is nice to be able to do this sort of thing, so keep it around in your bag of tricks to use as appropriate.

In the next chapter we'll build a complete YahooQuotes service and explore the WCF SOA programming model in greater detail.

Applying WCF: YahooQuotes

In this chapter you'll learn how to leverage ASP.NET to get a web service up and running fast. We'll also introduce the benefits of Microsoft's new web server, Internet Information Services 7.0 (IIS7). Just as Microsoft claims, IIS7 provides a secure, easy to manage platform for developing and reliably hosting web applications and services. Its automatic sandboxing of new sites lets you enjoy greater reliability and security, and its powerful new admin tools enable you to administer the server easily and efficiently.

Microsoft has done a really good job of reducing management complexity with this new feature-focused administration tool. IIS7 provides vastly simplified dialogs for common administrative tasks. In addition, the new command-line administration interface, Windows Management Instrumentation (WMI) provider, and .NET API make administration of web sites and applications more efficient, whether they are running on one server or many servers. IIS7 also makes hosting a web service using ASP.NET exceptionally easy.

Before going any further in this chapter, take the time to confirm that your IIS7 configuration is working. You should be able to open up the IIS Manager, as seen in Figure 11-1. With IIS7 fired up, you're ready to go.

Creating and Launching a Web Service

In this chapter you're going to build a simple web service that will provide stock quotes using Yahoo! Finance's publicly available stock-quote engine. When you're done, you should have an application that looks something like the one in Figure 11-2. In the following section, you'll write a simple WPF client to consume the web service you have created.

Figure 11-1. IIS7 as viewed from the new IIS Manager

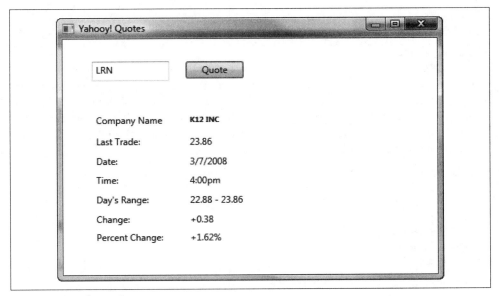

Figure 11-2. Yahooy! Quotes

Creating the Service

Start by creating a new project for your WCF service. Open up Microsoft Visual Studio 2008 and select New → Web Site from the File menu. In the ensuing dialog, choose the WCF Service option and name the file location *YahooQuotes*, as seen in Figure 11-3.

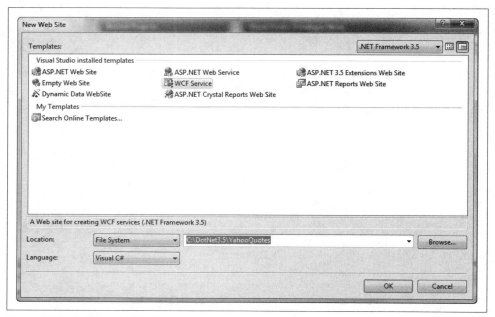

Figure 11-3. Creating the WCF service

Right off the bat, delete *IService.cs*. Then rename *Service.cs* and *Service.svc* to *YahooQuotes.cs* and *YahooQuotes.svc*, respectively. Drop into the *Web.config* file and replace all occurrences of "Service" with "YahooQuotes." You'll mix and match the interface (IYahooQuotes) and the implementation (YahooQuotes) in *YahooQuotes.cs*, which is why it was OK to get rid of the *IService.cs* file.

Start by declaring the namespaces you will need in *YahooQuotes.cs*:

```
using System;
using System.Collections.Generic;
using System.Text;
using System.Web;
using System.Net;
using System.IO;
using System.ServiceModel;
using System.Runtime.Serialization;
```

You'll need the bolded namespaces when you talk to Yahoo! Finance's quote service via an HTTP post.

The next thing you'll do is define the specifics of your service's contract. It is good practice to define the contract as an interface first and then create a concrete class to handle the implementation. This is, after all, the whole point of abstraction. In addition, it makes the boundary between the service and the implementation explicit (upholding one of the main tenets of SOA, as described in the previous chapter).

There will be two basic pieces to the IYahooQuotes interface: you'll want a method to test the service availability, and a mechanism to retrieve stock-quote data given a ticker symbol. To fulfill these objectives, you're going to create an interface that looks like this:

```
[ServiceContract]
public interface IYahooQuotes
{
    [OperationContract]
    string TestService(int intParam);

    [OperationContract]
    StockQuote GetQuoteForStockSymbol(String aSymbol);
}
```

 Although this interface definition is in code, as opposed to metadata, it provides a well-defined perimeter. It exposes only the minimum necessary to get back a StockQuote and a string that results from testing the service. It also preserves design-time and configuration-time flexibility.

Now you need to create a concrete YahooQuotes class to provide the implementation. You'll also use a data contract to separate the StockQuote type from the schema and XML-serialized types. Start with the YahooQuotes implementation:

```
public class YahooQuotes : IYahooQuotes
{
    public string TestService(int intParam)
    {
        return string.Format("You entered: {0}", intParam);
    }

    public StockQuote GetQuoteForStockSymbol(String tickerSymbol)
    {
        StockQuote sq = new StockQuote();
        string buffer;
        string[] bufferList;
        WebRequest webRequest;
        WebResponse webResponse;

        // Use the data dictionary at the end of the big listing to
        // decipher the end of this URL
        String url =
            "http://quote.yahoo.com/d/quotes.csv?s=" +
            tickerSymbol +
            "&f=l1d1t1pomvc1p2n";
```

```
// Now that you have a URL, go get some data. It will
// be returned to you in a nicely packaged CSV format.
webRequest = HttpWebRequest.Create(url);
webResponse = webRequest.GetResponse( );

// Put it in a stream buffer to make text replacement
// easier
using (StreamReader sr =
    new StreamReader(webResponse.GetResponseStream( )))
{
    buffer = sr.ReadToEnd( );
}

// Strip out the " marks
buffer = buffer.Replace("\"", "");
// Now put it in a char array
bufferList = buffer.Split(new char[] { ',' });

sq.LastTradePrice = bufferList[0]; // l1
sq.DateOfTrade = bufferList[1]; // d1
sq.TimeOfTrade = bufferList[2]; // t1
sq.PreviousClose = bufferList[3]; // p
sq.Open = bufferList[4]; // o
sq.DaysRange = bufferList[5]; // m
sq.Volume = bufferList[6]; // v
sq.Change = bufferList[7]; // c1
sq.PercentageChange = bufferList[8]; // p2
sq.CompanyName = bufferList[9]; // n

        return sq;
    }
}
```

The next step is to implement the StockQuote class. At first glance, this class appears to be little more than a dictionary of key/value pairs. Do not be fooled!

Data contracts are the desired mechanism for controlling serialization to and from XML. While data contracts can't handle *every* type of schema generation, their support for most schemas and their ease of use makes them a key tool in the .NET programmer's arsenal:

```
[DataContract]
public class StockQuote
{

    [DataMember]
    public String LastTradePrice
    {
        get;
        set;
    }

    [DataMember]
    public String DateOfTrade
```

```
{
   get;
   set;
}

[DataMember]
public String TimeOfTrade
{
   get;
   set;
}

[DataMember]
public String PreviousClose
{
   get;
   set;
}

[DataMember]
public String Open
{
   get;
   set;
}

[DataMember]
public String DaysRange
{
   get;
   set;
}

[DataMember]
public String Volume
{
   get;
   set;
}

[DataMember]
public String Change
{
   get;
   set;
}

[DataMember]
public String PercentageChange
{
   get;
   set;
}
```

```
    [DataMember]
    public String CompanyName
    {
        get;
        set;
    }

}
```

Here is the complete listing for *YahooQuotes.cs*:

```csharp
using System;
using System.Collections.Generic;
using System.Text;
using System.Web;
using System.Net;
using System.IO;
using System.ServiceModel;
using System.Runtime.Serialization;

/* A WCF service consists of a contract (defined below as IYahooQuote),
 * a class that implements that interface (see YahooQuote),
 * and configuration entries that specify behaviors associated with
 * that implementation (see <system.serviceModel> in web.config) */
[ServiceContract]
public interface IYahooQuotes
{

    [OperationContract]
    string TestService(int intParam);

    [OperationContract]
    StockQuote GetQuoteForStockSymbol(String aSymbol);

}

/*
 * Use a data contract as illustrated in the sample below to
 * add StockQuote types to service operations
 */

public class YahooQuotes : IYahooQuotes
{

    public string TestService(int intParam)
    {
        return string.Format("You entered: {0}", intParam);
    }

    public StockQuote GetQuoteForStockSymbol(String tickerSymbol)
    {
        StockQuote sq = new StockQuote();
        string buffer;
        string[] bufferList;
```

```csharp
        WebRequest webRequest;
        WebResponse webResponse;

        // Use the data dictionary at the end of the big listing to
        // decipher the end of this URL
        String url = "http://quote.yahoo.com/d/quotes.csv?s="
            + tickerSymbol + "&f=l1d1t1pomvc1p2n";

        // Now that you have a URL, go get some data. It will
        // be returned to you in a nicely packaged CSV format.
        webRequest = HttpWebRequest.Create(url);
        webResponse = webRequest.GetResponse();

        // Put it in a stream buffer to make text replacement
        // easier
        using (StreamReader sr =
            new StreamReader(webResponse.GetResponseStream()))
        {
            buffer = sr.ReadToEnd();
            sr.Close();
        }

        // Strip out the " marks
        buffer = buffer.Replace("\"", "");
        // Now put it in a char array
        bufferList = buffer.Split(new char[] { ',' });

        sq.LastTradePrice = bufferList[0]; // l1
        sq.DateOfTrade = bufferList[1]; // d1
        sq.TimeOfTrade = bufferList[2]; // t1
        sq.PreviousClose = bufferList[3]; // p
        sq.Open = bufferList[4]; // o
        sq.DaysRange = bufferList[5]; // m
        sq.Volume = bufferList[6]; // v
        sq.Change = bufferList[7]; // c1
        sq.PercentageChange = bufferList[8]; // p2
        sq.CompanyName = bufferList[9]; // n

        return sq;
    }
}

[DataContract]
public class StockQuote
{

    [DataMember]
    public String LastTradePrice
    {
        get;
        set;
    }
```

```csharp
[DataMember]
public String DateOfTrade
{
    get;
    set;
}

[DataMember]
public String TimeOfTrade
{
    get;
    set;
}

[DataMember]
public String PreviousClose
{
    get;
    set;
}

[DataMember]
public String Open
{
    get;
    set;
}

[DataMember]
public String DaysRange
{
    get;
    set;
}

[DataMember]
public String Volume
{
    get;
    set;
}

[DataMember]
public String Change
{
    get;
    set;
}

[DataMember]
public String PercentageChange
{
    get;
    set;
}
```

```
[DataMember]
public String CompanyName
{
    get;
    set;
}

}
```

Launching the Web Service

With the YahooQuotes service coded, the next step is to launch it. To prepare for the launch, you'll need to edit the services section of system.serviceModel inside *Web.config* so that it matches the bolded sections here:

```
<services>
    <service name="YahooQuotes"
        behaviorConfiguration="ServiceBehavior">
        <!-- Service Endpoints -->
        <endpoint address=""
            binding="wsHttpBinding"
            contract="IYahooQuotes">

            <!-- Upon deployment, the following identity element should be removed
            or replaced to reflect the identity under which the deployed service
            runs. If removed, WCF will infer an appropriate identity automatically.-->
            <identity>
                <dns value="localhost"/>
            </identity>
        </endpoint>
        <endpoint address="mex" binding="mexHttpBinding"
            contract="IMetadataExchange"/>
    </service>
</services>
```

Additionally, your *YahooQuotes.svc* file should read:

```
<%@ ServiceHost Language="C#" Debug="true" Service="YahooQuotes"
    CodeBehind="~/App_Code/YahooQuotes.cs" %>
```

With everything coded and configured correctly in your web service, you should be able to click on the *YahooQuotes.svc* file and launch the web service. Once you have done so, you should see a page like the one in Figure 11-4.

Consuming the Web Service

Now that you have successfully created and launched the YahooQuotes service, you need to be able to consume it. The fastest way to get going on that front is to use the *SvcUtil.exe* utility (usually found in *C:\Program Files\Microsoft SDKs\Windows\v6.0\Bin*) to create the proxies you will need. To accomplish this, enter the following command in your Command Prompt after navigating to the directory containing *SvcUtil.exe*:

```
svcutil.exe http://localhost:<port>/YahooQuotes/YahooQuotes.svc?wsdl
```

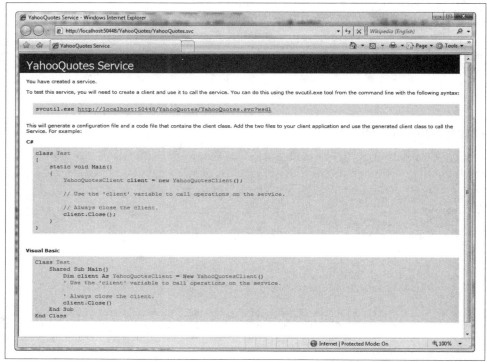

Figure 11-4. The YahooQuotes service in action

SvcUtil.exe reads the WSDL, which contains the metadata about the service. From this, it creates the proxy classes you can use in applications that wish to use the YahooQuotes service. *SvcUtil.exe* produces two files, *YahooQuotes.cs* and *Output.config* (see Figure 11-5). Be sure to put the *YahooQuotes.cs* file where you can find it later.

Figure 11-5. SvcUtil.exe output

Creating a WPF Client Application

Next, you're going to create a WPF Application called *StockQuotes*. Leaving the current Visual Studio application running (so you don't lose the port *YahooQuotes* is currently running on), start a new instance of Visual Studio 2008 and select New → Project from the File menu. In the ensuing dialog, choose WPF Application as the project type, and name the project *StockQuotes*.

When you've done this, make sure the XAML listing for *Window1.xaml* reads like this:

```
<Window x:Class="StockQuotes.Window1"
    xmlns="http://schemas.microsoft.com/winfx/2006/xaml/presentation"
    xmlns:x="http://schemas.microsoft.com/winfx/2006/xaml"
    Title="Yahooy! Quotes" Height="350" Width="500">
    <Grid>

    </Grid>
</Window>
```

Note that the Title, Height, and Width values for the Window element are different from the defaults. Please adjust your XAML accordingly.

Next, add a reference to the web service. To do this, right-click on the *References* folder in the Solution Explorer and select "Add Service Reference" (Figure 11-6).

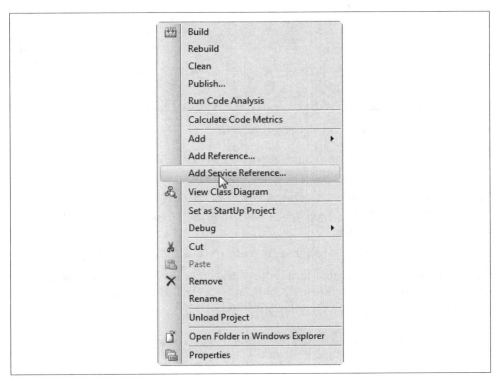

Figure 11-6. Adding a service reference

Cut and paste the YahooQuotes service URL (*http://localhost:<port>/YahooQuotes/ YahooQuotes.svc?wsdl*) into the Address text box. Clicking on the Go button should bring up the YahooQuotes service in the Services listbox, as shown in Figure 11-7.

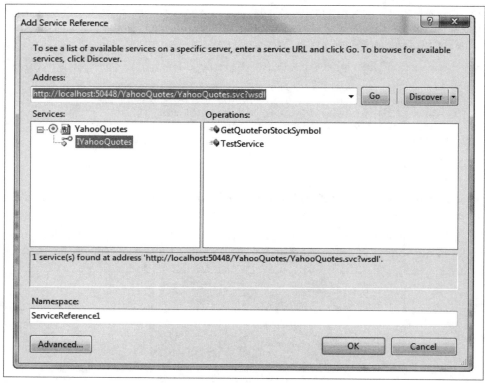

Figure 11-7. Using the WSDL URL to find YahooQuotes

Select IYahooQuotes, rename the namespace YahooQuotes, and press the OK button. Your project will now be configured to talk to this service.

Next, you need to add the *YahooQuotes.cs* file you created earlier with the *SvcUtil.exe* utility. Right-click on the *StockQuotes* folder and select Add → Existing Item, then add the *YahooQuotes.cs* file.

Once you have included this file, you are ready to start coding the application.

To begin, create a very simple form with a TextBox, a Button, and two Labels. You can either hand-type the following XAML into the *Window1.xaml* file or use Visual Studio's drag-and-drop toolbox to lay out *Window1*:

```
<Window x:Class="StockQuotes.Window1"
    xmlns="http://schemas.microsoft.com/winfx/2006/xaml/presentation"
    xmlns:x="http://schemas.microsoft.com/winfx/2006/xaml"
```

```
            Title="Yahooy! Quotes" Height="350" Width="500">
        <Grid>
            <TextBox Height="26"
                HorizontalAlignment="Left"
                Margin="38,30,0,0"
                Name="StockTickerTextBox"
                VerticalAlignment="Top"
                Width="100" />

            <Button Height="23"
                Margin="159,30,0,0"
                Name="GetTickerData"
                VerticalAlignment="Top"
                HorizontalAlignment="Left"
                Width="75"
                Click="GetQuote">Quote</Button>

            <Label Height="25.96"
                HorizontalAlignment="Left"
                Margin="38,95,0,0"
                Name="CompanyNameLabel"
                VerticalAlignment="Top"
                Width="100">Company Name</Label>

            <Label Height="25.96"
                Margin="159,95,16,0"
                Name="CompanyName"
                VerticalAlignment="Top"
                FontSize="10"
                FontWeight="Bold"></Label>
        </Grid>
    </Window>
```

Make sure you've named all the elements appropriately. Also note that you've assigned a method called GetQuote( ) to the Click attribute of your Button. Switch over to the *Window1.xaml.cs* view now and implement that method as follows:

```
public void GetQuote(object sender, RoutedEventArgs e)
{
    // This is just to quickly familiarize you with how
    // WPF applications work.

    String tickerSymbol = StockTickerTextBox.Text;
    CompanyName.Content = tickerSymbol;
}
```

Go ahead and run the application. Enter a ticker symbol, and observe how pressing the Quote button puts the ticker symbol into the Content of the CompanyName label, as shown in Figure 11-8.

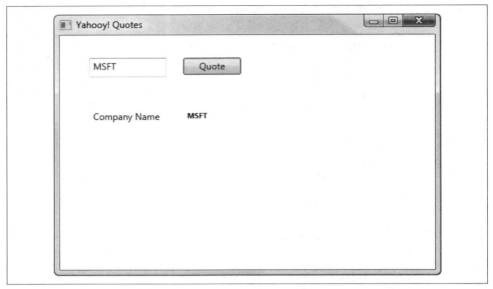

Figure 11-8. Simple WPF screen

Now you're going to actually call the service. To do this, you have to create a client of the service. You do this by instantiating a YahooQuoteClient in the following manner:

```
YahooQuoteClient client = new YahooQuoteClient( );
```

Modify the implementation of GetQuote( ) so it looks like this:

```
public void GetQuote(object sender, RoutedEventArgs e)
{
    String tickerSymbol = StockTickerTextBox.Text;
    StockQuote sq;

    YahooQuoteClient client = new YahooQuoteClient( );
    // Use the 'client' variable to call operations on the service

    sq = client.GetQuoteForStockSymbol(tickerSymbol);

    // Always close the client
    client.Close( );

    // Now we can set the variables on the page
    CompanyName.Content = sq.CompanyName;
}
```

Now when you run the WPF application, you should see that the company name associated with the ticker symbol you enter is retrieved from the web service and displayed in CompanyName.Content, as seen in Figure 11-9.

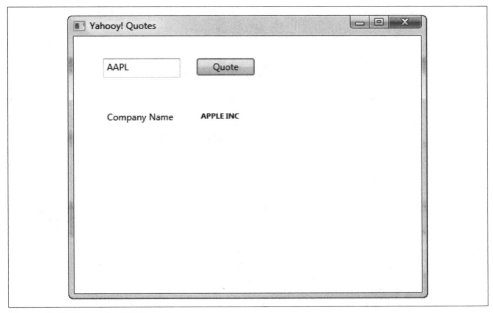

Figure 11-9. Using the WCF service

The service works! You can now focus on making its treatment of stock quotes more comprehensive. Try this listing for *Window1.xaml.cs*:

```
using System;
using System.Collections;
using System.Collections.Generic;
using System.Linq;
using System.Text;
using System.Windows;
using System.Windows.Controls;
using System.Windows.Data;
using System.Windows.Documents;
using System.Windows.Input;
using System.Windows.Shapes;
using System.Windows.Media;
using System.Windows.Media.Imaging;
using System.Windows.Navigation;

namespace StockQuotes
{
    /// <summary>
    /// Interaction logic for Window1.xaml
    /// </summary>

    public partial class Window1 : Window
    {
```

```csharp
        public Window1( )
        {
            InitializeComponent( );
        }

        public void GetQuote(object sender, RoutedEventArgs e)
        {
            String tickerSymbol = StockTickerTextBox.Text;
            StockQuote sq;

            YahooQuotesClient client = new YahooQuotesClient( );
            // Use the 'client' variable to call operations on the service

            sq = client.GetQuoteForStockSymbol(tickerSymbol);

            // Always close the client
            client.Close( );

            // Now you can set the variables on the page
            LastTradePrice.Content = sq.LastTradePrice;
            TradeDate.Content = sq.DateOfTrade;
            LastTradeTime.Content = sq.TimeOfTrade;
            DaysRange.Content = sq.DaysRange;
            DaysChange.Content = sq.Change;
            DaysPercentage.Content = sq.PercentageChange;
            CompanyName.Content = sq.CompanyName;
        }
    }
}
```

And this listing for *Window1.xaml*:

```xml
<Window x:Class="StockQuotes.Window1"
    xmlns="http://schemas.microsoft.com/winfx/2006/xaml/presentation"
    xmlns:x="http://schemas.microsoft.com/winfx/2006/xaml"
    Title="Yahooy! Quotes" Height="350" Width="510">
    <Grid>
        <TextBox Height="26"
            HorizontalAlignment="Left"
            Margin="38,30,0,0"
            Name="StockTickerTextBox"
            VerticalAlignment="Top"
            Width="100" />

        <Button Height="23"
            Margin="159,30,0,0"
            Name="GetTickerData"
            VerticalAlignment="Top"
            HorizontalAlignment="Left"
            Width="75"
            Click="GetQuote">Quote</Button>

        <Label Height="25.96"
            HorizontalAlignment="Left"
            Margin="38,95,0,0"
```

```
            Name="CompanyNameLabel"
            VerticalAlignment="Top"
            Width="100">Company Name</Label>

    <Label Height="25.96"
        Margin="159,95,16,0"
        Name="CompanyName"
        VerticalAlignment="Top"
        FontSize="10"
        FontWeight="Bold" />

    <Label Height="25.96"
        HorizontalAlignment="Left"
        Margin="38,123,0,0"
        VerticalAlignment="Top"
        Width="100">Last Trade:</Label>

    <Label Height="25.96"
        Margin="159,123,239,0"
        Name="LastTradePrice"
        VerticalAlignment="Top" />

    <Label HorizontalAlignment="Left"
        Margin="38,149,0,138.04"
        Width="100">Date:</Label>

    <Label Margin="159,149,239,138.04"
        Name="TradeDate" />

    <Label HorizontalAlignment="Left"
        Margin="38,0,0,114.04"
        Name="TimeLabel"
        Width="100"
        Height="25.96"
        VerticalAlignment="Bottom">Time:</Label>

    <Label Margin="159,0,239,114.04"
        Name="LastTradeTime"
        Height="25.96"
        VerticalAlignment="Bottom" />

    <Label Height="25.96"
        HorizontalAlignment="Left"
        Margin="38,0,0,88.04"
        VerticalAlignment="Bottom"
        Width="100">Day's Range:</Label>

    <Label Height="25.96"
        Margin="159,0,140,88.04"
        VerticalAlignment="Bottom"
        Name="DaysRange"/>

    <Label Height="25.96"
        HorizontalAlignment="Left"
```

```
            Margin="38,0,0,62.04"
            VerticalAlignment="Bottom"
            Width="100">Change:</Label>

        <Label Height="25.96"
            Margin="159,0,140,62.04"
            VerticalAlignment="Bottom"
            Name="DaysChange"/>

        <Label Height="25.96"
            HorizontalAlignment="Left"
            Margin="38,0,0,38.04"
            VerticalAlignment="Bottom"
            Width="100">Percent Change:</Label>

        <Label Height="25.96"
            Margin="159,0,239,38.04"
            VerticalAlignment="Bottom"
            Name="DaysPercentage" />

    </Grid>
</Window>
```

Compile and run the application now, and you should get something that looks like Figure 11-10.

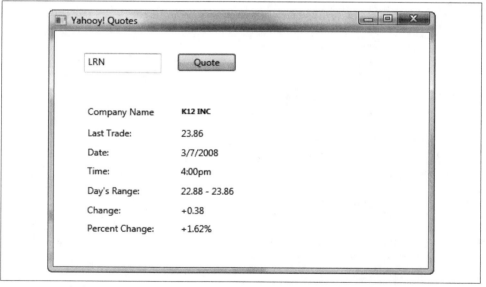

Figure 11-10. Yahooy! Quotes complete

This brief example should have given you a very good understanding of how to create, launch, and consume a WCF web service.

Introducing
Windows Workflow Foundation

Microsoft's Windows Workflow Foundation (WF) is a programming framework that facilitates the creation of *reactive programs* (described in the upcoming sidebar) designed to respond to external stimuli. It is an implementation of an important new idea that has recently found its way into programming: programmers, seeing the power of runtimes (such as the JVM and the CLR), are now starting to ask for the incorporation of design constructs as data in the same way type definitions are available as data.

Runtimes have shown the value of machine-readable representations. By way of example, most programmers almost immediately see the benefit of features such as reflection and serialization. The question naturally arises, "Why can't I model control flow, logic constructs, concurrency, and other design-time constructs as data in the same way I can model methods, fields, and classes?" The answer: there is no good reason.

Fortunately, the folks at Microsoft were thinking along the same lines, and they have given us an extensible meta-runtime in the form of WF. The meta approach taken by the architects of WF, under the leadership of Dharma Shukla, has resulted in a highly user-driven implementation (and by user, we mean you!). The WF programming model is organized around specific activities. WF is also inherently extensible, which makes it easier for you to capture the intentions of domain experts in the grammars/languages they know and understand.

In this chapter, you're going to build some simple applications. Our aim is to illustrate the core concepts of WF without specifically using the Microsoft tools. Then, after you've gained an appreciation of the heavy lifting involved, we'll take you though some of the simpler concepts involved in creating some small workflow applications using WF.

Conventional (Pre-WF) Flow Control

First, let's take a look at a couple of pre-WF examples that have one thing in common: either they deal with flow control in their own way, or they don't deal with it at all. Afterward, we'll see how WF changes the picture.

Reactive Programs

In the past, we created reactive programs to accomplish workflow-like activities. Reactive programs can be generally understood to be programs with the following characteristics:

- They pause during execution.
- The amount of time for which they pause is not predetermined.
- While paused, they await further input.

This is not really anything new to the world of computing. Collaboration between programs on the same and different machines has been an important goal since the very early days of computing. Over the years, technologies have been developed to assist in the communication between programs. From sockets to web services, computer scientists continue to evolve the mechanism through which inter-application communication occurs.

A Console Application: TalkBack

To get started with this first example, open Visual Studio 2008 and select New Project from the File menu. Create a new Console Application called *TalkBack*, as shown in Figure 12-1.

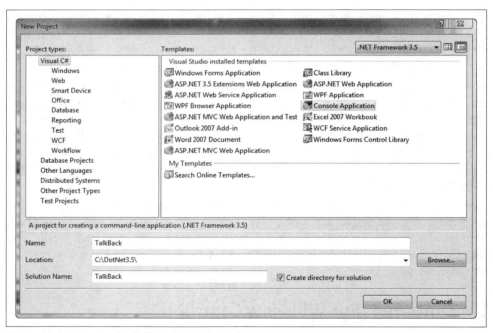

Figure 12-1. Creating the TalkBack console application

You will need to add the following code to *Program.cs*:

```csharp
using System;
using System.Collections.Generic;
using System.Text;

namespace TalkBack
{
    class Program
    {
        static void Main(string[] args)
        {
            // Print an instruction
            String key = DateTime.Now.GetHashCode().ToString();

            Console.WriteLine("Enter the following key to continue: "
                + key);

            String input = Console.ReadLine();

            if (key.Equals(input))
            {
                Console.WriteLine("We have a match: " + key + " = "
                    + input);
            }
            else
            {
            Console.WriteLine("Oops! " + key + " is not the same as "
                + input);

            }

            // Leave something on the screen and wait for input to exit
            Console.WriteLine("");
            Console.WriteLine("Press Enter to exit...");
            Console.ReadLine();
        }
    }
}
```

TalkBack is an example of a simple reactive program: it's a basic console application designed to gather input from the user, make a decision about that input, and display a result. As you can clearly see in Figure 12-2, this program pauses during execution for an unknown length of time, waiting for further input.

In many ways, this is like most of the computer programs with which we are all familiar. In the real world, we encounter reactive programs all the time. When you shop on Amazon.com or make travel reservations on Orbitz.com, these reactive programs are guided by your input. Likewise, when Amazon sends data to UPS about your order, or Orbitz books your seat on a United Airlines flight, UPS and United Airlines have reactive programs that are guided by input from other programs and that transfer the relevant information to the requesting company's programs.

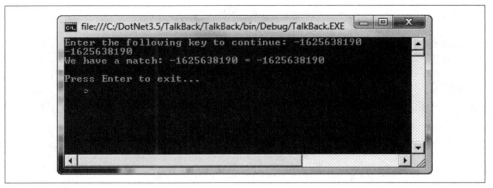

Figure 12-2. TalkBack: a simple reactive program

To further your understanding of workflow, next you'll write a simple order-status web service in ASP.NET.

An ASP.NET Web Service: OrderStatus

Create a new C#-based ASP.NET Web Service called *OrderStatus* in Visual Studio. Enter the following code in the *Service.cs* file:

```csharp
using System;
using System.Linq;
using System.Web;
using System.Web.Services;
using System.Web.Services.Protocols;
using System.Xml.Linq;

[WebService(Namespace = "http://tempuri.org/")]
[WebServiceBinding(ConformsTo = WsiProfiles.BasicProfile1_1)]
// To allow this web service to be called from script,
// using ASP.NET AJAX, uncomment the following line

// [System.Web.Script.Services.ScriptService]
public class Service : System.Web.Services.WebService
{
    public Service()
    {
        // Uncomment the following line if using designed components
        // InitializeComponent();
    }

    [WebMethod(EnableSession = true)]
    public string WelcomeInstructions()
    {
        String orderNumber = "W123456";
        Session["orderNumber"] = orderNumber;
        return "Please enter your order number: "
            + orderNumber + "\n\n";
    }
```

```
[WebMethod(EnableSession = true)]
public string GetOrderStatusForOrderNumber(String s)
{

    if (Session["orderNumber"].Equals(s))
    {
        return "Your order is being prepared for shipment";
    }
    else
    {
        return "Invalid order number...";
    }

}
}
```

This is a very simple reactive program implemented as a web service. The two methods are easy enough to understand, but there's no sense of the application flow; that is, there is nothing in the methods to prevent them from being called out of order. You'll need to implement the application flow by hand.

The first thing you'll need to do is add some flow control to the methods. As you'll see, it's fairly easy to write flow control into your code. In the code just shown, you saved the user's order number in an ASP Session variable. Next, you'll test the value of this variable to monitor the order in which the methods are called. Consider these additions (in bold) to the original code:

```
public string WelcomeInstructions( )
{
    bool orderNumberNotNull = (Session["orderNumber"] != null);

    if (orderNumberNotNull)
    {
        throw new InvalidOperationException( );
    }
    else
    {
        String orderNumber = "W123456";
        Session["orderNumber"] = orderNumber;
        return "Please enter your order number: " + orderNumber + "\n\n";
    }
}

public string GetOrderStatusForOrderNumber(String s)
{
    bool orderNumberIsNull = (Session["orderNumber"] == null);
    bool retrievedStatus = (Session["retrievedStatus"] != null);

    if (orderNumberIsNull)
    {
        throw new InvalidOperationException( );
    }
```

```
        else
        {
            if (retrievedStatus)
            {
                throw new InvalidOperationException();
            }
            else
            {
                if (Session["orderNumber"].Equals(s))
                {
                    Session["retrievedStatus"] = true;
                    return "Your order is being prepared for shipment";
                }
                else
                {
                    Session["retrievedStatus"] = true;
                    return "Invalid order number...";
                }
            }
        }
    }
```

These additions have returned flow control to your web service. If you compile it now it will run, and you should see a screen that describes the service inside your browser window (Figure 12-3).

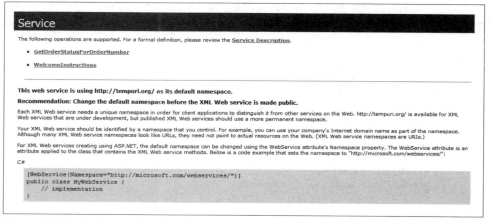

Figure 12-3. OrderStatus as a web service

You've taken advantage of ASP.NET's scalability in order to create and maintain state for a large number of sessions, but while doing so you have also introduced some serious problems.

For starters, to manage flow control, you are depending on a set of runtime checks that are hidden from the consumer of the service. Also, in this example the order number is shared by both operations (WelcomeInstructions and GetOrderStatusForOrderNumber)

---

and is manipulated as a key/value pair with nonspecific (weak) typing. If that were not enough, the order of operation is determined by testing to see whether the information needed to continue with the request is in place. All in all, this is no way to be writing reliable software.

To make matters worse, you haven't yet dealt with considerations such as threading or process agility. You'll need to be able to resume a workflow after it's been halted for an arbitrary period of time. That means you'll need a listener and a general-purpose runtime that can deal with resumption. Also, you haven't done any work to allow the program to be declared as data in a database or XAML.

Using Windows Workflow

And, you know what? Nowadays, that won't be necessary—WF will do the heavy lifting for you. In the rest of this chapter, we'll take a high-level view of the WF tools and toolkit, to provide you with an introduction to what WF can do for you.

Activities

Activities are the fundamental building blocks of WF workflows. As building blocks, they represent the basic steps within a workflow. In essence, a workflow is developed as a tree of activities, where a specific activity makes up an individual unit of execution. You will likely develop your WF solutions by assembling specific activities, which, as a result of their nature as reusable objects, can themselves be compositions of more than one activity.

The two types of WF activities are known as *basic activities* and *composite activities*. As its name suggests, a basic activity is custom-coded to provide its function set. It follows, then, that a composite activity is built out of other existing activities (both basic and composite).

A Simple Workflow Application: HelloWorkflow

Let's begin by creating a simple workflow. Open Visual Studio 2008 and choose New Project from the File menu. Select Sequential Workflow Console Application from the list of installed templates, and name the project (of all things) HelloWorkflow (see Figure 12-4).

Having successfully created your project, you should see an empty Sequential Workflow design pane like the one shown in Figure 12-5.

You should also see a toolbox pane containing several stock activities. You're going to use some of these activities to create a very simple workflow application. This application will use two Code activities (activities where the workflow will execute some user-provided code) and two Delay activities (activities where the workflow will be suspended for a period of time).

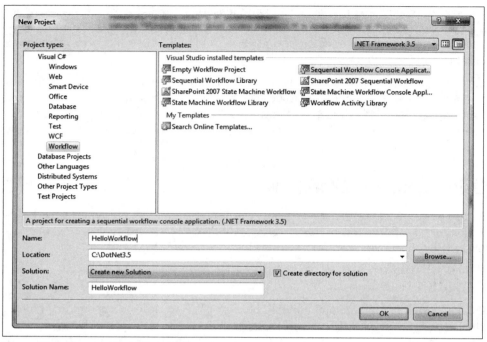

Figure 12-4. Creating the HelloWorkflow project

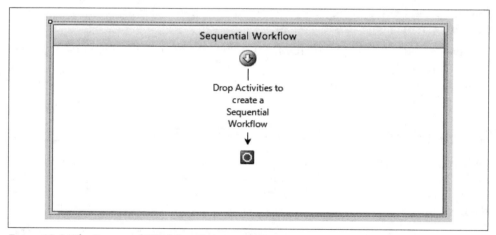

Figure 12-5. The Sequential Workflow design pane

Adding activities

Drag a Code activity onto the design surface, followed by a Delay activity. Repeat this process one more time, and you will have a sequential workflow that looks like the one in Figure 12-6. That was easy enough!

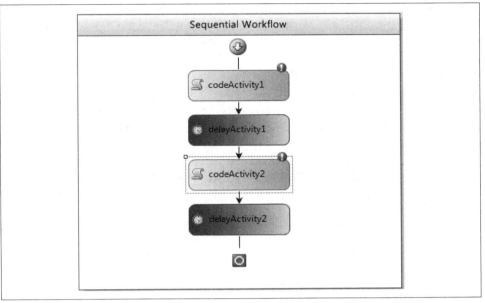

Figure 12-6. Simple workflow

Implementing the first Code activity

Now you need to implement the first Code activity. See those little exclamation points next to the Code activities? These indicate that there is nothing bound to their ExecuteCode events. To fix this, you need to implement the Code activities. Let's do the first one now.

Double-clicking on codeActivity1 automatically creates a stub method in your *Workflow1.cs* file and takes you to that method. Add a line to send output to the console. When you are done, the method will look like this:

```
private void codeActivity1_ExecuteCode(object sender, EventArgs e)
{
    Console.WriteLine("Hello Workflow!");
}
```

Next, double-click on codeActivity2, but just leave the method that gets created empty:

```
private void codeActivity2_ExecuteCode(object sender, EventArgs e)
{

}
```

At this point, you can run the application. But make sure you are watching very carefully!

What you may (or may not) have seen was a console application come into existence, quickly spit out the message "Hello Workflow," and then quickly disappear into inexistence. No worries—you can fix that by manipulating the Delay activities.

Adjusting the Delay activity's properties

Using the Properties inspector, adjust the TimeoutDuration property for delayActivity1 (see Figure 12-7). You can set it to any amount of time you like, but we have found five seconds to be sufficient. You might like something less, but you probably won't enjoy very much more.

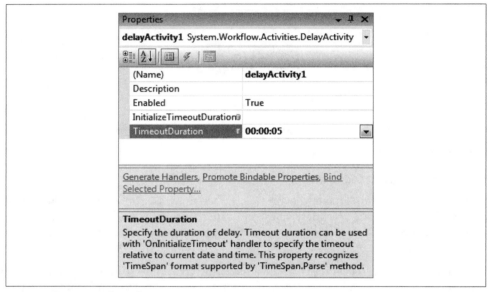

Figure 12-7. Setting the Delay activity's properties

Completing the workflow

Now, back in *Workflow1.cs*, add a Console.WriteLine() statement to the existing codeActivity2_ExecuteCode() method:

```
private void codeActivity2_ExecuteCode(object sender, EventArgs e)
{
    Console.WriteLine("Neat, it waited...");
}
```

Then, in the Properties inspector, set the TimeoutDuration of delayActivity2 to the same value you used for delayActivity1.

To review, in this simple workflow you have two Code activities and two (probably five-second) delays. Now when you compile and run the application, you should see a console application that looks similar to the one in Figure 12-8. Et voilà! A simple workflow.

Figure 12-8. Simple workflow in action

A More Sophisticated Workflow Application: WFOrderStatus

In the preceding example, you used some very simple activities from the base activity library that ships with WF. As you begin to explore the library in more detail, you will discover that there are activities for transaction management, local communication, flow control, web services, external event handlers, and a great deal more. In the next application, we will expand our tour of the base library.

Go ahead and create another Sequential Workflow Console Application, and call it *WFOrderStatus*. In this project you're going to utilize the IfElse activity, in addition to the Code and Delay activities introduced previously, to accomplish what you did programmatically at the beginning of this chapter when you created the *OrderStatus* web service.

To get started, you need some way of capturing the user's order number. To enable this, drag and drop a Code activity from the toolbox as the first activity in the sequential workflow. Double-click on the resulting codeActivity1 to take you to the code-behind. Here you will implement the following:

```
private void codeActivity1_ExecuteCode(object sender, EventArgs e)
{
    Console.WriteLine("Please enter your order tracking number: ");
    OrderNumber = Console.ReadLine();
}
```

You will also need to add a String called orderNumber inside the Workflow1 class:

```
public String orderNumber;
```

Adding the IfElse activity

Returning to the design view, add an IfElse activity to the second position in the workflow. You should now have a sequential workflow that looks very much like the one in Figure 12-9.

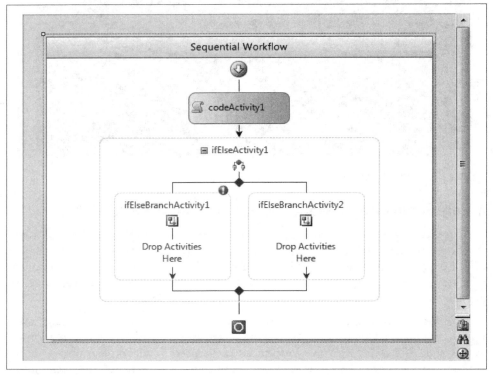

Figure 12-9. IfElse activity added

The IfElse activity itself is comprised of one or more IfElseBranch activities. These branches will be evaluated from left to right through the branches' Condition properties. You are required to set the Condition property for all but the last branch.

The first branch with a true condition will be the branch that executes. This means that if none of the branches has a true condition, nothing will execute. The one exception to this rule is when the last branch has no Condition property; in this case, it will execute by default.

Adding Code activities for the IfElseBranches

At this point, add two more Code activities, one to each branch of the IfElse activity. In addition, add a five-second Delay below the IfElse activity. Now for some "programming" by pointing and right-clicking.

Declarative rule conditions

Click on ifElseBranchActivity1 (the one on the left side), and go to the Properties window. Here, you will set the Condition property to be a declarative rule condition. After you do that, a little plus sign will appear just to the left of the Condition property. Click on it to expand the property values.

Selecting the ConditionName subproperty and then clicking on the ellipsis ("...") opens up a Select Condition panel. Click on "New" to open the Rule Condition Editor, as seen in Figure 12-10.

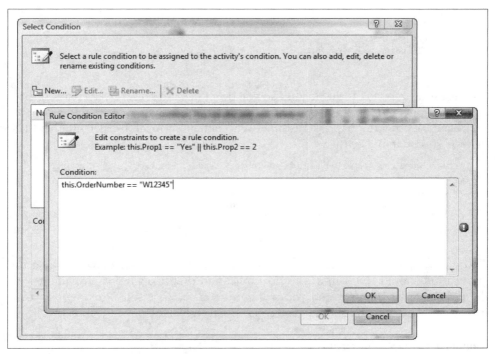

Figure 12-10. The Rule Condition Editor

Inside the editor, create a constraint that will constitute a rule condition. In this case, you want to see whether the order number provided is the same as the predetermined order number. Therefore, the constraint is `this.orderNumber == "W12345"`.

As you click through the OK sequence to close out these dialogs, you will notice that the condition becomes known as `Condition1`, and it is previewed for you in the Condition Preview section of the Select Condition pane. Clicking OK here drops you back to the Properties inspector for `ifElseBranchActivity1`, where you can see that `ConditionName` is now set to `Condition1`.

If this IfElseBranch activity is true, it will execute `codeActivity2`'s `ExecuteCode()` method. Because this is the condition where the user has supplied the correct order number, you want the console application to respond accordingly. Double-click on `codeActivity2` and enter the following:

```
private void codeActivity2_ExecuteCode(object sender, EventArgs e)
{
    Console.WriteLine(
        "Your order: " +
        orderNumber +
        "is being packaged for shipping!"
    );
}
```

`ifElseBranchActivity2` is the default, so you don't need to set its `Condition` property. However, you still must go back and double-click on `codeActivity3` to add an appropriate message for the hapless customer who enters an invalid order number. The method should look like this:

```
private void codeActivity3_ExecuteCode(object sender, EventArgs e)
{
    Console.WriteLine(
        "We're Sorry! Your order: " + OrderNumber +
        " was not found in the system!"
    );
}
```

Add a Delay activity and set the `TimeoutDuration` to 00:00:05. Now, running the application should result in a console application that takes input. Provide it with the correct order number, and you will get the expected result. Provide it with an invalid number, and you should get a console screen like the one in Figure 12-11.

Looping with the While activity

What if you wanted to make this a loop, so that customers can enter more than one order number? An easy way to handle this workflow scenario is to add in a While activity. The While activity works in a manner similar to the IfElse activity: it too has a `Condition` property, which can be set through either a declarative rule or a code condition. A While activity will evaluate this condition prior to each iteration and will continue to run as long as the condition returns true.

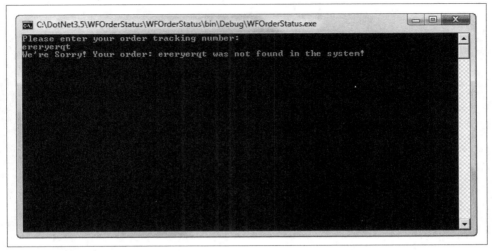

Figure 12-11. Good workflow, bad result!

To see this in action, drag a While activity into the Sequential Workflow design pane and place it between codeActivity1 and ifElseActivity1. Then drag ifElseActivity1 inside the newly created whileActivity1. You should now have a sequential workflow that looks like Figure 12-12.

Next, add the following bool variable to the top of your partial class in the *Workflow1.cs* code-behind:

```
bool keepGoing = true;
```

This variable will allow you to continue the While activity until it is no longer necessary. Also, since you know that codeActivity2's ExecuteCode( ) method will be executed when the user enters the right order number, you can use that method to set keepGoing to false as follows:

```
private void codeActivity2_ExecuteCode(object sender, EventArgs e)
{
    Console.WriteLine("Your order: " + orderNumber +
        " is being packaged for shipping!");
    keepGoing = false;
}
```

If the user enters an invalid order number, you'll need to let her know that she must re-enter the order number. Thus, you'll also need to modify the code-behind for codeActivity3's ExecuteCode( ) method, as shown here:

```
private void codeActivity3_ExecuteCode(object sender, EventArgs e)
{
    Console.WriteLine("We're Sorry! Your order: " + orderNumber +
        " was not found in the system!");
    Console.WriteLine("Please re-enter your order tracking number: ");
    orderNumber = Console.ReadLine( );
}
```

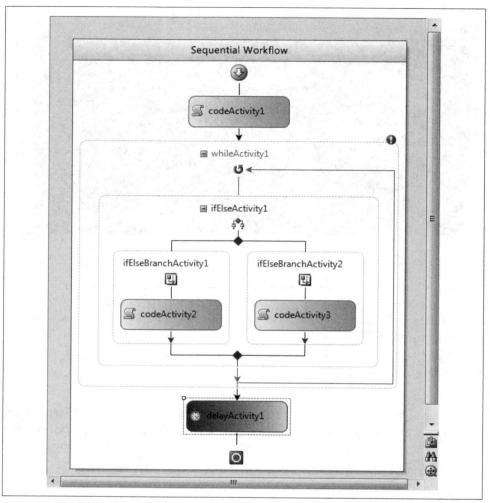

Figure 12-12. IfElse inside a While activity

The last thing you need to do is set whileActivity1's Condition property. You'll do that the same way you set the IfElseBranchActivity's Condition properties: simply set the declarative rule condition to keepGoing.

The complete listing of *Workflow1.cs* should be as follows:

```
using System;
using System.ComponentModel;
using System.ComponentModel.Design;
using System.Collections;
using System.Drawing;
using System.Linq;
using System.Workflow.ComponentModel.Compiler;
```

```
using System.Workflow.ComponentModel.Serialization;
using System.Workflow.ComponentModel;
using System.Workflow.ComponentModel.Design;
using System.Workflow.Runtime;
using System.Workflow.Activities;
using System.Workflow.Activities.Rules;

namespace WFOrderStatus
{
    public sealed partial class Workflow1: SequentialWorkflowActivity
    {
        public String OrderNumber;
        bool keepGoing = true;

        public Workflow1()
        {
            InitializeComponent();
        }

        private void codeActivity1_ExecuteCode(object sender, EventArgs e)
        {
            Console.WriteLine("Please enter your order tracking number: ");
            OrderNumber = Console.ReadLine();
        }

        private void codeActivity2_ExecuteCode(object sender, EventArgs e)
        {
            Console.WriteLine("Your order: " +OrderNumber +
                "is being packaged for shipping!");
            keepGoing = false;
        }

        private void codeActivity3_ExecuteCode(object sender, EventArgs e)
        {
            Console.WriteLine("We're Sorry! Your order: " + OrderNumber +
                " was not found in the system!");
            Console.WriteLine("Please re-enter your order tracking number: ");
            OrderNumber = Console.ReadLine();
        }

    }
}
```

With these simple changes, you have created an application that will continue prompting the user indefinitely until the correct order number is provided. When run, it should look like the application in Figure 12-13.

As you have just seen, the primary building block of any workflow solution is the activity. The workflow is defined by the activities in it, and by the steps and tasks included in the activities. WF ships with many more stock activities than we have included in our examples so far; we'll introduce many of these activities in the next chapter.

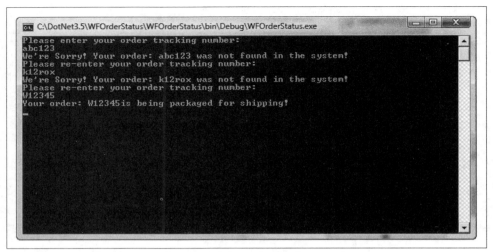

Figure 12-13. Application running with the While activity

Custom Activities

If you've been developing software for a long time, you probably already know that it's not usually possible to find a complete out-of-the-box solution that meets all the needs of a particular domain. Fortunately, WF allows you to develop custom activities that extend the functionality of the base activity classes. Even better, because the custom activities you write all derive (ultimately) from the base `Activity` class, Microsoft's workflow engine will make no distinction between your custom activities and the base class activities.

A powerful application of custom activities might be using them to create domain-specific languages for constructing workflow solutions. This is consistent with Microsoft's goal of creating an environment where the domain expert can assemble a solution using workflow activities without having to know a great deal about programming. The ability to create meaningful activities with domain-specific names should make communications between software engineers and business experts much more robust.

Imagine a scenario where a developer for a Human Resources department is assembling a workflow solution with her manager. Having an HR Manager deal with building blocks like `BeginOnlineInterview` and `SendOnlineInterviewResultsToHiringManagers` as opposed to `WebServiceInput` and `WebServiceOutput` will make things a lot easier when design conversations are ongoing. Activity names that make sense to the nontechnical domain expert *and* the software solutions expert allow for better collaboration and more productive results.

Understanding the WF Runtime

All running workflow instances are created and maintained by an in-process runtime engine commonly referred to as the *workflow runtime engine*. Accordingly, you might have several workflow runtime engines within an application domain, and each instance of the runtime engine can support multiple workflow instances, all running concurrently.

After a workflow model is compiled, it can be executed inside any Windows process (from console applications to web services). The workflow is hosted in-process, so it can easily communicate with its host application. As you can see in Figure 12-14, workflows, activities, and the runtime engine are all hosted inside a process on an application host.

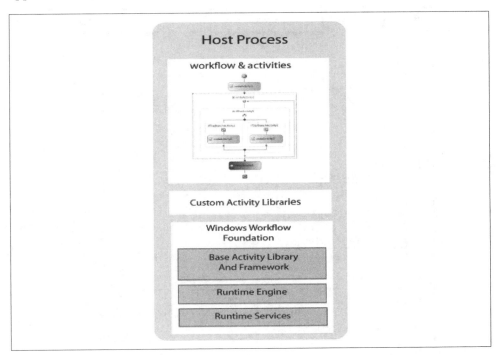

Figure 12-14. The host process

Workflow Services

WF includes classes to provide some important services, such as making workflows executable, schedulable, transactional, and persistent. We'll explore some of these services in greater detail in Chapter 13; for now, this section will provide a quick overview.

As discussed earlier, in order for a workflow to be executable it needs a runtime. *Runtime services* are provided by the WorkflowRuntime class. You can initialize a runtime by calling new WorkflowRuntime( ). Through WorkflowRuntime's AddService( ) method, you can make one or more services available to the runtime.

Once you have a new instance of the WorkflowRuntime and you have called StartRuntime( ), you begin the process that allows you to execute your workflow activities. The call to CreateWorkflow( ) returns an instantiated WorkflowInstance. You call that object's Start( ) method to begin the execution of the activities in your workflow, which continues until either the workflow is complete or an exception occurs. In both cases termination of the workflow is the end result, as depicted in Figure 12-15.

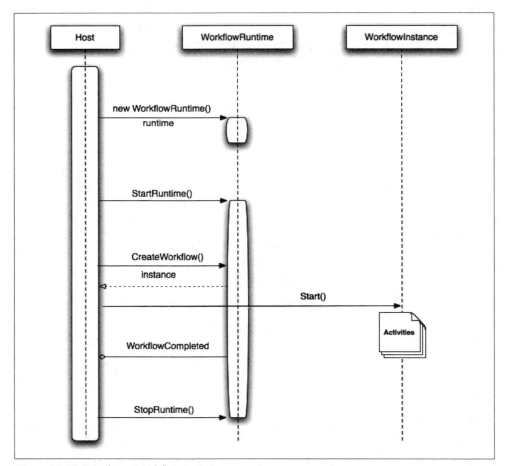

Figure 12-15. Windows Workflow in action

When it comes to *scheduling services*, you have two out-of-the-box options: the DefaultWorkflowSchedulerService class asynchronously creates the new threads necessary to execute workflows without blocking any application threads, and the ManualWorkflowSchedulerService class is available when you can spare some threads from the host application and you are not worried about synchronous execution on a single thread (or the reduction in scalability this can cause). As always, you can create and define your own scheduling service if these built-in mechanisms do not suit your needs.

If you have a requirement to maintain the internal state of a workflow, you might turn to the *transaction services* provided by the DefaultWorkflowTransactionService class. The DefaultWorkflowTransactionService class allows you to maintain the internal state in a durable store like SQL Server or some other relational database. As you might expect, the activities running inside a workflow instance, as well as the services connected to the same instance, will be able to share the same context for the transactions.

Persistence services are accomplished through the SQLWorkflowPersistenceService class. These services allow you to save the state of the workflow in a SQL Server database. If you have a long-running workflow, persistence will clearly be a requirement. Obviously, it isn't the optimal strategy to have a workflow dependent on persisting in memory for more than a few hours. Persistent storage allows you to pick up where you left off at any point in the future.

Monitoring and recording information about a given workflow is accomplished through the SQLTrackingService class. *Tracking services* utilize a tracking profile to tell the runtime about relevant information with respect to the workflow. Once the service has initiated a profile, it can open the tracking channel to receive data and events. Although the runtime does not start a tracking service as default behavior, you can configure a tracking service to help monitor service activity programmatically or through application configuration.

CHAPTER 13

Applying WF: Building a State Machine

When you are working with a set of predictable events, you will more often than not be engaged in sequential workflow. For instance, in the previous chapter you created an uncomplicated workflow example, *WFOrderStatus*, with simple rules that propelled you to completion. Even though the path of execution branched and looped, the rules you had defined dictated how you got from one part of the workflow to the next.

But what do you do when you are dependent on external events to advance your workflow? The answer is usually to build a *state machine*, which is a behavioral model composed of various activities, states, and transitions between those states. This is a task that traditionally has been easy to get almost right but terribly difficult to get completely correct. WF, however, makes creating state machines natural.

Perhaps more important, WF allows you to map a state machine to your problem domain neatly and directly, thereby dramatically reducing your cognitive load and allowing you to solve more complex problems with easier-to-maintain code.

State machines are often implemented as threads (or processes) that communicate with one another, triggered by consuming events, all as part of a larger application. As an example, an individual car in a traffic simulation might be implemented as an event-driven finite state machine (as, for that matter, might the entire traffic simulation itself).

Another way of thinking about this Cartesian split is this: decision-making *outside* the workflow will usually be made by a state machine, while decision making *inside* the workflow will be encoded using the Sequential Workflow design pane. (That said, the state machine itself will invariably have sequential workflow as part of its implementation.)

Windows Workflow and State Machines

In Windows Workflow, as events arrive they facilitate transitions between State activities. As the developer, you will specify the initial state. From there, the workflow will continue until it reaches a completed state.

EventDriven activities represent events in a state machine. By placing these activities inside State activities, you define the legal events for those states.

One level deeper, inside the EventDriven activities, you can embed your sequential workflow. These sequential activities will kick off after the arrival of the event. Under normal circumstances, the last activity in the sequence will be the SetState activity. As you might expect, this will define a transition to the next state.

Building an Incident Support State Machine

In the world of customer support, it's generally impossible to know in advance all the rules to apply to a request. Many companies have tried to make the workflow as sequential as possible, with the use of phone-based routing and resolution of issues. However, in many (most?) cases, customer support calls require some amount of ad-hoc decision making by a human being.

In this next example, you'll build a state machine that will track a support call from an open to a closed state. Over the life of the support call, the incident will be in one of the following states (and no other states; nor will it ever be in an undefined state):

- Call received
- Assigned to phone resolution
- Assigned to a service representative
- Awaiting further information
- Resolved

Your state machine will model these states and the transitions (edges) between them.

Let's get started. In Visual Studio 2008, choose File → New Project and create a State Machine Workflow Console Application. Name it *CustomerSupportStateMachine*, as shown in Figure 13-1.

You're not going to use *Workflow1.cs*, so you can delete that file. Then right-click on the project and choose Add → New Item. In the Templates area, choose "State Machine Workflow (with code separation)," as shown in Figure 13-2. Name the file *CustomerService.xoml*.

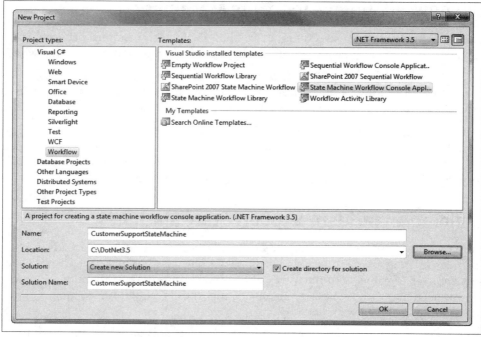

Figure 13-1. Creating the customer support state machine

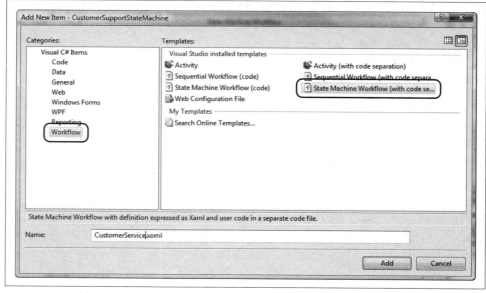

Figure 13-2. Adding CustomerService.xoml

Now, when you look at your project, you should see the workflow designer. Note that it has created the initial state for you (Figure 13-3).

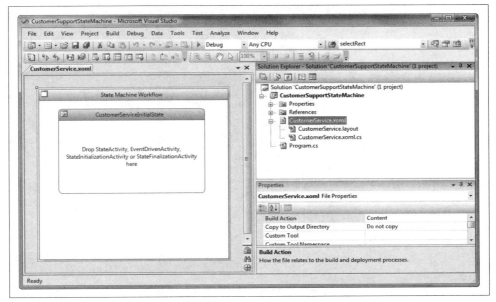

Figure 13-3. New state machine with initial state

Also note that the toolbox is available to you and is fully populated with activities from the Windows Workflow base library. This includes activities from both Windows Workflow v3.0 and v3.5, as seen in Figure 13-4.

As mentioned earlier, state machines are usually driven by external events. Typically, there will be a workflow and a host, and a mechanism by which data can be exchanged between the two. In this example, you're going to leverage a local communication service to facilitate that exchange. We won't worry about the implementation details, but you can assume that the workflow will utilize the local communication service to intercept communications, allowing it to do things like queue events until the workflow achieves the proper state to process those events.

As you might suspect, this type of activity will require a messaging contract. Contracts are defined in C# as interfaces; thus, you'll define an ICustomerCallService interface that will specify the five states that are legal in your state machine.

You'll also need to make sure that all objects you pass back and forth between the workflow and the host are serializable. Additionally, your events will need to derive from the ExternalDataEventArgs class to allow the external events to be handled.

To implement all of this, add a class named CustomerCallService to your project. The complete listing for this class is shown in Example 13-1.

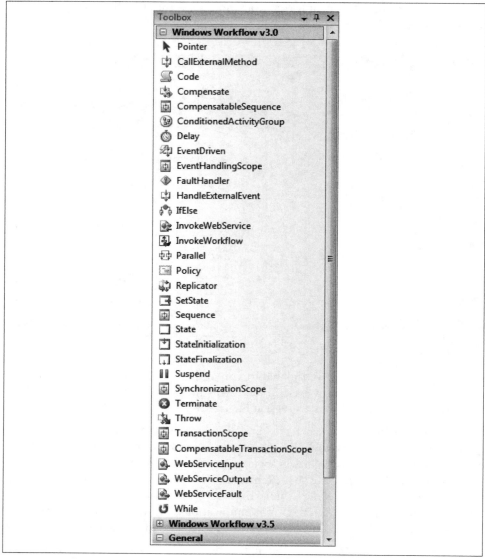

Figure 13-4. The WF toolbox

Example 13-1. CustomerCallService.cs

```
using System;
using System.Collections.Generic;
using System.Linq;
using System.Text;
using System.Workflow.Activities;

namespace CustomerSupportStateMachine
```

Example 13-1. CustomerCallService.cs (continued)

```csharp
{
    [ExternalDataExchange]
    public interface ICustomerCallService
    {
        event EventHandler<CallStateChangedEventArgs> CallRecieved;
        event EventHandler<CallStateChangedEventArgs> CallSentToPhoneResolution;
        event EventHandler<CallStateChangedEventArgs> CallAssignedToSupportPerson;
        event EventHandler<CallStateChangedEventArgs>
            CallEndedMoreInformationRequired;
        event EventHandler<CallStateChangedEventArgs> CallResolved;
    }

    [Serializable]
    public class Call
    {
        public string CallersFirstName { get; set; }
        public string Product { get; set; }
        public string AssignedTo { get; set; }
    }

    [Serializable]
    public class CallStateChangedEventArgs : ExternalDataEventArgs
    {
        public CallStateChangedEventArgs(Guid guid, Call aCall)
            : base(guid)
        {
            Call = aCall;
            WaitForIdle = true;
        }

        public Call Call { get; set; }

    }
}

public class CustomerCallService : ICustomerCallService
{
    public event EventHandler<CallStateChangedEventArgs> CallRecieved;
    public event EventHandler<CallStateChangedEventArgs> CallSentToPhoneResolution;
    public event EventHandler<CallStateChangedEventArgs>
        CallAssignedToSupportPerson;
    public event EventHandler<CallStateChangedEventArgs>
        CallEndedMoreInformationRequired;
    public event EventHandler<CallStateChangedEventArgs> CallResolved;

    public void CallRecieved(Guid guid, Call aCall)
    {
        if (CallRecieved != null)
            CallRecieved(null, new CallStateChangedEventArgs(guid, aCall));
    }

    public void CallSentToPhoneResolution(Guid guid, Call aCall)
```

Example 13-1. CustomerCallService.cs (continued)

```
    {
        if (CallSentToPhoneResolution != null)
            CallSentToPhoneResolution(null,
                new CallStateChangedEventArgs(guid, aCall));
    }

    public void CallAssignedToSupportPerson(Guid guid, Call aCall)
    {
        if (CallAssignedToSupportPerson != null)
            CallAssignedToSupportPerson(null,
                new CallStateChangedEventArgs(guid, aCall));
    }

    public void CallEndedMoreInformationRequired(Guid guid, Call aCall)
    {
        if (CallEndedMoreInformationRequired != null)
            CallEndedMoreInformationRequired(null,
                new CallStateChangedEventArgs(guid, aCall));
    }

    public void CallResolved(Guid guid, Call aCall)
    {
        if (CallResolved != null)
            CallResolved(null, new CallStateChangedEventArgs(guid, aCall));
    }
}
```

As mentioned earlier, the local communication service will require an interface. The
ICustomerCallService interface lays out the events that can be raised to provide data
to your workflow. The events correspond to the legitimate states for the customer's
service call:

```
[ExternalDataExchange]
public interface ICustomerCallService
{
    event EventHandler<CallStateChangedEventArgs> CallRecieved;
    event EventHandler<CallStateChangedEventArgs> CallSentToPhoneResolution;
    event EventHandler<CallStateChangedEventArgs>
        CallAssignedToSupportPerson;
    event EventHandler<CallStateChangedEventArgs>
        CallEndedMoreInformationRequired;
    event EventHandler<CallStateChangedEventArgs> CallResolved;
}
```

Note that in this example, communication is one-way only; you're simply laying out
a series of events that the workflow can invoke. If communication were two-way,
you would also have to define methods that the workflow could invoke.

The service will need to provide the information required by the workflow, using the
serializable Call object specifically created for this purpose. This object provides properties for the caller's name, the product, and who the call is assigned to. To have it play
nicely across different transport and storage mechanisms, it needs to be serializable:

```
[Serializable]
public class Call
{
    public string CallersFirstName { get; set; }
    public string Product { get; set; }
    public string AssignedTo { get; set; }
}
```

The next section of code is the implementation of ExternalDataEventArgs:

```
[Serializable]
public class CallStateChangedEventArgs : ExternalDataEventArgs
{
    public CallStateChangedEventArgs(Guid guid, Call aCall)
        : base(guid)
    {
        Call = aCall;
        WaitForIdle = true;
    }

    public Call Call { get; set; }

}
```

CallStateChangedEventArgs is a serializable event argument class, and this class is what allows you to pass the Call object between the host and the workflow. Because this is a local communication, you'll also leverage some additional properties of the class: specifically, you'll use the InstanceID (a globally unique identifier, or GUID), which you'll pass into the base constructor. This will guarantee that every workflow instance created by the runtime will be uniquely identified, which in turn ensures that events are routed to the appropriate instances.

In the implementation of CustomerCallService, you'll create a simple set of methods to raise events:

```
public class CustomerCallService : ICustomerCallService
{
    public event EventHandler<CallStateChangedEventArgs> CallRecieved;
    public event EventHandler<CallStateChangedEventArgs> CallSentToPhoneResolution;
    public event EventHandler<CallStateChangedEventArgs>
        CallAssignedToSupportPerson;
    public event EventHandler<CallStateChangedEventArgs>
        CallEndedMoreInformationRequired;
    public event EventHandler<CallStateChangedEventArgs> CallResolved;

    public void CallRecieved(Guid guid, Call aCall)
    {
        if (CallRecieved != null)
            CallRecieved(null, new CallStateChangedEventArgs(guid, aCall));
    }

    public void CallSentToPhoneResolution(Guid guid, Call aCall)
    {
        if (CallSentToPhoneResolution != null)
```

```
            CallSentToPhoneResolution(null,
                new CallStateChangedEventArgs(guid, aCall));
    }

    public void CallAssignedToSupportPerson(Guid guid, Call aCall)
    {
        if (CallAssignedToSupportPerson != null)
            CallAssignedToSupportPerson(null,
                new CallStateChangedEventArgs(guid, aCall));
    }

    public void CallEndedMoreInformationRequired(Guid guid, Call aCall)
    {
        if (CallEndedMoreInformationRequired != null)
            CallEndedMoreInformationRequired(null,
                new CallStateChangedEventArgs(guid, aCall));
    }

    public void CallResolved(Guid guid, Call aCall)
    {
        if (CallResolved != null)
            CallResolved(null, new CallStateChangedEventArgs(guid, aCall));
    }
}
```

Using this service from your console, you'll be able to raise events that will be routed to the workflow.

You're now ready to build the state machine.

State

As discussed earlier, the main component in a state machine workflow is the State activity. With events being captured at different points in a state machine workflow, states are entered to handle the tasks associated with those events.

During its lifetime, a workflow may leave and enter several different states. These states can be connected using the SetState activity.

After you add a new State activity into a workflow, you can then add the following types of child activities:

- EventDriven activities
- StateInitialization activities
- StateFinalization activities
- Additional State activity instances

An EventDriven activity is used when a State activity relies on an external event occurring in order for its child activities to execute.

You should note that when a child activity is executed more than once, a separate instance of the activity is created for each iteration. The instances execute independently (or in parallel, in the case of a Replicator activity), while the definition of the child activity in the template is not executed and is always in the intialized state.

You'll continue your development by using the toolbox to drop in a series of State activities, which you'll rename using the Properties window. You should wind up with the following additional State activities:

- `CallRecievedState`
- `CallSentToPhoneResolutionState`
- `CallAssignedToSupportPersonState`
- `CallEndedMoreInformationRequiredState`
- `CallResolvedState`
- `CustomerSatisfiedState`

When you create the `CustomerSatisfiedState` activity, you will need to right-click on it and select "Set as Completed State."

At this point, you should have a state machine layout that looks similar to Figure 13-5.

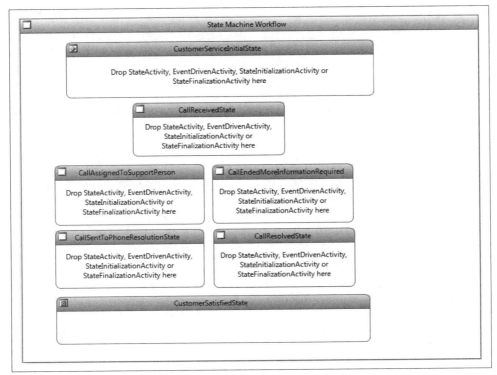

Figure 13-5. The State activities for your workflow

An Event-Driven State Machine

As mentioned in the previous section, there are four types of activity that you can drop into a State activity. The choice is clear for this workflow—you're going to start adding EventDriven activities.

Drag and drop an EventDriven activity from the toolbox into the CustomerServiceInitialState activity. In the Properties window, set its name to OnCallReceived. Then double-click on the newly named CustomerServiceInitialState activity to reveal a detail view that should look similar to Figure 13-6.

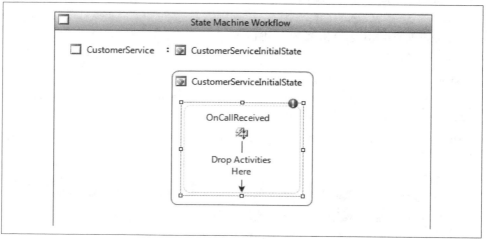

Figure 13-6. Detail view of CustomerServiceInitialState

OnCallReceived is now able to accept child activities. Remember that the first activity you drop into this sequence must support the IEventActivity interface. In this case you don't have much to worry about, because you're using a local communication service to generate events.

The next step is to drag a HandleExternalEvent activity from the toolbox onto the workflow. In the Properties window, change the name of this activity to handleCallReceivedEvent and set its InterfaceType property to ICustomerCallService. This will allow you to pick CallReceived from a list provided by Visual Studio, as you set the EventName property.

To wrap up this State activity, drag and drop a SetState activity just below the handleCallReceivedEvent activity. In the Properties window, rename this activity setCallRecievedState. There is only one other property to set: TargetStateName. This property will be the destination state. In this case, you'll set it to CallReceivedState. At this point, the CustomerServiceInitialState should look very much like Figure 13-7.

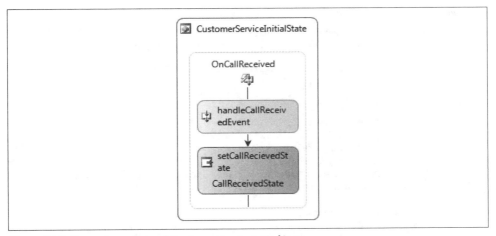

Figure 13-7. Properly configured CustomerServiceInitialState

Run 'Em If You Got 'Em

We're going to take the opportunity now to subject you to our core application development philosophy one more time: *get it running and keep it running*.

Let's see whether you can send your first event to the runtime. The complete listing (for now) will look like Example 13-2.

Example 13-2. Program.cs (initial listing)

```
using System;
using System.Collections.Generic;
using System.Linq;
using System.Text;
using System.Threading;
using System.Workflow.Runtime;
using System.Workflow.Runtime.Hosting;
using System.Workflow.Activities;
using System.Workflow.Runtime.Tracking;
using System.Workflow.Runtime.Configuration;

namespace CustomerSupportStateMachine
{
    class Program
    {
        static void Main(string[] args)
        {
            using (WorkflowRuntime workflowRuntime = new WorkflowRuntime())
            {
                AutoResetEvent waitHandle = new AutoResetEvent(false);
                workflowRuntime.WorkflowCompleted +=
                    delegate(object sender, WorkflowCompletedEventArgs e)
                    { waitHandle.Set(); };
```

Example 13-2. Program.cs (initial listing) (continued)

```
            workflowRuntime.WorkflowTerminated +=
                delegate(object sender, WorkflowTerminatedEventArgs e)
                {
                    Console.WriteLine(e.Exception.Message);
                    waitHandle.Set( );
                };

            ExternalDataExchangeService dataExchange;
            dataExchange = new ExternalDataExchangeService( );
            workflowRuntime.AddService(dataExchange);

            CustomerCallService customerCallService = new CustomerCallService( );
            dataExchange.AddService(customerCallService);

            WorkflowInstance instance =
                workflowRuntime.CreateWorkflow(typeof(CustomerService));
            instance.Start( );

            Call newCall = new Call( );

            newCall.CallersFirstName = "Alex";
            newCall.Product = "Widget Number Nine";

            customerCallService.ReceiveCall(instance.InstanceId, newCall);
            PrintStateMachineState(workflowRuntime, instance.InstanceId);

            waitHandle.WaitOne( );
        }
    }

    private static void PrintStateMachineState(
        WorkflowRuntime runtime, Guid instanceID)
    {
        StateMachineWorkflowInstance instance =
            new StateMachineWorkflowInstance(runtime, instanceID);

        Console.WriteLine("Workflow GUID: {0}", instanceID);
        Console.WriteLine("Current State: {0}", instance.CurrentStateName);
        Console.WriteLine("Transition States Available: {0}",
            instance.PossibleStateTransitions.Count);
        foreach (string transition in instance.PossibleStateTransitions)
        {
            Console.WriteLine("Transition to -> {0}", transition);
        }
    }

    }
}
```

Let's break this down. The `PrintStateMachineState()` static method enables you to actually print something meaningful to the console:

```
private static void PrintStateMachineState(
    WorkflowRuntime runtime, Guid instanceID)
{
    StateMachineWorkflowInstance instance =
        new StateMachineWorkflowInstance(runtime, instanceID);

    Console.WriteLine("Workflow GUID: {0}", instanceID);
    Console.WriteLine("Current State: {0}", instance.CurrentStateName);
    Console.WriteLine("Transition States Available: {0}",
        instance.PossibleStateTransitions.Count);
    foreach (string transition in instance.PossibleStateTransitions)
    {
        Console.WriteLine("Transition to -> {0}", name);
    }
}
```

Otherwise, running the application would produce a blank screen—after all, your state machine deals only in events. Additionally, you need a way to talk to the local communication service. The following lines of code get that up and running:

```
ExternalDataExchangeService dataExchange;
dataExchange = new ExternalDataExchangeService();
workflowRuntime.AddService(dataExchange);

CustomerCallService customerCallService = new CustomerCallService();
dataExchange.AddService(customerCallService);
```

These lines are followed by the section of code that creates the instance:

```
WorkflowInstance instance =
    workflowRuntime.CreateWorkflow(typeof(CustomerService));
instance.Start();
```

Then you set up a new call:

```
Call newCall = new Call();

newCall.CallersFirstName = "Alex";
newCall.Product = "Widget Number Nine";
```

and inform the service that a call has been received:

```
customerCallService.ReceiveCall(instance.InstanceId, newCall);
```

You can then print the state of the state machine to verify this:

```
PrintStateMachineState(workflowRuntime, instance.InstanceId);

waitHandle.WaitOne();
```

When everything is up and running, you should get a console view that looks like the one in Figure 13-8.

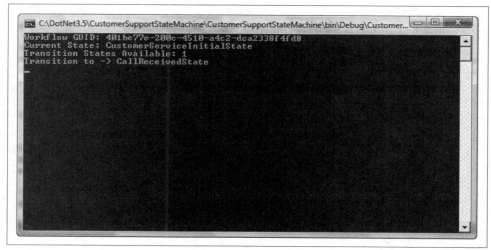

Figure 13-8. Running for the first time

Persisting Your State (Machine)

It's time to send more events—but before you can do that, you need to make sure that you can persist the state of the state machine beyond the simple event transaction. For this, you need some sort of persistence layer to mash up with the workflow.

Fortunately, Windows Workflow provides out-of-the-box support for persistence through the SQLWorkflowPersistenceService class. By this point in the book we're assuming that you have some version of Microsoft SQL Server installed. If not, go and get the free development version (SQL Express) from the Microsoft web site now.

Create a new database called WorkflowDataBase, as seen in Figure 13-9 (or, if you so choose, just use the default database).

Configure the database to handle workflow persistence and tracking. To do so, you only need to run the following scripts (all of which can be found in *C:\Windows\ Microsoft.NET\Framework\v3.0\Windows Workflow Foundation\SQL\EN*), in the order they're listed here:

- *SqlPersistenceService_Schema.sql*
- *SqlPersistenceService_Logic.sql*
- *Tracking_Schema.sql*
- *Tracking_Logic.sql*

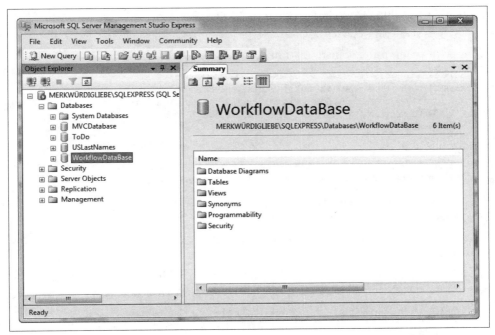

Figure 13-9. WorkflowDataBase in SQL Server 2008

These scripts will create the schemas and database logic required for the execution of your workflow, without consideration of the normal time/space continuum. In other words, one event can happen on a Monday and the next event can happen three months from Tuesday, and the workflow will chug along as if no time whatsoever has elapsed.

Next, add to the project an application configuration file with the following entry:

```
<?xml version="1.0" encoding="utf-8" ?>
<configuration>
    <connectionStrings>
        <add name="PersistentDataStore"
            connectionString="Data Source=(local);Initial Catalog=WorkflowDataBase;
            Integrated Security=true"/>
    </connectionStrings>
</configuration>
```

Also, add a reference to System.Configuration in the References section, to ensure that you can access your connection string programmatically.

Then add the following using statement to *Program.cs*:

```
using System.Configuration;
```

along with programmatic instantiation of tracking and persistence:

```
SqlWorkflowPersistenceService persistenceService;
persistenceService = new SqlWorkflowPersistenceService(
    ConfigurationManager.ConnectionStrings["PersistentDataStore"].
        ConnectionString, true, TimeSpan.MaxValue, TimeSpan.MinValue);
workflowRuntime.AddService(persistenceService);

SqlTrackingService trackingService;
trackingService = new SqlTrackingService(
    ConfigurationManager.ConnectionStrings["PersistentDataStore"].
        ConnectionString);
trackingService.UseDefaultProfile = true;
workflowRuntime.AddService(trackingService);
```

You'll need persistence in order to access the current state and tracking to access the history.

Speaking of history, you'll want to add another static method to the class to print the history of the state machine's instance. That method is as follows:

```
private static void PrintHistory(WorkflowRuntime runtime,Guid instanceID)
{
    StateMachineWorkflowInstance instance = new
        StateMachineWorkflowInstance(runtime, instanceID);
    Console.WriteLine(
        "History of State Machine instance's workflow: (From Last to First)");
    foreach (string history in instance.StateHistory)
    {
        Console.WriteLine("\t{0}", history);
    }
    Console.WriteLine("\n\n-----------------\n");
}
```

Back to Our Regularly Scheduled Programming

Now let's return to the State activities and make sure that they all have reasonable external event handler(s) and state setter(s). You need to ensure you have covered all the possible events and transitions for your call center.

Turning your attention to the CallReceivedState activity, add and configure four EventDriven activities:

- OnAssignToSupportPerson
- OnAssignToPhoneResolution
- OnEndCallNeedMoreInformation
- OnCallResolved

As you did earlier, you'll create these by dragging and dropping EventDriven activities from the toolbox into CallReceivedState. Change their names by editing their Name properties in the Properties window.

Next, double-click on OnAssignToSupportPerson and drop in a HandleExternal-Event activity and a SetState activity. Then set the HandleExternalEvent's Name property to handleAssignToSupportPerson, and configure its InterfaceType and EventName properties as CustomerSupportStateMachine.ICustomerCallService and CallEndedMoreInformationRequired, respectively. Set the SetState activity's Name property to setCallAssignedToSupportPersonState and its TargetStateName property to CallAssignedToSupportPerson.

Repeat these steps for the other three EventDriven activities in CallReceivedState, and you should wind up with a diagram that looks like Figure 13-10.

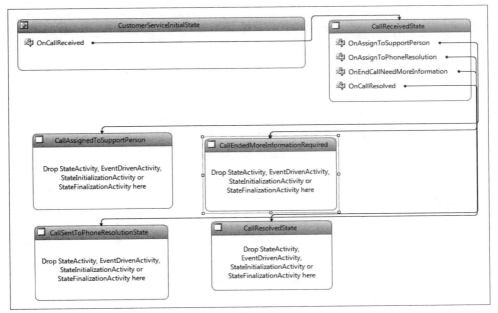

Figure 13-10. Correctly configured CallReceivedState

Follow this procedure for all the other State activities, and you should end up with a workflow that looks like the one in Figure 13-11.

Example 13-3 shows the complete listing for *Program.cs*.

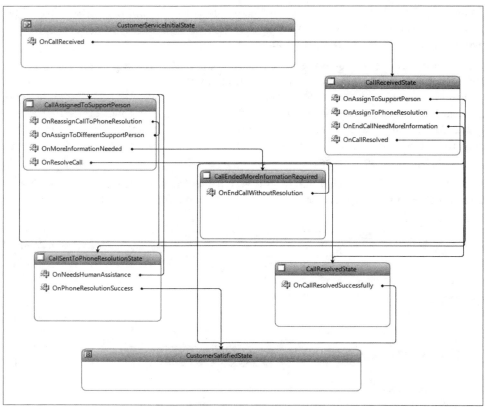

Figure 13-11. Workflow with all assignments

Example 13-3. Program.cs (complete listing)

```
using System;
using System.Collections.Generic;
using System.Linq;
using System.Text;
using System.Threading;
using System.Workflow.Runtime;
using System.Workflow.Runtime.Hosting;
using System.Workflow.Activities;
using System.Workflow.Runtime.Tracking;
using System.Workflow.Runtime.Configuration;
using System.Configuration;

namespace CustomerSupportStateMachine
{
    class Program
    {
        static void Main(string[] args)
        {
```

Example 13-3. Program.cs (complete listing) (continued)

```csharp
using (WorkflowRuntime workflowRuntime = new WorkflowRuntime())
{
    AutoResetEvent waitHandle = new AutoResetEvent(false);
    workflowRuntime.WorkflowCompleted +=
        delegate(object sender, WorkflowCompletedEventArgs e)
        { waitHandle.Set(); };
    workflowRuntime.WorkflowTerminated +=
        delegate(object sender, WorkflowTerminatedEventArgs e)
        {
            Console.WriteLine(e.Exception.Message);
            waitHandle.Set();
        };

    // Add persistence and tracking
    SqlWorkflowPersistenceService persistenceService;
    persistenceService = new SqlWorkflowPersistenceService(
        ConfigurationManager.ConnectionStrings["PersistentDataStore"].
        ConnectionString, true, TimeSpan.MaxValue, TimeSpan.MinValue);
    workflowRuntime.AddService(persistenceService);

    SqlTrackingService trackingService;
    trackingService = new SqlTrackingService(
        ConfigurationManager.ConnectionStrings["PersistentDataStore"].
        ConnectionString);
    trackingService.UseDefaultProfile = true;
    workflowRuntime.AddService(trackingService);

    // Set up the data exchange
    ExternalDataExchangeService dataExchange;
    dataExchange = new ExternalDataExchangeService();
    workflowRuntime.AddService(dataExchange);

    // Instantiate the local communication service
    CustomerCallService customerCallService = new CustomerCallService();
    dataExchange.AddService(customerCallService);

    // Create a new workflow instance
    WorkflowInstance instance =
        workflowRuntime.CreateWorkflow(typeof(CustomerService));
    instance.Start();

    // Create a new Call
    Call newCall = new Call();
    newCall.CallersFirstName = "Alex";
    newCall.Product = "Widget Number Nine";

    // Change the state using the service and events
    customerCallService.ReceiveCall(instance.InstanceId, newCall);
    customerCallService.SendCallToPhoneResolution(
        instance.InstanceId, newCall);
    customerCallService.AssignCallToSupportPerson(
        instance.InstanceId, newCall);
```

Example 13-3. Program.cs (complete listing) (continued)

```
            // Get a look at where you've wound up
            PrintStateMachineState(workflowRuntime, instance.InstanceId);

            // Change the state one last time
            customerCallService.ResolveCall(instance.InstanceId, newCall);

            // Print the history of your instance
            PrintHistory(workflowRuntime, instance.InstanceId);

            waitHandle.WaitOne();

            // Keep the console open until key strokes are entered
            // so that you can see what you've done...
            Console.ReadLine();
        }
    }

    private static void PrintStateMachineState(
        WorkflowRuntime runtime, Guid instanceID)
    {
        StateMachineWorkflowInstance myInstance =
            new StateMachineWorkflowInstance(runtime, instanceID);

        Console.WriteLine("Workflow GUID: {0}", instanceID);
        Console.WriteLine("Current State: {0}", myInstance.CurrentStateName);
        Console.WriteLine("Transition States Available: {0}",
            myInstance.PossibleStateTransitions.Count);
        foreach (string transition in myInstance.PossibleStateTransitions)
        {
            Console.WriteLine("Transition to -> {0}", transition);
        }
        Console.WriteLine("\n\n-----------------\n");
    }

    private static void PrintHistory(WorkflowRuntime runtime,Guid instanceID)
    {
        StateMachineWorkflowInstance instance =
            new StateMachineWorkflowInstance(runtime, instanceID);
        Console.WriteLine(
            "History of State Machine instance's workflow: (From Last to First)");
        foreach (string history in instance.StateHistory)
        {
            Console.WriteLine("\t{0}", history);
        }
        Console.WriteLine("\n\n-----------------\n");
    }

    }
}
```

When you run this program, you should see something that looks very similar to Figure 13-12.

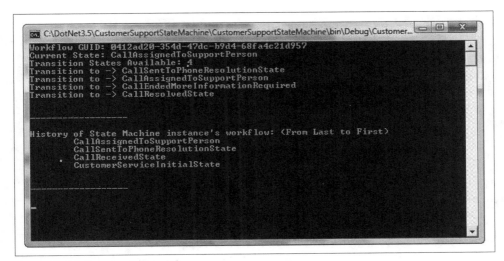

Figure 13-12. Running the workflow

CHAPTER 14

Using and Applying CardSpace: A New Scheme for Establishing Identity

Until now, identifying oneself on the Web has been a source of irritation, annoyance, security concerns, and risk. Web sites often require users to provide unique login IDs and passwords, and you may also have to supply some arbitrary level of personal identification. Because some sites contain information that may be of great value, or engage in transactions that may involve exchanging significant amounts of money, it is often in your interest to ensure that the passwords you use are secure. But unfortunately, at the present time there is no good, easy way to create secure passwords for all the sites that require them. By definition, a good password should be difficult for either a human or a computer algorithm to guess, and thus a good password will be difficult to remember. The usual solution to this is to write down all your passwords, which immediately makes them vulnerable to discovery.

Microsoft's first attempt at solving this problem was *Passport*. The idea behind Passport was that you would have a single identity with only a single password to remember. The problem with this approach, of course, is that you may not wish to have the same identity on every web site you visit. Also, many web users prefer to limit the information they give out to the absolute minimum required to perform the transactions they want on a given web site—and with good reason. All of us have experienced the tsunami of junk mail that can result from simply visiting the wrong web site.

A better solution, Microsoft determined, would be to allow users to create a number of "identity cards," each of which could provide its own level of validity, verifiability, reliability, and personal data. For example, you might choose to create a highly secure identity that reveals your most valuable information and provides the most verifiable and valid data, a day-to-day identity that provides a more limited amount of true information about you, an even more basic identity that reveals only a few personal details, and a false identity to use on casual web sites where you do not wish your true identity to be revealed.

Finally, you can imagine having certain special cards that represent trusted relationships between you and institutions with which you do ongoing business, such as your bank, brokerage firm, or employer.

Microsoft's solution to this problem is *CardSpace*.

About Windows CardSpace

The Windows CardSpace software ships with Microsoft's .NET 3.5 Framework. CardSpace functions as both an identity selector (a platform service for user-centric identity management) and an identity provider (a producer of assertions about the authenticity of an identity). It creates and stores references to a user's digital identities and allows the user to present his identity of choice in the form of an *information card*. Information cards appear on the screen very much like credit cards or other ID cards.

Microsoft has worked hard to ensure that CardSpace provides a consistent user experience through which users can easily select and use an identity on sites where CardSpace is accepted. CardSpace conforms to the Laws of Identity (see the upcoming sidebar "Kim Cameron's Laws of Identity in Brief") and provides the foundation for a unified, secure, privacy-protecting, interoperable identity layer for the Internet, which you as a developer can leverage today with relative ease.

Kim Cameron's Laws of Identity in Brief

Kim Cameron's Identityblog (*http://www.identityblog.com*) defines seven laws of identity:

1. User Control and Consent: Digital identity systems must only reveal information identifying a user with the user's consent.

2. Limited Disclosure for Limited Use: The solution which discloses the least identifying information and best limits its use is the most stable, long-term solution.

3. The Law of Fewest Parties: Digital identity systems must limit disclosure of identifying information to parties having a necessary and justifiable place in a given identity relationship.

4. Directed Identity: A universal identity metasystem must support both "omni-directional" identifiers for use by public entities and "unidirectional" identifiers for private entities, thus facilitating discovery while preventing unnecessary release of correlation handles.

5. Pluralism of Operators and Technologies: A universal identity metasystem must channel and enable the interworking of multiple identity technologies run by multiple identity providers.

6. Human Integration: A unifying identity metasystem must define the human user as a component integrated through protected and unambiguous human-machine communications.

7. Consistent Experience Across Contexts: A unifying identity metasystem must provide a simple consistent experience while enabling separation of contexts through multiple operators and technologies.

CardSpace allows you, as a user, to create personal (self-issued) information cards for yourself. An information card can contain one or more of 14 fields of identity information. For more secure transactions, users will use managed identity cards, typically issued by a third-party identity provider. These cards are different in that the providers—such as employers, financial institutions, or government agencies— make the claims on the user's behalf.

When CardSpace-enabled applications or information card-aware web sites wish to obtain information about a user, they ask the user for an identity card. At that point, CardSpace switches the display to the CardSpace service, which displays the user's stored identities on the screen (as illustrated in Figure 14-1). The user selects the card to use, at which point the CardSpace software contacts the issuer of the identity to obtain a digitally signed XML token that contains the requested information. It is important to note that the user chooses which identity to provide before the identity is validated.

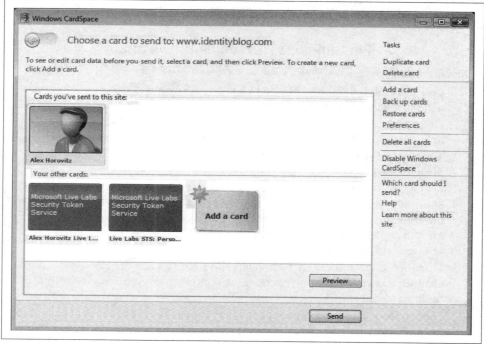

Figure 14-1. Selecting an identity

Built on top of the web services protocol stack, CardSpace leverages an open set of XML-based protocols. These include WS-Security, WS-Trust, WS-MetadataExchange, and WS-SecurityPolicy. As a direct result, any technology or platform that supports WS-* protocols can integrate with CardSpace.

To accept information cards, a web site developer only needs to declare an HTML OBJECT tag specifying the claims the web site requires from the user. Additionally, the site developer will need to implement code to process the returned token and to extract the claim values.

Identity providers who want to issue tokens must provide a means by which a user can obtain a managed card. They must also provide a Security Token Service (STS) that handles WS-Trust requests, including the return of an appropriate encrypted and signed token. Identity providers not wishing to build their own STS can obtain one from a variety of vendors, including BMC, Siemens, Sun, and Microsoft.

The basic interaction for a client is captured in Figure 14-2.

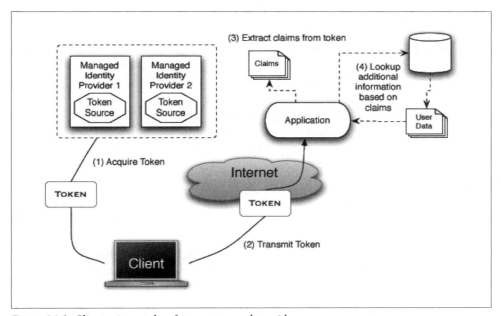

Figure 14-2. Client using a token from a managed provider

CardSpace and the Identity Metasystem on which it is based are token format-agnostic. Therefore, CardSpace does not compete directly with other Internet identity architectures. In some ways, these approaches to identity can be seen as complementary. As of this writing, CardSpace information cards can be used to sign into OpenID providers, Windows Live ID accounts, Security Assertion Markup Language (SAML) identity providers, and other kinds of services.

Understanding the Identity Metasystem

The main goal of the Identity Metasystem is to allow people to have a set of different identities, each of which may reveal more or less information than the others.

It was designed as an interoperable identity-delivery vehicle based on multiple underlying technologies. It allows for multiple implementations as well as multiple providers.

With this approach, customers can continue to use their existing identity-infrastructure investments. Then, when the time comes, they can choose the identity technology that works best for them and can easily migrate from their old technology to a better and newer technology without sacrificing interoperability.

By the nature of its design, the Identity Metasystem has three roles:

Identity provider
> The identity provider is an entity that issues an identity (in this case, in the form of an information card). With CardSpace, anyone can become an identity provider—you've just become one yourself!
>
> Just as in real life, however, your word might not be good enough to seal a transaction. Each identity provider comes with an established level of trust, and interactions are governed accordingly.

Relying party
> Similarly, anyone can be a relying party. The name comes from the dependency on a third party (the identity provider) to validate the claims made by identity tokens. The tokens contain the claims requested by the relying party and validated by the identity provider.

Subject
> The subject is most likely a person but might also be a device of some sort, such as a phone or a server. It is the entity about which claims are being made and validated.

The Identity Metasystem is built on a foundation of claims-based identities. The validation of an identity provider enables a relying party to assume that these assertions (claims) about the subject are true.

In the case of .NET 3.5, you rely on CardSpace to deliver claims to requesting parties and establish your own self-issued claims in the form of information cards. These cards currently support the following fields:

- First Name
- Last Name
- Email Address
- Street
- City
- State
- Postal Code
- Country/Region

- Home Phone
- Other Phone
- Mobile Phone
- Date of Birth
- Gender
- Web Page

Creating a CardSpace Identity

One of the best ways to understand Windows CardSpace is to walk through a use-case scenario as a CardSpace user. In this scenario, you will create a self-issued card and see what it means to use this card on a web site. Along the way, you'll take a look at some of the key issues surrounding the very meaning of identity.

What You Need for Our CardSpace Examples

If you already have version 3.5 of the .NET Framework installed, or if you are running Windows Vista, you are good to go.

Otherwise, you'll need to download and install the Microsoft .NET Framework 3.5 from *http://www.microsoft.com/downloads/*. This will also install Windows CardSpace.

Once that's done, open the Windows Control Panel and confirm that there is an icon for Windows CardSpace. You should see something like Figure 14-3. (If you are in Classic View, the icon will be the same but the view will be a little different.)

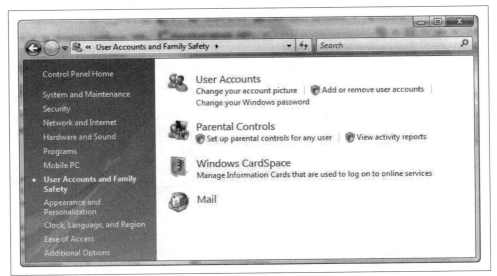

Figure 14-3. CardSpace successfully installed

CardSpace on Board, Ready to Create My Identity

If you don't already have one, to begin you'll need to create a CardSpace information card. Double-click on "Windows CardSpace" in the Windows Control Panel to launch CardSpace.

You will notice a task list running down the righthand side of the CardSpace control panel. Click on the "Add a card" link, and you should be presented with a window similar to the one shown in Figure 14-4.

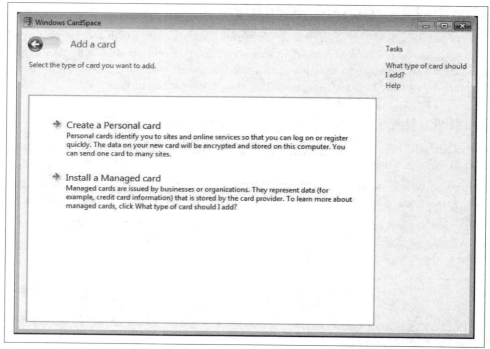

Figure 14-4. Adding a card

In Windows CardSpace, there are two kinds of "identity providers": cards can be "self-issued," with individuals making claims about themselves, or they can be supplied by a "managed" card provider, which supports claims made by one party about another. This distinction reflects the fact that different transactions require different levels of security. For example, if John Smith wants to get his dry cleaning back, he can identify himself by saying, "Hi, I'm John Smith." But if he wants to buy a plane ticket, he must provide a form of identification that has been issued by a trusted third party, such as a state or national government agency.

The driver's license or passport required by the Transport Security Administration are examples of managed cards provided by government agencies. Other examples of managed-card providers might include financial institutions, employers, and even businesses devoted to making assertions and claims about their customers that they are prepared to back financially.

For this example, you'll create a self-issued card. When you click on the "Create a Personal card" link, you should be presented with a screen similar to the one in Figure 14-5. On this screen you will provide information about yourself, to whatever level of detail you like.

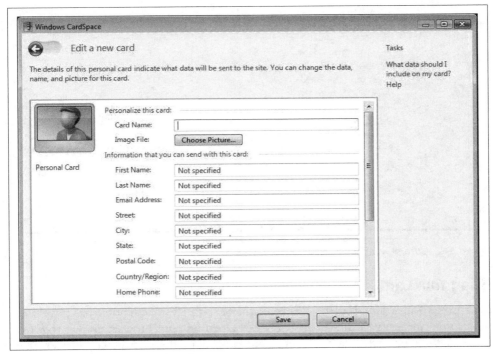

Figure 14-5. Creating a personal card

You are free to send this information via this card to one or more requesters. A requester can be any web site seeking identification from you.

It's important to remember that once you send your card to a requester, you have no control over how that information is used. Therefore, it is probably a good idea to set up various cards, each providing differing amounts of information, so that you can choose exactly how much to reveal to a given web site. In this manner, you can disclose details in proportion to your level of trust of the requester.

Once you have filled out and saved your cards, you will be able to preview each one (as shown in Figure 14-6).

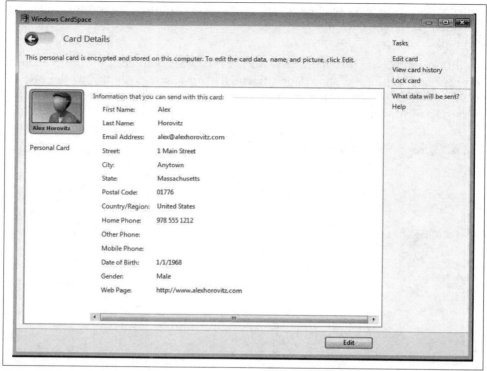

Figure 14-6. Card preview

Using Your Card

Microsoft's Kim Cameron (the author of the Seven Laws of Identity) has a web site where you can test your newly created card. Open up your browser and go to *http:// www.identityblog.com*. Click on the login button in the upper-right corner. You should see a page that looks like Figure 14-7.

Click on the "With an Information Card" link. This will bring you to the standard information page typically shown to users who have not previously identified themselves using CardSpace. This screen, shown in Figure 14-8, contains information about *www.identityblog.com* and asks you whether you want to send in a card to the site. This is one of the two decisions you will make as a user when interacting with a web site via CardSpace.

The information about the site, including the trusted authority that is verifying the site, is designed to offer you information to help you decide whether you want to continue, and what your level of trust is in terms of what card to supply. If you decide that the site is trustworthy and that you wish to present a card, click on the "Yes, choose a card to send" link. A screen like the one in Figure 14-9 will appear.

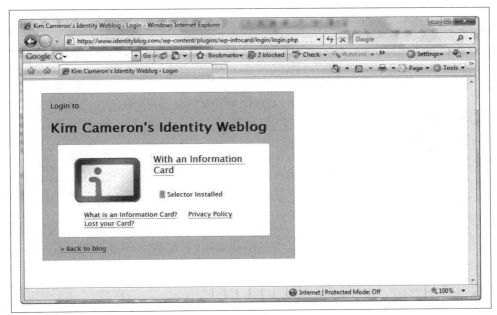

Figure 14-7. CardSpace login page at www.identityblog.com

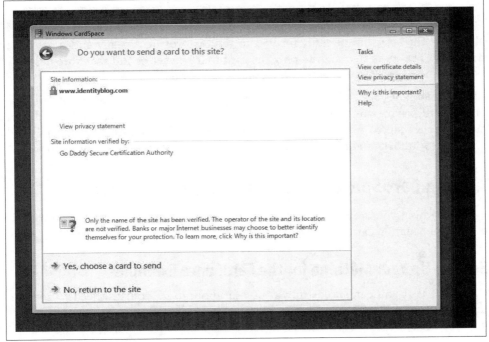

Figure 14-8. Do you want to send a card to this site?

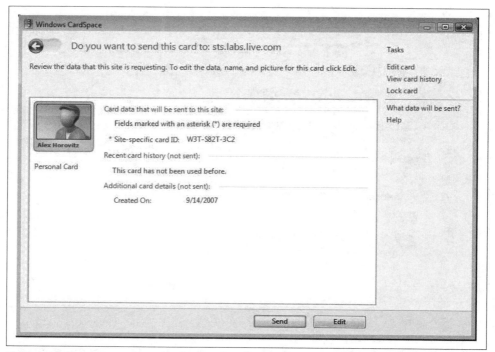

Figure 14-9. Sending a card

Note that the selection of cards for you to send is provided locally and not by the requester. The requester is given only the card that you select and therefore has only as much information about you as you choose to provide.

After you submit your card, you should get an email (if you have provided an address on the card) asking you to verify the submission. Assuming all goes as expected, you are now a registered user of Kim Cameron's Identityblog. This blog is a very good resource for understanding the issues that Windows CardSpace is meant to address.

Adding CardSpace Support to Your Application

The next thing you are going to do is build a sample ASP.NET application to process an information card.

Setting Up Your Machine for the CardSpace Examples

To ensure that you can successfully run your application, you will need to spend a little time setting up your computer.

IIS7

First, make sure IIS7 is installed (see the previous chapter for details).

If you're running Windows Vista, you'll also need to ensure that IIS 6.0 compatibility support is installed with IIS7. Otherwise, there is a chance that the certificates will not work correctly.

To ensure IIS6 compatibility, open the Control Panel and double-click "Programs and Features." Within the menu on the left, click on "Turn Window features on or off" (Figure 14-10). This will bring up a dialog box with that title. Navigate to and expand "Internet Information Services," then expand "Web Management Tools" and check and optionally expand "IIS 6 Management Compatibility," also shown in Figure 14-10.

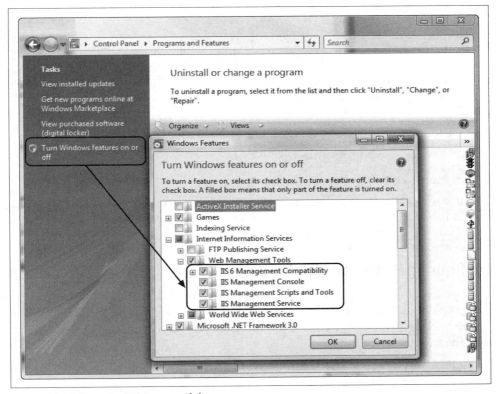

Figure 14-10. Ensuring IIS6 compatibility

With IIS7 installed and IIS6 compatibility ensured, point your browser to *http://tinyurl.com/2kp4x4*.

You'll want to download this sample, called "Introduction to CardSpace with Internet Explorer 7.0, August, Update," to a folder where you can find it later. Unzip the contents in that folder and then run the install script as the Administrator. This will install the sample certificates for the examples you are going to build.

About the certificates

The certificates installed by the script are for demonstration purposes only. The root certificate authority (CA) certificate is stored as an *.sst* (Microsoft Serialized Certificate Store) file. The web site certificates are all stored as *.pfx* files. The certificates are used for two categories of scenarios: browser scenarios and Windows Communication Foundation (WCF) scenarios.

The sample certificates are High-Assurance (HA) certificates that have embedded logo images in them. HA certificates come from a CA that has performed additional steps to verify the identity of the subject for whom the certificate is issued. In Internet Explorer 7.0, these HA certificates cause the address bar to change to green when the details are verified.

\etc\hosts

To ensure that you can see the address bar confirmation of the installed sample certificates, you need to make sure that your localhost (IP address 127.0.0.1) is correctly mapped to the certificate domains. To do this, run the Notepad application as the Administrator and open the *hosts* file (typically located at *C:\windows\system32\ drivers\etc\hosts*).

Add the following entries:

```
127.0.0.1 www.adatum.com adatum.com
127.0.0.1 www.contoso.com contoso.com
127.0.0.1 www.fabrikam.com fabrikam.com
```

If you have everything installed correctly, navigating to *https://www.fabrikam.com* should produce a page like Figure 14-11 in Internet Explorer 7.0—the address bar is green, but you'll have to take our word for it!

Configuring IIS for Your Application

If you want to add Windows CardSpace support to a web site, there are certain things you need to do. One of these involves making sure your site is able to use the Secure Sockets Layer (SSL); you can do this from the IIS Administration application with the easy-to-use GUI.

Using IIS7, you'll need to check that everything is properly configured prior to creating your test application:

1. Make sure you have created a dedicated directory, such as *C:\3.5\CardSpaces*.
2. Launch the IIS Manager from the Administrative Tools section of the Control Panel.
3. Expand the Connections tree until you can see "Default Web Site."
4. Right-click on "Default Web Site" and select "Add Virtual Directory."

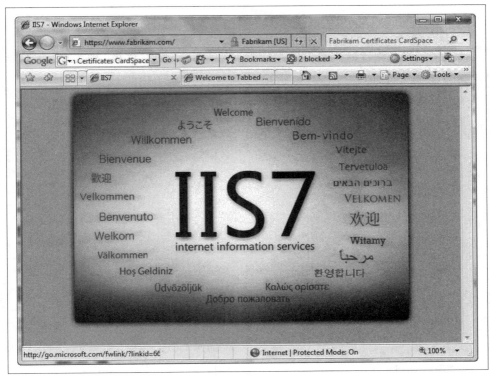

Figure 14-11. A green address bar means success

5. Name the alias directory *CardSpaces* and specify the path to your dedicated directory (*C:\3.5\CardSpaces*).

6. Right-click on "Default Web Site" again and select "Add Application."

7. Name the application *CardSpaceExample* and specify the same path you used for the virtual directory.

Creating a Sample ASP.NET Application

Launch Visual Studio 2008 as the Administrator, select File → New Web Site, and create a new ASP.NET Web Site (as shown in Figure 14-12). You will want to locate the site in your dedicated directory (*C:\3.5\CardSpaces*) and select Visual C# as the language. Also make sure you have selected .NET Framework 3.5 in the drop-down list in the top-right corner.

The first thing to do with your new application is add a new ASP.NET folder called *App_Code*. Inside this folder, you'll add two classes from Microsoft (available at *http://tinyurl.com/2ql3le*). To complete the upcoming exercise, you'll use specific sections of code from each. Take the time to download them now.

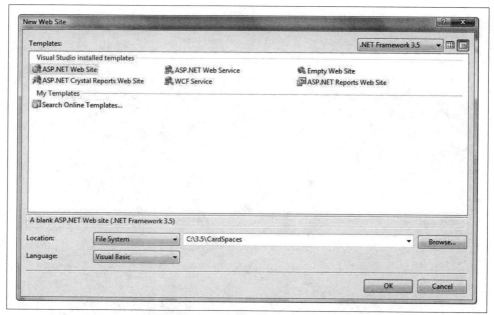

Figure 14-12. Creating the CardSpaces web application

 To follow along as we explore the Microsoft classes and what they are helping with in this chapter's example, you may want to open the *TokenProcessor.cs* file in your Visual Studio 2008 environment now. The relevant sections of code will be pointed out in the text.

When you run your application, and you are sure a CardSpace card has been submitted, you're going to make a call to initialize a new Token from the identityToken you've gathered from the HTTP request:

```
Token aToken = new Token(identityToken);
```

The Token class constructor uses the decryptToken( ) method to decrypt the XML data that you passed into the constructor. This is, as you will see, the gateway to the other activities you might want to perform. Before anything else can happen, you must be able to successfully decrypt the Token:

```
private static byte[] decryptToken(string xmlToken)
```

You'll use an XmlReader to iterate through the XML data:

```
XmlReader reader = new XmlTextReader(new StringReader(xmlToken));
```

Because of the strict nature of XML elements, very little flexibility exists. Thus, you'd like to be able to fail quickly (using an `ArgumentException`) if you come across an invalid token.

To start, you need to find the `EncryptionMethod` element. Its `Algorithm` attribute tells you the encryption method of the token:

```
if (!reader.ReadToDescendant(XmlEncryptionStrings.EncryptionMethod,
    XmlEncryptionStrings.Namespace))
    throw new ArgumentException("Cannot find token EncryptedMethod.");
encryptionAlgorithm =
    reader.GetAttribute(XmlEncryptionStrings.Algorithm).GetHashCode( );
```

Next, look for the `EncryptionMethod` attribute for the transient key, again getting the value of its `Algorithm` attribute. This is stored as its hash code:

```
if (!reader.ReadToFollowing(XmlEncryptionStrings.EncryptionMethod,
    XmlEncryptionStrings.Namespace))
    throw new ArgumentException("Cannot find key EncryptedMethod."); m_
keyEncryptionAlgorithm =
    reader.GetAttribute(XmlEncryptionStrings.Algorithm).GetHashCode( )
```

You'll find the thumbprint of the certificate (which you need for decryption) in the next element, `KeyIdentifier`:

```
if (!reader.ReadToFollowing(WSSecurityStrings.KeyIdentifier,
    WSSecurityStrings.Namespace))
    throw new ArgumentException("Cannot find Key Identifier.");
reader.Read( );
thumbprint = Convert.FromBase64String(reader.ReadContentAsString( ));
```

The `CipherValue` element contains the symmetric key in its encrypted form:

```
if (!reader.ReadToFollowing(XmlEncryptionStrings.CipherValue,
    XmlEncryptionStrings.Namespace))
    throw new ArgumentException("Cannot find symmetric key.");
reader.Read( );
symmetricKeyData =
    Convert.FromBase64String(reader.ReadContentAsString( ));
```

The `CipherValue` also contains the actual encrypted token:

```
if (!reader.ReadToFollowing(XmlEncryptionStrings.CipherValue,
    XmlEncryptionStrings.Namespace))
    throw new ArgumentException("Cannot find encrypted security token."); reader.Read(
);
securityTokenData =
    Convert.FromBase64String(reader.ReadContentAsString( ));
```

Finally, close the reader to free up resources:

```
reader.Close( );
```

Windows CardSpace ensures the encryption of the security token. With .NET 3.5, encryption is currently supported by one of two symmetric algorithms: AES and Triple DES. Use the encryption algorithm URI as a lookup:

```
SymmetricAlgorithm alg = null;
X509Certificate2 certificate = FindCertificate(thumbprint );

foreach( int i in Aes )
    if (encryptionAlgorithm == i)
    {
        alg= new RijndaelManaged( );
        break;
    }
if ( null == alg )
    foreach (int i in TripleDes)
    if (encryptionAlgorithm == i)
    {
        alg = new TripleDESCryptoServiceProvider( ); break;
    }
if (null == alg)
    throw new ArgumentException(
        "Could not determine Symmetric Algorithm"
    );
```

To get the symmetric key, decrypt it with the private key:

```
alg.Key=(certificate.PrivateKey as
    RSACryptoServiceProvider).Decrypt(symmetricKeyData,true);
```

Once you are finished with the discovery process, you know what algorithm has been used, so you can decrypt the token using the correct algorithm:

```
int ivSize = alg.BlockSize / 8;
byte[] iv = new byte[ivSize];

Buffer.BlockCopy(securityTokenData, 0, iv, 0, iv.Length);

alg.Padding = PaddingMode.ISO10126;
alg.Mode = CipherMode.CBC;
ICryptoTransform decrTransform = alg.CreateDecryptor(alg.Key, iv);

byte[] plainText =
    decrTransform.TransformFinalBlock(securityTokenData, iv.Length,
    securityTokenData.Length iv.Length);

decrTransform.Dispose( ); return plainText;
```

Thankfully, .NET 3.5 simplifies the deserialization of the decrypted Token through the WSSecurityTokenSerializer and facilitates its authentication through the use of the SamlSecurityTokenAuthenticator. The Token class supports SAML tokens out of the box. If you require a different token type, you simply need to provide an Authenticator to support the type in question.

Once the authenticator has validated the token, the Token class extracts the claims into a usable form:

```
public Token(String xmlToken)
{
    byte[] decryptedData = decryptToken(xmlToken);
    XmlReader reader = new XmlTextReader(new StreamReader(new
        MemoryStream(decryptedData), Encoding.UTF8));
    m_token =
        (SamlSecurityToken)
        WSSecurityTokenSerializer.DefaultInstance.ReadToken(
            reader, null);

    SamlSecurityTokenAuthenticator authenticator =
        new SamlSecurityTokenAuthenticator(
            new List<SecurityTokenAuthenticator>
            (
                new SecurityTokenAuthenticator[]{
                    new RsaSecurityTokenAuthenticator(),
                        new X509SecurityTokenAuthenticator() }),
                        MaximumTokenSkew
            );

    if (authenticator.CanValidateToken(m_token))
    {
        ReadOnlyCollection<IAuthorizationPolicy> policies =
            authenticator.ValidateToken(m_token);
        m_authorizationContext =
            AuthorizationContext.CreateDefaultAuthorizationContext(
                policies);
        FindIdentityClaims();
    }
    else
    {
        throw new Exception("Unable to validate the token.");
    }
}
```

As you can see, the Token class exposes several properties that simplify the extraction of claims from the security token:

IdentityClaims

A System.IdentityModel.Claims.ClaimsSet of the identity claims in the token.

AuthorizationContext

A System.IdentityModel.Policy.AuthorizationContext generated from the token.

UniqueID

The UniqueID (IdentityClaim) of the token. By default, the PPID and the issuer's public key are hashed together to generate a UniqueID. To use a different field, add a line like this:

```
<add name="IdentityClaimType" value=
    value="http://schemas.xmlsoap.org/ws/2005/05/identity/
    claims/privatepersonalidentifier" />
```

replacing the value with the URI for your unique claim.

Claims

A read-only String collection of the claims in the token. Provides support for the indexed claims accessor:

```
securityToken.Claims[ClaimsTypes.PPID]
```

IssuerIdentityClaim

The issuer's identity claim (most likely, the public key of the issuing authority).

In this example, you're going to get some of the claims, grab some of the decrypted data, and display it back in your return page. Go ahead and create that page now. Right-click on your web site in the Solution Explorer, select "Add New Item," and add a Web Form called *Results.aspx* (see Figure 14-13). This is the page you'll use to display the decrypted information you were able to gather from the CardSpace interaction with the user.

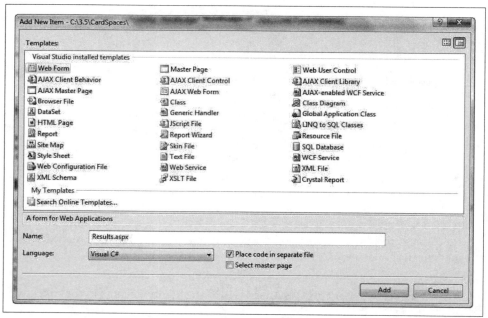

Figure 14-13. Adding the Results.aspx web form to your project

Next, you need to add two references to your web site. Right-click on your Card-Spaces web site icon and select "Add Reference" from the drop-down menu. You will need to add System.Identity.Model and System.Identity.Model.Selectors from the .NET tab, as seen in Figure 14-14.

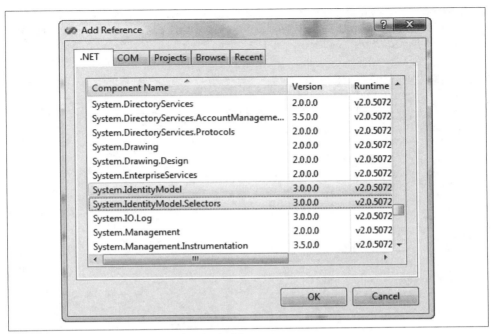

Figure 14-14. Adding the Systems.IdentityModel components

To continue with your project housekeeping, you're going to add a little information to your *Web.config* file. You need to identify the certificate subject, the store name, and the store location to use when attempting to process the Windows CardSpace authentication. In this case, you'll use the Fabrikam certificate that you installed earlier in this chapter.

Add the following appSettings element to your *Web.config* file:

```
<appSettings>
    <add key="CertificateSubject" value="www.fabrikam.com"/>
    <add key="StoreName" value="My"/>
    <add key="StoreLocation" value="LocalMachine"/>
    <add key="IdentityClaimType"
        value="http://schemas.xmlsoap.org/ws/2005/05/identity/claims/

    <add key="MaximumClockSkew" value="60"/>
</appSettings>
```

This will allow you to utilize the Fabrikam cert you loaded into IIS to decrypt the card's claims.

Next, remove the *Default.aspx* component from your web project. To do this, right-click on *Default.aspx* and select "Delete." Replace this page with a regular HTML page called *Default.htm* (see Figure 14-15).

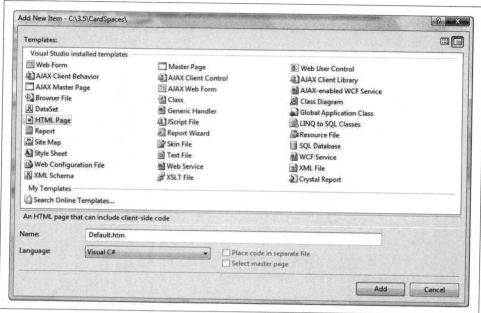

Figure 14-15. Adding Default.htm

Here's the complete listing for *Default.htm*:

```
<!DOCTYPE html PUBLIC "-//W3C//DTD XHTML 1.0 Transitional//EN"
    "http://www.w3.org/TR/xhtml1/DTD/xhtml1-transitional.dtd">

<html xmlns="http://www.w3.org/1999/xhtml">
<head>
    <title>Programming .NET 3.5 :: CardSpaces Demo</title>
</head>
<body>
    <form method="post" action="Results.aspx">
    <div>
        <object type="application/x-informationcard" name="identityToken">
            <param name="tokenType"
                value="urn:oasis:names:tc:SAML:1.0:assertion" />
            <param name="issuer"
                value="http://schemas.xmlsoap.org/ws/2005/05/identity/issuer/self" />
            <param name="requiredClaims" value ="
                http://schemas.xmlsoap.org/ws/2005/05/identity/claims/givenname
                http://schemas.xmlsoap.org/ws/2005/05/identity/claims/surname
                http://schemas.xmlsoap.org/ws/2005/05/identity/claims/locality
                http://schemas.xmlsoap.org/ws/2005/05/identity/claims/country
                http://schemas.xmlsoap.org/ws/2005/05/identity/claims/dateofbirth
```

```
          http://schemas.xmlsoap.org/ws/2005/05/identity/claims/emailaddress
          http://schemas.xmlsoap.org/ws/2005/05/identity/claims/
               privatepersonalidentifier"/>
     </object>

     <input type="submit" name="SignInButton"
        value="Authenticate using CardSpace!" />
  </div>
  </form>
</body>
</html>
```

Embedded in this HTML document is the line `<object type="application/x-informationcard" name="identityToken">`. This is the object that does the work of calling Windows CardSpace. In this example you're binding its activation to a Submit button because the object is attached to the form. It will direct the results to your *Results.aspx* page. A quick look at the parameters of the object shows how you will interact with CardSpace.

The first parameter sets up the token type:

```
          <param name="tokenType"
               value="urn:oasis:names:tc:SAML:1.0:assertion" />
```

The next parameter is where you identify the issuer:

```
          <param name="issuer"
               value="http://schemas.xmlsoap.org/ws/2005/05/identity/issuer/self" />
```

In this case, you're willing to accept a self-signed certificate as opposed to one that you created and distributed.

Last, you list all the claims that you require your users to provide:

```
          <param name="requiredClaims" value ="
               http://schemas.xmlsoap.org/ws/2005/05/identity/claims/givenname
               http://schemas.xmlsoap.org/ws/2005/05/identity/claims/surname
               http://schemas.xmlsoap.org/ws/2005/05/identity/claims/locality
               http://schemas.xmlsoap.org/ws/2005/05/identity/claims/country
               http://schemas.xmlsoap.org/ws/2005/05/identity/claims/dateofbirth
               http://schemas.xmlsoap.org/ws/2005/05/identity/claims/emailaddress
               http://schemas.xmlsoap.org/ws/2005/05/identity/claims/
                    privatepersonalidentifier"/>
```

You'll be able to access these values after decryption. Once you have a Token, you can simply extract the claims like this:

```
     aToken.Claims[ClaimTypes.GivenName]
```

In this example, you'll get back a string for the user's first name.

The complete specification for these parameters is as follows:

```
     <?xml version="1.0" encoding="utf-8" ?>
     <!--
     Copyright &#169; 2006-2007 Microsoft Corporation, Inc. All rights reserved.
     -->
```

```
<xs:schema
    targetNamespace="http://schemas.xmlsoap.org/ws/2005/05/identity/claims"
    xmlns:tns="http://schemas.xmlsoap.org/ws/2005/05/identity/claims"
    xmlns:xs="http://www.w3.org/2001/XMLSchema" elementFormDefault="qualified"
    blockDefault="#all" version="0.1">
    <xs:import namespace="http://www.w3.org/XML/1998/namespace"
        schemaLocation="http://www.w3.org/2001/xml.xsd" />
    <xs:simpleType name="StringMaxLength255MinLength1">
        <xs:restriction base="xs:string">
            <xs:maxLength value="255" />
            <xs:minLength value="1" />
        </xs:restriction>
    </xs:simpleType>
    <xs:simpleType name="Base64BinaryMaxSize1K">
        <xs:restriction base="xs:base64Binary">
            <xs:maxLength value="1024" />
        </xs:restriction>
    </xs:simpleType>
    <!--
    Gender claims are serialized as follows: 0-Unspecified, 1-Male, 2-Female
    -->
    <xs:simpleType name="GenderType">
        <xs:restriction base="xs:token">
            <xs:enumeration value="0" />
            <xs:enumeration value="1" />
            <xs:enumeration value="2" />
        </xs:restriction>
    </xs:simpleType>
    <!--
    Standard claim types defined by the information card model
    -->
    <xs:element name="givenname" type="tns:StringMaxLength255MinLength1" />
    <xs:element name="surname" type="tns:StringMaxLength255MinLength1" />
    <xs:element name="emailaddress" type="tns:StringMaxLength255MinLength1" />
    <xs:element name="streetaddress" type="tns:StringMaxLength255MinLength1" />
    <xs:element name="locality" type="tns:StringMaxLength255MinLength1" />
    <xs:element name="stateorprovince" type="tns:StringMaxLength255MinLength1" />
    <xs:element name="postalcode" type="tns:StringMaxLength255MinLength1" />
    <xs:element name="country" type="tns:StringMaxLength255MinLength1" />
    <xs:element name="primaryphone" type="tns:StringMaxLength255MinLength1" />
    <xs:element name="dateofbirth" type="xs:date" />
    <xs:element name="privatepersonalidentifier" type="tns:Base64BinaryMaxSize1K" />
    <xs:element name="gender" type="tns:GenderType" />
    <xs:element name="webpage" type="tns:StringMaxLength255MinLength1" />
</xs:schema>
```

Run your application now. To properly connect to the site, change the URL Visual Studio automatically created to *https://www.fabrikam.com/CardSpaces/Default.aspx*.

You should get a Windows CardSpace request to supply a card, similar to the one in Figure 14-16. Notice that the claims listed as being required by the site are the same ones that you listed in the requiredClaims parameter.

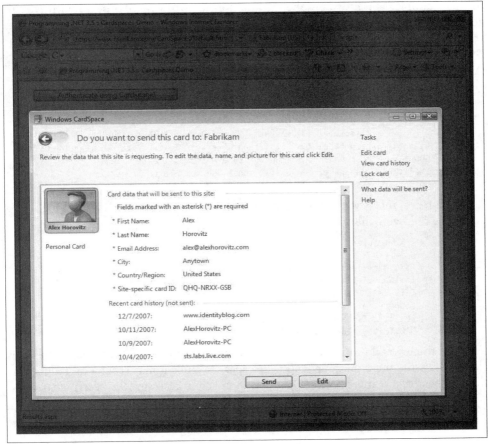

Figure 14-16. The data to be sent is marked with an asterisk (*)

More likely than not, you got a blank page when you submitted the card. This is OK, because you have not written the results component yet. You'll do that next.

Processing the Information Card

As discussed previously, you're going to grab the following information from the CardSpace information card:

- First Name
- Last Name
- Email Address
- City
- Country/Region
- Site-specific card ID

In this example, you'll display the information in two ways. To begin with, you're going to fill in a number of asp:Labels on your page with the decrypted values that you retrieve from the card.

Your *.aspx* file will contain these lines:

```
The Identity Card provided contains the following information:
<br />
<br />
Name:       <asp:Label ID="FirstName" runat="server" Text=""/>
            <asp:Label ID="LastName" runat="server" Text="" /><br />
City:       <asp:Label ID="City" runat="server" Text=""/><br />
Country:    <asp:Label ID="Country" runat="server" Text=""/><br />
Email:      <asp:Label ID="Email" runat="server" Text=""/><br />
Unique ID:  <asp:Label ID="UID" runat="server" Text=""/><br />
```

As you can see, this is very straightforward. In your *.aspx.cs* code, you'll set these values in the following manner:

```
Token aToken = new Token(identityToken);

FirstName.Text = aToken.Claims[ClaimTypes.GivenName];
LastName.Text = aToken.Claims[ClaimTypes.Surname];
City.Text = aToken.Claims[ClaimTypes.Locality];
Country.Text = aToken.Claims[ClaimTypes.Country];
Email.Text = aToken.Claims[ClaimTypes.Email];
UID.Text = aToken.UniqueID;
```

The next thing you'll want to do is leverage *TokenHelper.cs* to iterate through the set of claims and write them out longhand (so to speak). While it may seem a bit redundant, this emphasizes that there is more than one approach to accessing the decrypted claims.

To accomplish this, you're going to add an asp:Literal element to your *.aspx* file:

```
<asp:Literal ID="ResultsLiteral" runat="server" />
```

At runtime, you'll use code to build up an HTML table that will get inserted into this element's Text property. To start with, you'll define the top of the table and the headers as follows:

```
ResultsLiteral.Text += "<table border=\"1\" width=\"640\"><tr>
    <th width=\"200\">Type</th><th width=\"240\">Resource</th></tr>";
```

Next, you'll instantiate a new TokenHelper using the identityToken passed in by CardSpace. As when you instantiated a Token object using Microsoft's TokenProcessor class, this instantiation will handle the decryption for you:

```
TokenHelper tokenHelper = new TokenHelper(identityToken);
```

Now it is simply a matter of iterating over each Claim in the TokenHelper's IdentityClaims collection and building the rows of the table:

```
foreach (Claim aClaim in tokenHelper.IdentityClaims)
{
    ResultsLiteral.Text += "<tr>";
    ResultsLiteral.Text += "<td width=\"200\">" +
        aClaim.ClaimType + "</td>";
```

```
        ResultsLiteral.Text += "<td width=\"240\">" +
            aClaim.Resource.ToString() + "</td>";
        ResultsLiteral.Text += "</tr>";
    }
```

Finally, when you've run out of claims, you need to close out the HTML table:

```
        ResultsLiteral.Text += "</table>";
    }
```

Now add the complete listings to your project.

Please note that you need to make sure you are not validating the incoming request (i.e., set ValidateRequest="false"), as the request comes across with the card as embedded XML and will cause the validation engine to kick it back. Here is the complete listing for *Results.aspx*:

```
<%@ Page Language="C#" AutoEventWireup="true" CodeFile="Results.aspx.cs"
    Inherits="Results" ValidateRequest="false" %>

<!DOCTYPE html PUBLIC "-//W3C//DTD XHTML 1.0 Transitional//EN"
    "http://www.w3.org/TR/xhtml1/DTD/xhtml1-transitional.dtd">

<html xmlns="http://www.w3.org/1999/xhtml">
<head id="Head1" runat="server">
    <title>Programming .NET 3.5 :: CardSpaces Results</title>
    <style type="text/css">
        .cardspaceTable
        {
            font-family: Verdana;
            font-size: x-small;
            font-weight: normal;
        }
    </style>
</head>
<body>

    <form id="identityForm" runat="server">
    <div class="cardspaceTable">
        The Identity Card provided contains the following information:
        <br />
        <br />
        Name: <asp:Label ID="FirstName" runat="server" Text=""/>
            <asp:Label ID="LastName" runat="server" Text="" /><br />
        City: <asp:Label ID="City" runat="server" Text=""/><br />
        Country: <asp:Label ID="Country" runat="server" Text=""/><br />
        Email: <asp:Label ID="Email" runat="server" Text=""/><br />
        Unique ID: <asp:Label ID="UID" runat="server" Text=""/><br />
        <br /><br />In the form of these decrypted claims:</br>
        <asp:Literal ID="ResultsLiteral" runat="server" />
    </div>
    </form>

</body>
</html>
```

And here's the complete listing for *Results.aspx.cs*:

```
using System;
using System.Data;
using System.Configuration;
using System.Collections;
using System.Web;
using Microsoft.IdentityModel.TokenProcessor;
using Microsoft.IdentityModel.Samples;
using System.IdentityModel.Claims;
using System.IdentityModel.Tokens;
using System.Web.Security;
using System.Web.UI;
using System.Web.UI.WebControls;
using System.Web.UI.WebControls.WebParts;
using System.Web.UI.HtmlControls;

public partial class Results : System.Web.UI.Page
{
    protected void Page_Load(object sender, EventArgs e)
    {
        String identityToken;
        identityToken = Request.Params["identityToken"];

        if (identityToken == null || identityToken == "")
        {
            identityToken = "Oops! Someone forgot to tell us who they were...";
        }
        else
        {
            Token aToken = new Token(identityToken);

            FirstName.Text = aToken.Claims[ClaimTypes.GivenName];
            LastName.Text = aToken.Claims[ClaimTypes.Surname];
            City.Text = aToken.Claims[ClaimTypes.Locality];
            Country.Text = aToken.Claims[ClaimTypes.Country];
            Email.Text = aToken.Claims[ClaimTypes.Email];
            UID.Text = aToken.UniqueID;

            ResultsLiteral.Text += "<table border=\"1\" width=\"640\"><tr>
                <th width=\"200\">Type</th><th width=\"240\">Resource</th></tr>";

            TokenHelper tokenHelper = new TokenHelper(identityToken);

            foreach (Claim aClaim in tokenHelper.IdentityClaims)
            {
                ResultsLiteral.Text += "<tr>";
                ResultsLiteral.Text += "<td width=\"200\">" +
                    aClaim.ClaimType + "</td>";
                ResultsLiteral.Text += "<td width=\"240\">" +
                    aClaim.Resource.ToString() + "</td>";
                ResultsLiteral.Text += "</tr>";
            }

            ResultsLiteral.Text += "</table>";
```

```
            }
        }
    }
```

Assuming all went well, you should be able to run the application now. Don't forget to use SSL by specifying *https://* instead of *http://*, as in *https://www.fabrikam.com/CardSpaceExample/Default.htm*. If you don't use SSL, you'll get the following exception: "The page you are trying to access is secured with Secure Sockets Layer (SSL)."

Also, if you interact directly with the browser page that opens up when you run the application in Visual Studio, instead of changing the URL from *localhost* to *www.fabrikam.com*, you will get the following stack trace:

```
at Microsoft.IdentityModel.TokenProcessor.Token.decryptToken(
String xmlToken)
in c:\\3.5\\CardSpaces\\App_Code\\TokenProcessor.cs:line 364\r\n
at Microsoft.IdentityModel.TokenProcessor.Token..ctor(String xmlToken)
in c:\\3.5\\CardSpaces\\App_Code\\TokenProcessor.cs:line 145\r\n
at Results.Page_Load(Object sender, EventArgs e)
in c:\\3.5\\CardSpaces\\Results.aspx.cs:line 31\r\n
at System.Web.Util.CalliHelper.EventArgFunctionCaller(
IntPtr fp, Object o, Object t, EventArgs e)\r\n
at System.Web.Util.CalliEventHandlerDelegateProxy.Callback(
Object sender, EventArgs e)\r\n
at System.Web.UI.Control.OnLoad(EventArgs e)\r\n   at System.Web.UI.Control.
LoadRecursive()\r\n   at System.Web.UI.Page.ProcessRequestMain(
Boolean includeStagesBeforeAsyncPoint,
Boolean includeStagesAfterAsyncPoint)
```

This is a fancy way of saying that the web site could not identify the encryption you were using (in no small part because you weren't actually using encryption).

On the other hand, if you hit the correct URL through SSL, you should get a page that looks like the one in Figure 14-17.

Summary

CardSpace provides the identification and authentication required for web-based transactions, while allowing the end user to select exactly how much information to provide to a given web site. It is expected that a typical web user will create a small number of specific identities: perhaps one fake identity to avoid junk email, one with minimal identification for casual membership, one with typical identification for shopping, and finally one with strong identification for commercial transactions, banking, and so forth. As CardSpace gains wider acceptance, we can anticipate that institutions such as banks and brokerage houses will begin to issue individualized cards. Over time, there may be an ebb and flow between individualized and more generalized cards.

One of the key aspects that will govern the success of CardSpace and the Identity Metasystem will be user acceptance. That is, users will have to find the technology compelling, valuable, trustworthy, and easy to use and understand.

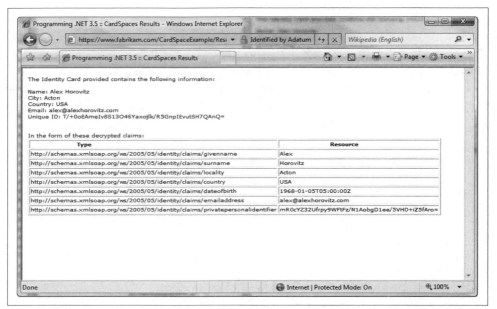

Figure 14-17. A successful run

Traditionally, this has been a hard problem when it comes to security tokens and transactions. You only have to go to your local grocery store to see how difficult it is for a new technology to gain acceptance. Wait a while, and you're sure to see someone write out a check rather than using a debit or credit card. More often than not, the check-writers are older people who, when asked, will tell you they have never used a debit card because checks are "so convenient." They simply don't find the debit card compelling. Many who do find credit/debit cards compelling don't find them trustworthy, especially when they're used over the Internet. Identity systems that are both compelling *and* trustworthy are usually not easy to use and easy to understand. Whether CardSpace will meet all these needs and gain sufficient acceptance remains an open question at the time of this writing.

Epilogue

Jesse happens to hate epilogues. He thinks, and sometimes I agree, that they are a waste of time. Mostly, no one ever reads them. However, our editors at O'Reilly disagree, and without them our children might go hungry. So, on the off chance that you'll take a look, I've written one for you.

In this book, we have given you a complete tour of .NET 3.5. You have seen how it increases your productivity on a wide range of systems, from your desktop to the data center. By now, you should have a deep appreciation that .NET 3.5 provides a solid foundation for building connected and appealing applications.

In our opinion, the features you will find most compelling in .NET 3.5 are as follows:

- Deep integration of Language INtegrated Query (LINQ) and data awareness
- Support for Web 2.0 AJAX-style applications and services in ASP.NET and WCF
- Full tooling support for WF, WCF, and WPF, including the new workflow-enabled services technology

Hopefully, you have come away with the sense that this book is a great introduction to each of the "silos" that make up the .NET 3.5 platform. If you're ready to dive deeper into the areas that interest you most, we suggest the following titles (also from O'Reilly):

Programming WPF, by Chris Sells and Ian Griffiths
Learning WCF: A Hands-on Guide, by Michele Bustamante
Programming WCF Services, by Juval Lowy
Programming C# 3.0, by Jesse Liberty and Donald Xie
Programming Silverlight 2, by Jesse Liberty and Tim Heuer
Programming ASP.NET MVC, by Alex Horovitz

As a developer, you will also want to keep a close eye on emerging .NET 3.5 technologies. ADO.NET has the Entity Framework. ASP.NET has the MVC Framework.

Increasingly, Microsoft is depending on external developer communities to drive features and new ideas. You can, through active participation, impact the future of your development tools.

So, get out there and write some code!

—Alex Horovitz

Index

We'd like to hear your suggestions for improving our indexes. Send email to *index@oreilly.com*.

About the Authors

Jesse Liberty is a senior program manager at Microsoft in the Silverlight Development division. His business card reads "Silverlight Geek," and he is responsible for fostering a Silverlight Developer community, primarily through Silverlight.net.

Jesse is the author of numerous books, including O'Reilly's *Programming Silverlight 2* and the perennial bestseller *Programming C# 3.0*. Jesse has two decades of experience as a developer, author, and consultant, and has been a distinguished software engineer at AT&T, a software architect for PBS/Learning Link, and a vice president at Citibank. He provides full support for his writing, and access to his blogs, at *http://www.JesseLiberty.com*.

Alex Horovitz is a creative and analytical technologist. He brings a strong aesthetic sense coupled with rich conceptual thinking abilities to his work. He is currently the chief technology officer at The Brookeside Group, Inc., where he designs and implemenets enterprise applications leveraging the Model-View-Controller design pattern and reusable frameworks.

Prior to The Brookeside Group, Alex was most recently the senior director of Enterprise Architecture and Standards at K12, Inc., after his company Emergency Vault Data Solutions was acquired by them in 2007. During the 1990s and early 2000s, Alex worked at NeXT Computer and later at Apple.

You can contact him through his web site, *http://alexhorovitz.com*.

Colophon

The animal on the cover of *Programming .NET 3.5* is a giant petrel, a large seabird from the genus *Macronectes*, which encompasses both the southern, or Antarctic, giant petrel (*Macronectes giganteus*) and the northern giant petrel (*Macronectes halli*). While much of the two species' habitat range overlaps and both are restricted to the southern hemisphere, only the southern petrel nests as far south as Antarctica. They are also physically similar; most individuals have gray plumage, though they can range from black and brown, to white in some southern petrels. They have long, pale-orange bills, but northern petrels can be distinguished by their reddish-pink billtips, versus the light-green tip of the southern petrels. Giant petrels are so named due to their impressive size; they can grow up to 34 inches long with wingspans of around 77 inches, and they weigh as much as 11 pounds.

Although they are sometimes mistaken for albatrosses, giant petrels—unlike the albatross—forage on both sea and land. At sea, they feed on fish, squid, crustaceans, and refuse from ships. On land, they feed primarily on penguin, whale, seal, or seabird carrion, earning them a reputation as the "vultures of the Antarctic." They are capable of killing birds as large as the king penguin and can be quite vicious in their attacks.

Whalers have nicknamed the giant petrel "stinker" due in part to its carrion-feeding tendencies, but also to one particularly nasty talent: it is able to spit, with great precision, a foul-smelling glob of oil and regurgitated food at attackers. Giant petrels are very susceptible to disturbance during breeding season and will abandon their nests if threatened, so one theory is that the birds may have developed this spitting ability as a way to ward off intruders.

The cover image is from the *Dover Pictorial Archive*. The cover font is Adobe ITC Garamond. The text font is Linotype Birka; the heading font is Adobe Myriad Condensed; and the code font is LucasFont's TheSansMonoCondensed.

Related Titles from O'Reilly

.NET and C#

ADO.NET Cookbook

ADO.NET 3.5 Cookbook,
  2nd Edition

ASP.NET 2.0 Cookbook,
  2nd Edition

ASP.NET 2.0: A Developer's
  Notebook

Building an ASP.NET Web 2.0 Portal

C# 3.0 in a Nutshell, *3rd Edition*

C# Cookbook, *2nd Edition*

C# Design Patterns

C# in a Nutshell, *2nd Edition*

C# Language Pocket Reference

Exchange Server 2007
  Administration: The Definitive
  Guide

Head First C#

Learning ASP.NET 2.0 with AJAX

Learning C# 2005, *2nd Edition*

Learning WCF

MCSE Core Elective Exams in a
  Nutshell

.NET and XML

.NET Gotchas

Programming Atlas

Programming ASP.NET, *3rd Edition*

Programming ASP.NET AJAX

Programming C#, *4th Edition*

Programming MapPoint in .NET

Programming .NET 3.5

Programming .NET Components,
  2nd Edition

Programming .NET Security

Programming .NET Web Services

Programming Visual Basic 2005

Programming WCF Services

Programming WPF, *2nd Edition*

Programming Windows Presentation
  Foundation

Programming the .NET Compact
  Framework

Visual Basic 2005: A Developer's
  Notebook

Visual Basic 2005 Cookbook

Visual Basic 2005 in a Nutshell,
  3rd Edition

Visual Basic 2005 Jumpstart

Visual C# 2005: A Developer's
  Notebook

Visual Studio Hacks

Windows Developer Power Tools

XAML in a Nutshell

The O'Reilly Advantage

Stay Current and Save Money

70502